DOCUMENTARY HISTORY OF WESTERN CIVILIZATION
edited by Eugene C. Black and Leonard W. Levy

ANCIENT AND MEDIEVAL HISTORY OF THE WEST

Morton Smith: ANCIENT GREECE

A. H. M. Jones: A HISTORY OF ROME THROUGH THE FIFTH CENTURY
Vol. I: *The Republic*
Vol. II: *The Empire*

Deno Geanakopolos: BYZANTINE EMPIRE

Marshall W. Baldwin: CHRISTIANITY THROUGH THE CRUSADES

Bernard Lewis: ISLAM THROUGH SULEIMAN THE MAGNIFICENT

David Herlihy: HISTORY OF FEUDALISM

William M. Bowsky: RISE OF COMMERCE AND TOWNS

David Herlihy: MEDIEVAL CULTURE AND SOCIETY

EARLY MODERN HISTORY

Hannah Gray: CULTURAL HISTORY OF THE RENAISSANCE

Florence Edler De Roover: MONEY, BANKING & COMMERCE, 13TH-16TH CENTURIES

V. J. Parry: THE OTTOMAN EMPIRE

Ralph E. Giesey: EVOLUTION OF THE DYNASTIC STATE

J. H. Parry: THE EUROPEAN RECONNAISSANCE

Hans J. Hillerbrand: THE PROTESTANT REFORMATION

John C. Olin: THE CATHOLIC COUNTER-REFORMATION

Orest Ranum: THE CENTURY OF LOUIS XIV

Thomas Hegarty: RUSSIAN HISTORY THROUGH PETER THE GREAT

Marie Boas-Hall: THE SCIENTIFIC REVOLUTION

Barry E. Supple: HISTORY OF MERCANTILISM

_____: IMPERIALISM, WAR & DIPLOMACY,1550-1763

Herbert H. Rowen: THE LOW COUNTRIES

C. A. Macartney: THE EVOLUTION OF THE HABSBURG & HOHENZOLLERN DYNASTIES

Lester G. Crocker: THE ENLIGHTENMENT

Robert Forster: EIGHTEENTH CENTURY EUROPEAN SOCIETY

A volume
in
DOCUMENTARY HISTORY
of
WESTERN CIVILIZATION

THE EUROPEAN RECONNAISSANCE
Selected Documents

edited by
J. H. PARRY

WALKER AND COMPANY
New York

Library of Congress Catalog Card Number: 68-13329.

Printed in the United States of America.

Published in the United States of America in
1968 by Walker and Company, a division of the
Walker Publishing Company, Inc.

Published simultaneously in Canada by
The Ryerson Press, Toronto.

Volumes in this series are published in association
with Harper & Row, Publishers, Inc., from
whom paperback editions are available in Harper
Torchbooks.

Contents

V.   INDONESIA, CHINA, AND JAPAN

VI.   THE AMERICAS

VII.   THE PACIFIC

VIII.   BY THE ARCTIC TO CATHAY

Maps

(to be found in a group following page 70)

1. The East Indies.
2. The Pacific.
3. The Caribbean Sea.
4. Wind Chart of the World.
5. The World according to Ptolemy's description. From *Geographia* by Ptolemy (Ulm, 1482). Photo: British Museum.
6. The Indian Ocean.

Acknowledgments

I wish to thank the following for permission
to quote extracts from copyright works:
The Council of the Hakluyt Society
(nos. 1–7, 9, 10, 13, 15, 17, 21, 22, 26–29).
Messrs. Chas. J. Sawyer, Booksellers,
12 Grafton Street, London, W.1. (no. 8).
The University of California Press (no. 12).
Mr. Frederick J. Pohl (no. 14).
Messrs. Routledge and Kegan Paul, Ltd.,
London (no. 16).
The University of New Mexico Press (no. 18).
The University of Toronto Press (no. 22 [2]).
The Queen's Printer, Ottawa
(no. 22 [3] and no. 24).
Messrs. Jackson and Co. (Booksellers) Ltd.,
Glasgow (no. 25).
I should also like to thank Professor C. R. Boxer
and Professor L. A. Vigneras for their
courtesy and help in connection with extracts
from their translations.

J. H. P.

I. *Introduction*

The field of Reconnaissance

The documents which comprise the greater part of this book are concerned with the process of maritime discovery. Most of them are either eyewitness accounts written by men who took part in voyages of discovery; or else comments by contemporaries who were in a position to assess their achievements. The voyages themselves were incidents in a persistent, determined, and ultimately successful European endeavor to establish direct contact, first with West Africa, subsequently with Asia; more specifically, to link individual centers in western Europe with places in India, the Indonesian islands, China, and Japan; places known or believed to exist, and reputed to be of high civilization and great commercial importance. The main purpose of the voyages was to discover, not new lands, but new routes to old lands. They reflected not only a keen commercial demand in Europe for goods of Oriental origin, but an intense curiosity among Europeans about the East itself.

This interest was not reciprocated. The only Asians who had any serious concern with Europe in the later Middle Ages were Ottoman rulers and soldiers engaged in the conquest and plunder of the ancient Byzantine Empire; and the Levantine Arab merchants who sold Oriental goods at great profit to Italian traders in Alexandria or Aleppo. Elsewhere in Asia there was no demand for European goods and no interest in Europe itself. Throughout the Reconnaissance, therefore, the initiative was European. Europe sought out Asia, not Asia Europe. When Reconnaissance achieved its purpose, when contact was established, this active-passive relation persisted. Europeans eagerly absorbed all they could of the

East—goods, information, ideas. Most Asiatics—except where their livelihood, safety, or sovereignty seemed directly threatened—reacted to the presence of Europeans in small numbers off their coasts or in their harbors merely with indifference or distaste. This generalization remained true for more than two hundred years after Vasco da Gama's landing at Calicut. Pugnacious and formidable though Europeans could be, it was not until the eighteenth century that Asiatics came to take them seriously.

The voyages which these documents describe were nearly all made within the span of about a hundred years, roughly the second half of the fifteenth century and the first half of the sixteenth. In the history of maritime discovery, this is a fairly well-defined span. European shipping, in the middle of the fifteenth century, was almost confined to European waters: the Baltic, the coasts of the northeast Atlantic, the Mediterranean, and the Black Sea. The only maritime powers whose ships covered the whole stretch of European waters, or most of it, were Italian—Venice, Genoa, Florence. Shipping of the Atlantic seaboard passed the Straits of Gibraltar comparatively seldom. Western Europe got its supplies of Oriental imports, in small quantity at high prices, from Italian intermediaries, who had them from Arab intermediaries on terms negotiated with powerful and sometimes hostile Muslim rulers. In the middle of the fifteenth century even that long-established trade seemed likely to be interrupted.

A hundred years later, a sea route to India had been found by western Europeans—by men of the Atlantic seaboard—and was in regular commercial use. An alternative, but longer and more dangerous route had been explored, into the south Atlantic and westward to southeast Asia. Trade had been opened with Malaya and some of the Indonesian islands. South China and Japan had been visited. Some of the ancient myths had been exploded. "Prester John" had turned out to be not a major Asian potentate, but a hard-pressed African one—the Negus of Abyssinia, a Christian of sorts, to be sure, but otherwise disappointing. Of all the major reported kingdoms of the East, only Marco Polo's "Cathay"—not yet identified with northern China—still eluded the European search. This is not to say, of course, that the whole of southern Asia was open to the trade of all Europe; far from it. In the East, except in the few harbors where Portuguese had settled and were entrenched, trade was limited to what Asian rulers would permit. In the Atlantic, the two Iberian sovereigns each jealously guarded his monopoly of the ocean route which his subjects had discovered. Further exploration had already indicated that these were the only sea routes; no others existed; none, at least, through warm or temperate latitudes. Other Europeans, it appeared, could trade by sea to the East only by defying Portuguese and Spanish naval power, which none of them was yet equipped to do; or else by finding a passage to "Cathay," east or west, through the Arctic ice. In the second half of the sixteenth century many northern Europeans turned their attention to the "northern passages," risking men, money, and ships in a hazardous and—as it proved—fruitless search. Others, again, turned back to the Levant and came to terms with the Turk, as the Venetians had done a hundred years before. In this sense too, the middle of the sixteenth century marked the end of a chapter in the story of maritime discovery.

Although the establishment of direct contact with the East was the main purpose and principal achievement of voyages of discovery in our period, it was not necessarily the only purpose and certainly not the only outcome. In the course of their search the explorers found an ocean bigger than the Atlantic, a continent as big as Europe and Africa combined. Within that continent Spaniards quickly established a territorial empire whose vast riches, in the middle of the sixteenth century, were just beginning to appear. More generally, the explorers discovered that the world as a whole was larger by far than any then accepted authority, ancient or medieval, had taught. They proved that the salt seas of the world, with a few insignificant exceptions, were all connected, so that a seaman, with courage, adequate provisions, and a "sufficient" ship, could in time reach any country in the world which possessed a sea coast. They encountered curious animals, unfamiliar plants, strange natural phenomena, in such variety that the purveyors of fabulous tales were almost put out of business, unable to compete with the truthful narratives of sober explorers. The human inhabitants of this vast and varied world similarly displayed an infinite variety, ranging from naked cannibals to the urbane officials of great and civilized empires, compared with which the kingdoms of Europe were disorderly petty states. Pious Europeans learned, with a sense of incredulous shock, that the peoples of the world, far from being divided (with a few trivial exceptions) between two great religions, one divinely, the other diabolically inspired, followed many faiths, and that some of these faiths contained elements worthy of a limited respect, so that their adherents were more to be pitied than blamed for their pagan ignorance.

The knowledge brought home by the discoverers, and spread about by the new device of printing, affected every aspect of European life and thought. Geographical exploration is the most empirical of all forms of inquiry, depending as it does on eye-witness experience. Practical navigators put the theories of revered authorities in cosmography to the test, and often proved them wrong. Inevitably men of inquiring mind were encouraged to question, by observation and experiment, accepted authority in other branches of knowledge. Again, appreciation of the number and diversity of human societies led Europeans to look with new and critical eyes at their own society and institutions. Unknown lands caught the imagination of philosophers, poets, and painters. On a more immediate and practical plane, discovery made Europe richer. Exotic goods, some rare and little known, others totally new, gradually became common in European markets; while the metals of the New World helped to finance the extension, eventually the predominance, of European commerce in the Old.

We must, of course, take care not to anticipate. These far-reaching changes did not occur overnight. Europeans took a long time to absorb the implications and exploit the opportunities revealed by an immense widening of their geographical horizon. Oceanic trade was speculative and dangerous, though tempting. Sailors knew this all too well, but it was some years before businessmen saw that new forms of organization, new methods of mobilizing capital and spreading risks, above all a new conception of long-term investment, would be needed to make it lucrative and safe. In the realm of science and philosophy, similarly, with evidence before their eyes that seamen were discovering lands formerly unknown and unsuspected, learned men hesitated at first to draw analogies in other fields of inquiry. The idea that there might be an America of learning and understanding beyond the horizon of the classics, ancient philosophy, and the teachings of religion was in those days new and strange, the vision of comparatively few men. Even in the field of geography itself, book-learning and sea-going experience drew together but slowly. Learned men were willing enough to place their cosmographical theories at the disposal of inquiring explorers, and to revise those theories in the light of the explorers' discoveries; but often the explorers failed to tell them what they really wanted to know. The great discoverers, like the rulers and investors who sent them out, were practical men. They were not primarily concerned with the enlargement of knowledge. Distant, unknown continents and islands, unless obviously productive of gold or other precious things, were of little interest to them. The cartographical techniques available for recording their discoveries were limited and laborious, and naturally they concentrated their labor and skill upon the places and routes of known wealth. The knowledge which they accumulated, vast in extent, was sketchy, rough, and uneven. For the most part it concerned only hastily explored coastlines and commercially useful harbors. It lacked precision; it left many gaps; and while it discredited some long-lived myths, it perpetuated others. In the story of discovery in the broadest sense, therefore, our period was a time of tentative, though splendid, beginnings. "Reconnaissance" seems the most appropriate term by which to describe it.

When all these qualifications have been stated, the bare facts remain: in the hundred years or so of Reconnaissance, European seamen achieved an enlargement of geographical knowledge astounding both in its extent and in its speed. In this respect no other century in the history of the world, before or since, is remotely comparable. For the first time, Europeans were enabled, with the confidence of experience and firsthand report, to think of the world as a whole and all seas as one. Why was this dramatic Reconnaissance undertaken at that particular time? How was it conducted? Why was it so strikingly successful? In considering these and similar questions we must not only trace the course of discovery, as narrated in the documents which follow, but also try to identify its preconditions: the knowledge, the will, and the means.

The knowledge

Western Europeans in the early fifteenth century were not wholly ignorant of the non-European, non-Christian world. In the Near East, Venetian and Genoese merchants occupied permanent factory compounds in most of the major trading centers, and current prices at Kaffa or Cairo or Damascus were commonplace talk on the Rialto. Numbers of other Europeans also regularly visited the area, at considerable expense it is true, but without great hazard. They went not as armed crusaders in the manner of their ancestors, but as pilgrims, impelled by a powerful mixture of piety, curiosity, and social emulation. The pilgrim traffic was highly organized, by the standards of the time, and was highly profitable both to the Christians who provided the transport and the Muslims who controlled access to the shrines. There existed a considerable volume of writing describing the Holy Land and neighboring countries, from which intending travelers could learn the routes they should follow, the authorities they should propitiate, and the tolls they would have to pay.

Europeans naturally knew much less of the vast and varied half-world of Asia beyond the termini of pilgrimages and Mediterranean trade routes. Ignorance was not total. For a hundred years or so, between the mid-thirteenth and the mid-fourteenth centuries, the military and administrative unification forced upon much of Asia by the Tartar Khans had made it possible to travel overland in reasonable security across the whole length of the continent. A number of European merchants and missionary ambassadors had traveled in the Great Khan's dominions, and a small community of Catholic Christians grew up in Peking itself, with, for a time, its own archbishop. Some of those who made journeys to the East wrote accounts of their experiences. These accounts were incorporated or summarized in other books: in serious historical or geographical treatises compiled by learned clerics, and in books of imaginary travels written to amuse an increasingly literate laity. They became part of the general stock of European knowledge; but, as the scribes went on copying them, they became increasingly out of date. After the middle of the fourteenth century such journeys ceased to be possible. Clavijo's embassy to Tamerlane in 1405 was an isolated incident; and Clavijo got nowhere near India or China. The "safe road to Peking," calmly so described in a fourteenth-century merchants' handbook,[1] had become extremely unsafe, and no European had followed it for many years. After John of Marignolli[2] in the mid-fourteenth century, indeed, there is no surviving eyewitness account of European travel in southern Asia until that of Nicolò de' Conti[3] in the mid-fifteenth, no account of eastern Asia until the sixteenth. The writings of Marco Polo are of immense, almost unique value to historians; but to an actual traveler in the fifteenth century they would have been about as helpful as the writings of A. W. Kinglake would be today.

Knowledge of Africa was even more sketchy and partial. The accounts of the great African travelers—Masudi, Ibn Haukal, El-Bekri, Ibn Battuta—were unknown to Europeans in their original form. Scraps of information derived from them, which filtered into Europe through Sicily or Spain, appear in the famous Catalan Atlas, drawn by the Jew Abraham Cresques in Majorca in 1375. The Arab travelers were far better informed about Africa than any Europeans. On the other hand, some of their geographical theories were both misleading and discouraging. Masudi, for example, believed the "green sea of darkness" (the Atlantic) to be unnavigable, and the frigid and torrid zones of the earth to be uninhabitable; and in these opinions he was followed by many later writers, both Muslim and Christian. As far as firsthand information went, Europeans knew something of the power and wealth of Mamluk Egypt. The Maghreb was known, through its long and intimate connection with the Iberian peninsula. Occasional reports also reached Europe of the kingdoms, mostly founded by Moorish

[1] Francesco Balducci Pegolotti, ed. A. Evans: *La practica della mercatura* (Cambridge, Mass., 1936).

[2] The Franciscan John of Marignolli was sent to "Cathay" in 1338, returned by sea to Quilon, thence via the Holy Land back to Avignon in 1353. H. Yule: *Cathay and the Way Thither* (2nd edn, London 1913–16), III, 249–250.

[3] See document 3 below.

adventurers, which flourished in the later Middle Ages along the southern fringe of the Sahara. These kingdoms imported manufactured goods and salt by trans-Saharan caravan and paid for them in gold. At least one enterprising Florentine made this arduous journey in the fourteenth century, and sold a consignment of Lombard cloth in Timbuktu. When the Portuguese in 1415, in the course of a crusading expedition of the old-fashioned kind, seized the fortress of Ceuta, they must have learned something of the caravan routes, and must have speculated—despite Masudi—on the possibility of reaching the southern Saharan kingdoms by water. Such a notion would not have been entirely new. The Catalan Atlas shows near Timbuktu a large lake from which one river, probably the Senegal, flows westward to the sea, and another, presumably intended to represent the Niger, eastward to join the Nile.

The lack of up-to-date reports based on firsthand knowledge, the absence of any firm criteria for judging the veracity of such reports as there were, no less than the intellectual habits of their time, drove students of geography in the early fifteenth century to a heavy reliance on "authorities." Academic treatises on cosmography and geography existed in profusion. Some, in the strait scholastic tradition, concerned themselves with symmetry and orthodoxy rather than with scientific verisimilitude, and drew their information chiefly from scriptural and patristic sources and from the handful of ancient writers long accepted as respectable. Others made extensive use of more recently recovered works of ancient science, coming to Europe chiefly through Arabic translations. Roger Bacon, to name an outstanding example, had a wide acquaintance with Arab writers. In the geographical section of his *Opus majus* of 1264, he maintained, on literary evidence, that Asia and Africa extended southward across the Equator, and that (contrary to Masudi and his followers) the torrid zone was habitable. Bacon exerted a powerful influence on the last great scholastic geographer, Cardinal Pierre d'Ailly, whose *Imago Mundi* was completed about 1410. This is a vast mine of scriptural and Aristotelian erudition, bearing little relation to travelers' experience—its author knew nothing, for instance, of Marco Polo. It had a widespread influence throughout the fifteenth century. It was printed at Louvain about 1483. Columbus' copy, with his marginal annotations, survives in the Colombina at Seville. Like all theorists of whom Columbus approved, d'Ailly, following Bacon, exaggerated the east-west extent of Asia and the proportion of land to sea in the area of the globe. Apart from his influence on Columbus, d'Ailly's work is of interest to us because of his acquaintance, wider even than Bacon's, with Arab authors and with little-known classical writers. D'Ailly not only summarized the best medieval academic thought on geographical questions; he was also the herald of a new and exciting series of classical recoveries and of geographical writings based on their inspiration.

Any fifteenth-century scholar—in the absence of firsthand experience, and outside the realm of revealed religion—would have preferred the testimony of a classical author to that of one of his own contemporaries, where the two conflicted. More influential even than *Imago Mundi* was the *Geography* of Claudius Ptolemaeus, which appeared in Latin translation at about the same time. Ptolemy was a Hellenized Egyptian who wrote about the middle of the second century A.D., at the time of the greatest territorial extension of the Roman Empire. He endeavored to summarize in his writings the entire geographical and cosmographical knowledge of his day. His works—both the *Geography* and an Astronomy known as the *Almagest*—were well known in the Arab learned world; the *Almagest* was translated by Gerard of Cremona, and briefly summarized by Sacrobosco in the thirteenth century under the title *De Sphaera Mundi*. Thanks to Sacrobosco, it was at least common knowledge among educated people in the later Middle Ages that the earth was round. All the more curious that the *Geography* remained so long unknown in Europe. It was translated not from an Arabic manuscript, but from a Greek one brought to Rome from Constantinople. The appearance of this translation was one of the most important events in the growth of European geographical knowledge.

In form the *Geography*—at least that part of the text which has survived—is an elaborate treatise on the construction of maps. Ptolemy divided his sphere into the familiar 360 degrees of latitude and longitude, and from his estimate of the circumference of the earth deduced the length of a degree of the Equator or of a meridian. He gives a method of adjusting the length of a degree of longitude for any given latitude, and explains how to construct a grid of parallels and meridians for maps drawn on a conical projection. This device, to fifteenth-century cartographers, was new and revolutionary. The main part of Ptolemy's text is a detailed development of this basic device; it consists of an exhaustive gazetteer of places, arranged by regions, with a latitude and longitude assigned to each place. Ptolemy, however, had no compass and no reliable means of observing longitude; and the number of reliably observed latitudes known to him was small. He could ascertain the positions of little-known places only by plotting their reported distance, along vaguely indicated lines of direction, from places better known; and calculating differences of latitude and longitude by means of plane—not spherical—triangles. Consequently, the positions which he gives for many places outside the well-known area of the Mediterranean are wildly inaccurate. Moreover, Ptolemy's general calculations embody two basic errors. From the many Greek estimates of the circumference of the earth—some of which were remarkably accurate—Ptolemy selected that of Posidonius, which was too small by about one sixth. Further, he assumed that the "known" world of his day—the land mass—covered exactly 180 degrees of longitude; he numbered these eastward from the furthest reported land in the west—the Canaries or Fortunate Islands—and stretched the continent of Asia eastward accordingly. In this exaggeration of the longitudinal extent of Asia, arriving at their conclusions independently and by very different routes, Ptolemy, Marco Polo, and Pierre d'Ailly all concurred.

Whether Ptolemy himself drew maps to accompany his text is unknown; but many fifteenth-century maps were drawn on his projection and in accordance with his instructions, and from 1477 were used to illustrate printed editions of the *Geography*. These Ptolemaic maps were greatly superior to medieval *mappaemundi*, and they covered areas not usually touched by the makers of marine charts. They were, nevertheless, misleading, and to mariners thinking of a sea route to India, entirely discouraging. They show, in addition to a detailed and reasonably accurate (though elongated) Mediterranean, the continents of Europe, Asia, and Africa. Africa is broad and truncated, India even more truncated, Ceylon greatly exaggerated in size. To the east of India is drawn another and larger peninsula, the Golden Chersonese; to the east of that again, a great arm of the sea, the Great Gulf; and finally, near the easternmost extremity of the map, the country of the Sinae. The country of the Sinae is joined continuously to the southern part of Africa, making the Indian Ocean a landlocked sea; and all around, to the east and south, is solid land, *Terra Australis Incognita*.

Ptolemy's theories were both stimulating and potentially enslaving; the advancement of geographical knowledge required that they should first be mastered and then superseded. It was a principal task of the Reconnaissance to challenge belief in the necessary superiority of ancient wisdom. In every branch of science there came a moment when western Europe, so to speak, at last caught up with the ancient world, and a few bold men, understanding and revering what the ancients had taught, were nevertheless ready to dispute their conclusions. Doubt and disputation are the business of scholars. Ptolemy was for more than a hundred years the leading academic source of geographical knowledge in Europe. Such an authority could not be lightly challenged; yet throughout the fifteenth century there were some scholars who kept open minds, who were willing to consider the possibility that Ptolemy—who, after all, had never been to India or China—might in some particulars be mistaken. Much more remarkable, in the last quarter of the century there were some hard-headed investors and practical seamen who were willing to gamble on the possibility; so urgent was the desire to make contact with the East, and so strong the will to achieve it.

The will

The European Reconnaissance has often been described as a continuation or adaptation of the Crusades. This is to oversimplify. The traditional pattern of crusade—a direct campaign against Muslim rulers in the eastern Mediterranean lands, with the object of capturing the Holy Places and establishing Christian principalities on the shores of the Levant—had by the fifteenth century long been abandoned as hopeless. The infidel was too strong to be dislodged, too clever and too irretrievably the Devil's to be converted. For the rulers of eastern Europe, with Ottoman power expanding and the Byzantine Empire slowly foundering before their eyes, crusading had become a stark matter of self-defense, a desperate *sauve-qui-peut*. In divided western Europe it was politically outmoded, driven from the minds of most rulers by other, more pressing concerns. It survived, however, in religious, literary, and social convention. The idea of smiting the infidel still had power to fire the imagination of men of gentle birth and adventurous impulses. This was true especially among the nobilities of Castile and Portugal, who were generally both belligerent and pious in the old-fashioned way, and who had close at hand the last remaining areas where the infidel might still be smitten effectively. These areas were Granada, a civilized but decayed remnant of a once-great Muslim empire, and Morocco. Here, minor and limited crusades could still be mounted with good hope of glory, profit, and lasting success. The Portuguese capture of Ceuta in 1415 was an example of such a crusade. Azurara, the chronicler, states that it was undertaken because Prince Pedro and Prince Henry wished to win their spurs in battle with the infidel; and this explanation accords entirely with the convention of the time and with what we know of the characters of the Princes. There were to be many subsequent assaults by Spanish and Portuguese expeditions on North African harbors, all undertaken in the same spirit of pious aggression.

These latter-day crusades were not part of the Reconnaissance, of the movement for oceanic discovery; on the contrary, they competed with it for money and royal attention. If, as is very probable, Prince Henry obtained in Ceuta information about the trans-Sahara gold caravans, which encouraged him to seek the source of the gold by sea, the connection must have been fortuitous. Such intelligence was not—so far as we know—among the objects of the expedition, and it did not divert Henry from conventional crusading. He was always ready to drop Atlantic and West African exploration in favor of direct military assaults upon Morocco, whenever his royal relatives could be persuaded to mount these costly and often fruitless adventures. Henry, however, though a dedicated crusader, was an unsuccessful one. He was given command of an assault on Tangier in 1437, which proved a disastrous failure. Thereafter his energies were concentrated principally upon the exploration of the Guinea coast. Guinea had separate, and quite different, attractions to offer. There was profit to be made from a trade in gold, ivory, gum-arabic, and slaves; and a religious duty to be discharged in the conversion of primitive pagans to Christianity. Moreover, Guinea might still have an indirect bearing on the crusade; the assiduous exploration of West African rivers reflected the old desire to establish contact with "Prester John," as a possible ally against the Saracen enemies of the Faith.

It is difficult to say when the search for a sea route to India became a serious object of Portuguese endeavor. Azurara does not mention it among Prince Henry's purposes;[4] though it must have been in his mind, if only as a symbol and a day-dream. In the twenty years after Henry's death, the attention of Portuguese ocean-going seamen was absorbed in fighting the Castillians—unsuccessfully, as it turned out—for possession of the Canaries, and in organizing the Guinea trade. These nearer objects competed with the enterprise of India not only in an economic and military sense, but geographically also. The Gulf of Guinea is a *cul-de-sac*, well off the route of a sailing ship bound for India. This began to be apparent about 1474, when the southerly trend of the Gaboon coast was discovered; but more than twenty years elapsed before the Portuguese government could formulate, and could venture to face, the unwelcome fact. Not until after the accession of João II in 1481 were ships sent south from Gaboon to look for the extremity of Africa—if Africa had an extremity. When that point had been settled (and Ptolemy confuted) the understandable hesitations of wary investors and an impecunious government had still to be overcome. It was not until the end of the century that the enterprise of India was separated from the enterprise of Guinea, and a fleet was despatched for India direct.

If the search for India had been only a matter of balancing possible profit against financial and maritime risk, the decision to attempt it might have been still longer delayed; but the pull

[4] See document 3 below.

which India exerted on the European imagination was not commercial only. The bull *Romanus pontifex* of 1455, which granted exclusive rights on the Guinea coast to Prince Henry's Order of Christ, stated that the Prince ". . . would best perform his duty to God in this matter [of exploration] if by his effort and industry that sea [to the south and east] might become navigable as far as the Indians who are said to worship the name of Christ. . . ." European Christendom in the fifteenth century was isolated and confined. Its bastions against Islam were falling, its territory was shrinking, and in the face of danger the Church was divided within itself. The leaders in the great Councils, who planned and negotiated to heal the schisms, looked longingly for reunion, not only within the Roman communion, but with all the communities of Christians throughout the world. They knew, or had heard, of many such communities: the Orthodox Greeks, fighting their losing battle against the Turk; Armenians, Syrians, and Copts, living within the boundaries of Muslim power; Chaldeans on the eastern flank of Islam; Ethiopian, Indian, even Cathayan Christians; and some Christian lands whose very existence was matter of hearsay—St. Brendan's Isle, and Antilla of the Seven Cities. Interest in these places was partly political and strategic, a search for sympathy, reassurance, and possible military support; but mixed with these practical ends was another, harder to define: a search for Christian perfection. Though fifteenth-century Europe was assured of its possession of Christian revelation, it had good grounds for doubting that its own institutions were the most perfect embodiment of that revelation. For some, at least, of its spiritual and intellectual leaders, perfection was not here, not now; it had existed long ago in time; it might be found again surviving far away in space. Of all the distant and reputedly Christian lands to which these plans and dreams became attached, the most appealing was India, where St. Thomas had preached and suffered martyrdom, and where the descendants of his followers—it was believed—still lived. When Vasco da Gama actually reached India, he explained to his reluctant hosts that he had come in search of Christians and spices—not spices and unbelievers, as a conventional crusader might have put it, or spices alone, as a mere merchant would have said.

Merchants, of course, had their part to play, and without their participation the Reconnaissance could not have taken place. Voyages of discovery were expensive and hazardous. Ships had to be hired, men recruited—for this was before the age of professional navies—and cargoes of trade goods provided. Rulers, whose income from taxation and feudal incidents barely sufficed for their ordinary needs, expected merchants to subscribe the necessary capital. Merchants would risk large sums in speculative undertakings only if they were assured of high returns in the event of success. An oceanic expedition could be an attractive investment, in fifteenth-century terms, only if it seemed likely to open up new and relatively cheap supplies of goods in high demand in Europe. Two classes of luxury goods were of particular interest: silks and spices. Silk—both raw silk and manufactured fabrics—had been the principal object of the journeys which the Polos and their successors had made across the length of Asia. Chinese silk was of good quality and relatively cheap to buy; its selling price in Europe much more than covered all the trouble and cost of overland transport. In the fourteenth century overland communications were much interrupted, and even if there had been a convenient alternative route by sea, the increasing isolation of the Ming Empire in the later fifteenth century would have prevented its extensive use. The extravagant Renaissance taste in clothes, however, caused a constant rise in the European demand for silk; so Italian dealers in it sought other sources of supply. Persian silk, though more expensive than Chinese, could be had in considerable quantity in Black Sea ports such as Trebizond, much frequented by the Genoese, and in Syria; and sericulture, in the fifteenth century, was widely expanded in Italy itself. There was no good reason to suppose that any better or cheaper supply could be found by any oceanic route.

Spices were another matter. The European craving for spices—indeed the necessity for spices, to preserve meat and make it palatable, especially in winter conditions in northern Europe—is well known. Apart from common salt, and a few minor spices such as saffron, Europe produced none of these preservative and flavoring substances. The best condiment and preservative spices grew in southeast Asia: cinnamon in Ceylon, pepper in Java and Sumatra, nutmeg and its derivative mace in Borneo and Celebes, cloves—the most valuable of all—in the Moluccas and the Banda islands at the eastern end of the Malay archipelago. These details, however, were unknown to fifteenth-century Europe. Europeans tended to lump together large areas of Asia under the general name of India, and they had heard or read of certain harbors in India—Calicut in particular—as markets where spices were sold. So far as they knew, these Malabar ports, or their hinterland, were the original sources of supply. Spices intended directly for the Arab and Ottoman areas, or indirectly for sale to Europeans, were carried from Malabar across the Indian Ocean by Arab shippers. They went to Ormuz, up the Persian Gulf to Basra, up the Mesopotamian rivers to Baghdad, to Damascus, and to the ports of Syria; or alternatively to Aden, up the Red Sea, and overland via Cairo to Alexandria, where Venetian traders bought them for transmission to Italy and to western Europe. Of course every middleman took his profit, and every ruler on the way his toll; but if the costs were high, so was the demand and so the ultimate margin of profit. If it were true that the Malabar ports were inhabited wholly or in part by Christians, and if those ports could be reached by a continuous ocean passage, it should be possible—so the Portuguese reasoned—to establish friendly commercial relations, at once to obtain spice cargoes, and eventually perhaps to divert the whole trade between India and Europe to their own ships. By so doing, they would cut out a series of rapacious middlemen, deprive the Saracen, in part at least, of the means of financing war against Christendom, and make immense and continuing profits.

Contact with India was an international preoccupation. The Portuguese were first in the field, and the Cape route long remained a Portuguese monopoly; but other European governments had similar aims, seeking other routes to India or to other parts of Asia. This competitive ambition called for a new type of specialist—the professional explorer. The exploring activity of the late fifteenth and early sixteenth centuries was dominated by a small group of men, regularly employed in difficult and dangerous tasks. They were not for the most part learned men. The fifteenth-century revival of ancient learning affected them only at second hand; that, no doubt, was one reason why they were not intimidated by Ptolemy. They were not Renaissance humanists consumed by intellectual curiosity. They had their full share of geographical curiosity, of course; that is one of the basic qualities of an explorer; but to judge from the scanty surviving records, their curiosity in other directions was limited. They investigated carefully, and fully reported, navigational data; the evidence of commercial wealth, political power, and military strength, in the countries they visited; and sundry customs, such as *sati*, nakedness, cannibalism, which struck them as specially remarkable or shocking. They were not dedicated missionaries; though they recognized a duty to attempt the conversion of heathen people, they saw no incongruity in enslaving and selling, when convenient, those who were to be converted. They were conventionally pious, aware of the value of Christian allies, ready enough to smite the infidel if they were strong enough, but also willing to trade or treat with him. They were not great men by birth; some indeed, were of humble origin, though most of them had enough training in arms and diplomatic courtesies to negotiate with civilized rulers. They were practical men. Some of them were simply bold and competent seamen, sent out to investigate ideas suggested by scholarly theorists; but others were themselves cosmographers as well as sailors, possessing the knowledge and the imagination to initiate proposals for discovery, and the persuasiveness and force of character to urge them upon rulers and investors. For the most part their national allegiance sat lightly upon them; like *condottieri* ashore, they were qualified and willing to serve any prince who would employ them. Drawing upon a common fund of geographical knowledge and surmise, they carried from court to court information which their employers would have preferred to keep secret; but such was the value set upon their skill that they were welcome wherever they chose to settle. The Portuguese government was more successful than most in employing its own subjects and keeping its own secrets; but eventually it was a Portuguese sailor of fortune in the service of Spain who discovered the passage to the South Sea and commanded the first expedition which was to circumnavigate the globe.[5]

The explorers were supremely bold gamblers, backing their skill and knowledge, their geographical intuition, their powers of leadership, staking their reputations and their lives. They ran greater risks than any *condottiere*; the odds were against a man returning

[5] See document 20 below.

alive from a long voyage of oceanic exploration. The prizes they sought, for their employers and for themselves, were far bigger than those for which the *condottieri* were hired to fight. They expected, in the event of success, to be well rewarded with royal honors, with grants of land and office, and with the profits of privileged private trade. Above all, as men of the Renaissance would, they expected individual recognition, reputation, and respect among their contemporaries and fame in posterity. Some of them were so rewarded. Vasco da Gama's rewards were munificent; del Cano was knighted—no empty honor then; Columbus died rich, though disgruntled; Vespucci gave his name, in his lifetime, to a continent. Their hazardous calling, in the stratified societies in which they lived, offered one of the very few ladders by which an obscure man might mount quickly to wealth and fame. It was a ladder which only the bold, the clever, and the lucky could hope to use.

The means

The men who sought the sea route to India, in the middle and later fifteenth century, were probably no bolder and no luckier than oceangoing seamen of preceding centuries. Nor, in geographical matters, were they significantly better informed; the knowledge available to them of the world outside Europe was largely derived from accounts of thirteenth- and early fourteenth-century travel, and much of it was misleading and out of date. Fifteenth-century ocean navigators, however, possessed some important advantages over their predecessors of earlier times. They had more powerful backing, more consistent encouragement and support; and they were much better equipped. These advantages were, indeed, crucial to the success of the Reconnaissance.

The most essential item of a sailor's equipment is his ship. The fifteenth century was a period of rapid change and development in the design of European seagoing ships. The development was not, to any significant extent, a response to the particular demands of oceanic discovery; on the contrary, the great voyages of discovery, with their immensely long passages through unknown oceans, were made in ships built for the everyday trades of western Europe. The fifteenth-century advance in the design of such ships was a necessary precondition of the Reconnaissance. It came about largely because of increasing commercial intercourse between the Mediterranean and Atlantic Europe. The ship-building fashions of northern and southern Europe in the later Middle Ages were local and distinct. Northern ships were usually clinker-built, in most cases with light frames inserted after the shaping of the hull. They were beamy, buoyant, and comparatively small. Their rig was normally a simple, indeed somewhat primitive square rig, usually with a single mast and a single sail. The Mediterranean was the home of a much more sophisticated maritime tradition. Two- and three-masted ships were common, with stout frames, their planking set edge to edge and pinned to the timbers of the frame. The commonest Mediterranean rig was the lateen, derived originally from the Indian Ocean or the Levant, and modified over the centuries for Mediterranean wind conditions. Mediterranean shipping had long tended toward specialization in two opposite directions: the development of large, deep, heavily timbered sailing ships for the carriage of bulky cargoes such as grain; and reliance upon oared vessels for fighting, for the carriage of valuable cargoes of small bulk, for all work requiring maneuvrability and speed. Neither the primitive, though seaworthy, northern "cog" nor the more specialized Mediterranean types were suited for voyages of discovery, which involved both long ocean passages and intricate coastal exploration. The aptest ships for such work were hybrids. Many small and medium-sized vessels, built on the Atlantic coasts of Spain and Portugal in the fifteenth century for the purposes of fishing, coastal trade, and island settlement, combined the virtues of both traditions: the stout frame and carvel planking of the south, the buoyant lines and bold sheer of the north. In the second half of the century the rig of these Iberian vessels displayed a remarkable versatility. They stepped two, three, even occasionally four masts, and used a variety of sail plans, including both square and lateen sails. Square sails on fore, or fore and main, gave them a large area of canvas combined with simplicity and ease of handling; lateens on the remaining mast or masts gave maneuvrability and better performance on a wind. The experienced Venetian, Cadamosto, considered Portuguese caravels to be the most versatile and seaworthy craft afloat in his day. They were the product of bold experiment and intelligent selection and borrowing. Prince Henry's choice of Sagres as the site of his little ocean-loving court was symbolic in more ways than one. Sagres Point was not only a bold headland jutting into the Ocean Sea; it stood, so to speak, on the street corner of Europe, between Atlantic and Mediterranean, and it overlooked one of the busiest and most varied shipping lanes in the western world.

In pilotage and navigation, as in the design of ships, Iberian seamen in the fifteenth century combined and developed two distinct traditions. Mediterranean navigators since the thirteenth century had used magnetic compasses and had possessed well-drawn marine charts based on a network of compass bearings. Most of these portolan charts were drawn in Italy; but in the later fifteenth century the art of making them was carried to Lisbon and Seville by the Genoese, who conducted much of the financial and commercial business of both cities. As exploration proceeded, therefore, the results could be recorded in graphic form, not indeed with mathematical accuracy—since no satisfactory plane projection had yet been invented—but with some degree of versimilitude, by both Iberian and Italian cartographers. In northern Europe, compasses were less widespread and charts almost unknown; but seamen who frequented the shallow waters of the continental shelf had collected a great body of tidal lore and had developed the use of the sounding lead for purposes of pilotage to a fine art. This skill, obviously essential for the exploration of strange coasts, was also acquired in the course of the fifteenth century by Spanish and Portuguese sailors who made trading and fishing voyages to northern Europe, sometimes as far as Iceland.

Men who proposed to make long passages in unfamiliar oceans, however, needed other skills in addition to those of chart navigation and pilotage. They had to be able to fix the position of a ship or a newly discovered coast or island, at least approximately, in order to return safely themselves, and in order to enable others to follow their track. For this, estimated bearing and distance from the point of departure were not enough; both could at best be only approximate, at a time when compass variation was not understood and no reliable method was known of estimating a ship's speed. It was necessary, or at least highly desirable, to record positions in terms of fixed coordinates, and this called for precise astronomical observation. Celestial navigation of a rough-and-ready kind is a comparatively primitive skill. European seamen had been aware for centuries that the altitude of the Pole Star at any particular place is constant, or nearly so, and that it changes in direct relation to distance north or south of the point of departure. Tenth-century Norse seamen, who had no compasses, probably sailed due east or due west across the north Atlantic by maintaining a constant polar altitude. Medieval methods of measuring altitude were rough indeed—so many spans, or the height of a man, or—as Cadamosto put it[6]—"about a third of a lance" above the horizon. Already in Cadamosto's day, however, this kind of eye-estimate was giving way to measurement with instruments. Portuguese navigators, sailing to and from the Atlantic islands or down the African coast, took to sea greatly simplified versions of appliances—astrolabe, quadrant, cross-staff—which had long been used for celestial observations by astronomers ashore. With these, in favorable conditions, they could measure differences of latitude to the nearest half degree. As they sailed through the Tropics and lost sight of the Pole Star, they looked for other heavenly bodies which could be used for the same purpose. The Southern Cross they found unsuitable; but in the 1480's, Portuguese astronomers, with royal encouragement, produced simplified vernacular versions of the solar almanac, giving tables of the sun's declination day by day throughout the year. With the help of these tables, an intelligent and literate navigator could calculate his latitude from the altitude of the sun at midday. By the end of the fifteenth century some Portuguese charts already carried scales of latitude, marked along a single meridian, usually that of Cape St. Vincent. Longitude was a much more intractable problem, not solved until the invention of ships' chronometers in the eighteenth century; though some early explorers, notably Vespucci[7] and Sebastian Cabot, made serious attempts to grapple with it. Meanwhile, however, knowledge of compass variation was

[6] See document 5 below.
[7] See document 14 below.

enlarged by observation at sea, and methods of estimating course and speed made good were steadily improved, so that difference of longitude could be calculated, at least roughly, from departure. At the end of the fifteenth century, therefore, a skilled navigator, using a combination of dead reckoning and observed latitude, could grope his way about the world with some approach to confidence; and regular trade could, in many waters, follow close upon discovery.

There remained the problem of human opposition. Dias, Columbus, Cabot, went in search of India, or Cipango, or Cathay, in small ships designed for coastwise trade, with few arms beyond the personal weapons of the ships' companies. Presumably they counted on a friendly reception, should their search prove successful. Their confidence was misplaced, as the Portuguese discovered on arrival in the East. Vasco da Gama's first voyage confirmed the hostile presence of Muslim rulers or traders in all the harbors which he visited. Da Gama's first fleet carried twenty small guns in three ships; enough for defense and for ceremonial display. His second expedition, and the expedition of Cabral which preceded it, were made in powerful fleets carrying large numbers of men and formidable armament. The Portuguese used their armed strength not only in self-defense, but in reprisals for real or fancied injuries, in demonstrations to force minor Indian rulers to allow trade, and soon in outright aggression. They were not always and everywhere successful; they received a severe mauling, for instance, from an Egyptian and Gujerati fleet off Chaul in 1508; but in general, when competently led they could defeat at sea any fleet which the eastern rulers could send against them. They owed their success chiefly to the stout construction of their ships, to the physical and moral effect of the firearms which they carried, and to an intelligent tactical use of these advantages. Guns and gunpowder, it is true, were not European monopolies, nor, in the fifteenth century, were they more highly developed in Europe than in some parts of the East, as the defenders of Constantinople had found. The use of guns as a major part of the armament of ships, however, was first developed by western Europeans. In the fifteenth century all guns were of iron, and only small and weak guns of the forged or built-up type were mounted in ships; but early in the sixteenth century techniques were developed for the casting

of much larger pieces in brass or bronze. The ability to manufacture such guns and to mount them along the broadsides of
sailing ships ensured the permanence of the European footholds
in the East.

Portugal and Castile had the ships and the sailors, the instruments and the weapons, the motives and the opportunity for
oceanic exploration. The major voyages of discovery mostly started
from Iberian harbors and the ships were manned mostly by Spaniards and Portuguese. Iberian seamen of the middle fifteenth century already possessed a great store of experience in oceanic work,
accumulated not only in trading, fishing, sealing, and slaving all
the way from Iceland to Cape Verde, but also in settling and
fighting in the Atlantic islands—Madeira, the Canaries, the Azores
—which were soon to become essential way-stations for the longer
oceanic voyages. In addition, Iberian seamen—the Portuguese
especially—enjoyed in the fifteenth century the advantage of consistent royal backing, which for the first time made possible a
systematic, step-by-step approach to the whole business of exploration. The Spanish and Portuguese governments, however,
lacked the capital, the commercial experience, and the financial
organization to mount frequent large expeditions and to exploit
the discoveries which their subjects made. It was the rapid growth
of the international money market in the later fifteenth century
which made adequate financial backing possible. Italian and German commercial and banking houses maintained networks of agen-
cies in all the principal trading and financial centers of western
Europe. The example of their business methods and their great
resources of capital for investment were available, at a price, to
the Spaniards and the Portuguese in the development of the
discoveries. Among the leading Italian traders, only the Venetians
held aloof—naturally, since their precious monopoly was threatened; they even egged on the Mamluk rulers of Egypt to attack
Portuguese fleets in the Indian Ocean. Other Italians were very
ready to support the Portuguese and Spanish enterprises and to
trade with India direct. Genoese residents in Seville invested in
Columbus' first and second voyages and were the chief backers
of Sebastian Cabot's expedition to the Río de la Plata. The Florentine house of Marchionni, established in Lisbon since 1443, invested
in Vasco da Gama's first voyage and in many subsequent ventures.

As for the Germans, the houses of Fugger, Höchstetter, and Welser all invested heavily in the early sixteenth-century Portuguese voyages to India, and the Fuggers, through their Spanish agent Cristóbal de Haro, provided the trade goods carried by Magellan's fleet. The international financiers retained their grip upon the trade and products of the Indies, East and West, because of the insistent financial needs of the Iberian governments. Though the beginnings of the Reconnaissance, the first great moves in oceanic discovery, were the work, for the most part, of adventurous Portuguese and Spaniards, the development of discovery, the foundations of settlement, trade, and empire were paid for by capitalists whose bases were in the older commercial centers of the Mediterranean and South Germany. To those centers, the profits mostly returned. International finance made the Reconnaissance the concern of all Europe.

II. *Theories, Rumors, and Travelers' Tales*

1. The cosmographical ideas of Sir John Mandeville

The Book of John Mandeville is a compilation of travelers' tales, thinly disguised as a guide to the Holy Land, but including descriptions and anecdotes of almost every country in the Near, Middle, and Far East whose name was known in Europe. Whether its author had ever visited the Holy Land is doubtful; he had certainly never traveled further east, and may never have been further afield than Liége, where he wrote his book and where, in 1372, he died. The information in the book is derived from other books. Mandeville's chief sources were the *Speculum historiale* and the *Speculum naturale* of Vincent of Beauvais; but he was a widely read man, if not in the technical sense a learned one, and he incorporated scraps from many other writers, some genuine travelers, some academic theorists, and some armchair travelers like himself. He delighted in monsters and marvels; nothing came amiss; and he freely assumed the pose of an eyewitness to lend verisimilitude to his tales. The skill with which he combined his diverse material to make a coherent whole was all his own. The book is well constructed, well written, and very entertaining; and this, no doubt, was what its author chiefly intended.

It may appear frivolous to include spurious travelers' tales in a collection of documents on discovery; but Mandeville had his influence in the Reconnaissance. He was widely read, in manuscript in the fifteenth century, in print in the sixteenth. He was much enjoyed by his readers, and probably at least half believed by many, who had no means of knowing whether his tales were true or false. His ideas—unlike those of, say, Ptolemy—encouraged exploration. Finally, for all his romancing, Mandeville gives a clear summary of the stock of cosmographical knowledge and theory available to an educated European of the later Middle Ages.

Mandeville wrote in French, but his work was quickly translated into

English. The extract which follows is part of a modernized version of
the Egerton text, from *Mandeville's Travels, Texts and Translations*, by
Malcolm Letts (2 vols., London, Hakluyt Society, 1953), I, 128–32.

A<small>ND</small> ye shall understand that in this land,[1] and in many other
thereabout, men may not see the star that is called *Polus Articus*,
which stands even north and stirs never, by which shipmen are
led, for it is not seen in the south. But there is another star which
is called Antarctic, and that is even against the tother star; and by
that star are shipmen led there, as shipmen are led here by *Polus
Articus*. And right as that star may not be seen here, on the same
wise this star may not be seen there. And thereby may men see
well that the world is all round; for parts of the firmament which
may be seen in some country may not be seen in another. And
that may men prove thus. For if a man might find ready shipping
and good company and thereto had his health and would go to
see the world, he might go all about the world, both above and
beneath. And that prove I thus after that I have seen. For I have
been in Brabant and seen by the astrolabe that the Pole Arctic is
there fifty-three degrees high and in Almayne towards Bohemia
it has fifty-eight degrees, and furthermore towards the north it
has sixty-two degrees of height and some minutes. All this I
perceived by the astrolabe. And ye shall understand that in the
south, even anent this star, is the star that is called Pole Antarctic.
These two stars stir nevermore; and about them moves the firmament, as a wheel does about an axletree. And so the line that is
between these two stars departs all the firmament in two parts,
either alike mickle. Afterwards I went toward the south, and I
found that in Libya see men first the star Antarctic; and as I went
further, I found that in high Libya it has in height eighteen degrees and some minutes, of which minutes sixty make a degree.
And so, passing by land and by sea toward the country that I
spake of, and other lands and isles that are beyond, I found that
this star Antarctic had in height thirty-two degrees. And if I had
had company and shipping that would have gone further, I trow
forsooth that we should have seen all the roundness of the firma-

---

[1] He is writing of one of the Indonesian kingdoms. [Ed.]

ment, that is to say both the hemispheres, the uppermore and the nethermore. For, as I said you before, half the firmament is between these two stars; the which I have seen. And of the tother I saw a part toward the north, that is to say sixty-two degrees and ten minutes under the Pole Arctic; and another part I saw toward the south, that is to say thirty-three degrees and sixteen minutes under the Pole Antarctic. And half the firmament contains but nine score degrees, of which I have seen sixty-two degrees of Arctic and ten minutes, and of Antarctic towards the south I have seen thirty-three degrees and sixteen minutes. These are four score and fifteen degrees and near half a degree. And so there lack but four score and four degrees and more than half a degree, that I have seen all the firmament. For the fourth part contains four score and ten degrees. And so the three parts have I seen and five degrees more and near a half. And therefore I say sickerly that a man might go all the world about, both above and beneath, and come again to his own country, so that he had his health, good shipping and good company, as I said before. And always he should find men, lands, isles and cities and towns, as are in their countries. For ye wot well that those men that dwell even under the Pole Antarctic are foot against foot to those that dwell even under the Pole Arctic, as well as we and those men that dwell against us are foot against foot; and right so it is of other parts of the world. For ilk a part of the earth and of the sea has his contrary of things which are even against him. And ye shall understand that, as I conjecture, the land of Prester John, emperor of India, is even under us. For if a man shall go from Scotland or England unto Jerusalem, he shall go always upward. For our land is the lowest part of the west and the land of Prester John is in the lowest part of the east. And they have day when we have night, and night when we have day. And, als mickle as a man ascends upward out of our countries to Jerusalem, als mickle shall he go downward to the land of Prester John; and the cause is for the earth and the sea are round. For it is the common word that Jerusalem is in midst of the earth; and that may well be proved thus. For, and a man there take a spear and set it even in the earth at midday, when the day and the night are both alike long, it makes no shadow til no part. And David also bears witness thereof, where he says *Deus autem rex noster ante secula operatus est salutem in medio terre*,[2] that is to say, "God our king before the beginning of the world wrought health in midst of the earth." And therefore they that go out of our countries of the west toward Jerusalem, als many journeys as they make to go thither upward, als many journeys shall they make to go into the land of Prester John downward from Jerusalem. And so he may go into those isles environing all the roundness of the earth and of the sea til he come even under us. And therefore I have oft-times thought on a tale that I heard, when I was young, how a worthy man of our country went on a time for to see the world; and he passed India and many isles beyond India, where are more than five thousand isles, and he went so long by land and by sea, environing the world, that he found an isle where he heard men speak his own language. For he heard one drive beasts, saying to them such words as he heard men say til oxen in his own country going at the plough; of which he had great marvel, for he wist not how it might be. But I suppose he had so long went on land and on sea, environing the world, that he was come in to his own marches; and, if he had passed furthermore, he should have come even to his own country. But for he heard that marvel and might get shipping no farther, he turned again as he came; and so he had a great travail. And it befell afterward that he went into Norway; and a tempest of wind in the sea drove him, so that he arrived in an isle. And when he was there, he wist well it was the isle in which he had been before and heard his own speech, as men drove beasts. And that might right well be; for all it be that simple men of cunning trow not that men may go under the earth but if they fall unto the firmament. For as us think that those men are under so, so think them that we are under them. For, if a man might fall from the earth to the firmament, by more skill [reason] the earth and the sea that are so heavy should fall unto the firmament. But that may not be, as God witnesses himself where he says, *Non timeas me, qui suspendi terram ex nichilo*,[3] that

---

[2] Psalm lxxiv, 12.

[3] Job xxvi, 7. This was a great point made by the supporters of the flat-earth theory. If the world were in fact round, the people on the sides and on the antipodes would be walking sideways or upside down, trees would be growing downwards and rain and hail falling upwards, and how could men walking upside down tread the serpent underfoot? Cosmas, who wrote about 540, a flat-earth enthusiast, drew a plan of the Antipodes in derision,

is to say, "Have no dread of me, that hanged the earth of nought."

And if all it be possible that a man may go all about the earth, nevertheless of a thousand peradventure one should not do it in all his life, for to take the right way all about the earth till he come til his own country again that he came from. For there are so many ways and countries that a man should lightly fail, but if it were by special grace of God. For the earth is right great and large, and it contains in roundness about, above and beneath, twenty thousand four hundred and twenty-five mile,[4] after the opinion of old wise men that say it, which I will not reprove, but after my feeble wit methinks, save their grace, that it is mickle more about. And for to make you to understand how, I imagine a figure of a great compass; and about the point of that compass, which is called the centre, be another little compass departed by lines in many parts and that all those lines meet sammen [together] on the centre, so that as many parts or lines as the great compass has be on the little compass, if all the space be less. Now be the great compass set for the firmament, the which by astronomers is divided in twelve signs, and ilk a sign is divided in thirty degrees; this is three hundred and sixty degrees, that it is about. Now, be the less compass set for the earth and departed in als many parts as the firmament, and ilk one of those parts answers to a degree of the firmament; these are in all seven hundred and twenty. Now, be these all multiplied three hundred times and sixty, and it shall amount in all til thirty-one thousand mile and five, ilk a mile of eight furlongs, as miles are in our country. And so mickle has the earth in roundness all about, after mine opinion and mine understanding. And ye shall understand, after the opinion of old wise philosophers and astronomers, that England, Scotland, Wales ne Ireland are not reckoned in the eight of the earth, as it seems well by all the books of astronomy. For the height of the earth is departed in seven parts, the which are called seven climates after

---

showing a round ball with a man on the top, two men at right angles on the sides and one upside down. Mandeville may have had this in mind. See generally Beazley: *Dawn of Modern Geography*, i, p. 294.

[4] Brunetto Latini (i. 3. III) gives the measurements as 20,427 miles, but Mandeville's computation comes probably from Eratosthenes by way of Vincent of Beauvais (*Spec. Nat.* vi. 13): "stadiorum ducentorum quinquaginta duorum millia, id est miliaria xxx et unum milia et D".

the seven planets that are called climates; and til ilk one of these planets is appropriated one of the climates. And these countries that I spake of are not in those climates, for they are downward toward the west. And also isles of India, which are even against us, are not reckoned in the climates, for they are toward the east. These climates environ all the world. Nevertheless some astronomers appropriate these foresaid countries to the moon, which is the lowest planet, and swiftliest makes his course. Now will I turn again to my matter where I left, and tell you of more countries and isles, which are in India and beyond.

2. Mandeville on the Great Chan of Cathay

Western Europeans in the late thirteenth and early fourteenth centuries were better informed about the Far East than they had ever been before, or than they were to be again for nearly two hundred years. The Tartar Khans, the successors of Chingis Khan the conqueror, governed, first from Karakorum and later from Peking, an empire which covered northern China and the greater part of Central Asia. They kept order on the caravan routes and tolerated, even welcomed, foreign ambassadors, missionaries, and traders. A number of Europeans made the arduous journey, partly or wholly overland, to the court of "Cathay," and some wrote detailed accounts and descriptions. Of surviving writings, the most informative are those of the missionary-ambassadors John of Plano Carpini and William of Rubruck, one despatched by the Pope in 1245, the other by Saint Louis in 1251; Marco Polo, the Venetian merchant who became a trusted official and spent nearly twenty years in the service of Kublai Khan; and Friar Odoric of Pordenone, who traveled to the East, partly by sea, between 1316 and 1318, and spent three years in Peking. Extracts from some of these eyewitness accounts were quickly incorporated in academic treatises such as the *Speculum historiale* of Vincent of Beauvais and Haiton's *Fleurs des histoires d'Orient*. The author of the *Book of John Mandeville* knew most of this literature well. For his descriptions of the Far East he drew most heavily upon Odoric of Pordenone, somewhat less upon Marco Polo, and upon Carpini, whose writings he knew indirectly from the pages of Vincent of Beauvais.

The chapter quoted here was lifted chiefly from Odoric; but the detail about the panther (panda?) skins came from Vincent and the comment on Cathayan contempt for the intelligence of foreigners, from Haiton.

In the middle of the fourteenth century, all this coming and going ceased. The Black Death inhibited travel. The militant Muslim power of the Ottoman Turks imposed a new barrier between East and West. The Tartar Empire broke up. In 1368 the descendants of Kublai Khan were driven from their Peking throne by a native dynasty, the Mings, who brought back the traditional official distaste and contempt for western barbarians. Mandeville, therefore, in popularizing information derived from Odoric, Marco Polo, and the rest, was not only fixing Cathay in the European mind as a symbol of wealth and splendor; he was also describing a political situation which, when he wrote in the 1360's, was passing away, to be replaced by one far less favorable to western contact. No news of this overturn reached Europe. The notions which Mandeville put about could not effectively be questioned. When Columbus, over a hundred years later, tried to reach Cathay by sailing west—an enterprise which Mandeville would surely have applauded—he carried letters of credence for the Great Khan.

The extract which follows is from *Mandeville's Travels, Texts and Translations*, by Malcolm Letts (2 vols., London, Hakluyt Society, 1953) I, 148–54: Chapter XXIII, "Of the Great Chan of Cathay; of the royalty of his palace, and how he sits at meat; and of the great number of officers that serve him."

THE land of Cathay is a great country, fair and good and rich and full of good merchandise. And thither come merchants ilk a year for to fetch spicery and other manner of merchandise more commonly than til other countries. And ye shall understand that merchants that come from Venice or Genoa or other places of Lombardy or Romany, they travel by sea and by land eleven months or twelve ere they come to Cathay, which is the chief realm of the Great Caan. And toward the east is an old city and near to that city the Tartarenes have made another city which they call Gaydon. This city has twelve gates and ever betwixt a gate and another is a mile, and so all the umgang [circuit] of this city is twenty mile and four. In this city is the siege and the see of the Great Caan in a right fair palace, of which the walls about are two mile and more; and within these walls are many other fair palaces. And in the garden of the great palace is a hill upon which is another palace, a fair and a rich; there is not such another in all the world. And all about the palace and the hill are many trees bearing divers manners of fruit; and without them are deep dykes and broad, and without them are many vivers [ponds] and stanks [lakes], whereon are many fowls of river, as swans and cranes, herons butours [bitterns] and mallards and such other. Without them also are all manner of wild beasts of venery, as harts and hinds, buck and deer and roe and many other. And aye when the Great Caan will have his disport in ryvaying or hunting, he may [have] wild fowl slain with hawks, and deer slain with hounds or other gins, and pass not his chamber. This palace with his see is wonder fair and great; and the hall of that palace is richly dight. For within the hall are twenty-four pillars of gold; and all the walls are covered with red skins of beasts, that are called panthers. And they are wonder fair beasts and well smelling, and because of the good smell of the skins, there may no wicked air come therein. These skins are als red as any blood and so fair shining against the sun that men may unnethe look on them or behold them for great brightness. The folk of that country worship that beast where they see it, for the great virtue and the sweet savour that come thereof; and they prize the skin thereof als mickle as it were of fine gold. In the midward of the palace is made an ascensory for the Great Caan, enorned [adorned] with gold and precious stones; and at the four corners are made four dragons of gold. And this ascensory is covered above with cloth of silk, barred overthwart with gold and silver, and many great precious stones are hanging about it. And under the ascensory are conduits full of drink, that they that are of the emperor's court drink of; and beside the conduits are vessel set of gold, that men may drink of when they will. This hall is nobly and worshipfully arrayed and ordained in all things. First, up at the high dais, even in the midst, is ordained the throne for the emperor, where he sits at his meat, well high from the pavement. His table, on which he eats, is made

of precious stones set in fine gold, and it is well bordered about
with fine gold set full of precious stones. And the grees [steps],
where he goes up til his throne, are all of precious stones en-
dented in gold. And at the left side of his throne is the seat of
his first wife, a gree lower than his throne; and it is of jasper,
with sides of fine gold set full of precious stones, and her board
is of jasper bordered with gold set full of precious stones. The
seat of his second wife is a gree lower than the tother; and both
her seat and her board are enorned worshipfully as the tother is.
The seat also of the third wife and her table are a gree lower than
the second. For he has evermore three wives with him, whereso-
ever he ride, far or near. Next his third wife, upon the same side,
sit other ladies of the emperor's kin, ilk one a gree lower than
other, after they are near of blood to the emperor. All the women
of that country that are wedded have standing on their heads as it
were a man's foot made of gold and precious stones and pea-
cock feathers that are shining curiously and well dight, in tokening
that they are under man's subjection; and they that are not wedded
have none such. Upon the right hand of the emperor sits his eldest
son that shall reign after him, a gree lower than his father. His
seat and his board are arrayed in all things as the emperor's are.
And then sit other lords of the emperor's kin, ilk one as they are
of degree, as ladies do on the tother side. And ilk one of them
has a board by himself, and right so have the ladies; and they are
either of jasper or of crystal or of amethyst or of *lignum aloes*,
which comes out of Paradise, or of ivory. And all their boards
are bordered about with gold set full of precious stones, so that
there is none of them that they ne are worth a great treasure.
Under the emperor's table at his feet sit four clerks that write
all the words that he speaks at his meat, whether they be good or
ill. For all that ever he says behoves [to] be holden and done in
deed; for his word may not be again called for no thing.

There are brought forth upon solemn days before the emperor
tables of gold, fair and great, in the which stand peacocks of gold
and many other manners of fowls of gold, curiously and subtly
wrought. And these fowls are so wonderfully made by craft of man
that it seems as they leaped and danced and beat with their wings,
and played them on other divers wise; and it is right wonderful to

the sight, how that such things may be done. By what craft they move so can I not say; but a [one] thing wot I well, that that folk are wonder subtle of wit touching anything that they will do, forbye any other folk of the world. For they pass all the nations of the world in subtlety of wit, whether it touch ill or good; and that know themselves well. And therefore they say that they look with two eyes and Christian men with one; for they hold Christian men most subtle and wise after themselves. Folk of other nations, they say, are blind without eyes, as anent cunning and working. I busied me greatly for to wit and perceive by what craft these foresaid things were done; but the master of the work said me that he was so bound by vow til his god that he might show that craft to no man but til his eldest son. Above the emperor's table and about a great part of the hall is made a great vine of fine gold; and it is wonder curiously wrought with many branches and grapes like unto grapes of vines growing, of which some are white, some yellow, some red, some black, some green. All those that are red are made of rubies or cremas or alabandines; the white are made of crystal or of beryl, the yellow are made of topazes or chrysolites; the green of emeralds, the black of onyxes or geraudes. And this vine is thus made of precious stones so properly and so curiously that it seems as it were a vine growing.

And before the emperor's table stand great lords and barons for to serve the emperor; and none of them is so hardy to speak word, but if the emperor speak first to them, out-taken minstrels that sing him songs, or say him jests, or tell japes or bourds [jests] for solace of the emperor. All the vessels that are served into his hall or his chamber, and namely at his own board or at boards where great lords sit, are of jasper or of crystal or of amethysts or of fine gold. And all their cups are of smaragds or of sapphires or topazes or of other precious stones. Vessels of silver make they none, ne set no price by silver. For they will never eat ne drink of the vessels that are made thereof; but they make thereof grees, pillars and pavements to halls and chambers. Before the hall door stand certain lords and many other knights for to keep that none enter in at the door but they that the emperor will, unless when he be of the household or a minstrel; other dare there none come near.

And ye shall understand that my fellows and I were dwelling soldiers with the Great Caan sixteen months against the king of Mancy, for they were at war when we were there. And the cause of our dwelling with him was for that we desired greatly to see his great noblay and the state and the ordinance of his court, and the great excellence of his riches, to wit whether it were such as we had heard tell before. And sickerly we found it more rich and noble than we heard say thereof; and we should never have trowed it if we had not seen it with our eyes. There is no such court here in this land. For kings and lords in these parts hold als few men in their courts as they may; but the Great Caan has ilk a day in his court at his cost folk without number. But ye shall understand that meat and drink is more honestly arrayed in our country than it is there; and also in this country men sit more honestly at the meat than they do there. For all the commons of his court have their meat laid on their knees when they eat, without any cloth or towel, and for the most part they eat flesh, without bread, of all manner of beasts; and when they have eaten they wipe their hands on their skirts. And they eat but once on a day. This is the array and the manner of the commons of the court of the Great Caan. But the array of himself and other lords that sit with him is noble and royal, passing all earthly men.

[For sickerly under the firmament is not so great a lord ne so rich, he not so mighty as is the Great Caan of Tartary. Not Prester John, that is emperor of India the less and the more, ne the sultan of Babylon, ne the emperor of Persia, ne none other may be made comparison of til him. Certes it is mickle harm that he ne were a Christian man; and not forbye he will gladly hear speak of God and suffer Christian men dwell in his empire. For no man is forbidden in his land to trow in what law that him list.] And if all some men peradventure will not trow me of this that I have said and will say it is but trifle that I tell of the noblay and the great excellence and riches of the Great Caan and of his court, and the multitude of men therein that I spake of before, I reck not mickle. But he that will trow it, trow it; and he that will not, leave.

3. Travel in disguise

The barrier between East and West remained almost continuously intact for a century and a half. Many Europeans traveled, for purposes of trade or pilgrimage, to the western fringe of the barrier in the countries of the Levant, for the Mediterranean commerce of Venice and other Italian cities soon accommodated itself to the facts of Turkish power. Very few Europeans, between the middle of the fourteenth century and the end of the fifteenth, succeeded in penetrating further, and those few did so by means of hazardous subterfuge: by traveling disguised as Ārabs and adopting at least the outward forms of Islam. Of this handful of travelers in disguise, the best known and most influential was Nicolò de' Conti, a Venetian trader who spent twenty-five years in the East; who visited Mesopotamia, India, Burma, the Indonesian archipelago, the approaches to the Red Sea, and Egypt; and who returned to tell the tale in 1441. Conti recounted his experiences to Poggio Bracciolini, secretary to Pope Eugenius IV. Poggio was a humanist scholar of formidable learning, who had himself traveled widely within Europe in the course of his ecclesiastical duties, and who was an enthusiastic amateur of travel further afield. He was interested in facts, in so far as they could be ascertained, rather than in tall stories, and he used the information given him by Conti as the basis of one section of his own book of historical reflection, *De varietate fortunae*. The section soon became detached from the rest of the work, circulated widely in manuscript, and was printed in 1492 under the title *India recognita*—the Indies rediscovered. Europe—at least Mediterranean Europe—was thirsting for knowledge of the East, and the Bracciolini-Conti account exerted considerable influence on geographical thought. Signs of its influence can be seen in maps, notably the so-called Genoese world map of 1457, and in the descriptions of India in the *Historia rerum ubique gestarum* of Aeneas Silvius Piccolomini, Pope Pius II. One of Conti's important contributions was to distinguish between Ceylon and Sumatra, which had long been confused under the Ptolemaic name of Taprobana.

The extract which follows is from *India in the Fifteenth Century,* edited by R. H. Major (London, Hakluyt Society, 1857): "The travels of Nicolò Conti . . . as related by Poggio Bracciolini, in his work entitled *Historia de varietate fortunae*, Lib. IV," pp. 3–21.

A CERTAIN Venetian named Nicolò, who had penetrated to the interior of India, came to pope Eugenius (he being then for the second time at Florence) for the purpose of craving absolution, inasmuch as, when, on his return from India, he had arrived at the confines of Egypt, on the Red Sea, he was compelled to renounce his faith, not so much from the fear of death to himself, as from the danger which threatened his wife and children who accompanied him. I being very desirous of his conversation (for I had heard of many things related by him which were well worth knowing), questioned him diligently, both in the meetings of learned men and at my own house, upon many matters which seemed very deserving to be committed to memory and also to writing. He discoursed learnedly and gravely concerning his journey to such remote nations, of the situation and different manners and customs of the Indians, also of their animals and trees and spices, and in what place each thing is produced. His accounts bore all the appearance of being true, and not fabrications. He went farther than any former traveller ever penetrated, so far as our records inform us. For he crossed the Ganges and travelled far beyond the island of Taprobana, a point which there is no evidence that any European had previously reached, with the exception of a commander of the fleet of Alexander the Great, and a Roman citizen[1] in the time of Tiberius Claudius Caesar, both of whom were driven there by temptests.

Nicolò, being a young man, resided as a merchant in the city of Damascus in Syria. Having learnt the Arabic language, he departed

---

[1] This refers to a story related by Pliny (*Hist. Nat.*, lib. vi, cap. 22), to the effect that a freedman of one Annius Plocamus, being overtaken by a tempest when off the coast of Arabia, was, after being tossed about for a fortnight, driven on shore at Hypuros, in the island of Taprobana. The king of this island, having questioned the freedman respecting the Romans, was so much struck by his answers that he became desirous of their friendship, and forthwith despatched ambassadors to Rome. The description given by these ambassadors of their island of Taprobana is inserted by Pliny in his history, and forms the twenty-second chapter of the sixth book.

thence with his merchandise in company with six hundred other merchants (who formed what is commonly called a caravan), with whom he passed over the deserts of Arabia Petræa, and thence through Chaldæa until he arrived at the Euphrates. He says that on reaching the border of these deserts, which are situated in the midst of the province, there happened to them a very marvellous adventure; that about midnight, while they were resting, they heard a great noise, and thinking that it might be Arabs who were coming to rob them, they all got up, through fear of what might be about to happen. And while they stood thus they saw a great multitude of people on horseback, like travellers, pass in silence near their tents without offering them any molestation. Several merchants who had seen the same thing before, asserted that they were demons, who were in the habit of passing in this manner through these deserts.

On the river Euphrates there is a noble city, a part of the ancient city of Babylon, the circumference of which is fourteen miles, and which is called by the inhabitants thereof by the new name of Baldochia.[2] The river Euphrates flows through the centre of the city, the two parts of which are connected together by a single bridge of fourteen arches, with strong towers at both ends. Many monuments and foundations of buildings of the ancient city are still to be seen. In the upper part of the city there is a very strong fortress, and also the royal palace.

Sailing hence for the space of twenty days down the river, in which he saw many noble and cultivated islands, and then travelling for eight days through the country, he arrived at a city called Balsera,[3] and in four days' journey beyond at the Persian Gulf, where the sea rises and falls in the manner of the Atlantic Ocean. Sailing through this gulf for the space of five days he came to the port of Colcus, and afterwards to Ormuz (which is a small island in the said gulf), distant from the mainland twelve miles. Leaving this island and turning towards India for the space of one hundred miles, he arrived at the city of Calacatia, a very noble emporium of the Persians. Here, having remained for some time, he learned the Persian language, of which he afterwards made great use, and also adopted the dress of the country, which he

[2] Baghdad.
[3] Bussorah.

continued to wear during the whole period of his travels. Subsequently he and some Persian merchants freighted a ship, having first taken a solemn oath to be faithful and loyal companions one to another.

Sailing in this wise together, he arrived in the course of a month at the very noble city of Cambay, situated in the second gulf[4] after having passed the mouth of the river Indus. In this country are found those precious stones called sardonixes. It is the custom when husbands die, for one or more of their wives to burn themselves with them, in order to add to the pomp of the funeral. She who was the most dear to the deceased, places herself by his side with her arm round his neck, and burns herself with him; the other wives, when the funeral pile is lighted, cast themselves into the flames. These ceremonies will be described more at length hereafter.

Proceeding onwards he sailed for the space of twenty days, and arrived at two cities situated on the sea shore, one named Pacamuria, and the other Helly. In these districts grows ginger, called in the language of the country *beledi*, *gebeli*, and *neli*. It is the root of a shrub, which grows to the height of two cubits, with great leaves, similar to those of the blue lilies called *Iris*, with a hard bark. They grow like the roots of reeds, which cover the fruit. From these the ginger is obtained, on which they cast ashes and place it in the sun for three days, in which time it is dried.

Departing hence, and travelling about three hundred miles inland, he arrived at the great city of Bizenegalia, situated near very steep mountains. The circumference of the city is sixty miles: its walls are carried up to the mountains and enclose the valleys at their foot, so that its extent is thereby encreased. In this city there are estimated to be ninety thousand men fit to bear arms. The inhabitants of this region marry as many wives as they please, who are burnt with their dead husbands. Their king is more powerful than all the others kings in India. He takes to himself twelve thousand wives, of whom four thousand follow him on foot wherever he may go, and are employed solely in the service of the kitchen. A like number, more handsomely equipped, ride on horseback. The remainder are carried by men in litters, of whom two thousand or three thousand are selected as his wives on condition that

[4] The Gulf of Cambay.

at his death they should voluntarily burn themselves with him, which is considered to be a great honour for them.

The very noble city of Pelagonda is subject to the same king; it is ten miles in circumference, and is distant eight days' journey from Bizenegalia. Travelling afterwards hence by land for twenty days he arrived at a city and seaport called Peudifetania, on the road to which he passed two cities, viz., Odeschiria and Cenderghiria, where the red sandal wood grows. Proceeding onwards the said Nicolò arrived at a maritime city which is named Malepur, situated in the Second Gulf beyond the Indus.[5] Here the body of Saint Thomas lies honourably buried in a very large and beautiful church: it is worshipped by heretics, who are called Nestorians, and inhabit this city to the number of a thousand. These Nestorians are scattered over all India, in like manner as are the Jews among us. All this province is called Malabar. Beyond this city there is another, which is called Cahila, where pearls are found. Here also there grows a tree which does not bear fruit, but the leaf of which is six cubits in length and almost as many broad, and so thin that when pressed together it can be held in the closed hand.[6] These leaves are used in this country for writing upon instead of paper, and in rainy weather are carried on the head as a covering to keep off the wet. Three or four persons travelling together can be covered by one of these leaves stretched out. In the middle of the gulf there is a very noble island called Zeilam,[7] which is three thousand miles in circumference, and in which they find, by digging, rubies, saffires, garnets, and those stones which are called cats' eyes. Here also cinnamon grows in great abundance. It is a tree which very resembles our thick willows, excepting that the branches do not grow upwards, but are spread out horizontally: the leaves are very like those of the laurel, but are somewhat larger. The bark of the branches is the thinnest and best, that of the trunk of the tree is thicker and inferior in flavour. The fruit resembles the berries of the laurel: an odoriferous oil is extracted from it adapted for ointments, which are much

[5] The Bay of Bengal. Mylapore, reputed burial place of St. Thomas, is now a suburb of Madras.

[6] The Fan Palm, or Palmyra tree (*Borassus flabelliformis*, L.): but the thinness of the leaves is enormously exaggerated.

[7] Ceylon.

used by the Indians. When the bark is stripped off the wood is used for fuel.[8]

In this island there is a lake, in the middle of which is a city three miles in circumference.[9] The islands are governed by persons who are of the race of bramins, and who are reputed to be wiser than other people. The bramins are great philosophers, devoting the whole of their life to the study of astrology, and cultivating the virtues and refinements of life.

He afterwards went to a fine city of the island Taprobana, which island is called by the natives Sciamuthera.[10] He remained one year in this city (which is six miles in circumference and a very noble emporium of that island), and then sailed for the space of twenty days with a favorable wind, leaving on his right hand an island called Andamania,[11] which means the island of gold, the circumference of which is eight hundred miles. The inhabitants are cannibals. No travellers touch here unless driven so to do by bad weather, for when taken they are torn to pieces and devoured by these cruel savages. He affirms that the island of Taprobana is six thousand miles in circumference. The men are cruel and their customs brutal. The ears both of the men and women are very large, in which they wear earrings ornamented with precious stones. Their garments are made of linen and silk, and hang down to their knees. The men marry as many wives as they please. Their houses are extremely low, in order to protect them against the excessive heat of the sun. They are all idolators. In this island pepper, larger than the ordinary pepper, also long pepper, camphor, and also gold are produced in great abundance. The tree which produces the pepper is similar to the ivy, the seeds are green and resemble in form those of the juniper tree: they dry them in the sun, spreading a few ashes over them. In this island there also grows a green fruit, which they call *duriano*,[12]

[8] This account of the cinnamon is remarkably exact.

[9] There are no longer any traces of a lake in the center of Ceylon of sufficient magnitude to contain a city three miles in circumference.

[10] Sumatra.

[11] The Andaman Isles. The three principal islands lying in close contiguity with each other may have been mistaken by Conti for one island.

12 *Durio Zibthinus*, L., one of the most highly esteemed fruits of the Malay Islands, but extremely offensive to those who are unaccustomed to it, on account of its nauseous odour.

of the size of a cucumber. When opened five fruits are found
within, resembling oblong oranges. The taste varies, like that of
cheese.

In one part of the island called Batech, the inhabitants eat
human flesh, and are in a state of constant warfare with their
neighbours.[13] They keep human heads as valuable property, for
when they have captured an enemy they cut off his head, and having eaten the flesh, store up the skull and use it for money. When
they desire to purchase any article, they give one or more heads
in exchange for it according to its value, and he who has most
heads in his house is considered to be the most wealthy.

Having departed from the island of Taprobana he arrived, after
a stormy passage of sixteen days, at the city of Ternassari,[14] which
is situated on the mouth of a river of the same name. This district abounds in elephants and a species of thrush.

Afterwards, having made many journeys both by land and sea,
he entered the mouth of the river Ganges, and, sailing up it,
at the end of fifteen days he came to a large and wealthy city,
called Cernove. This river is so large that, being in the middle
of it, you cannot see land on either side. He asserts that in some
places it is fifteen miles in width. On the banks of this river there
grow reeds extremely high, and of such surprising thickness that
one man alone cannot encompass them with his arms:[15] they make
of these fishing boats, for which purpose one alone is sufficient,
and of the wood or bark, which is more than a palm's breadth in
thickness, skiffs adapted to the navigation of the river. The distance
between the knots is about the height of a man. Crocodiles and
various kinds of fishes unknown to us are found in the river. On
both banks of the stream there are most charming villas and
plantations and gardens, wherein grow vast varieties of fruits,
and above all those called *musa*,[16] which are more sweet than

[13] Batta; a district extending from the river Singkell to the Tabooyong,
and inland to the back of Ayer Bañgis. Marsden, in his *History of Sumatra*
(p. 390, 3rd edn.), gives instances of canibalism among this people as late
as the year 1780.

[14] Tenasserim, the capital of a district of the same name in the Birman
Empire.

[15] Bamboos.

[16] Bananas. *Musa Paradisiaca*, L.

honey, resembling figs, and also the nuts which we call nuts of India.[17]

Having departed hence he sailed up the river Ganges for the space of three months, leaving behind him four very famous cities, and landed at an extremely powerful city called Maarazia, where there is a great abundance of aloe wood, gold, silver, precious stones, and pearls. From thence he took the route towards some mountains situated towards the east, for the purpose of procuring those precious stones called carbuncles, which are found there. Having spent thirteen days on this expedition, he returned to the city of Cernove, and thence proceeded to Buffetania. Departing thence he arrived, at the end of a month's voyage, at the mouth of the river Racha,[18] and navigating up the said river, he came in the space of six days to a very large city called by the same name as the river, and situated upon the bank thereof.

Quitting this city he travelled through mountains void of all habitations[19] for the space of seventeen days, and then through open plains for fifteen days more, at the end of which time he arrived at a river larger than the Ganges, which is called by the inhabitants Dava.[20] Having sailed up this river for the space of a month he arrived at a city more noble than all the others, called Ava, and the circumference of which is fifteen miles.

In this city he said there were several shops of ridiculous and lascivious things, about which I have written for the fun of it; in these shops only women sell things which we call "ringers" because they ring out like bells; they are made of gold, silver or brass, and are as big as a small nut. The men, before they take a wife, go to these women (otherwise the marriage would be broken) who cut the skin of the virile member in many places and put between the skin and the flesh as many as twelve of these "ringers" (according to their pleasure). After the member is sewn up, it heals in a few days. This they do to satisfy the wantonness of the women: because of these swellings, or tumour,

[17] Cocoanuts, formerly called *Nuces Indicæ*.
[18] Aracan.
[19] The Youmadoung Mountains, forming the western boundary of Burmah Proper.
[20] The Irrawaddy.

of the member, the women have great pleasure in coitus. The members of some men stretch down between their legs so that when they walk they ring out and may be heard. But Nicolò, scorned by the women because he had a small member and invited to rectify this, was not willing through his pain to give others pleasure.

This province, which is called by the inhabitants Macinus,[21] abounds in elephants. The king keeps ten thousand of these animals, and uses them in his wars. They fix castles on their backs, from which eight or ten men fight with javelins, bows, and those weapons which we call crossbows. Their manner of capturing these elephants is said to be generally as follows, and it agrees with the mode stated by Pliny (lib. 8, c. 8): In the rutting season they drive tame female elephants into the woods, where they are left until the wild male elephants seek them; the female then gradually withdraws, feeding, into a place set apart for this purpose, surrounded by a wall and furnished with two large doors, one for the entrance and another for exit. When the elephant perceives the female to be there and enters by the first door to come to her, she, as soon as she sees him, runs out through the other, and the doors are then immediately closed. As many as a thousand men then enter, through apertures made for that purpose in the walls, with very strong ropes with running nooses; a man then presents himself to the beast in the forepart of the enclosure. As soon as the elephant sees him he runs furiously at him to kill him, while the men behind throw the nooses over his hind feet as he raises them, and then drawing the cords tight fasten them to a pole fixed into the ground, and leave the elephant there for three or four days, giving him only a little grass daily. In the course of fifteen days he becomes quiet. They afterwards tie him between two tame elephants and lead him through the city, and thus in ten days he is rendered as tame as the others.

It is also related by Nicolò, that in other parts they tame them thus. They drive the elephants into a small valley enclosed on all sides, and having removed the females they leave the males shut up there, and tame them by hunger. At the end of four days

[21] This province cannot be Mangi, as supposed by Ramusio, but is most probably Siam, formerly called Sian.

they drive them thence and conduct them to narrow places constructed for the purpose, and there make them gentle. The kings purchase these for their own use. The tame elephants are fed upon rice and butter, and the wild ones eat branches of trees and grass. The tame elephants are governed by one man, who guides them with an iron hook, which is applied to the head. This animal is so intelligent, that when he is in battle he frequently receives the javelins of the enemy on the sole of his foot, in order that those whom he carries on his back may not be injured. The king of this province rides on a white elephant, round the neck of which is fastened a chain of gold ornamented with precious stones, which reaches to its feet.

The men of this country are satisfied with one wife; and all the inhabitants, as well men as women, puncture their flesh with pins of iron, and rub into these punctures pigments which cannot be obliterated, and so they remain painted for ever. All worship idols: nevertheless when they rise in the morning from their beds they turn towards the east, and with their hands joined together say, "God in Trinity and His law defend us."

In this country there is a kind of apple, very similar to a pomegranate, full of juice and sweet.[22] There is also a tree called *tal*,[23] the leaves of which are extremely large, and upon which they write, for throughout all India they do not use paper excepting in the city of Cambay. This tree bears fruit like large turnips, the juice contained under the bark becoming solid, forms very agreeable sweet food.

This country produces frightful serpents[24] without feet, as thick as a man, and six cubits in length. The inhabitants eat them roasted, and hold them in great esteem as food. They also eat a kind of red ant, of the size of a small crab, which they consider a great delicacy seasoned with pepper.

There is here also an animal which has a head resembling that of a pig, a tail like that of an ox, and on his forehead a horn similar to that of the unicorn, but shorter, being about a cubit

[22] Probably the Jamboo apple: *Eugenia Jambos*. L.
[23] The Fan Palm. See fn. 6 above.
[24] A species of python.
[25] The rhinoceros.

in length.[25] It resembles an elephant in size and colour, with which it is constantly at war. It is said that its horn is an antidote against poisons, and is on that account much esteemed.

In the upper part of this country, towards Cathay, there are found white and black bulls, and those are most prized which have hair and a tail like that of a horse, but the tail more full of hair and reaching to their feet. The hair of the tail, which is very fine and as light as a feather, is valued at its weight in silver. Of this kind of hair they make fans, which are used for the service of their idols and of their kings. They also place them over the crupper of their horses in a gold or silver cone, so that they may completely cover the hinder parts of the animal: they also fasten them to the neck, so that, hanging down, they may form an ornament to the breast. This is considered a distinguished kind of embellishment. The cavalry also carry the hair at the head of their lances as a mark of high nobility.

Beyond this province of Macinus is one which is superior to all others in the world, and is named Cathay. The lord of this country is called the Great Khan, which in the language of the inhabitants means emperor. The principal city is called Cambaleschia.[26] It is built in the form of a quadrangle, and is twenty-eight miles in circumference. In the center is a very handsome and strong fortress, in which is situated the king's palace. In each of the four angles there is constructed a circular fortress for defense, and the circuit of each of these is four miles. In these fortresses are deposited military arms of all sorts, and machines for war and the storming of cities. From the royal palace a vaulted wall extends through the city to each of the said four fortresses, by which, in the event of the people rising against the king, he can retire into the fortresses at his pleasure. Fifteen days distant from this city there is another, very large, called Nemptai,[27] which has been built by this king. It is thirty miles in circumference, and more populous than the others. In these two cities, according to the statement of Nicolò, the houses and palaces and other ornaments are similar to those in Italy: the men, gentle and dis-

---

[26] Cambaluc, or Peking.

[27] Nemptai is supposed to be the same as the city called, in the time of Marco Polo, Hăng-chow-Keun-che, and in common parlance Keun-che, whence the corruption Quin-sai. Its present name is Hăng-chow-foo.

creet, wise, and more wealthy than any that have been before mentioned.

Afterwards he departed from Ava and proceeded towards the sea, and at the expiration of seventeen days he arrived at the mouth of a moderately sized river,[28] where there is a port called Xeythona; and having entered the river, at the end of ten days he arrived at a very populous city called Panconia, the circumference of which is twelve miles.[29] He remained here for the space of four months. This is the only place in which vines are found, and here in very small quantity: for throughout all India there are no vines, neither is there any wine. And in this place they do not use the grape for the purpose of making wine. They have pine apples, oranges, chestnuts, melons, but small and green, white sandal wood, and camphor. The camphor is found within the tree, and if they do not sacrifice to the gods before they cut the bark, it disappears and is no more seen.

In central India there are two islands towards the extreme confines of the world, both of which are called Java. One of these islands is three thousand miles in circumference, the other two thousand. Both are situated towards the east, and are distinguished from each other by the names of the Greater and the Less. These islands lay in his route to the ocean. They are distant from the continent one month's sail, and lie within one hundred miles of each other.[30] He remained here for the space of nine months with his wife and children, who accompanied him in all his journeys.

The inhabitants of these islands are more inhuman and cruel than any other nation, and they eat mice, dogs, cats, and all other kinds of unclean animals. They exceed every other people in cruelty. They regard killing a man as a mere jest, nor is any punishment allotted for such a deed. Debtors are given up to their creditors to be their slaves. But he who, rather than be a slave, prefers death, seizing a naked sword issues into the street and kills all he meets, until he is slain by some one more powerful than himself: then comes the creditor of the dead man and cites him by whom he was killed, demanding of him his debt, which he is constrained by the judges to satisfy.

[28] Most probably the river Pegu.
[29] Pegu is the city which corresponds most nearly with this description.
[30] Perhaps Java and Sumatra? Or Java and Sumbawa?

If any one purchase a new scimiter or sword and wish to try it, he will thrust it into the breast of the first person he meets neither is any punishment awarded for the death of that man. The passers by examine the wound, and praise the skill of the person who inflicted it if he thrust the weapon in direct. Every person may satisfy his desires by taking as many wives as he pleases.

The amusement most in vogue amongst them is cock-fighting. Several persons will produce their birds for fighting, each maintaining that his will be the conqueror. Those who are present to witness the sport make bets amongst themselves upon these combatants, and the cock that remains conquerer decides the winning bet.

In Great Java a very remarkable bird is found, resembling a wood pigeon, without feet, of slight plumage, and with an oblong tail; it always frequents trees. The flesh of this bird is not eaten, but the skin and tail are highly prized, being used as ornaments for the head.[30]

At fifteen days' sail beyond these islands eastward, two others are found: the one is called Sandai, in which nutmegs and maces grow; the other is named Bandan; this is the only island in which cloves grow, which are exported hence to the Java islands. In Bandan three kinds of parrots are found, some with red feathers and a yellow beak, and some party-coloured, which are called *nori*,[31] that is *brilliant*, both kinds of the size of doves: also some white of the size of hens. These last are called *cachi*,[32] which means the more excellent: they excel in talking, imitating human speech in a wonderful manner, and even answering questions. The inhabitants of both islands are black. The sea is not navigable beyond these islands, and the stormy atmosphere keeps navigators at a distance.

Having quitted Java, and taken with him such articles as were useful for commerce, he bent his course westward to a maritime city called Ciampa, abounding in aloes wood, camphor, and gold, In that journey he occupied one month; and departing thence, he,

[30] A bird of Paradise?
[31] A lory?
[32] A cockatoo?

in the same space of time, arrived at a noble city called Coloen,[33] the circumference of which is twelve miles. This province is called Melibaria,[34] and they collect in it ginger, called by the natives *colobi*, pepper, brazil wood, and cinnamon, which is known there by the name of *crassa*. There are also serpents without feet, six ells in length, wild, but harmless unless irritated. They are pleased with the sight of little children, and by this means are enticed into the presence of men.[35] In the same province, and also in another called Susinaria, there is found another kind of serpent with four feet, and an oblong tail like that of large dogs, which are hunted for food. It is as harmless as kids or goats, and the flesh is prized as the best kind of food.

This region also produces other serpents of a remarkable form, one cubit in length and winged like bats. They have seven heads arranged along the body, and live in trees. They are extremely rapid in flight, and the most venomous of all, destroying men by their breath alone. There are also flying cats, for they have a pellicle extending from the fore to the hinder feet and attached to the body, which is drawn up when they are at rest.[36] They fly from tree to tree by extending their feet and shaking their wings. When pursued by hunters they fall to the earth when fatigued by flying, and so are taken. A tree grows here in great abundance, the trunk of which produces fruit resembling the pineapple, but so large as to be lifted with difficulty by one man; the rind is green and hard, but yields nevertheless to the pressure of the finger. Within are from two hundred and fifty to three hundred apples, resembling figs, very sweet to the taste, and which are separated from each other by follicles. They have a kernel within, resembling the chestnut in hardness and flavour, flatulent, and which is cooked in the same manner as the chestnut; when thrown upon live embers, unless previously incised somewhat, it bounces up with a crackling noise. The external bark is used as provender for cattle.[37] The fruit of this tree is some-

[33] Quilon?
[34] Malabar.
[35] The python.
[36] The Galeopithecus.
[37] The tree here described is clearly the Jack (*Artocarpus integrifolia*, L.) The subsequent reference to incised leaves, however, suggests confusion with the breadfruit, *Artocarpus incisa*. [Ed.]

times found under the earth in its roots; these excel the others in flavour, and for this reason it is the custom to set these apart for royal use. This fruit has no kernel. The tree is like a large fig tree, the leaves being intercised like those of the palm: the wood is equal to boxwood, and is therefore much prized for its applicability to many purposes. The name of this tree is *cachi*. There is also another fruit, called *amba*,[38] green and resembling very much a nut, but larger than the nectarine; the outer rind is bitter, but within it is sweet like honey: before they are ripe they steep them in water to remove the acidity, in the same manner as we are in the habit of steeping green olives.

Having quitted Coloen he arrived, after a journey of three days, at the city Cocym.[39] This city is five miles in circumference, and stands at the mouth of a river, from which it derives its name. Sailing for some time in this river he saw many fires lighted along the banks, and thought that they were made by fishermen. But those who were with him in the ship exclaimed, smiling, "Icepe, Icepe." These have the human form, but may be called either fishes or monsters, which, issuing from the water at night, collect wood, and procuring fire by striking one stone against another, ignite it and burn it near the water; the fishes, attracted by the light, swim toward it in great numbers, when these monsters, who lie hid in the water, seize them and devour them. They said that some which they had taken, both male and female, differed in no respect as to their form from human beings. In this district the same fruits are found as in Coloen.

He then visited in succession Colanguria, which is placed at the mouth of another river, Paliuria, and then Meliancota, which name in the language of the country signifies great city. This last city is eight miles in circumference. He next proceeded to Calicut, a maritime city, eight miles in circumference, a noble emporium for all India, abounding in pepper, lac, ginger, a larger kind of cinnamon, myrobalans, and zedoary. In this district alone the women are allowed to take several husbands, so that some have ten and more. The husbands contribute amongst themselves to the maintenance of the wife, who lives apart from her husbands. When one visits her he leaves a mark at the door of the house,

[38] The Mango (*Mangifera Indica*, L.).
[39] Cochin?

which being seen by another coming afterwards, he goes away
without entering. The children are allotted to the husbands at
the will of the wife. The inheritance of the father does not
descend to the children, but to the grandchildren. Departing from
Calicut, he proceeded next westward to Cambay, which he reached
in fifteen days. Cambay is situated near to the sea, and is twelve
miles in circuit; it abounds in spikenard, lac, indigo, myrobalans,
and silks. There are priests here who are called bachari, who only
marry one wife. The wife is, by law, burnt with the body of
her husband. These priests do not eat any animal food, but live
upon rice, milk, and vegetables. Wild cattle are found in great
abundance, with manes like those of horses, but with longer hair,
and with horns so long that when the head is turned back they
touch the tail. These horns being extremely large, are used like
barrels for carrying water on journeys.

Returning to Calicut, he spent two months on the island of
Sechutera, which trends westward, and is distant one hundred
miles from the continent.[40] This island produces Socotrine aloes,
is six hundred miles in circumference, and is for the most part
inhabited by Nestorian Christians.

Opposite to this island, and at a distance of not more than five
miles, there are two other islands, distant from each other one
hundred miles, one of which is inhabited by men and the other
by women. Sometimes the men pass over to the women, and
sometimes the women pass over to the men, and each return to
their own respective islands before the expiration of six months.
Those who remain on the island of the others beyond this fatal
period die immediately. Departing hence, he sailed in five days to
Aden, an opulent city, remarkable for its buildings. He then sailed
over to Æthiopia, where he arrived in seven days, and anchored
in a port named Barbora. He then, after sailing for a month,
landed at a port in the Red Sea called Gidda,[41] and subsequently
near Mount Sinai, having spent two months in reaching this place
from the Red Sea, on account of the difficulty of the navigation.
He afterwards travelled through the desert to Carras,[42] a city of

---

[40] This must be the island of Socotra, and the continent mentioned in the
text the African continent; but the size of the island is much exaggerated.
[41] Jeddah?
[42] Cairo?

Egypt, with his wife and four children and as many servants. In this city he lost his wife, and two of his children, and all his servants by the plague. At length, after so many journeys by sea and land, he arrived in safety at his native country, Venice, with his two children.

III. *Africa*

4. Prince Henry of Portugal

Between 1420 and 1460 Madeira and the Azores were settled by Portuguese adventurers, and a series of Portuguese expeditions explored the West African coast as far south as Sierra Leone. Most of these expeditions—at least those of which record remains—were undertaken by the command, or with the encouragement, of Prince Henry of Portugal, the "Navigator," most famous of the precursors and inspirers of the Reconnaissance. The waters between Cape St. Vincent, the Canaries, and the northwest coast of Morocco were already known in his day to adventurous Portuguese fishermen. Prince Henry placed gentlemen of his own household in command of the ships, and set them definite geographical objects to be reached and passed. Thus from the habit of making fishing and casual trading voyages along a relatively short stretch of coast, there developed a program of progressive, though intermittent, exploration much further south. In the extract quoted here, Azurara, the contemporary chronicler of Prince Henry's achievements, lists the motives which impelled the Prince to support these enterprises. They were the traditional motives of an orthodox medieval prince. Even the last—Prince Henry's desire to fulfill the predictions of his horoscope—was a conventional late medieval attitude, and a reminder that in his day astronomical knowledge was still more commonly applied to fortune-telling than to navigation. Azurara, it is true, wrote as a panegyrist in Prince Henry's lifetime; but that is all the more reason for supposing that he emphasized traits in which Henry himself took pride—his rigid piety, his personal asceticism, his obsession with the idea of the Crusade.

Henry's activities attracted considerable interest in learned circles in Italy; Poggio Bracciolini, among others, addressed adulatory letters to the Prince. Yet Henry himself, it is clear, was no Renaissance humanist. There is no evidence that he shared the omnivorous curiosity, the intellectual excitement, the passion for the revival of classical learning and ancient science, of a man like Poggio. He was not particularly learned himself, and unlike his royal brothers he left no writings. Henry was a generous patron of sailors and cartographers; but the story of a school of astronomy and mathematics at Sagres is pure invention.

The extract which follows is from *The Chronicle of the Discovery and Conquest of Guinea,* by Gomes Eannes de Azurara, translated and edited by Charles Raymond Beazley and Edgar Prestage (2 vols., London, Hakluyt Society, 1896), I, 27–30: Chapter VII, "in which five reasons appear why the Lord Infant was moved to command the search for the lands of Guinea."

WE imagine that we know a matter when we are acquainted with the doer of it and the end for which he did it. And since in former chapters we have set forth the Lord Infant as the chief actor in these things, giving as clear an understanding of him as we could, it is meet that in this present chapter we should know his purpose in doing them. And you should note well that the noble spirit of this Prince, by a sort of natural constraint, was ever urging him both to begin and to carry out very great deeds. For which reason, after the taking of Ceuta he always kept ships well armed against the Infidel, both for war, and because he had also a wish to know the land that lay beyond the isles of Canary and that Cape called Bojador, for that up to his time, neither by writings, nor by the memory of man, was known with any certainty the nature of the land beyond that Cape. Some said indeed that Saint Brandan had passed that way; and there was another tale of two galleys rounding the Cape, which never returned. But this doth not appear at all likely to be true, for it is not to be presumed that if the said galleys went there, some other ships would not have endeavoured to learn what voyage they had made. And because the said Lord Infant wished to know the truth of this,—since it seemed to him that if he or some other lord did not endeavour to gain that knowledge, no mariners or merchants would ever dare to attempt it—(for it is clear that none of them ever trouble themselves to sail to a place where there is not a sure and certain hope of profit)—and seeing also that no other prince took any pains in this matter, he sent out his own ships against those parts, to have manifest certainty of them all. And to this he was stirred up by his zeal for the service of God and of the King Edward his Lord and brother, who then reigned. And this was the first reason of his action.

The second reason was that if there chanced to be in those lands some population of Christians, or some havens, into which it would be possible to sail without peril, many kinds of merchandise might be brought to this realm, which would find a ready market, and reasonably so, because no other people of these parts traded with them, nor yet people of any other that were known; and also the products of this realm might be taken there, which traffic would bring great profit to our countrymen.

The third reason was that, as it was said that the power of the Moors in that land of Africa was very much greater than was commonly supposed, and that there were no Christians among them, nor any other race of men; and because every wise man is obliged by natural prudence to wish for a knowledge of the power of his enemy; therefore the said Lord Infant exerted himself to cause this to be fully discovered, and to make it known determinately how far the power of those infidels extended.

The fourth reason was because during the one and thirty years that he had warred against the Moors, he had never found a Christian king, nor a lord outside this land, who for the love of our Lord Jesus Christ would aid him in the said war. Therefore he sought to know if there were in those parts any Christian princes, in whom the charity and the love of Christ was so ingrained that they would aid him against those enemies of the faith.

The fifth reason was his great desire to make increase in the faith of our Lord Jesus Christ and to bring to him all the souls that should be saved, understanding that all the mystery of the Incarnation, Death, and Passion of our Lord Jesus Christ was for this sole end—namely the salvation of lost souls—whom the said Lord Infant by his travail and spending would fain bring into the true path. For he perceived that no better offering could be made unto the Lord than this; for if God promised to return one hundred goods for one, we may justly believe that for such great benefits, that is to say for so many souls as were saved by the efforts of this Lord, he will have so many hundreds of guerdons in the kingdom of God, by which his spirit may be glorified after this life in the celestial realm. For I that wrote this history saw so many men and women of those parts turned to the holy faith, that even if the Infant had been a heathen, their prayers would have been enough to have obtained his salvation. And not only did I see the first captives, but their children and grandchildren as true Christians as if the Divine grace breathed in them and imparted to them a clear knowledge of itself.

But over and above these five reasons I have a sixth that would seem to be the root from which all the others proceeded: and this is the inclination of the heavenly wheels. For, as I wrote not many days ago in a letter I sent to the Lord King, that although it be written that the wise man shall be Lord of the stars, and that the courses of the planets (according to the true estimate of the holy doctors) cannot cause the good man to stumble; yet it is manifest that they are bodies ordained in the secret counsels of our Lord God and run by a fixed measure, appointed to different ends, which are revealed to men by his grace, through whose influence bodies of the lower order are inclined to certain passions. And if it be a fact, speaking as a Catholic, that the contrary predestinations of the wheels of heaven can be avoided by natural judgment with the aid of a certain divine grace, much more does it stand to reason that those who are predestined to good fortune, by the help of this same grace, will not only follow their course but even add a far greater increase to themselves. But here I wish to tell you how by the constraint of the influence of nature this glorious Prince was inclined to those actions of his. And that was because his ascendent was Aries, which is the house of Mars, and exaltation of the sun, and his lord in the XIth house, in company of the sun. And because the said Mars was in Aquarius, which is the house of Saturn, and in the mansion of hope, it signified that this Lord should toil at high and mighty conquests, especially in seeking out things that were hidden from other men and secret, according to the nature of Saturn, in whose house he is. And the fact of his being accompanied by the sun, as I said, and the sun being in the house of Jupiter, signified that all his traffick and his conquests would be loyally carried out, according to the good pleasure of his king and lord.

5. West Africa in the fifteenth century

The motives of the Portuguese in exploring the West African coast were at least in part commercial. They hoped to wrest from foreign and often hostile hands the considerable trade between Guinea and Morocco, and to divert it from the trans-Saharan caravans to their own ships. In this they achieved some success. Besides fishing and sealing off the Mauretanian coast, they exported cloth, trinkets, and later horses, to Upper Guinea, and procured there slaves, gums and resins, a little ivory, a little gold dust. The returns helped to enrich the Order of Christ, which had provided some of the capital for the trade, and of which Prince Henry was the Grand Master. The Prince secured from the Portuguese Crown a monopoly of West African trade, and from the Papacy, in 1454 and 1455, bulls conferring on the Order a monopoly of missionary work in the area. Within the general terms of his monopoly, he was liberal in licensing the trade of other investors. Among those who sailed under his license and with his support was the Venetian Alvise da Ca' da Mosto, who made two voyages, probably in 1455 and 1456. Although almost certainly the first European to report sighting the Cape Verde Islands, Cadamosto was a businessman and not primarily an explorer. He shared, however, the open-minded curiosity characteristic of Renaissance Italy. He had a good eye for detail himself and was assiduous in collecting information from others. The fabulous and the sensational had no place in the story he had to tell. He wrote by far the best of the accounts of the upper Guinea coast which survive from the time when that coast was first becoming known to Europeans. His narrative was first published in the collection *Paesi novamente retrovati*, printed at Vicenza in 1507, and was later, in 1550, included by Ramusio in the first volume of his *Navigationi*.

The extract which follows is from *The Voyages of Cadamosto*, translated and edited by G. R. Crone (London, Hakluyt Society, 1937), pp. 14–23, 27–8, 61–2: Chapters IX, XI, XIV, and part of XXXIX.

Chapter IX: The description of Capo Bianco and the islands nearest to it

W E set sail from this island[1] making due south towards Ethiopia; and in a few days reached Capo Blanco about 770 miles from the Canaries. It is to be noted that, leaving these islands to sail towards this cape, one goes along the coast of Africa which is constantly on the left hand; you sail well offshore, however, and do not sight land, because the Isole di Canaria are very far out to sea to the west, each one further than its neighbour. Thus you keep a course far out from land, until you have covered at least two-thirds of the passage from the islands to Capo Bianco and then draw near on the left hand to the coast until land is sighted, in order not to run past the said Cape without recognising it, because beyond it no land is seen for a considerable distance. The coast runs back at this cape, forming a gulf which is called the "Forna dargin."[2] This name Dargin is derived from an islet in the gulf called Argin by the people of the country. This gulf runs in more than fifty miles, and there are three more islands, to which the Portuguese have given these names: Isola Bianca, from its sands: Isola da le Garze,[3] because the first Portuguese found on it so many eggs of these sea birds that they loaded two boats from the caravels with them: the third Isola de Cuori. All are small, sandy, and uninhabited. On this Dargin there is a supply of fresh water, but not on the others.

Note that when you set out beyond the Strecto de Zibelterra [keeping this coast on the left hand, that is, of Barbary] towards Ethiopia, you do not find it inhabited by these Barbari except as far as the Cauo de Chantin.[4] From this cape along the coast to Capo Blanco commences the sandy country which is the desert

[1] Palma. The distance is about 570 nautical miles.

[2] Arguim, discovered in 1443 by Nuno Tristão, where a fort was erected by Prince Henry in 1448 for the protection of merchants. Its good water and safe anchorage quickly made it a valuable *entrepôt*, and it became an important trading centre. The Arab name was "Ghir", and Azurara calls it "Gete".

[3] Island of Herons (Azurara: I, p. 63, and II, pp. 320–1), one of the Arguim Islands. The big expedition of 1444 rested here and refreshed themselves on the multitude of young birds.

[4] Cape Cantin, 32° 36′ N., 9° 14′ W.

that ranges on its northern confines with the mountains, which cut off our Barbary from Tunis, and from all these places of the coast. This desert the Berbers call Sarra:[5] on the south it marches with the Blacks of lower Ethiopia: it is a very great desert, which takes well-mounted men fifty to sixty days to cross—in some places more, and some less. The boundary of this desert is on the Ocean Sea at the coast, which is everywhere sandy, white, arid, and all equally low-lying: it does not appear to be higher in one place than another, as far as the said Capo Bianco, which is so called because the Portuguese who discovered it saw it to be sandy and white, without signs of grass or trees whatsoever. It is a very fine cape, like a triangle, that is, on its face; it has three points, distant the one from the other about a mile.

On this coast there are very large fisheries[6] of various and most excellent large fish without number, like those of our Venetian fisheries, and other kinds. Throughout this Forna Dargin there is little water, and there are many shoals, some of sand, others of rock. There are strong currents in the sea, on account of which one navigates only by day, with the lead in hand, and according to the state of the tide. Two ships have already been wrecked upon these banks. The aforesaid Cauo de Chantin stands approximately north-east of Capo Bianco.

You should also know that behind this Cauo Bianco on the land, is a place called Hoden,[7] which is about six days inland by camel. This place is not walled, but is frequented by Arabs, and is a market where the caravans arrive from Tanbutu,[8] and from other places in the land of the Blacks, on their way to our nearer Barbary. The food of the peoples of this place is dates, and barley, of which there is sufficient, for they grow in some of these places, but not abundantly. They drink the milk of camels

[5] Sahara. The mountains are the Atlas range.
[6] The fishing fields were already being exploited under Prince Henry's license.
[7] Wadan, an important desert market about 350 miles east of Arguim. Later, in 1487, when the Portuguese were endeavouring to penetrate the interior they attempted to establish a trading factory at Wadan which acted as a feeder to Arguim, tapping the north-bound caravan traffic and diverting some of it to the west coast.
[8] Timbuktu.

and other animals, for they have no wine. They also have cows and goats, but not many, for the land is dry. Their oxen and cows, compared with ours, are small.

They are Muhammadans, and very hostile to Christians. They never remain settled, but are always wandering over these deserts. These are the men who go to the land of the Blacks, and also to our nearer Barbary. They are very numerous, and have many camels on which they carry brass and silver from Barbary and other things to Tanbuto and to the land of the Blacks. Thence they carry away gold and pepper,[9] which they bring hither. They are brown complexioned, and wear white cloaks edged with a red stripe: their women also dress thus, without shifts. On their heads the men wear turbans in the Moorish fashion, and they always go barefooted. In these sandy districts there are many lions, leopards, and ostriches, the eggs of which I have often eaten and found good.

You should know that the said Lord Infante of Portugal has leased this island of Argin to Christians [for ten years], so that no one can enter the bay to trade with the Arabs save those who hold the license. These have dwellings on the island and factories where they buy and sell with the said Arabs who come to the coast to trade for merchandise of various kinds, such as woollen cloths, cotton, silver, and "alchezeli,"[10] that is, cloaks, carpets, and similar articles and above all, corn, for they are always short of food. They give in exchange slaves whom the Arabs bring from the land of the Blacks,[11] and gold *tiber*.[12] The Lord Infante therefore caused a castle[13] to be built on the island to protect this trade for ever. For this reason, Portuguese caravels are coming and going all the year to this island.

These Arabs also have many Berber horses,[14] which they trade,

[9] Malaguetta pepper.

[10] Probably the coarse cloth called by El Bekri in the eleventh century "chigguiza," which was doubtless the "shigge" purchased by Barth in Timbuktu in the nineteenth century (Barth: *Travels*, iv, p. 443).

[11] The Portuguese had now established in West Africa the insidious practice of inciting the coast tribes to raid their neighbours for slaves.

[12] The Arabic *thibr* or *tibar*, meaning gold dust.

[13] Built by Prince Henry in 1448.

[14] Leo Africanus, writing in the sixteenth century, makes several references to the trade in Barbary horses for which there was an excellent market

and take to the Land of the Blacks, exchanging them with the
rulers for slaves. Ten or fifteen slaves are given for one of these
horses, according to their quality. The Arabs likewise take articles
of Moorish silk, made in Granata and in Tunis of Barbary, silver,
and other goods, obtaining in exchange any number of these
slaves, and some gold. These slaves are brought to the market
and town of Hoden; there they are divided: some go to the
mountains of Barcha,[15] and thence to Sicily, [others to the said
town of Tunis and to all the coasts of Barbary], and others again
are taken to this place, Argin, and sold to the Portuguese lease-
holders. As a result every year the Portuguese carry away from
Argin a thousand slaves.[16] Note that before this traffic was organized, the Portuguese caravels, sometimes four, sometimes more,
were wont to come armed to the Golfo d'Argin, and descending
on the land by night, would assail the fisher villages, and so
ravage the land. Thus they took of these Arabs both men and
women, and carried them to Portugal for sale: behaving in a
like manner along all the rest of the coast, which stretches from
Cauo Bianco to the Rio di Senega and even beyond. This is a
great river, dividing a race which is called Azanaghi[17] from the
first Kingdom of the Blacks. These Azanaghi are brownish, rather
dark brown than light, and live in places along this coast beyond
Cauo Bianco, and many of them are spread over this desert inland. They are neighbours of the above mentioned Arabs of Hoden.

They live on dates, barley, and camel's milk: but as they are
very near the first land of the Blacks, they trade with them,
obtaining from this land of the Blacks millet and certain vegetables, such as beans, upon which they support themselves. They
are men who require little food and can withstand hunger, so
that they sustain themselves throughout the day upon a mess of

---

in the Sudan. Later the Portuguese regularly shipped out horses to barter for
slaves.

[15] Barca in Cyrenaica.

[16] According to Azurara (II, p. 288), up to the year 1448 the total number
of Africans who had been carried captive to Portugal during Prince Henry's
time was only 927. This passage indicates how rapidly the slave trade was
increasing.

[17] The Azanaghi or Azaneguys, as Azurara calls them, were the Sanhaja,
historically the most important of the Tuareg tribes, and widely distributed
over the western Sahara.

barley porridge. They are obliged to do this because of the want of victuals they experience. These, as I have said, are taken by the Portuguese as before mentioned and are the best slaves of all the Blacks. But, however, for some time all have been at peace and engaged in trade. The said Lord Infante will not permit further hurt to be done to any, because he hopes that, mixing with Christians, they may without difficulty be converted to our faith, not yet being firmly attached to the tenets of Muhammad, save from what they know by hearsay.

These same Azanaghi have a strange custom: they always wear a handkerchief on the head with a flap[18] which they bring across the face, covering the mouth and part of the nose. For they say that the mouth is a brutish thing, that is always uttering wind and bad odours so that it should be kept covered, and not displayed, likening it almost to the posterior, and that these two portions should be kept covered. It is true that they never uncover it, except when they eat, and not otherwise for I have seen many of them.

There are no lords among them, save those who are richer: these are honoured and obeyed to some degree by the others. They are a very poor people, liars, the biggest thieves in the world, and exceedingly treacherous. They are men of average height, and spare. They wear their hair in locks down to their shoulders, almost in the German fashion—but their hair is black, and anointed every day with fish oil, so that it smells strongly, the which they consider a great refinement.

Chapter XI[19]: The exchange of salt for gold: and the distance it travels

That woman who has the largest breasts is considered more beautiful than the others: with the result that each woman, to increase their size, at the age of seventeen or eighteen when the breasts are already formed, places across her chest a cord, which she binds around the breasts, and draws tight with much force; in

[18] The *litham*, still worn by the Tuareg; hence their name Muleththemin, meaning the Veiled People. In Roman and Byzantine times they appear not to have worn the veil, and when or why they took to it remains a problem to which no acceptable solution has been found. Its use appears always to have been restricted to the men.

[19] This and subsequent chapters are misnumbered in the original version.

this way the breasts are distended, and frequent pulling every day causes them to grow and lengthen so much that many reach the navel. Those that have the biggest prize them as a rare thing.

You should know that these people have no knowledge of any Christians except the Portuguese, against whom they have waged war for [thirteen or] fourteen years, many of them having been taken prisoners, as I have already said, and sold into slavery. It is asserted that when for the first time they saw sails, that is, ships, on the sea (which neither they nor their forefathers had ever seen before), they believed that they were great sea-birds with white wings, which were flying, and had come from some strange place: when the sails were lowered for the landing, some of them, watching from far off, thought that the ships were fishes. Others again said that they were phantoms that went by night, at which they were greatly terrified. The reason for this belief was because these caravels within a short space of time appeared at many places, where attacks were delivered, especially at night, by their crews. Thus one such assault might be separated from the next by a hundred or more miles, according to the plans of the sailors, or as the winds, blowing hither and thither, served them. Perceiving this, they said amongst themselves, "If these be human creatures, how can they travel so great a distance in one night, a distance which we could not go in three days?" Thus, as they did not understand the art of navigation, they all thought that the ships were phantoms. This I know is testified to by many Portuguese who at that time were trading in caravels on this coast, and also by those who were captured on these raids. And from this it may be judged how strange many of our ways appeared to them, if such an opinion could prevail.

Beyond the said mart of Edon [Oden], six days journey further inland, there is a place called Tagaza, that is to say in our tongue "cargador,"[20] where a very great quantity of rock-salt is mined. Every year large caravans of camels belonging to the above mentioned Arabs and Azanaghi, leaving in many parties, carry it to Tanbutu,[21] thence they go to Melli,[22] the empire of the Blacks,

[20] "A load, or charge"; other texts have "bisaccia d'oro", i.e. wallet of gold, the gold not being obtained locally, but in exchange for salt.
[21] Timbuktu.
[22] Mali.

where, so rapidly is it sold, within eight days of its arrival all
is disposed of at a price of two to three hundred *mitigalli*[23] a load,
according to the quantity: [a *mitigallo* is worth about a ducat:]
then with the gold they return to their homes.

In this empire of Melli it is very hot, and the pasturage is
very unsuitable for fourfooted animals: so that of the majority
which come with the caravans no more than twenty-five out of
a hundred return. There are no quadrupeds in this country, because they all die, and many also of the Arabs and Azanaghi
sicken in this place and die, on account of the great heat. It is
said that on horseback it is about forty days from Tagaza to
Tanbutu, and thirty from Tanbutu to Melli.

I enquired of them what the merchants of Melli did with this
salt, and was told that a small quantity is consumed in their
country. Since it is below the meridional and on the equinoctial,
where the day is constantly about as long as the night, it is extremely hot at certain seasons of the year: this causes the blood
to putrefy, so that were it not for this salt, they would die. The
remedy they employ is as follows: they take a small piece of the
salt, mix it in a jar with a little water, and drink it every day.
They say that this saves them. The remainder of this salt they
carry away on a long journey in pieces as large as a man can,
with a certain knack, bear on his head.

You must know that when this salt is carried to Melli by camel
it goes in large pieces [as it is dug out from the mines], of a
size most easily carried on camels, two pieces on each animal.
Then at Melli, these blacks break it in smaller pieces, in order
to carry it on their heads, so that each man carries one piece, and
thus they form a great army of men on foot, who transport
it a great distance. Those who carry it have two forked sticks,
one in each hand: when they are tired, they plant them in the
ground, and rest their load upon them. In this way they carry it
until they reach certain waters: I could not learn from them
whether it is fresh or sea water, so that I do not know if it is
a river or the sea, though they consider it to be the sea. [I think
however it must be a river, for if it were the sea, in such a
hot country there would be no lack of salt.] These Blacks are

[23] One *mithgal* or *mitkal* equalled about ⅛ oz. of gold.

obliged to carry it in this way, because they have no camels or
other beasts of burden, as these cannot live in the great heat. It
may be imagined how many men are required to carry it on foot,
and how many are those who consume it every year. Having
reached these waters with the salt, they proceed in this fashion:
all those who have the salt pile it in rows, each marking his own.
Having made these piles, the whole caravan retires half a day's
journey. Then there come another race of blacks who do not
wish to be seen or to speak. They arrive in large boats, from
which it appears that they come from islands, and disembark.
Seeing the salt, they place a quantity of gold opposite each pile,
and then turn back, leaving salt and gold. When they have gone,
the negroes who own the salt return: if they are satisfied with
the quantity of gold, they leave the salt and retire with the gold.
Then the blacks of the gold return, and remove those piles which
are without gold. By other piles of salt they place more gold,
if it pleases them, or else they leave the salt. In this way, by
long and ancient custom, they carry on their trade without seeing
or speaking to each other. Although it is difficult to believe this,
I can testify that I have had this information from many merchants, Arab as well as Azanaghi, and also from persons in whom
faith can be placed.

*Chapter XIV: The Rio de Senega, which divides the desert from
the fertile land*

When we had passed in sight of this Cauo Bianco, we sailed on
our journey to the river called the Rio de Senega, the first river
of the Land of the Blacks, which debouches on this coast. This
river separates the Blacks from the brown people called Azanaghi,
and also the dry and arid land, that is, the above mentioned
desert, from the fertile country of the Blacks. The river is large;
its mouth being over a mile wide, and quite deep. There is another
mouth a little distance beyond, with an island between. Thus it
enters the sea by two mouths, and before each of them about a
mile out to sea are shoals and broad sand-banks. In this place
the water increases and decreases every six hours, that is, with
the rise and fall of the tide. The tide ascends the river more than
sixty miles, according to the information I have had from Portuguese who have been [many miles] up it [in caravels]. He who

wishes to enter this river must go in with the tide, on account
of the shoals and banks at the mouth. From Cauo Bianco it is
380 miles to the river: all the coast is sandy within about twenty
miles of the mouth. It is called Costa de Antte rotte, and is of
the Azanaghi, or brown men.

It appears to me a very marvellous thing that beyond the river
all men are very black, tall and big, their bodies well formed;
and the whole country green, full of trees, and fertile: while on
this side, the men are brownish, small, lean, ill-nourished, and
small in stature: the country sterile and arid. This river is said
to be a branch of the river Nile, of the four royal rivers: it
flows through all Ethiopia, watering the country as in Egypt:
passing through "lo caiero," it waters all the land of Egypt.

Chapter XXXIX: *The elevation of our* North Star; *and the six stars opposite*

During the days we spent at the mouth of this river,[24] we saw the
pole star once only; it appeared very low down over the sea,
therefore we could see it only when the weather was very clear.
It appeared about a third of a lance above the horizon. We also
had sight of six stars low down over the sea, clear, bright, and
large. By the compass, they stood due south, in the following
fashion.[25]

*   *
   *   *   *   *
       *

This we took to be the southern wain, though we did not see the
principal star, for it would not have been possible to sight it
unless we had lost the north star. In this place we found the
night to be 13 [eleven and a half] hours, and the day 11 [twelve
and a half] hours, that is, in the first days of July, or more accurately on the second of the month.

This country is hot at all seasons of the year. It is true that
there is some variation, and what they call a winter: thus beginning in the aforesaid month [of July] until the end of October
it rains continuously almost every day from noon, in the following way: clouds rise continually over the land from the E.N.E.,

[24] The Gambia.
[25] The first recorded notice of the Southern Cross.

or from the E.S.E., with very heavy thunder, lightning and thunderbolts. Thus an excessive quantity of rain falls, and at this season the negroes begin to sow in the same manner as those of the kingdom of Senega. Their sustenance is entirely millet and vegetables, flesh and milk.

I understand that in the interior of this country, [on account of the great heat of the air] the rain which falls is warm. In the morning, when day breaks, there is no dawn at the rising of the sun, as in our parts, where between dawn and sunrise there is a short interval before the shadows of night disperse: the sun appears suddenly, though it is not light for the space of half an hour, as the sun is dull and, as it were, smoky on first rising. The cause of this appearance of the sun early in the morning, contrary to what happens in our country, cannot, I think, arise from any other circumstance than the extreme lowness of the land, devoid of mountains, and all my companions were of this opinion.

6. The Cape of Good Hope

When Prince Henry died in 1460 his rights in West Africa passed to the Portuguese Crown, and a pall of silence descended. Between Cadamosto's voyages and the first voyage of Vasco da Gama there are no surviving eyewitness reports. Partly, no doubt, this was due to an official policy of secrecy about valuable discoveries; partly to the destroying hand of time. Whatever the cause, we know nothing at first hand of Fernão Gomes, the Crown lessee whose captains explored the Bights of Benin and Biafra; of Diogo d'Azambuja, who in 1482 built the factory-fort of São Jorge da Mina on what became the Gold Coast, to protect Portuguese trade in gold dust, slaves, and *malagueta* pepper; of Lopo Gonçalves and Rui de Sequeira, who discovered the southerly trend of the Gaboon coast—a sore disappointment to men who were beginning to think that India lay round the corner; of Diogo Cão, who defied that disappointment, discovered the mouth of the Congo and explored the Angola coast. In 1488 Bartholomeu Dias passed the Cape of Good Hope. With this event began the long story of Portuguese navigation, trade and piracy in the Indian Ocean; yet still we have no first-hand report. Even the chroniclers have little to say. Neither Ruy de Pina nor Garcia de Resende describes the event. Barros gives a brief account; to him we owe the story that Dias named his cape the Cape of Storms, and that the King renamed it the Cape of Good Hope; but Barros wrote more than sixty years after the event, and his dates and details are unreliable.

The brief description of the Cape and account of its discovery which is quoted here comes neither from an eyewitness nor from a chronicle, but from a book of sailing directions and a treatise on navigation and cosmography. Its author, Duarte Pacheco Pereira, was a distinguished sea officer who served in India and in West Africa. His last public employment, indeed, was as governor of São Jorge da Mina. He knew the African coastline as well as any man, and he knew Dias personally. His account is cursory indeed, but we have nothing better, from so early a date. Pacheco's oddly named book was probably written between 1505 and 1508. It is incomplete, and parts of it may well have come under the censor's ban. It was not published until 1892. The extract which follows is from *Esmeraldo de situ orbis* by Duarte Pacheco Pereira, translated and edited by George H. T. Kimble (London, Hakluyt Society, 1937), pp. 153–6: Chapter VII, "Concerning the discovery of Cabo de Bõa Esperança, where Africa ends."

Eight leagues beyond Ponta da Praya is a beautiful promontory which we call Cabo de Bõa Esperança[1]; it lies N.N.W. and S.S.E. with the Ponta da Praya and is 34° 30′ south of the Equator. It was with good reason that this promontory was called Cabo de Bõa Esperança, for Bertholameu Diaz, who discovered it at the command of the late King John in the year 1488, when he saw that the coast here turned northwards and northeastwards towards Ethiopia under Egypt and on to the Gulf of Arabia, giving great hope of the discovery of India, called it the "Cape of Good Hope." Its latitude is 34° 30/ (or half a degree) south, as we have said above. The land is very high and shaped as appears in our picture. During its winter, from the month of April till the end of the month of September, it is very cold and

[1] Ponta da Praya is Green Point in Table Bay. The true latitude of the Cape of Good Hope is 34° 21′ S.

stormy.[2] The negroes of this region are heathen, bestial people, and they wear skins and sandals of raw hide; they are not as black as the negroes of Jalofo, Mandingua and other parts of Guinea. There is no trade here, but there are many cows, goats and sheep and there is plenty of fish. In this country there are large cats called "baboys," almost of the size of a man, with large beards, which one has to see in order to believe.[3] Some say that this Cape is the promontory called Plaso[4] of which Ptolemy spoke, but I do not think so; I think rather it must be the Montes Lunae in which Ptolemy says the Nile rises, for in the very position which Ptolemy gave to these mountains, in $34\frac{1}{2}°$ south of the Equator, there the promontory of Bõa Esperança is found, so that the distance from the Equator in degrees answers to the Montes Lunae; moreover the shape of this country answers to Ptolemy's description of the said mountains, so that they appear to be one and the same. For these reasons the Cape is easy to find; it can also be found by the course of the sun, for, at whatever time of the year a person may be here, the sun will always be to the north of him and the shadow to the south, the exact contrary of what happens in the part of the world in which we live, for with us the sun is always to the south and the shadow to the north. At this promontory Africa comes to an end in the Ocean [i.e. Atlantic], and is divided from Asia;[5] from this point the boundary of Africa runs due north following the course of the Nile, through the midst of the Ethiopias of Trogouditas[6] to Damiata on the sea of Egypt; here, near

[2] While gales are not infrequent accompaniments of winter, the mean winter temperature in the Cape region is 53° F., i.e. 4° F. higher than that of Lisbon.

[3] I.e. the leopard.

[4] I.e. Prasum Promontorium, Ptolemy's "farthest south" in East Africa: it is commonly regarded as being identical with C. Delgado to the south of Zanzibar.

[5] In book 1, chap. 5, Pacheco indicates the limits of Africa commencing at the mouth of the Nile. In conformity with the general classical view he makes the Nile the continental frontier and since the Nile rose in the "Mountains of the Moon" which he erroneously identifies with the mountains of Cape Province, it was quite natural that he should regard the Cape as the southern boundary point.

[6] I.e. the Troglodytes (or cave-dwellers) who according to Herodotus and later writers inhabited a mountainous region in the Sahara near the Garamantes, some 30 days' journey south from Tripoli.

Libya it turns and follows the coast of Carthage until it terminates in the great city of Cepta; thence it follows Tingitania and the coast of the Atlantic and the Ethiopias of Guinea, as described in this book, until it comes to an end again in the Cabo de Bõa Esperança, as we stated in the middle of the fifth chapter of the first book. This is the circumference of Africa, as may be seen in the painting of the map of the world and general description given in that chapter. The circumference of Africa is 3,850 leagues; its length, beginning at the Rio de Çanaguá and running due east to the river Nile, is 840 leagues; its breadth, going due south from Tripoli in Berbery to the sea of Guinea at the Rio dos Escravos, is 500 leagues; and this is its circumference, length and breadth, as we have said, and these are its boundaries and coasts, which do not have gulfs running into them, as they do in Europe and Asia. All this we have ascertained in great detail. On this promontory of Bõa Esperança herbs, like those of Portugal, are to be found: for here there is much mint and camomile and cress; there are also many other herbs of the same nature as those in this country [i.e. Portugal]. There are also wild olives, oaks and heather which yields berries, and other trees like ours. The cause of this [similarity] is the movement of the sun which gives life to all things, for Lisbon is about the same number of degrees north of the Equator as Cabo de Bõa Esperança is south of it; for this reason Portugal and this country are alike in their trees and herbs and fruits. However, the seasons are opposite; when it is winter here, it is summer there, and when it is summer here, it is winter there; for the sun in its movement away from us, and towards us, being the same degrees distant from the Equator towards the Cape as towards the other [i.e. Lisbon] produces the same herbs and fruits and trees, although the seasons are different, as we have learnt by experience.

Aqui Mapa

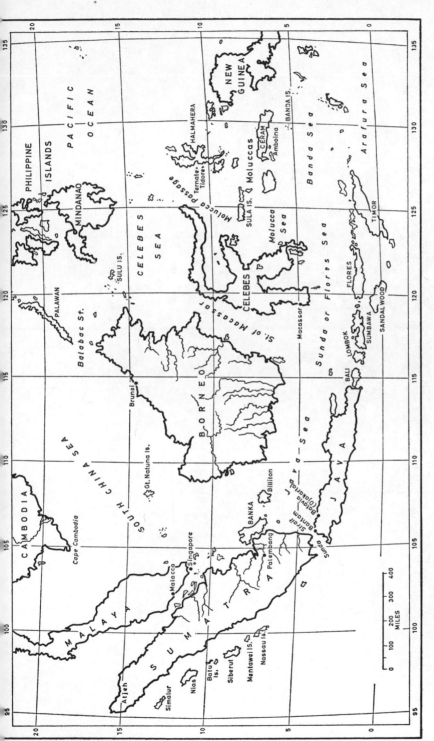

1. The East Indies.

2. The Pacific.

NEW MEXICO

Gulf of California

NEW SPAIN

• Mexico

Acapulco

• Huatulco

Tehuantepec

Panamá

Gulf of San Miguel

• Quito

• Túmbez

Cajamarca • PERU

• Lima

Pachacámac • Cuzco

CHILE

• Santiago

Magellan's Strait

TIERRA DEL FUEGO

3. The Caribbean Sea.

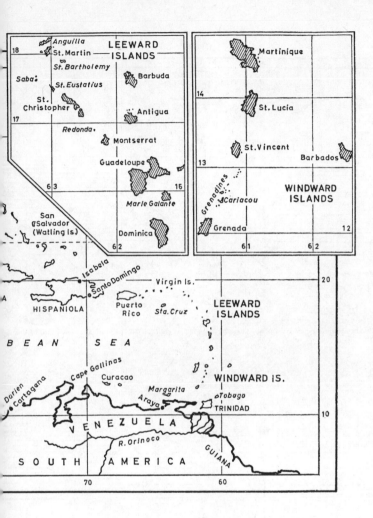

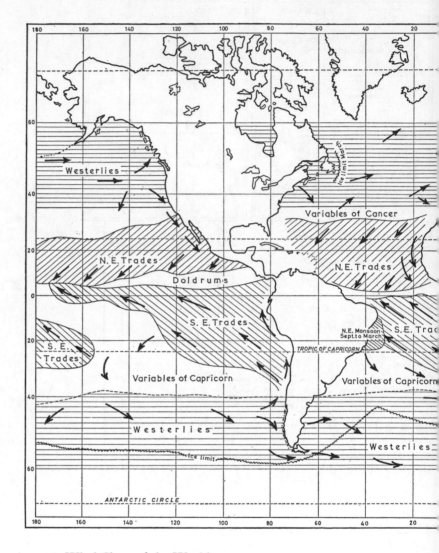

4. Wind Chart of the World.

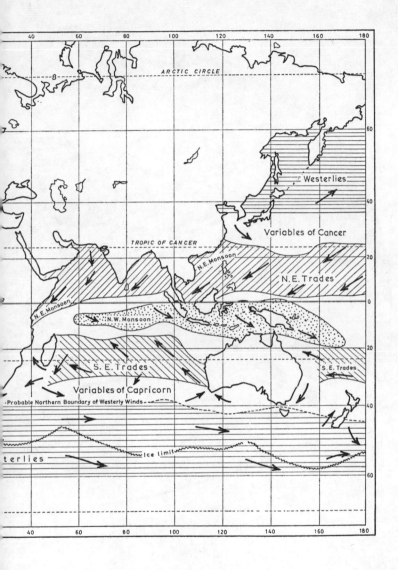

5. The world according to Ptolemy's description. From *Geograph*

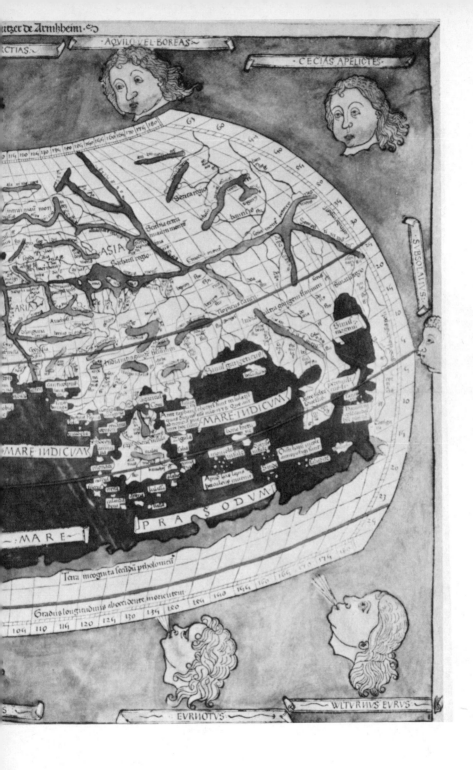

y Ptolemy (Ulm, 1482). Photo: British Museum.

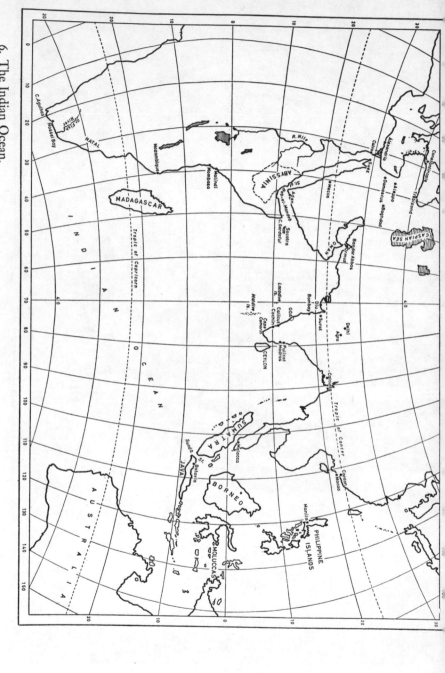

6. The Indian Ocean.

IV . *India*

7. From Mombasa to Malabar

Ten years elapsed between Dias' discovery of the seaway into the Indian Ocean and Vasco de Gama's arrival in India. The delay was probably due to political uncertainties, and to the illness and death of John II,
who was succeeded by Manoel "the Fortunate" in 1495; but inciden-
tally it allowed time for the collection of valuable information. In the
1480's a number of explorer-ambassadors were sent from Portugal to
various places in the Near and Middle East, both to discover what they
could about India, and to establish relations with any Christian princes
they might encounter on the way there. The most successful of these
Portuguese travelers was Pedro da Covilhã, who left Lisbon in 1487,
the same year in which Dias sailed for the Cape. Covilhã was a pica-
resque individual who had formerly been employed as a spy in Spain
and Morocco. He traveled disguised as a Muslim merchant—he spoke
Arabic—via Cairo and Suakin to Aden, where he shipped in an Arab
dhow to Calicut. There he made a reconnaissance of the ports of the
Malabar coast, including Goa, the terminus of the Arabian horse trade
to India. From Malabar he sailed to Ormuz, the great commercial *entrepôt* of the Persian Gulf; and from there to Sofala, where he carried out
a corresponding survey of the Arab trade along the East African coast.
He then returned to Cairo, arriving there late in 1490. Eventually, after
three more years of fantastic adventure, including a "pilgrimage" to
Mecca, he reached Abyssinia, and there spent the remaining thirty
years of his life as a powerful and trusted (but probably captive) servant of the emperor. He had indeed found "Prester John." During his
stay in Cairo in 1490 he had induced a messenger to carry a report of
his travels back to John II. If this letter reached the king—and though
positive evidence is lacking, there is reason to believe it did—then Vasco
da Gama could have been told what Indian Ocean harbors to make for
and what kind of reception to expect; though the unsuitability of the

presents and trade goods he carried shows how sketchy this information must have been.

The ten years' interval may also have been used for further maritime reconnaissance. Before sending an expensive expedition all the way to India, it may well have been thought prudent to investigate more thoroughly the wind system and other navigational peculiarities of the central and south Atlantic; perhaps even to reconnoiter the Muslim harbors in East Africa. There is a reference, in an Arabic book of sailing directions, to Portuguese vessels wrecked off Sofala in 1495;[1] though the story is not confirmed in any known Portuguese source. Be that as it may, Vasco da Gama's navigation through the Atlantic, by a route very different from that of Dias, was bold, well informed, and accurate. In the East African ports also he showed a self-confidence which suggested reliable intelligence. When he set sail from Malindi to cross the Indian Ocean, however, he was in waters totally unknown to European pilots. He required a remarkable stroke of luck, as well as courage and skill, to bring his three ships safely to anchor in Calicut Road in May 1498.

The Portuguese chroniclers naturally had much to say about this famous voyage; but as usual firsthand evidence is scanty. All reports, logs, and trading accounts brought back by the fleet have disappeared. While they survived, they must have been treated as highly secret. Some of the chroniclers used them. Of the secondary descriptions of the voyage, the best are in the *Decades* of João de Barros and in Damião de Gois' *Chronicle of King Manoel*. Barros was a *Casa da India* official and Gois an official archivist; both had access to documents; but they wrote many years after the event, and neither was a sailor. Of the voyage as a triumphantly successful maritime operation—which it was—they tell us very little.

The only surviving eyewitness account of the voyage is the *Roteiro*, part of which is quoted here. In some ways it is a disappointing document, but apart from the chronicles it is the foundation of our knowledge. It is not a true *roteiro*,[2] but a simple diary. Its author has never been identified and we do not know his rank or duties; but he was not in the flagship and does not seem to have participated in the inner councils of the fleet. He may have been a soldier; he does not write like a seaman. He tells us little about navigation. Perhaps the most tantalizing sentence in the whole document is the casual reference to "the pilot

[1] T. A. Shumovskii, trans. M. Malkiel-Jirmounsky: *Tres roteiros desconhecidos de Ahmad ibn-Mādjid, o piloto árabe de Vasco da Gama* (Lisbon, 1960).

[2] See p. 322 below.

whom the king had given us" at Malindi. This man is described in the chronicles as a Gujerati, but a modern scholar has identified him as the celebrated Arab astronomer-pilot Ahmad ibn Mádjid, the best-known Asian navigator of his day, and author of a distinguished collection of rutters and nautical instructions.[3] Why he happened to be in Malindi, and how he was persuaded to accompany the fleet, we do not know. His services were crucial to the success of the enterprise.

Vasco da Gama's expedition was not primarily a voyage of discovery —the commercial importance and the general position of India were well known—but an armed commercial embassy and reconnaissance. On this side of the fleet's activities the *Roteiro* is more informative. The writer understood that the vested interests of Arab traders, both in East Africa and in India, and of the Malabar Muslims—the *Moplahs*—stood in the way of Portuguese commercial plans at Calicut. He saw also the contempt with which the goods carried in the fleet were regarded by upper-class Malabaris; and unwittingly he revealed the unfavorable impression which the behavior of the Portuguese, compounded of ignorance, arrogance, and suspicion, made upon their hosts. He shared his commanding officer's delusion that the Hindus of Malabar, like the Nestorians, were a heretical kind of Christian—a delusion in which many Portuguese, with what seems to us singular obtuseness, long persisted. Vasco da Gama was a sea commander of great determination, courage, and skill. As a commercial ambassador he was much less successful. His first visit to Calicut made it clear that his countrymen could break into the Indian Ocean trades only by force of arms.

The manscript of the *Roteiro* was deposited for many years in the Convent of Santa Cruz at Coimbra. From there it was transferred to the public library of Oporto. It was first published, in a Portuguese edition by D. Kopke and A da Costa Paiva, in 1838. The extract which follows is from *A Journal of the First Voyage of Vasco da Gama*, translated and edited by E. G. Ravenstein (London, Hakluyt Society, 1898), pp. 31–63.

[*Mombaça*]

O N Saturday [April 7] we cast anchor off Mombaça, but did not enter the port. No sooner had we been perceived than a *zavra*[1] manned by Moors came out to us; in front of the city

---

[3] G. Ferrand: *Introduction à l'astronomie nautique arabe* (Paris, 1928), p. 196. See above, p. oo. note.

[1] Zavra or zabra is a small open vessel, sharp at the stern, with a square sail of matting.

there lay numerous vessels all dressed in flags.[2] And we, anxious not to be outdone, also dressed our ships, and we actually surpassed their show, for we wanted in nothing but men, even the few whom we had being very ill. We anchored here with much pleasure, for we confidently hoped that on the following day we might go on land and hear mass jointly with the Christians reported to live there under their own *alcaide*[3] in a quarter separate from that of the Moors.

The pilots who had come with us told us there resided both Moors and Christians in this city; that these latter lived apart under their own lords, and that on our arrival they would receive us with much honour and take us to their houses. But they said this for a purpose of their own, for it was not true. At midnight there approached us a *zavra* with about a hundred men, all armed with cutlasses [tarçados] and bucklers. When they came to the vessel of the captain-major they attempted to board her, armed as they were, but this was not permitted, only four or five of the most distinguished men among them being allowed on board. They remained about a couple of hours, and it seemed to us that they paid us this visit merely to find out whether they might not capture one or the other of our vessels.

On Palm Sunday [April 8] the King of Mombaça sent the captain-major a sheep and large quantities of oranges, lemons and sugar-cane, together with a ring, as a pledge of safety, letting him know that in case of his entering the port he would be supplied with all he stood in need of. This present was conveyed to us by two men, almost white, who said they were Christians, which appeared to be the fact. The captain-major sent the king a string of coral-beads as a return present, and let him know that he purposed entering the port on the following day. On the same day the captain-major's vessel was visited by four Moors of distinction.

Two men were sent by the captain-major to the king, still further to confirm these peaceful assurances. When these landed they were followed by a crowd as far as the gates of the palace.

[2] The Swahili "dress" their vessels at the feast that follows the Ramadan month.

[3] *Alcaide*, from the Arabic *Alkadi*, the Judge.

Before reaching the king they passed through four doors, each guarded by a doorkeeper with a drawn cutlass. The king received them hospitably, and ordered that they should be shown over the city. They stopped on their way at the house of two Christian merchants, who showed them a paper [carta], an object of their adoration, on which was a sketch of the Holy Ghost.[4] When they had seen all, the king sent them back with samples of cloves, pepper and corn,[5] with which articles he would allow us to load our ships.

On Tuesday [April 10], when weighing anchor to enter the port, the captain-major's vessel would not pay off, and struck the vessel which followed astern. We therefore again cast anchor. When the Moors who were in our ship saw that we did not go on, they scrambled into a *zavra* attached to our stern; whilst the two pilots whom we had brought from Moçambique jumped into the water, and were picked up by the men in the *zavra*. At night the captain-major "questioned" two Moors [from Moçambique] whom we had on board, by dropping boiling oil upon their skin, so that they might confess any treachery intended against us. They said that orders had been given to capture us as soon as we entered the port, and thus to avenge what we had done at Moçambique. And when this torture was being applied a second time, one of the Moors, although his hands were tied, threw himself into the sea, whilst the other did so during the morning watch.

About midnight two *almadias*, with many men in them, approached. The *almadias* stood off whilst the men entered the water, some swimming in the direction of the *Berrio*, others in that of the *Raphael*. Those who swam to the *Berrio* began to cut the cable. The men on watch thought at first that they were tunny fish, but when they perceived their mistake they shouted to the other vessels. The other swimmers had already got hold

[4] Burton (*Camoens*, iv, p. 241) suggests that this picture of the Holy Ghost may have been a figure of Kapot-eshwar, the Hindu pigeon-god and goddess, an incarnation of Shiva and his wife, the third person of the Hindu Triad.

[5] Trigo tremez, corn that ripens in three months. This would be sorghum (the "matama" of the Swahili), which is sent in shiploads to Arabia and the Persian Gulf.

of the rigging of the mizzen-mast. Seeing themselves discovered, they silently slipped down and fled. These and other wicked tricks were practised upon us by these dogs, but our Lord did not allow them to succeed, because they were unbelievers.

Mombaça is a large city seated upon an eminence washed by the sea. Its port is entered daily by numerous vessels. At its entrance stands a pillar, and by the sea a low-lying fortress. Those who had gone on shore told us that in the town they had seen many men in irons; and it seemed to us that these must be Christians, as the Christians in that country are at war with the Moors.

The Christian merchants in the town are only temporary residents, and are held in much subjection, they not being allowed to do anything except by the order of the Moorish King.

It pleased God in his mercy that on arriving at this city all our sick recovered their health, for the climate ["air"] of this place is very good.

After the malice and treachery planned by these dogs had been discovered, we still remained on Wednesday and Thursday [April 11 and 12].

[Mombaça to Malindi]

We left in the morning [April 13], the wind being light, and anchored about eight leagues from Mombaça, close to the shore. At break of day [April 14] we saw two boats [barcas] about three leagues to the leeward, in the open sea, and at once gave chase, with the intention of capturing them, for we wanted to secure a pilot who would guide us to where we wanted to go. At vesper-time we came up with one of them, and captured it, the other escaping towards the land. In the one we took we found seventeen men, besides gold, silver, and an abundance of maize and other provisions; as also a young woman, who was the wife of an old Moor of distinction, who was a passenger. When we came up with the boat they all threw themselves into the water, but we picked them up from our boats.

That same day [April 14] at sunset, we cast anchor off a place called Milinde [Malindi], which is thirty leagues from Mombaça. The following places are between Mombaça and Milinde, viz., Benapa, Toça and Nuguoquioniete.

[*Malindi*]⁶

On Easter Sunday [April 15] the Moors whom we had taken in the boat told us that there were at this city of Melinde four vessels belonging to Christians from India, and that if it pleased us to take them there, they would provide us, instead of them, Christian pilots and all we stood in need of, including water, wood and other things. The captain-major much desired to have pilots from the country, and having discussed the matter with his Moorish prisoners, he cast anchor off the town, at a distance of about half a league from the mainland. The inhabitants of the town did not venture to come aboard our ships, for they had already learnt that we had captured a vessel and made her occupants prisoners.

On Monday morning [xApril 16] the captain-major had the old Moor taken to a sandbank in front of the town, where he was picked up by an *almadia*. The Moor explained to the king the wishes of the captain-major, and how much he desired to make peace with him. After dinner the Moor came back in a *zavra*, accompanied by one of the king's cavaliers and a sharif: he also brought three sheep. These messengers told the captain-general that the king would rejoice to make peace with him, and to enter into friendly relations; that he would willingly grant to the captain-major all his country afforded, whether pilots or anything else. The captain-major upon this sent word that he proposed to enter the port on the following day, and forwarded by the king's messengers a present consisting of a *balandrau*,⁷ two strings of coral, three wash-hand basins, a hat, little bells and two pieces of *lambel*.⁸

Consequently, on Tuesday [April 17] we approached nearer

---

⁶ The ruins of the ancient town of Malindi lie to the south of the modern village of that name, and are of great extent. They include the remains of a town wall. Persian and Arabic inscriptions have been discovered, but, with the exception of Vasco da Gama's pillar, no traces of occupation by the Portuguese. Malindi Road, or Port Melinda of the Admiralty chart, lies about three miles to the south of the town, but Vasco da Gama anchored off the town, and not in this sheltered road. The anchorage is less than half a mile from the town in four fathoms and a half.

⁷ *Balandrau*, a surtout worn by the Brothers of Mercy in Portugal.

⁸ *Lambel*, a striped cotton stuff which had a large sale at the beginning of the African trade.

to the town. The king sent the captain-major six sheep, besides quantities of cloves, cumin, ginger, nutmeg and pepper, as also a message, telling him that if he desired to have an interview with him he (the king) would come out in his *zavra*, when the captain-major could meet him in a boat.

On Wednesday [April 18], after dinner, when the king came up close to the ships in a *zavra*, the captain-major at once entered one of his boats, which had been well furnished, and many friendly words were exchanged when they lay side by side. The king having invited the captain-major to come to his house to rest, after which he (the king) would visit him on board his ship, the captain-major said that he was not permitted by his master to go on land, and if he were to do so a bad report would be given of him. The king wanted to know what would be said of himself by his people if he were to visit the ships, and what account could he render them? He then asked for the name of our king, which was written down for him, and said that on our return he would sent an ambassador with us, or a letter.

When both had said all they desired, the captain-major sent for the Moors whom he had taken prisoner, and surrendered them all. This gave much satisfaction to the king, who said that he valued this act more highly than if he had been presented with a town. And the king, much pleased, made the circuit of our ships, the bombards of which fired a salute. About three hours were spent in this way. When the king went away he left in the ship one of his sons and a sharif, and took two of us away with him, to whom he desired to show his palace. He, moreover, told the captain that as he would not go ashore he would himself return on the following day to the beach, and would order his horsemen to go through some exercises.

The king wore a robe [royal cloak] of damask trimmed with green satin, and a rich *touca*. He was seated on two cushioned chairs of bronze, beneath a round sunshade of crimson satin attached to a pole. An old man, who attended him as page, carried a short sword in a silver sheath. There were many players on *anafils*, and two trumpets of ivory, richly carved, and of the size of a man, which were blown from a hole in the side, and made sweet harmony with the *anafils*.

On Thursday [April 19] the captain-major and Nicolau Coelho rowed along the front of the town, bombards having been placed in the poops of their long-boats. Many people were along the shore, and among them two horsemen, who appeared to take much delight in a sham-fight. The king was carried in a palanquin from the stone steps of his palace to the side of the captain-major's boats. He again begged the captain to come ashore, as he had a helpless father who wanted to see him, and that he and his sons would go on board the ships as hostages. The captain, however, excused himself.

We found here four vessels belonging to Indian Christians. When they came for the first time on board Paulo da Gama's ship, the captain-major being there at the time, they were shown an altar-piece representing Our Lady at the foot of the cross, with Jesus Christ in her arms and the apostles around her. When the Indians saw this picture they prostrated themselves, and as long as we were there they came to say their prayers in front of it, bringing offerings of cloves, pepper, and other things.

These Indians are tawny men; they wear but little clothing and have long beards and long hair, which they braid. They told us that they ate no beef. Their language differs from that of the Arabs, but some of them know a little of it, as they hold much intercourse with them.

On the day on which the captain-major went up to the town in the boats, these Christian Indians fired off many bombards from their vessel, and when they saw him pass they raised their hands and shouted lustily *Christ! Christ!*[9]

That same night they asked the king's permission to give us a night-fête. And when night came they fired off many bombards, sent up rockets, and raised loud shouts.

These Indians warned the captain-major against going on shore, and told him not to trust to their "fanfares," as they neither came from their hearts nor from their good will.

On the following Sunday, the 22nd of April, the king's *zavra* brought on board one of his confidential servants, and as two days had passed without any visitors, the captain-major had this

[9] Burton (*Camoens*, IV, p. 420) suggests that they cried *Krishna*, the name of the eighth Incarnation of Vishnu, the second person of the Hindu Trinity, and the most popular of Indian gods.

man seized, and sent word to the king that he required the pilots whom he had promised. The king, when he received this message, sent a Christian pilot,[10] and the captain-major allowed the gentleman, whom he had retained in his vessel, to go away.

We were much pleased with the Christian pilot whom the king had sent us. We learnt from him that the island of which we heard at Moçambique as being inhabited by Christians was in reality an island subject to this same King of Moçambique; that half of it belonged to the Moors and the other half to the Christians; that many pearls were to be found there, and that it was called Quyluee.[11] This is the island the Moorish pilots wanted to take us to, and we also wished to go there, for we believed that what they said was true.

The town of Malindi lies in a bay and extends along the shore. It may be likened to Alcouchette.[12] Its houses are lofty and well white-washed, and have many windows; on the landside are palm-groves, and all around it maize and vegetables are being cultivated.

We remained in front of this town during nine days, and all this time we had fêtes, sham-fights, and musical performances ["fanfares"].

[Across the Gulf—the Arabian Sea]

We left Malindi on Tuesday, the 24th of the month [of April] for a city called Qualecut [Calecut], with the pilot whom the king had given us. The coast there runs north and south, and the land encloses a huge bay with a strait. In this bay,[13] we were told, were to be found many large cities of Christians and Moors, including one called Quambay [Cambay), as also six-hundred known islands, and within it the Red Sea and the "house" [Kaabah] of Mecca.

On the following Sunday [April 29] we once more saw the North Star, which we had not seen for a long time.

[10] See introductory note, p. 73.

[11] The island in question is Kilwa.

[12] Alcochete, a town on the left bank of the estuary of the Tagus, above Lisbon.

[13] The "Bay" is the Arabian Sea, which the "Strait" of Bab el Mandeb joins to the Red Sea. Cambay (Khambhat), in Gujarat, when the Portuguese first came to India, was one of the most flourishing marts of commerce. The silting up of the Gulf accounts, in a large measure, for its commercial decline since then.

On Friday, the 18th of May, after having seen no land for twenty-three days, we sighted lofty mountains, and having all this time sailed before the wind we could not have made less than 600 leagues. The land, when first sighted,[14] was at a distance of eight leagues, and our lead reached bottom at forty-five fathoms. That same night we took a course to the S.S.W., so as to get away from the coast. On the following day [May 19] we again approached the land, but owing to the heavy rain and a thunderstorm,[15] which prevailed whilst we were sailing along the coast, our pilot was unable to identify the exact locality. On Sunday [May 20] we found ourselves close to some mountains,[16] and when we were near enough for the pilot to recognise them he told us that they were above Calecut, and that this was the country we desired to go to.

[Calecut]

[Arrival] That night [May 20] we anchored two leagues from the city of Calecut, and we did so because our pilot mistook Capua,[17] a town at that place, for Calecut. Still further there is another town called Pandarani.[18] We anchored about a league and a half from the shore. After we were at anchor, four boats [almadias] approached us from the land, who asked of what nation we were. We told them, and they then pointed out Calecut to us.

On the following day [May 21] these same boats came again alongside, when the captain-major sent one of the convicts to

[14] Mount Eli (Dely) was probably the land first sighted, a conspicuous hill forming a promontory about 16 miles to the north of Cananor, and named thus from the Cardamoms which are largely exported from this part of Malabar, and are called Ela in Sanscrit (Yule's *Marco Polo*, ii, p. 321).

[15] The rains in Malabar begin about April or May, and continue until September or October. They are synchronous with the S.W. monsoon, and are heaviest in June, July, and August. The annual rainfall exceeds 150 inches!

[16] Cotta Point, or Cape Kadalur, the "Monte Formosa" of the Portuguese, 15 miles N.N.W. of Calecut.

[17] Castanheda and Barros call this place Capocate. It was seven miles N.N.W. of Calecut, at the mouth of the Elatur River.

[18] Pandaramy (Pandarani) is Batuta's Fandarain. Barros calls it Pandarane. It is identical with Pantharini Kollam, the northern Kollam or Quillan, and boasts one of the nine original mosques built on the Malabar coast by Malik Ibn Dinar. It is 14 miles N.N.W. of Calecut. The author of the MS elsewhere spells Pandaramy and Pandarin.

Calecut, and those with whom he went took him to two Moors from Tunis, who could speak Castilian and Genoese. The first greeting that he received was in these words: "May the Devil take thee! What brought you hither?" They asked what he sought so far away from home, and he told them that we came in search of Christians and of spices. They said: "Why does not the King of Castile, the King of France, or the Signoria of Venice send hither?" He said that the King of Portugal would not consent to their doing so, and they said he did the right thing. After this conversation they took him to their lodgings and gave him wheaten bread and honey. When he had eaten he returned to the ships, accompanied by one of the Moors, who was no sooner on board, than he said these words: "A lucky venture, a lucky venture! Plenty of rubies, plenty of emeralds! You owe great thanks to God, for having brought you to a country holding such riches!" We were greatly astonished to hear his talk, for we never expected to hear our language spoken so far away from Portugal.

[*A description of Calecut*] The city of Calecut is inhabited by Christians. They are of a tawny complexion. Some of them have big beards and long hair, whilst others clip their hair short or shave the head, merely allowing a tuft to remain on the crown as a sign that they are Christians. They also wear moustaches. They pierce the ears and wear much gold in them. They go naked down to the waist, covering their lower extremities with very fine cotton stuffs. But it is only the most respectable who do this, for the others manage as best they are able.[19]

The women of this country, as a rule, are ugly and of small stature. They wear many jewels of gold round the neck, numerous bracelets on their arms, and rings set with precious stones on their toes. All these people are well-disposed and apparently of mild temper. At first sight they seem covetous and ignorant.

[*A message sent to the King*] When we arrived at Calecut the king was fifteen leagues away. The captain-major sent two

[19] The visitors thus became at once acquainted with the various castes constituting the population of Calecut, including the *Nairs*, or fighting caste of Malabar, who eat meat (which shows a servile origin), but wear the thread of the Dwija (twice-born), rank next to the Brahmans, and practise polyandry; and the turbulent *Moplah*, who are descendants of Arab fathers and native women. These latter are the "native" Moors.

men to him with a message, informing him that an ambassador had arrived from the King of Portugal with letters, and that if he desired it he would take them to where the king then was.

The king presented the bearers of this message with much fine cloth. He sent word to the captain bidding him welcome, saying that he was about to proceed to Qualecut [Calecut]. As a matter of fact, he started at once with a large retinue.

[*At anchor at Pandarani*, May 27] A pilot accompanied our two men, with orders to take us to a place called Pandarani, below the place [Capua] where we anchored at first. At this time we were actually in front of the city of Calecut. We were told that the anchorage at the place to which we were to go was good, whilst at the place we were then it was bad, with a stony bottom, which was quite true; and, moreover, that it was customary for the ships which came to this country to anchor there for the sake of safety. We ourselves did not feel comfortable, and the captain-major had no sooner received this royal message than he ordered the sails to be set, and we departed. We did not, however, anchor as near the shore as the king's pilot desired.

When we were at anchor, a message arrived informing the captain-major that the king was already in the city. At the same time the king sent a *bale*,[20] with other men of distinction, to Pandarani, to conduct the captain-major to where the king awaited him. This *bale* is like an *alcaide*, and is always attended by two hundred men armed with swords and bucklers. As it was late when this message arrived, the captain-major deferred going.

[*Gama goes to Calecut*] On the following morning, which was Monday, May 28th, the captain-major set out to speak to the king, and took with him thirteen men, of whom I was one. We put on our best attire, placed bombards in our boats, and took with us trumpets and many flags. On landing, the captain-major was received by the *alcaide*, with whom were many men, armed and unarmed. The reception was friendly, as if the people were pleased to see us, though at first appearances looked threatening, for they carried naked swords in their hands. A palanquin was provided for the captain-major, such as is used by men of distinction in that country, as also by some of the merchants, who

[20] *Bale*, in the Arabic *Wali*, governor. *Alcaide*, in Portuguese, has this same meaning.

pay something to the king for this privilege. The captain-major
entered the palanquin, which was carried by six men by turns.
Attended by all these people we took the road of Qualecut,
and came first to another town, called Capua. The captain-major
was there deposited at the house of a man of rank, whilst we
others were provided with food, consisting of rice, with much
butter, and excellent boiled fish. The captain-major did not wish
to eat, and when we had done so, we embarked on a river close
by, which flows between the sea and the mainlaind, close to the
coast.[21] The two boats in which we embarked were lashed together,
so that we were not separated. There were numerous other boats,
all crowded with people. As to those who were on the banks I
say nothing; their number was infinite, and they had all come
to see us. We went up that river for about a league, and saw
many large ships drawn up high and dry on its banks, for there
is no port here.

When we disembarked, the captain-major once more entered
his palanquin. The road was crowded with a countless multitude
anxious to see us. Even the women came out of their houses
with children in their arms and followed us.

[*A Christian Church*][22] When we arrived [at Calecut] they took
us to a large church, and this is what we saw:—

The body of the church is as large as a monastery, all built
of hewn stone and covered with tiles. At the main entrance rises
a pillar of bronze as high as a mast, on the top of which was
perched a bird, apparently a cock. In addition to this, there was
another pillar as high as a man, and very stout. In the centre of
the body of the church rose a chapel,[23] all built of hewn stone,
with a bronze door sufficiently wide for a man to pass, and
stone steps leading up to it. Within this sanctuary stood a small
image which they said represented Our Lady. Along the walls,

[21] This river is the Elatur.

[22] This "church" was, of course, a pagoda or temple. The high pillar in
front of it is used for suspending the flag which indicates the commencement
of the Temple festival. It is of wood, but usually covered with copper or
silver. The cock, which surmounts it, is the symbol of the War-god Sub-
raumainar. The smaller pillar supports the coco-oil lamps during the festival.

[23] *Corucheo*, which literally means spire or minaret; but further on the
authors calls this sanctuary a chapel, *capella*.

by the main entrance, hung seven small bells.[24] In this church the
captain-major said his prayers, and we with him.[25]

We did not go within the chapel, for it is the custom that only
certain servants of the church, called *quafees*,[26] should enter. These
quafees wore some threads passing over the left shoulder and
under the right arm, in the same manner as our deacons wear
the stole. They threw holy water over us, and gave us some
white earth,[27] which the Christians of this country are in the habit
of putting on their foreheads, breasts, around the neck, and on
the forearms. They threw holy water upon the captain-major
and gave him some of the earth, which he gave in charge of
someone, giving them to understand that he would put it on later.

Many other saints were painted on the walls of the church,
wearing crowns. They were painted variously, with teeth pro-
truding an inch from the mouth, and four or five arms.

Below this church there was a large masonry tank, similar to
many others which we had seen along the road.

[*Progress through the Town*] After we had left that place, and
had arrived at the entrance to the city [of Calecut] we were
shown another church, where we saw things like those described
above. Here the crowd grew so dense that progress along the
street became next to impossible, and for this reason they put
the captain into a house, and us with him.

The king sent a brother of the *bale*, who was a lord of this
country, to accompany the captain, and he was attended by men
beating drums, blowing *anafils* and bagpipes, and firing off match-
locks. In conducting the captain they showed us much respect,
more than is shown in Spain to a king. The number of people

[24] These bells are struck by the Brahmans when they enter the temple,
but must not be touched by people of inferior castes.

[25] It is just possible that some of the Portuguese doubted whether these
Hindu Gods and images represented the saints of their own churches. Castanheda (i, p. 57) says that when João de Sá knelt down by the side of
Vasco da Gama, he said: "If these be devils, I worship the true God"; at
which his chief smiled. But however this may be, it is equally true that the
reports furnished by the heads of the expedition described these Hindus as
Christians, and that the king believed them to be so.

[26] The "*quafees*" are, of course, Brahman priests. The Rev. J. J. Jaus
suggests *kāz* (Arabic), meaning "judge".

[27] The "white earth" is a mixture of dust, cow-dung, sacrificial ashes,
sandal wood, etc., cemented in rice-water.

was countless, for in addition to those who surrounded us, and among whom there were two thousand armed men, they crowded the roofs and houses.

[*The King's Palace*] The further we advanced in the direction of the king's palace, the more did they increase in number. And when we arrived there, men of much distinction and great lords came out to meet the captain, and joined those who were already in attendance upon him. It was then an hour before sunset. When we reached the palace we passed through a gate into a courtyard of great size, and before we arrived at where the king was, we passed four doors, through which we had to force our way, giving many blows to the people. When, at last, we reached the door where the king was, there came forth from it a little old man, who holds a position resembling that of a bishop, and whose advice the king acts upon in all affairs of the church. This man embraced the captain when he entered the door. Several men were wounded at this door, and we only got in by the use of much force.

[*A Royal Audience, May 28*] The king was in a small court, re-clining upon a couch covered with a cloth of green velvet, above whiich was a good mattress, and upon this again a sheet of cotton stuff, very white and fine, more so than any linen. The cushions were after the same fashion. In his left hand the king held a very large golden cup [spittoon], having a capacity of half an almude [8 pints]. At its mouth this cup was two palmas [16 inches] wide, and apparently it was massive. Into this cup the king threw the husks of a certain herb which is chewed by the people of this country because of its soothing effects, and which they call *atambo*r.[28] On the right side of the king stood a basin of gold, so large that a man might just encircle it with his arms: this contained the herbs. There were likewise many silver jugs. The canopy above the couch was all gilt.

The captain, on entering, saluted in the manner of the country:

[28] *Atambor*, a corruption of the Arabic *tambur*, the betel-nut. It is the fruit of Areca Catechu, and is universally chewed throughout India, the Indian Archipelago and Southern China. Its juice discolours the teeth, but is said to make the breath sweet, and to be conducive to health. "Erva" (herb) is quite inapplicable to this fruit. Usually it is cut up into four slices, which are wrapped up in a leaf of Betel-pepper (*Piper Betle*), and chewed with an admixture of lime and catechu.

by putting the hands together, then raising them toward Heaven, as is done by Christians when addressing God, and immediately afterwards opening them and shutting the fists quickly. The king beckoned to the captain with his right hand to come nearer, but the captain did not approach him, for it is the custom of the country for no man to approach the king except only the servant who hands him the herbs, and when anyone addresses the king he holds his hand before the mouth, and remains at a distance. When the king beckoned to the captain he looked at us others, and ordered us to be seated on a stone bench near him, where he could see us. He ordered that water for our hands should be given us, as also some fruit, one kind of which resembled a melon, except that its outside was rough and the inside sweet, whilst another kind of fruit resembled a fig, and tasted very nice.[29] There were men who prepared these fruits for us; and the king looked at us eating, and smiled; and talked to the servant who stood near him supplying him with the herbs referred to.

Then, throwing his eyes on the captain, who sat facing him, he invited him to address himself to the courtiers present, saying they were men of much distinction, that he could tell them whatever he desired to say, and they would repeat it to him (the king). The captain-major replied that he was the ambassador of the King of Portugal, and the bearer of a message which he could only deliver to him personally. The king said this was good, and immediately asked him to be conducted to a chamber. When the captain-major had entered, the king, too, rose and joined him, whilst we remained where we were. All this happened about sunset. An old man who was in the court took away the couch as soon as the king rose, but allowed the plate to remain. The king, when he joined the captain, threw himself upon another couch, covered with various stuffs embroidered in gold, and asked the captain what he wanted.

And the captain told him he was the ambassador of a King of Portugal, who was Lord of many countries and the possessor of great wealth of every description, exceeding that of any king of these parts; that for a period of sixty years his ancestors had annually sent out vessels to make discoveries in the direction of

[29] These fruits were the Jack (*Artocarpus integrifolia*) and bananas.

India, as they knew that there were Christian kings there like themselves. This, he said, was the reason which induced them to order this country to be discovered, not because they sought for gold or silver, for of this they had such abundance that they needed not what was to be found in this country. He further stated that the captains sent out travelled for a year or two, until their provisions were exhausted, and then returned to Portugal, without having succeeded in making the desired discovery. There reigned a king now whose name was Dom Manuel, who had ordered him to build three vessels, of which he had been appointed captain-major, and who had ordered him not to return to Portugal until he should have discovered this King of the Christians, on pain of having his head cut off. That two letters had been intrusted to him to be presented in case he succeeded in discovering him, and that he would do so on the ensuing day; and, finally, he had been instructed to say by word of mouth that he [the King of Portugal] desired to be his friend and brother.

In reply to this the king said that he was welcome; that, on his part, he held him as a friend and brother, and would send ambassadors with him to Portugal. This latter had been asked as a favour, the captain pretending that he would not dare to present himself before his king and master unless he was able to present, at the same time, some men of this country.

These and many other things passed between the two in this chamber, and as it was already late in the night, the king asked the captain with whom he desired to lodge, with Christians or with Moors? And the captain replied, neither with Christians nor with Moors, and begged as a favour that he be given a lodging by himself. The king said he would order it thus, upon which the captain took leave of the king and came to where we were, that is, to a veranda lit up by a huge candlestick. By that time four hours of the night had already gone.

[*A Night's Lodging*] We then all went forth with the captain in search of our lodgings, and a countless crowd with us. And the rain poured down so heavily that the streets ran with water. The captain went on the back of six men [in a palanquin], and the time occupied in passing through the city was so long that the captain at last grew tired, and complained to the king's factor, a Moor of distinction, who attended him to the lodgings. The

Moor then took him to his own house, and we were admitted to a court within it, where there was a veranda, roofed in with tiles. Many carpets had been spread, and there were two large candlesticks like those at the Royal palace. At the top of each of these were great iron lamps, fed with oil or butter, and each lamp had four wicks, which gave much light. These lamps they use instead of torches.

This same Moor then had a horse brought for the captain to take him to his lodgings, but it was without a saddle, and the captain refused to mount it.[30] We then started for our lodgings, and when we arrived we found there some of our men [who had come from the ships] with the captain's bed, and with numerous other things which the captain had brought as presents for the king.

[*Presents for the King*] On Tuesday [May 29] the captain got ready the following things to be sent to the king, viz., twelve pieces of *lambel*, four scarlet hoods, six hats, four strings of coral, a case containing six wash-hand basins, a case of sugar, two casks of oil, and two of honey. And as it is the custom not to send anything to the king without the knowledge of the Moor, his factor, and of the *bale*, the captain informed them of his intention. They came, and when they saw the present they laughed at it, saying that it was not a thing to offer a king, that the poorest merchant from Mecca, or any other part of India, gave more, and that if he wanted to make a present it should be in gold, as the king would not accept such things. When the captain heard this he grew sad, and said that he had brought no gold, that, moreover, he was no merchant, but an ambassador; that he gave of that which he had, which was his own [private gift] and not the king's;[31] that if the King of Portugal ordered him to return he would intrust him with far richer presents; and that if King Camolim[32] would not accept these things he would send them back to the ships. Upon this they declared that they would not for-

---

[30] It is still the practice in Calecut to ride horses without a saddle, and no slight seems therefore to have been intended.

[31] As a matter of fact, Vasco da Gama was very poorly provided with suitable merchandise.

[32] Zamorin. It is a title; according to some a corrupt reading of Tamuri Rajah, Tamuri being the name of the most exalted family of the Nair caste, whilst others derive it from "Samudriya Rajah," that is, "King of the Coast."

ward his presents, nor consent to his forwarding them himself. When they had gone there came certain Moorish merchants, and they all depreciated the present which the captain desired to be sent to the king.

When the captain saw that they were determined not to forward his present, he said, that as they would not allow him to send his present to the palace he would go to speak to the king, and would then return to the ships. They approved of this, and told him that if he would wait a short time they would return and accompany him to the palace. And the captain waited all day, but they never came back. The captain was very wroth at being among so phlegmatic and unreliable a people, and intended at first, to go to the palace without them. On further consideration, however, he thought it best to wait until the following day. As to us others, we diverted ourselves, singing and dancing to the sound of trumpets, and enjoyed ourselves much.

[*A Second Audience, May 30*] On Wednesday morning the Moors returned, and took the captain to the palace, and us others with him. The palace was crowded with armed men. Our captain was kept waiting with his conductors for fully four long hours, outside a door, which was only opened when the king sent word to admit him, attended by two men only, whom he might select. The captain said that he desired to have Fernão Martins with him, who could interpret, and his secretary. It seemed to him, as it did to us, that this separation portended no good.

When he had entered, the king said that he had expected him on Tuesday. The captain said that the long road had tired him, and that for this reason he had not come to see him. The king then said that he had told him that he came from a very rich kingdom, and yet had brought him nothing; that he had also told him that he was the bearer of a letter, which had not yet been delivered. To this the captain rejoined that he had brought nothing, because the object of his voyage was merely to make discoveries, but that when other ships came he would then see what they brought him; as to the letter, it was true that he had brought one, and would deliver it immediately.

The king then asked what it was he had come to discover: stones or men? If he came to discover men, as he said, why had he brought nothing? Moreover, he had been told that he carried with him the golden image of a Santa Maria. The captain said that the Santa Maria was not of gold, and that even if she were he would not part with her, as she had guided him across the ocean, and would guide him back to his own country. The king then asked for the letter. The captain said that he begged as a favour, that as the Moors wished him ill and might misinterpret him, a Christian able to speak Arabic should be sent for. The king said this was well, and at once sent for a young man, of small stature, whose name was Quaram. The captain then said that he had two letters, one written in his own language and the other in that of the Moors; that he was able to read the former, and knew that it contained nothing but what would prove acceptable; but that as to the other he was unable to read it, and it might be good, or contain something that was erroneous. As the Christian was unable to *read* Moorish, four Moors took the letter and read it between them, after which they translated it to the king, who was well satisfied with its contents.

The king then asked what kind of merchandise was to be found in his country. The captain said there was much corn, cloth, iron, bronze, and many other things. The king asked whether he had any merchandise with him. The captain replied that he had a little of each sort, as samples, and that if permitted to return to the ships he would order it to be landed, and that meantime four or five men would remain at the lodgings assigned them. The king said no! He might take all his people with him, securely moor his ships, land his merchandise, and sell it to the best advantage.

8. Vijayanagar

Most of the early sixteenth-century accounts of European visits to the East were written by Portuguese seamen or officials, and the Portuguese government endeavored, on the whole successfully, to prevent their publication. They remained in manuscript until at least the second half of the century, some much longer; and some have entirely disappeared.

When, occasionally, a non-Portuguese traveler succeeded in getting to the East, he could publish his experiences without much fear of contradiction and in the expectation of a ready sale. The *Itinerary* of Ludovico di Varthema of Bologna first appeared in Rome in 1510. Unlike most sixteenth-century commentators (but like Conti in the preceding century) Varthema went to the East over the land routes of the Levant, learned colloquial Arabic and accepted Islam, passing himself off as a Christian born, but captured in early youth. He arrived in South India in 1504, six years after Vasco da Gama's first visit, six years before Alboquerque's capture of Goa, during the early struggle of the Portuguese to establish armed trading posts on the Malabar coast. In 1505 Varthema—according to his own account—rounded Cape Comorin by sea, touched at several places on the east coast of India, and visited Tenasserim, Pegu, Malacca, Sumatra, the Moluccas, Borneo, and Java. Doubts have been cast on the authenticity of these travels east of Cape Comorin. If the dates usually ascribed to them are correct, and if Varthema really visited all the places he claimed to have visited, his journey must have been somewhat hurried; and certainly his descriptions of Burma, Malaya, and the islands are shorter, vaguer, and less detailed than those of South India. It is fairly generally conceded, however, that the journey was possible; and whether or not the information which Varthema recorded was all derived from personal knowledge, it is of great interest. He preceded the first Portuguese expeditions by a few years in all the places in which they were principally interested. He described Malacca, one of the most celebrated trading centers of the East, six years before Alboquerque's people took the place; and the Moluccas, the longed-for-Spice Islands, six years before Antonio de Abreu went in search of them, eight years before Abreu's lieutenant Francisco Serrão was wrecked in the Banda Sea and made his way to Amboina and Ternate. Varthema returned to Calicut late in 1505, and after a series of escapades there took employment with the Portuguese at Cochin. He was knighted for his services, and sailed for Lisbon in 1508 with a Portuguese fleet, in a ship belonging to the Florentine house of Marchionni. From Lisbon he went on to Rome to arrange for the publication of his book.

The *Itinerary* is at least plausible; in its day it was influential; Magellan is said to have used it in the arguments which he laid before Charles I of Spain. If modern scholars do not entirely believe Varthema, his contemporaries in Europe did. The book was an immediate success. It appeared in six Italian editions between 1510 and 1535, and was translated into Latin, German, and Spanish; later in the century into French, Dutch, and English. Varthema's descriptions of South India, in particu-

lar, are vivid and apparently accurate. Most interesting among them is
his brief account of the great Hindu kingdom of Vijayanagar. Later in
the century, at Talikot in 1565, Vijayanagar was to be defeated and
dismembered by a league of Muslim princes; but in Varthema's day it
was still strong, prosperous, and secure, the suzerain power of most of
Hindu South India. Today its capital city is a vast deserted ruin. Varthema wrote the best description we have of Vijayanagar, the Sanskrit
"City of Victory," at the height of its splendor.

The extract which follows is from *The Itinerary of Ludovico di
Varthema of Bologna from 1502 to 1508*, translated by J. W. Jones,
edited by R. C. Temple (London, Argonaut Press, 1928), pp. 51-3.

T HE said city of Bisinegar [Vijayanagar] belongs to the King
of Narsinga [i.e. Narsingha, King of Vijayanagar], and is very
large and strongly walled. It is situated on the side of a mountain,
and is seven miles in circumference. It has a triple circle of
walls. It is a place of great merchandise, is extremely fertile, and
is endowed with all possible kinds of delicacies. It occupies the
most beautiful site, and possesses the best air that was ever seen:
with certain very beautiful places for hunting and the same for
fowling, so that it appears to me to be a second paradise. The
king of this city is a pagan, with all his kingdom, that is to say,
idolators. He is a very powerful king, and keeps up constantly
40,000 horsemen. And you must know that a horse is worth at
least 300, 400, and 500 *pardai*, and some are purchased for 800
pardai, because horses are not produced there, neither are many
mares found there, because those kings who hold the seaports
do not allow them to be brought there.

The said king also possesses 400 elephants and some dromedaries, which dromedaries run with great swiftness. It occurs to
me here to touch upon a subject worthy of notice, viz., the
discretion, the intelligence, and the strength of the elephant. We
will first say in what manner he fights. When an elephant goes
into battle he carries a saddle, in the same manner as they are
borne by the mules of the kingdom of Naples, fastened underneath by two iron chains. On each side of the said saddle he
carries a large and very strong wooden box, and in each box
there go three men. On the neck of the elephant, between the
boxes, they place a plank the size of half a span, and between

the boxes and the plank a man sits astride who speaks to the elephant, for the said elephant possesses more intelligence than any other animal in the world; so that there are in all seven persons who go upon the said elephant; and they go armed with shirts of mail, and with bows and lances, swords and shields. And in like manner they arm the elephant with mail, especially the head and the trunk. They fasten to the trunk a sword two *braccia* long, as thick and as wide as the hand of a man. And in that way they fight. And he who sits upon his neck orders him: "Go forward," or "Turn back," "Strike this one," "Strike that one," "Do not strike any more," and he understands as though he were a human being. But if at any time they are put to flight it is impossible to restrain them; for this race of people are great masters of the art of making fireworks, and these animals have a great dread of fire, and through this means they sometimes take to flight. But in every way this animal is the most discreet in the world and the most powerful. I have seen three elephants bring a ship from the sea to the land, in the manner as I will tell you. When I was in Canonor, some Moorish merchants brought a ship on shore in this manner, after the custom of Christians. They beach ships the prow foremost, but here they put the side of the vessel foremost, and under the said ship they put three pieces of wood, and on the side next the sea I saw three elephants kneel down and with their heads push the ship on to dry land. Many say that the elephant has no joints, and I say that it is true that they have not the joints so high as other animals, but they have them low. I tell you, moreover, that the female elephant is stronger and more proud than the male, and some of the females are mad. The said elephants are as large as three buffaloes, and they have a skin like that of the buffalo, and eyes like those of a pig, and a trunk reaching to the ground, and with this they put their food into their mouth as also their drink; for their mouth is situated beneath their throat, and almost like a pig or a sturgeon. This trunk is hollow within, and I have many times seen them fish up a *quattrino* from the ground with it. And with this trunk I have seen them pull down a branch from a tree which twenty-four of our men could not pull to the ground with a rope, and the elephant tore it down with three pulls. The two teeth which are seen are in the upper jaw. The ears are two *palmi* every way, some more, some less. Their legs are almost as large at the lower extremity as at the upper. Their feet are round like a very large trencher for cutting meat on, and around the foot there are five nails as large as the shell of an oyster. The tail is as long as that of a buffalo, about three *palmi* long, and has a few scattered hairs. The female is smaller than the male. With respect to the height of the said elephant, I have seen a great many thirteen and fourteen *palmi* high, and I have ridden on some of that height; they say, moreover, that some are found fifteen *palmi* high. Their walk is very slow, and those who are not accustomed to it cannot ride them, because it upsets their stomach, just as it does in travelling by sea. The small elephants have a pace like that of a mule, and it is a pleasure to ride them. When the said elephants are to be ridden, the said elephant lowers one of the hind legs, and by that leg it is mounted; nevertheless, you must help yourself or be helped to mount. You must also know that the said elephants do not carry a bridle or halter, or anything bound on the head. The said elephant, when he wishes to generate, goes into a secret place, that is, into the water in certain marshes, and they unite and generate like human beings. In some countries, I have seen that the finest present which can be made to a king is the parts of an elephant, which said king eats the said parts; for in some countries an elephant is worth fifty ducats, in some other countries it is worth one thousand and two thousand ducats. So that, in conclusion, I say that I have seen some elephants which have more understanding, and more discretion and intelligence, than any kind of people I have met with.

This King of Narsinga is the richest king I have ever heard spoken of. This city is situated like Milan, but not in a plain. The residence of the king is here, and his realms are placed as it might be the realm of Naples and also Venice; so that he has the sea on both sides. His Brahmins, that is, his priests, say that he possesses a revenue of 12,000 *pardai* per day. He is constantly at war with several Moorish and pagan kings. His faith is idolatrous, and they worship the devil, as do those of Calicut. When the proper time comes we will state in what manner they worship

him. They live like pagans. Their dress is this: the men of condition
wear a short shirt, and on their head a cloth of gold and silk
in the Moorish fashion, but nothing on the feet. The common
people go quite naked, with the exception of a piece of cloth
about their middle. The king wears a cap of gold brocade two
spans long, and when he goes to war he wears a quilted dress
of cotton, and over it he puts another garment full of golden
piastres, and having all around it jewels of various kinds. His
horse is worth more than some of our cities, on account of the
ornaments which it wears. When he rides for his pleasure he is
always accompanied by three or four kings, and many other lords,
and five or six thousand horse. Wherefore he may be considered
to be a very powerful lord.

His money consists of a *pardao*, as I have said. He also coins
a silver money called *tare*, and others of gold, twenty of which
go to a *pardao*, and are called *fanom*. And of these small ones
of silver, there go sixteen to a *fanom*. They also have another
coin called *cas;* sixteen of which go to a *tare* of silver. In this
kingdom you can go everywhere in safety. But it is necessary
to be on your guard against some lions which are on the road. I
will not speak of their food at the present time, because I wish
to describe it when we shall be in Calicut, where there are the
same customs and the same manner of living. This king is a
very great friend of the Christians, especially of the King of
Portugal, because he does not know much of any other Christians.
When the Portuguese arrive in his territories they do them great
honour.

9. The Portuguese in South India

After an initial rebuff at Calicut the Portuguese established themselves,
by agreement with the local ruler, in a fortified factory compound at
Cochin. Their intrusion into the spice trade provoked universally hostile reactions among the Muslim rulers of the whole Indian Ocean lit-

toral, led by the Sultan of Egypt, egged on by the Venetians. King Manoel quickly became convinced of the need for a secure base in India, under Portuguese control. In 1510 Affonso d'Alboquerque, in alliance with a Hindu corsair named Timoja, captured the island city and harbour of Goa from its Muslim ruler, and began to develop it both as a naval base and as the administrative and commercial center of Portuguese activity throughout the East. From Goa expeditions went out in attempts to seize other points of strategic and commercial importance, both on the Indian Ocean coasts and in the Malay archipelago. Portuguese superiority in naval armament, especially in gunnery, gave these attempts an initially rapid success. In the second decade of the sixteenth century the Portuguese established an effective though, as it turned out, short-lived monopoly of the supply of spices to Europe.

The *Book* of Duarte Barbosa describes the situation in the East in the middle of this decade of Portuguese success. Barbosa served in India as a government official between 1501 and 1516 or 1517. He learned Malayalam, knew South India thoroughly, and described it well; his *Book*, though it describes perfunctorily many other places in the East, is chiefly concerned with India.

So valuable and informative a manuscript, as might be expected, was allowed only a very limited circulation in Portugal, but a copy was supplied, no doubt clandestinely, to an Italian translator in 1524, and the Italian version appeared in print as part of the first volume of Ramusio's *Navigationi* in 1550. This was the only version known to scholars until 1812, when a Portuguese manuscript copy came to light and was published in Portugal. The differences between the two versions are slight: a tribute to Ramusio's skill as an editor.

Of the four brief chapters quoted here, three describe the cities in South India in which the Portuguese did most of their Indian business at the time when Barbosa wrote; the fourth is a summary of the nature and price of the chief commodities handled. The extracts are from *The Book of Duarte Barbosa*, translated and edited by Mansel Longworth Dames (2 vols., London, Hakluyt Society, 1918–21), I, 170–81; II, 84–95; II, 227–9.

§ 73. *Goa*

FURTHER along the coast there is a very fine river which sends out two branches to the sea. Between these two is an island on which stands the city of Goa. It belongs to the Daquem, and was a seignory over itself and over other lands around it further inland. There rules a great lord, a vassal of the said king, whom they call Sabayo,[1] on whom this seignory of Goa was bestowed because he was a bold horseman and valiant in war, in order that he might wage war thence against the king of Narsyngua,[2] as he did continually thenceforth until the day of his death; on which this city remained in the possession of his son the çabaym Hydalcam.

The inhabitants thereof are Moors of distinction, many of whom are foreigners from divers lands. They were white men,[3] among whom, as well as merchants of great wealth, there were also many husbandmen. The land, by reason that the harbour was exceeding good, had great trade, and many ships of the Moors came thither from Meca, the city of Adem, Ormus, Cambaya and Malabar. The Hydalcam had there a captain with many men at arms, who guarded it, and no man entered the island except under a strict regulation and a pass. He also kept there magistrates, scriveners and guards, who stopped every man who would enter, writing down who and whence he was, and what were his dis· tinguishing marks; in this manner they allowed men to come in or to go forth. The city is very great, with good houses, well girt about with strong walls, with towers and bastions. Around it are many vegetable and fruit gardens, with fine trees and tanks of sweet water, with mosques and heathen temples. The surrounding country is exceeding fertile. Here the Hydalcam had a great revenue as well from the land as from the sea.

Having heard the news of the overthrow of the Rumes before Dio by the Viceroy Dom Francisco Dalmeida[4] as I have stated

---

[1] *Sabayo, Cabaym,* or *Savain* was the title of Yusuf Adhil Khan, one of the chief vassal princes of the Deccan, and overlord of Goa at the time of Alboquerque's attack on the city in 1510. He was of Turkish origin.

[2] The Hindu kingdom of Vijayanagar.

[3] White men. Varthema says that the Savain was at the head of 400 Mamelukes like himself. These were mainly Turks, Persians, Kurds, Abysinnians or captives from Christian countries, and must all have appeared white in comparison with the natives of the Konkan. There were also settlers and adventurers in great numbers from the countries lying round the Red Sea and Persian Gulf in all the ports of Western India at this period. The kingdoms of the Deccan depended mainly on these men for their armies. The native Musalman population of Goa are called by De Barros Naiteas.

[4] Yūsuf 'Adil Khan, himself a "Mamlūk" like Mir Husain, the Egyptian admiral, who was a Kurd by birth, was evidently from the beginning in the

above in its proper place, he sent to summon all those who had escaped thence, and they, leaving their Captain Mirocem in the kingdom of Guzarate, came to Goa. The Hydalcam received them well and determined to give them all the aid and succour of which they stood in need, and to set them up again by the help of other Moorish kings and of the merchants, to the end that they might wage war against our people; in such a way, that having gathered together a great sum of money they began to build in the Goa river fair galleys and brigantines after our fashion and style, as well as many pieces of ordnance of iron and copper and all other munitions of war needful for the sea, and made such good speed that in a short time a great part of the fleet was ready, as well as many great store-houses full of all necessaries in great perfection. Thus they were so confident that they put out to sea in *atalayas* and *fustas* to the *zambucos*, which were passing by with safe-conducts from the Captains of the King our Lord and from Afonso D'Alboquerque, who was then Captain-in-Chief of the Indian Sea, and took them. And as this continued to increase, the said Afonso D'Alboquerque, having information thereof, determined to pay them a visit and persuade them to change their intentions; so gathering together all his ships, caravels and galleons he entered the river, and attacking the said city, took it by force of arms. In this attack many noteworthy events took place, which I do not here relate, in order to cut my story short, "for it is not my intention to write a chronicle, but only a short summary of that which can in truth be ascertained regarding the chief places in India."

But, to return to the subject: In this fight perished much people of the city, and of the ships which they had made ready some were taken and more were burnt, and he brought the city forthwith under the rule and governance of the King our Lord, even as it now is, and built for its defence strong fortresses. It is, at this time present, inhabited by Portuguese, Moors and Heathen, in great numbers.

Duties on the fruits and produce of the land yield the King

---

combination of Muhammadan powers against the Portuguese, and after the sack of Dābhōl by D'Almeida he was eager for revenge. Hence the combination of the naval powers which Barbosa alludes to, and the activity in the Goa River which led to the attack on it made by Alboquerque.

our Lord yearly twenty thousand cruzados, in addition to the port dues.

In this port of Goa there is great trade in many kinds of goods, from the whole of Malabar, Chaul, Dabul and the great kingdom of Cambaya, which are consumed on the mainlands, and from the kingdom of Ormus come every year many ships laden with horses, and great numbers of dealers from the great kingdom of Narsyngua and from Daquem come hither to buy them. They pay for them at the rate of two to three hundred cruzados a piece, as the case may be, and take them away to sell them to the kings and lords of their lands, and by this means one and all they make great gains, and the King our Lord as well, who receives a duty of forty cruzados on each horse. [The King of Portugal collects forty thousand ducats in revenue; although they now pay less than in the time of the Moors, nevertheless the said port makes him good returns.—*Ramusio*].

[In this kingdom of Decam there are many great cities and many towns and villages in the inland country, inhabited by Moors and Heathen. The country is exceeding fertile, yielding much food, and with great traffic.]

The Ormus merchants take hence in their ships cargoes of rice (great store) sugar, iron, pepper, ginger and other spices of divers kinds, and drugs, which they carry thither: and in all their dealings they are by the order of the King our Lord treated with greater mildness than by the Moorish kings.

The king of this land[5] and of the whole *Daquem* kingdom is named *Soltan Mahamude*. He is a Moor, and resides always in one city which is called *Bider*, where there is great luxury, leading a very pleasant life. He does not govern himself, nor do anything concerning his government, but makes it all over to certain Moorish noblemen to govern, and each of these has charge of certain towns and cities, and governs those entrusted to him by the king. If any one of these rises against him the others all help him against the rebel, and bring him back to his obedience or destroy him. These Governors are often at war one with the other; they have many horsemen and are good archers, with

[5] Mahmud Shah, ruler of the Bahmani kingdom of Bidar, who still retained his nominal suzerainty over a very large area of the Deccan, although superseded in real power by his vassals.

Turkish bows. They are fair men and tall, and are attired in fine
cotton garments, with turbans on their heads. They come from
divers countries, and he pays them right well; they speak Arabic,
Persian and Daquanim,[6] which is the native tongue of the land.

The Moorish noblemen in general take with them tents, with
which they form encampments, on the halting-grounds, when
they travel, or when they take the field to attack any town.

They ride on high-pommelled saddles, and make much use of
zojares, and fight tied to their saddles, with long light lances
which have heads a cubit long, square and very strong. They
wear short coats padded with cotton, and many of them kilts of
mail; their horses are well caparisoned with steel headpieces. They
carry maces and battle-axes and two swords (each with its dagger), two or three Turkish bows hanging from the saddle, with
very long arrows, so that every man carries arms enough for
two. When they go forth to fight they take their wives with
them, and they employ pack-bullocks on which they carry their
baggage as they travel. Their king is often at war with the king
of Narsyngua, from whom he has taken many towns, who in
his turn endeavours to recover them. They are but seldom at peace,
and were so even more seldom while the Sabayo yet lived. The
Heathen of this Daquem kingdom are black and well-built, the
more part of them fight on foot, but some on horseback, yet
these are few. The foot-soldiers carry swords and daggers, bows
and arrows. They are right good archers, and their bows are long
like those of England. They go bare from the waist up, but
are clad below; they wear small turbans on their heads. They
eat flesh of all kinds, save beef, which is forbidden by their
idolatrous religion, which they follow very strictly. When they die
they order their bodies to be burnt, and their wives burn themselves alive as I shall relate below when dealing with the kingdom
of Narsyngua.

§ 89. *The Kingdom Of Calecut*

Leaving this Kingdom [of Cananor] and going southward, on the
further side of this same river of Tremopatam is a town belonging

---

[6] Daquanim, *i.e.*, *Dakkhanī*, means the language of the Deccan, that is,
Marāthī.

to the Moors of the country which is called *Tiramuingate*,[7] where there are many ships and much traffic by sea. Beyond this place is a river on which lies a large Moorish town called *Manjaim*,[8] also a place of sea traffic, with many ships and much trade.

Beyond this is another place also of the Moors which they call *Chamobai*,[9] a place of much sea traffic. Inland from these three places the country is thickly peopled by *Nayres* who are very fine men and give obedience to no King, they are divided between two lords who rule them.

Passing by these places there is a river which they call *Pedirpatam*,[10] on which stands a Moorish town with much trade and navigation, and from this place begins the Kingdom of Calecut.

Passing thereby is another town on the coast called *Tircore*[11] and passing this there is another which they call *Pandanare*[12] beyond which there is yet another with a small river which they call *Capucate*.[13] This is a place of great trade and many ships, where on the strand are found many soft sapphires.

Two leagues beyond this place is the city of *Calecut*,[14] wherein more trade was carried on, and yet is, by foreigners than by the natives of the land, where also the King our Lord, with the full assent of the King thereof, holds a very strong fortress. To the south of this city there is a river on which lies another town called *Chiliate*,[15] where dwell many Moors, natives of the land who are merchants, and have many ships in which they sail; and beyond this town and river there is another city belonging to the King of Calecut, called *Propriamguary*,[16] of both Moors and Heathen, a place of trade. Passing this there are two Moorish towns, five leagues apart one from the other, one named *Para-*

[7] Modern Tellicherry.
[8] Modern Mahé.
[9] Chombala.
[10] Modern Badagara. Its population is still Muslim.
[11] Modern Tikkodi.
[12] Pantalayini.
[13] Kappata, referred to in the *Roteiro* as Capua. It is now a mere village.
[14] Vasco da Gama's first port of call. Despite the factory-fort to which Barbosa refers, the Portuguese never effectively controlled the place.
[15] Chalyam.
[16] Parappanangadi.

nanor,[17] and the other *Tanor*,[18] and inland thence is a Lord who rules over them (and has many Nayres in his pay) and at times rebels against the King of Calecut, and does not obey him. These towns trade in goods of many kinds, and merchants of substance dwell therein.

Beyond these on the coast southward is a river, whereon stands a city of the Moors natives of the land, also some Heathen, which they call *Pananee*.[19] In it are many merchants who possess ships in great numbers, and from it the King of Calecut draws a great revenue in dues.

And advancing thence, there is another river which they call *Chatua*,[20] on which higher up, are a number of Heathen villages, and by this river comes out the greater part of the pepper [grown in the country].

And yet further along the coast is another river which forms the frontier with the Kingdom of Cochim, on the hither bank of which is a place called *Cranganor*, where the king of Cochim[21] holds certain dues. In these places dwell many Moors, Christians and Heathen Indians. The Christians follow the doctrine of the Blessed Saint Thomas, and they hold here a Church dedicated to him, and another to Our Lady. They are very devout Christians, lacking nothing but true doctrine whereof I will speak further on, for many of them dwell from here as far as Charamandel, whom the Blessed Saint Thomas left established here when he died in these regions.

"And after passing this town of *Cranganore* along the shore of the sea, the land of the King of Cochim begins in the inland region, and above Cochim, the lands of Calecut extend," and this land, or rather the whole land of Malabar is covered along the strand with palm-trees as high as lofty cypresses, the trunk

[17] Parapani.

[18] Tanur.

[19] Ponnani, a thriving port on the Ponnani River, the largest river in Malabar. It is still a Muslim city. It was attacked by Almeida in 1507 and by Menezes in 1525.

[20] Modern Chetwai. It was traditionally the landing place of St. Thomas.

[21] Cranganore had been an important harbour, but owing to silting it had been superseded by Cochin, which at the time of the Portuguese arrival was the chief harbour of Malabar.

whereof is extremely clean and smooth, and on the top a crown of branches among which grows a great fruit which they call *cocos*, it is a fruit of which they make great profit, and whereof they load many cargoes yearly. They bear their fruit every year without fail, never either more or less. All the folk of Malabar have these palms, and by their means they are free from any dearth, even though other food be lacking, for they produce ten or twelve things all very needful for the service of man, by which they help and profit themselves greatly, and everything is produced in every month of the year.

In the first place they produce these cocos, a very sweet and grateful fruit when green; from them is drawn milk like that of almonds, and each one when green, has within it a pint of a fresh and pleasant water, better than that from a spring. When they are dry this same water thickens within them into a white fruit as large as an apple which also is very sweet and dainty. The coco itself after being dried is eaten, and from it they get much oil by pressing it, as we do. And from the shell which they have close to the kernel is made charcoal for the goldsmiths who work with no other kind. And from the outer husk which throws out certain threads, they make all the cord which they use, a great article of trade in many parts. And from the sap of the tree itself they extract a *must*, from which they make wine, or properly speaking a strong water,[22] and that in such abundance that many ships are laden with it, for export. From this same *must* they make very good vinegar, and also a sugar of extreme sweetness[23] which is much sought after in India. From the leaf of the tree they make many things, in accordance with the size of the branch. They thatch the houses with them, for as I have said above, no house is roofed with tiles, save the temples or the palaces; all others are thatched with palm-leaves. From the same tree they get timber for their houses and firewood as well, and all this in such abundance that ships take in cargoes thereof for export.

Other palm-trees there are of a lower kind whence they get

[22] Palm toddy; arrack.
[23] Jaggery sugar.

the leaves on which the Heathen write; it serves as paper.[24] There
are other very slender palms the trunks of which are of extreme
height and smoothness; these bear a fruit as large as walnuts
which they call Areca,[25] which they eat with betel. Among them
it is held in high esteem. It is very ugly and disagreeable in taste.
It is so abundant that ships take many cargoes of it for Cambaia
and Daquem and many other countries, whither they take it preserved and dried.

§ *90   The Kingdom Of Cochin*

Further in advance along the coast is the Kingdom of *Cochin*,
in which there is much pepper which grows throughout the land
on trees like unto ivy, and it climbs on other trees and on palms,
also on trellises to a great extent. The pepper grows on these
trees in bunches. Here also grows very much fine belide[26] ginger,
cardamoms, myrobalans, canafistula,[27] zerumba, zedoary,[28] wild cinnamon.[29] This Kingdom possesses a very large and excellent river,
which here comes forth to the sea by which come in great ships
of Moors and Christians, who trade with this Kingdom. On the
banks of this river is a city of the Moors natives of the land,
wherein also dwell Heathen Chatims, and great merchants. They
have many ships and trade with Charamandel, the great Kingdom of Cambaia, Dabul, and Chaul, in *areca* (great store), cocos,
pepper, *jagara*, and palm sugar. At the mouth of the river the
King our Lord possesses a very fine fortress, which is a large
settlement of Portuguese and Christians, natives of the land, who
became Christians after the establishment of our fortress. And
every day also other Christian Indians who have remained from
the teaching of the Blessed Saint Thomas come there also from

[24] The Palmyra or fan palm.
[25] *Areca Catechu.* The nut is wrapped in betel leaf for chewing.
[26] Native ginger, from the Arabic *baládi.*
[27] Presumably *cassia fistula*, a purgative.
[28] *Curcuma zedoaria*, sold in India as a cure for indigestion.
[29] *Canela Brava or* Wild Cinnamon. This, no doubt, was the wild plant
of Malabar which is inferior to the fine cinnamon of Ceylon. They are both
from the same plant, *Cinnamomum Zeylanicum.*

Coilam[30] and other places. In this fort and settlement of Cochim[31] the King our Lord carries out the repairs of his ships, and other new ships are built, both galleys and caravels in as great perfection as on the Lisbon strand. Great store of pepper is here taken on board, also many other kinds of spices, and drugs which come from Malacca, and are taken hence every year to Portugal. The King of Cochim has a very small country and was not a King before the Portuguese discovered India, for all the Kings who had of late reigned in Calecut had held it for their practice and rule to invade Cochim and drive the King out of his estate, taking themselves possession thereof,[32] thereafter, according as their pleasure was, they would give it back to him or not. The King of Cochim gave him every year a certain number of elephants, but he might not strike coins, nor roof his palace with tiles under pain of losing his land. Now that the King our Lord has discovered India he has made the King independent and powerful in his own land, so that none can interfere with it, and he strikes whatsoever money he will.

The Divers Kinds of Spices, Where They Grow, What They Are Worth At Calicut, and Whither They Are Carried

OF PEPPER

In the first place, in the whole of Malabar and in Calicut pepper grows. A *bahar* thereof sells at Calicut at from 200 to 300 *fanams* of which one, as we have already said, is worth a silver real of Spain. Each *bahar* weighs 4 *quintals* (old weight) of

[30] Quilon.

[31] *The Fortress of Cochin.* This fortress was founded by the two Alboquerques, Afonso and Francisco, who arrived in 1503 with instructions from the King to build a fort there. They were just in time to rescue the few Portuguese left there by Cabral and V. da Gama, who were beseiged by the invading King of Calicut. It became the headquarters of the Portuguese in India until Goa took its place. It was again besieged by the Calicut forces in 1504, but bravely and successfully defended by Duarte Pacheco.

[32] The Raja of Cochin found in the Portuguese powerful allies against his ancient enemy of Calicut, and Barbosa is probably right in stating that his state would soon have been annexed to Calicut had not the Portuguese interfered. They were glad to be on friendly terms with Cochin, for the harbour there was the best on the Malabar coast, far superior to that of Calicut, and the King was willing to allow of the construction of a fort.

Portugal, by which all spices are sold at Lisbon. To the King of Calicut a duty of 12 *fanams* a *bahar* is paid. The merchants have the practice of taking it to Cambaya, Persia, Adem and Meca, and thence to Cairo and Alexandria. At the present day they give it to the King of Portugal at 6,562 *maravedis* the *bahar* (including the duties which are 193¼ *fanams*), partly because there is not there such a concourse of merchants to purchase it, and partly on account of the contract made by the King of Portugal with that King, and with the Moors and merchants of the country.

Much pepper grows as well in the Island of Çamatra near Malaca, which is fairer and larger than that of Malabar but not so good or strong as the aforesaid. This is taken to Bengala and China, and some quantity is smuggled into Meca unknown to the Portuguese who do not permit it to be taken thither. It is worth in Çamatra 400 to 600 *maravedis* the *quintal* (new weight); and between the new and old there is a difference of 2 ounces to the *arratel*, the old being 14 ounces and the new 16 ounces.

OF CLOVES

Cloves grow in the islands called Molucos; they take them to Malaca and thence to Calicut in Malabar. At Calicut a *bahar* is worth from 500 to 600 *fanams*, and if very clean and picked, 700; duty is paid at 18 *fanams* the *bahar*. In Moluco where they grow they are sold at one to two ducats the *bahar*, according to the number of purchasers who go there for it, and at Malaca from ten to fourteen, according to the market.

OF CINNAMON

The good Cinnamon grows in the Island of Ceilão and the bad in Malabar. The good is cheap in Ceilão, but if fresh and well picked it fetches 300 *fanams* the *bahar* at Calicut.

OF BELEDI GINGER

Beledi Ginger grows around the town of Calicut at from six to nine miles distance. Each *bahar* is worth 40 *fanams*, sometimes 50; they bring it in from the mountains to the town for retail sale. The Indian merchants buy it and collect it, and when the ship arrives to take cargoes of it they sell it to the Moors at the price of from 90 to 110 *fanams*, for by then it is very heavy.

DELY GINGER

Dely Ginger grows from Mount Dely up to Cananor. It is small and not so white nor so good. A *bahar* at Cananor is worth 40 *fanams*, and the duty is 6 *fanams* on each *bahar*.

CONSERVE OF GREEN GINGER

In Bengal also there is much Beledi Ginger of which they make abundance of very good Conserve with sugar, and carry it for sale in Martaban jars to Malabar. Each *farazola* (*i.e.*, 22 *arratels* and 6 ounces) fetches 14, 15 or 16 *fanams*. That which is fresh is preserved at Calicut, and is worth 25 *fanams*, sugar being dear there, and this green ginger sold to be preserved is worth ¾ of a *fanam* the *farazola*.

Of Drugs and of their Prices at Calicut and in the Land of Malabar

	Fanams
Good Martaban lac, the *farazola*, *i.e.*, 22 arratels 6½ ounces new weight of Portugal	18
Country lac .... the *farazola*	123
Tincal (good), in large pieces .... Do.	30 and 40 to 50
Coarse camphor in loaves	70 to 80
Camphor for anointing idols, a *fanam* and a half the *mitigal*, 6½ of which make an ounce	
Camphor for eating and for the eyes, per *mitigal*	3
Aguila (eagle-wood, aloes-wood) per *farazola*	300 to 400

V . *Indonesia, China, and Japan*

10. The Portuguese in Malacca and the Spice Islands

The eastern luxury goods in which Portuguese factors were chiefly interested were products not of India, but of islands in the Malay archipelago; nor were the Malabar ports the only markets, or even the principal markets, where such goods were bought and sold. Arab merchants shipping to the Red Sea and the Persian Gulf could easily elude Portuguese interference by making their purchases in one or other of the Malayan or Indonesian markets, of which Malacca was the best known. Malacca had a strategic as well as a commercial importance, because most shipping between the archipelago and the Bay of Bengal passed through the Malacca Strait. The Portuguese commanders in India soon grasped that in order to establish a monopoly of the supply of spices to Europe they would have to destroy the trade of their Arab competitors; and that in order to achieve this end they must control Malacca. If they could establish their own factories still further east, and make their own spice purchases, or some of them, in the actual places of origin, so much the better.

Malacca was taken by a Portuguese force under Affonso d'Albuquerque in 1511. It became, like Goa, a fortified Portuguese base, and remained so until 1641. In 1512 Alboquerque sent a fleet of three ships under Antonio de Abreu to reconnoiter the "spicery." Abreu got as far as the Banda Islands before returning to Malacca. His navigator, Francisco Rodrigues, wrote a brief report on maritime routes in the East— a rudimentary "China rutter"—illustrated by views and sketch charts, partly drawn from Javanese originals, which provided the Portuguese government (and subsequently, through "leakage," the Spanish government) with their first reliable cartographical information on the eastern archipelago. Another of Abreu's officers, Francisco Serrão, was shipwrecked, and made his way to Amboina and thence to Ternate in the Moluccas, where he spent the rest of his life as an adviser to the Muslim

ruler and as an occasional, and somewhat unreliable, informant to Europeans on island affairs. Ternate was at that time one of the very few
islands in which cloves were grown. With the information so acquired
and the contacts so established, the Portuguese at Malacca, shortly after
Abreu's return, began regular trade with the Moluccas and, by agreement with the ruler, established a factory (but not a fort) on the island
of Ternate.

Tomé Pires served from 1512 to 1515 as accountant (*contador*) of
the royal factory at Malacca. It was a comparatively humble office and
Pires, the son of an apothecary, was a comparatively humble person;
but he was a competent and trustworthy official and his connection
with eastern trade made him a rich man. He was also an intelligent and
accurate observer, who knew the East well. The *Suma Oriental* was
written partly in Malacca, partly in Goa, and completed in 1515. It is a
description of the whole of the East, but is primarily concerned with
commercial matters, and well reflects the commercial euphoria of the
Portuguese in the second decade of the sixteenth century. On India,
Pires was less well informed than Duarte Barbosa; but he wrote by far
the best contemporary account of Malacca and the islands immediately
after the Portuguese arrival in the area. The *Suma Oriental* must have
been of great interest and use to the authorities in Lisbon. Like Barbosa's *Book*, it was treated as a secret document. Ramusio got hold of
part of the book—that dealing with India, Ceylon, Burma, China, Japan,
Borneo, and the Philippines—and published it in 1550; but information
on Malacca, Sumatra, Java, and the Spiceries was more closely guarded,
and these portions of the *Suma Oriental* remained unpublished until
1944.

The extract which follows is from *The Suma Oriental of Tomé
Pires*, translated and edited by Armando Cortesão (2 vols., London,
Hakluyt Society, 1944), II, 283-7; I, 212-23.

Malacca

Malacca is growing richer in junks; the Malacca merchants
buy junks; they are rebuilding new godowns. The country is
improving; they are beginning to pour in, and there is need for
rule and ordinance at this outset, and permanent laws. A Solomon
was needed to govern Malacca, and it deserves one.

Java trade. The owner fits out his junk with everything that is
necessary. If you want a cabin (*peitaca*), or two, you set two or
three men to look after and manage it, and note what you take;

and when you come back to Malacca you pay twenty per cent on what you put in the junk in Malacca. And you, the owner of the merchandise, give a present on what you bring back. And if you loaded a hundred *cruzados'* worth in Malacca, when you get back you have two hundred before paying the owner of the junk.

If I am a merchant in Malacca and give you, the owner of the junk, a hundred *cruzados* of merchandise at the price then ruling in Malacca, assuming the risk myself, on the return they give me a hundred and forty and nothing else; and the payment is made, according to the Malacca ordinance, forty-four days after the arrival of the junk in port.

The voyage of Java is made at the beginning of January, in the first monsoon, and they come back from May onwards, up to August or September of the same year.

For Sunda they give you fifty per cent, because they can bring black pepper and slaves. It is a land of merchandise and trade; the profit is greater. The voyage takes little time and is plain sailing.

All four places here give you fifty per cent, the loader taking the sea risk. The voyages are all almost plain sailing. They pay in the manner aforesaid.

These three places pay, according to the law of the land, thirty-five per cent the voyage. The sailing is safer and shorter.

Siam and Pegu pay fifty per cent, the risk being as aforesaid. If you load merchandise on the return voyage, you get two for one, and after paying all dues there remains one for one and sometimes more. And they take eight or nine months on the journeys.

These two places make the voyage year by year. These give one for one, according to the ordinance, or eighty or ninety per cent; and whoever loads up for these two places sometimes makes three for one.

China is a profitable voyage, and moreover whoever loads up, hiring cabins (*peitacas*), sometimes makes three for one, and in good merchandise which is soon sold.

And because this loading of the junks is a very profitable matter, as they sail in regular monsoons, the king of Malacca derived great profit from it. They gave the king one third [more] than they give to others, and the king made the man who dealt

with his money exempt from dues, so that it was found that from
this loading of the junks great store of gold was brought in, and
it could not be otherwise. And here come the kings of Pahang,
and Kampar, and Indragiri, and others, through their factors, to
employ money in the said junks. This is very important for anyone with capital, because Malacca sends junks out, and others
come in, and they are so numerous that the king could not help
but be rich. And the said merchant who dealt with the king's
money had a share; he got pride and freedom, and they welcomed him gladly and paid him in due time. For this the king
had officials to receive the merchandise and grant the said rights,
and this was attached to the custom-house, in charge of *Ceryna
De Raja*, the *Bemdara's* brother.

If when the time is up the said merchant has no gold to pay
with, he pays in merchandise according to the value in the
country, and when he pays in merchandise it is more profitable
for one settled there. This is the custom if you have not con-
tracted to be paid in gold. But the merchant prefers merchandise
to gold, because from day to day the merchandise goes up in
price, and because trade of every kind from all parts of the world
is done in Malacca.

And should anyone ask what advantage to his exchequer the
King our Lord can derive from Malacca, there is no doubt that
—once the influence is finished that this ex-king of Malacca
still exercises, and also once Java has been visited, to win the
confidence of the merchants and navigators, and of the kings
who still trust the false words of the king of Bintang, who does
more mischief among relatives in one day than we can undo in a
year—there is no doubt that Malacca is of such importance and
profit that it seems to me it has no equal in the world.

Anyone may note that if someone came to Malacca, capable of
sending each year a junk to China, and another to Bengal, and
another to Pulicat, and another to Pegu, and the merchants of
Malacca and for the other parts took shares in these; if a factor
of the King our Lord came to tax money and merchandise, so
much per cent as aforesaid; and if someone else with officials
came to take charge of the custom-house to collect dues; who can
doubt that in Malacca bahars of gold will be made, and that
there will be no need of money from India, but it will go from

here to there? And I do not speak of Banda and the Moluccas, because it is the easiest thing in the world for all the spices to reach there [India] without any trouble, because Malacca pays wages and maintenance, and it will make money, and will send all the spices if they are acquired and traded and controlled, and if it has the people such as it deserves. Great affairs cannot be managed with few people. Malacca should be well supplied with people, sending some and bringing back others. It should be provided with excellent officials, expert traders, lovers of peace, not arrogant, quick-tempered, undisciplined, dissolute, but sober and elderly, for Malacca has no white-haired official. Courteous youth and business life do not go together; and since this cannot be had in any other way, at least let us have years, for the rest cannot be found. Men cannot estimate the worth of Malacca, on account of its greatness and profit. Malacca is a city that was made for merchandise, fitter than any other in the world; the end of monsoons and the beginning of others. Malacca is surrounded and lies in the middle, and the trade and commerce between the different nations for a thousand leagues on every hand must come to Malacca. Wherefore a thing of such magnitude and of such great wealth, which never in the world could decline, if it were moderately governed and favoured, should be supplied, looked after, praised and favoured, and not neglected for Malacca is surrounded by Mohammedans who cannot be friends with us unless Malacca is strong, and the Moors will not be faithful to us except by force, because they are always on the look-out, and when they see any part exposed they shoot at it. And since it is known how profitable Malacca is in temporal affairs, how much the more is it in spiritual [affairs], as Mohammed is cornered and cannot go farther, and flees as much as he can. And let people favour one side, while merchandise favors our faith; and the truth is that Mohammed will be destroyed, and destroyed he cannot help but be. And true it is that this part of the world is richer and more prized than the world of the Indies, because the smallest merchandise here is gold, which is least prized, and in Malacca they consider it as merchandise. Whoever is lord of Malacca has his hand on the throat of Venice. As far as from Malacca, and from Malacca to China, and from China to the Moluccas, and from the Moluccas to Java, and from Java to Malacca [and]

Sumatra, [all] is in our power. Who understands this will favour
Malacca; let it not be forgotten, for in Malacca they prize garlic
and onions more than musk, benzoin, and other precious things.

Moluccas

We have reached the Molucca (*Maluqo*) islands, because it is not
our intention to go farther on from here, as there is no need for
this, but just the clove islands, and from there I will turn back
home.

The Molucca islands which produce cloves are five, to wit,
the chief one is called Ternate and another Tidore and another
Motir (*Motes*) and another Makyan (*Maqujem*) and another
Bachian (*Pacham*). And there is also a great deal of wild cloves
in the port of Gillolo (*Jeilolo*) in the land of the island of Gillolo
(*Batochina*). According to what they say, Mohammedanism in
the Molucca islands began fifty years ago. The kings of the islands
are Mohammedans, but not very deeply involved in the sect.
Many are Mohammedans without being circumcised, and there
are not many Mohammedans. The heathen are three parts and
more out of four. The people of these islands are dark-skinned;
they have sleek hair. They are at war with one another most of
the time. They are almost all related.

These five islands must produce about six thousand bahars of
cloves a year—sometimes a thousand more, or a thousand less.
It is true that merchandise bought in Malacca for five hundred
reis will buy a bahar of cloves in the Moluccas. The bahar is
by Malacca weight, because they weigh it in accordance with
that, and the merchants take the scales, as it is sometimes worth
more, sometimes less, just a little. There are six crops of cloves
every year. Eight junks used at one time to go from Malacca
to Banda and the Moluccas, and three or four [of them were]
from Grisee, and as many more from Malacca. The ones from
Malacca belonged to *Curia Deva*, a Chetti merchant, and those
from Grisee to *Pate Cuçuf* who had the trade there; and there
were other merchants as well, both Javanese and Malay, but
these two were the chief merchants; each of them has made a
large sum of gold in this trade. Cloves were always worth nine
or ten *cruzados* a bahar in Malacca when they were plentiful,
and twelve cruzados a bahar when they were scarce.

The chief island of all the five is the island of Ternate. The king is a Mohammedan. He is called Sultan *Bem Acorala*. They say he is a good man. His island produces at least a hundred and fifty bahars of cloves every year. Two or three ships can anchor in the port of this island; this is a good village. This king has some foreign merchants in his country. They say that the island must contain up to two thousand men, and up to two hundred will be Mohammedans. This king is powerful among his neighbors. His country is abundant in footstuffs from the land, although many foodstuffs come to the Molucca kings from other islands, as will be told later. Only the king of Ternate is called Sultan; the others are called Raja. He is at war with his father-in-law, *Raja Almançor*, king of the island of Tidore. He has as many as a hundred *paraos*. The island must be six leagues round. There is a mountain in the middle of this island, which yields a great deal of sulphur, which burns in great quantities.[1] This king has half the island of Motir (*Motei*) for his own, whence he gets many foodstuffs. [The people of] Ternate are more tractable than those in any of the other [islands], although another has a better port, and more trade because of it. They say that this king dispenses justice. He keeps his people obedient. He says he would be glad to see Christian priests, because if our faith seemed to him good he would forsake his sect and turn Christian.

This king of Ternate, being a man of good judgement, when he heard that Francisco Serrão was in Amboina, sent for him and for other Portuguese who were wrecked in the voyage of António de Abreu, and received them in his country and did them honour; and the said king wrote letters to Malacca saying how he and his lands were the slaves of the King our lord, as will be seen at greater length in his letters, which were brought by António de Miranda who went to Banda and sent to Amboina whither the letters had arrived, having been brought by Francisco Serrão, who returned to Ternate, because that was the arrangement.

The people of Ternate are knights among those of the Moluccas. They are men who drink wines of their kind. Ternate has

[1] Ternate Island, eight miles long from north to south, and six miles broad, is composed almost exclusively of a conical volcano, 5184 feet (1580 m) in height, which has been in a state of constant activity for more than 300 years.

good water. It is a healthy country with good air. The king of
Ternate has four hundred women within his doors, all daughters
of men of standing; he has many daughters by them. When the
king goes to war he rallies forth with a crown of gold, and his
sons wear them also as a mark of dignity. These crowns are of
moderate value.

The country produces cloves. A great deal of iron comes from
outside, from the islands of Banggai (*Bemgaia*),[2] iron axes, chop-
pers, swords, knives. Gold comes from other islands. It has some
little ivory; it has coarse native cloth. A great many parrots
come from the islands of Morotai (*Mor*),[3] and the white parrots
come from Ceram.

Coarse cloth from Cambay is of value in the Moluccas; and
for the finer sort, all the *enrolado* cloth from *Bonuaquelim*, with
large, medium or small *ladrilho*, *patolas*, all the coarse and white
cloth, as for instance, *synhauas*, *balachos*, *panchavelizes*, *coto-
balachos;* but the principal merchandise is cloth from Cambay
and the tails of white oxen and cows which they bring from
Bengal.

Cloves have six crops a year; others say that there are cloves
all the year round, but that at six periods in the year there are
more. After flowering it turns green and then it turns red; then
they gather it, some by hand and some beaten down with a pole,
and red as it is they spread it out on mats to dry, and it turns
black. They are small trees. Cloves grow like myrtle berries, a
great many heads grow together. All this fruit is in the hands of
the natives, and it all comes through their hands to the seacoast.

Although this island of Ternate is the most distant of all from
Amboina, and the next in order ought to be the nearest to
Amboina, which is Bachian (*Pachão*), yet as Ternate is the best,
it has been described first, and also because the king is a vassal
of the King our lord; and now I will go towards Amboina, describing the islands.

After leaving Ternate for Amboina [and] sailing three leagues,

---

[2] Banggai Island is one of the more important in the Banggai archipelago,
which lies 300 miles southwest of Ternate, off Banggai peninsula, on the
east coast of central Celebes.

[3] Morotai or Morti Island lies thirteen miles east of the northeastern point
of Gillolo, with the small Rau Island and some islets close by.

you see the island of Tidore. It is an island which is about ten leagues round. The king of this island is a Mohammedan, an enemy of the king of Ternate and his father-in-law. This king has about two thousand men in his country, about two hundred of whom are Mohammedans and the others are heathens. The king is called *Raja Almançor*. He has many wives and children. His country produces about one thousand four hundred bahars of cloves a year. There is no port in this island where ships can anchor. He is as powerful a king as the king of Ternate. He is always at war. These two are the most important in the Moluccas, and they compute that this king must have eighty *paraos* in his country. This king has the king of Makyan (*Maqiem*) for his vassal.

Half the island of Motir is also subject to this king. His country produces many foodstuffs: rice, meat, fish. They say he is a man of good judgement. This king is very desirous of trading with us, because the Moluccas Islands are going to ruin, and for the last three years they have only gathered a few cloves, because of the drop in navigation since the capture of Malacca.

Six leagues sail from this island of Tidore is the island of Motir. This island is about four or five leagues round. It has a mountain in the middle. Half the island obeys the king of Ternate and the other half the king of Tidore; each of them has stationed his captain in his own land. This island is entirely heathen; it has about six hundred men. This island produces about one thousand two hundred bahars of cloves a year; each captain will have four or five small lancharas. This island produces many foodstuffs, and each part supports its own lord. The captains of these islands are heathens, knightly men, important people, and they are friends.

Both the king of Tidore and this island of Motir bring their cloves in *paraos* to the island of Makyan to be sold, because the port where the junks come and anchor is there.

Five leagues away from the island of Motir, the island of Makyan appears. This island of Makyan is eight or nine leagues round; it has about three thousand men; it has a hundred and thirty *paraos*. It produces about one thousand five hundred bahars of cloves a year. The king is called *Raja Ucem*. He is a Mohammedan, and [so are] about three hundred men in his country.

This island of Makyan has a very good port. This is the island where the junks load, and they bring the cloves to be sold here from all the islands, with the exception of Ternate, whither [some people] also go because of the port where they can anchor. The king has almost as many foodstuffs as the others, and he has more people and *paraos* than Tidore.

The *Raja Ucem*, king of this island of Makyan, is a first cousin of the *Raja Almançor*, king of Tidore, and this king is to some extent subject to the said king of Tidore. There are a few foreigners in this port, and they greatly long for peace with us. They say that he is a good man, and this is a land with more trade than the others, and thus the junks come and anchor here. The port is safe and good. Almost all the people are heathens. They come to this island with merchandise from many islands. They have an abundance of foodstuffs and good water, and they say that the people on the sea-coast are tractable.

From this island of Makyan which I have described, it is almost fourteen leagues to the islands of Bachian.[4] These islands of Bachian are ten or twelve. The island called Bachian produces cloves, the others do not. The king of this island is called *Raja Cuçuf*. He has more land and more people than any of the kings of the Moluccas, and more *paraos*. This king is a half-brother of the king of Ternate; they are great friends. Almost all the people are heathens. They have good ports. Those who have to load cargoes in the Moluccas come here to sight this land, and they go from here to other islands. Bachian is a chain of islands which goes up to Ceram opposite Amboina. This island produces about five hundred bahars of cloves every year. It produces a great deal of pitch; it does not produce many foodstuffs, but they bring plenty of them from the other islands. They do a great deal of trade in their land. This island has parrots, mats and other things which people come there to buy.

According to information I obtained, it is a very short time since the cloves in this island were wild—in the same way as

[4] Bachian Island is the largest and southernmost of the five true Moluccas. There are many islands near Bachian, the largest of which are Great Tawali or Kasiruta, and Mandioli near the western part; about fifteen miles northwards lie the Ombi Islands, eighty miles north of the northwestern part of Ceram.

wild plums become cultivated plums and wild olives become cultivated olives—and they say that originally these cloves were not made use of, because the trees were covered up in wild places, and that during the last ten years the cloves have been made as good as any of the others, and that the cloves in this island are increasing greatly. It is forty leagues from this island to the island of Amboina. All the cloves from these five islands are of equal goodness if they are gathered when they are perfectly ripe.

In this island they also dry the branches of the trees with many leaves on. This is merchandise, because in our part of Europe the said leaves are used instead of betel, and since dried betel has no flavour they put the leaves in its place. It is a merchandise which they used to take to Venice by way of Alexandria, and it must be quite twenty years that I have been using the said leaves in Portugal instead of the said *folio Indio* which is betel.[5]

That ends the account of the five Molucca islands, coming from Ternate to Amboina; and if that is not in order, go back in the account from Amboina to Ternate, beginning with Bachian. Do not say that the navigation from Malacca to the Moluccas is dangerous, for it is a good route and convenient for our ships, and with monsoon winds you can sail to Banda or Amboina in a month, and from there to the Moluccas in a day or two. Our well-equipped ships will not linger in Amboina; they must go on to the Moluccas, especially anyone who has been able to learn and investigate how to come from Portugal to the Moluccas in such a short time; anyone will be able, as is known, when his turn comes and if he works—anyone who is jealous that things should be accomplished in the service of the King our lord—to make the journey of the Moluccas not by way of the coast of Java, but by Singapore, and from Singapore to Borneo and from Borneo to the island of Buton (*Butum*)[6] and then to the Moluccas. Anyone who has sailed to the Moluccas has always found this a very good way, in a monsoon, and quick. The Java way

[5] Pires was wrong in identifying *folio indio* with betel. But it seems that the leaves of the clove tree (*Caryophyllus aromaticus* Linn.) were used as a substitute for the *folium indum*.

[6] Buton Island appears like a prolongation of the southeastern peninsula of Celebes. Banda lies due east of the north part of Buton.

to the Moluccas was officially established in this manner: the route from Borneo to the Moluccas suits us well, and the Java way suits the merchants of Malacca; the Borneo one suits us because we do not put in to ports from country to country, selling here, selling there, making money in each place in such a way that the time draws out; and as they have little capital and the sailors are slaves they make their journeys long and profitable, because from Malacca they take merchandise to sell in Java, and from Java merchandise to sell in Bima and Sumbawa, and from these islands they take cloth for Banda and the Moluccas, and that which they have kept in reserve for Malacca. The people of Banda and the Moluccas adore them. And so they do their trade, which they could not do along the way by Borneo and Buton and Macassar.

We do not seize the opportunity of adding to our profits in their crude way, nor are we as leisurely as they, because we take paid people only. We take on liberal supplies and good cloth and set out on our journey. We do our trade like Portuguese who are not accustomed to it, and the petty cloths of the royal merchants are carefully kept because they regret [they cannot take the richer?] merchandise; and thus we make our way quickly. Therefore the Borneo route suits us better, because we already know (God be praised!) that it is good and fairly profitable.

After the Moluccas I have spoken of five islands; now I should also like to speak of the island of Gillolo on account of the port of Gillolo, which has a great deal of cloves, and is near to our friend Ternate.[7]

The island of Gillolo is a long arm of land. One end of it is opposite to Amboina and Ceram and on the other side it extends towards the north to the islands of Morotai. It is very large. It is entirely heathen. It has many foodstuffs and many people and many *paraos*. Some of them go pillaging; some of them go trading—like all other nations. It is six leagues from Ternate to this island. This is the port which is called Gillolo (*Jeilolo*). This

[7] *Batochina*, or *Batochina do Moro*, was the early name given by the Portuguese to Gillolo Island, or Halmaheira, which has a length of about 190 miles from north to south; its width across the centre is about 40 miles. Gillolo bay and roadstead, and Gillolo village, lie about 20 miles northwest of Ternate.

is the only port in the island of Gillolo. It has a Mohammedan king. His port has many foodstuffs. He is an enemy of the king of Ternate, and they raid and rob one another. Like the island of Bachian, this island of Gillolo (*Jeilolo*) has a great deal of wild cloves; they say that they are working to make it good. This island has a good port, and the people are somewhat whiter than those in the Moluccas.

There are a great many other islands around the Moluccas: towards the north there are the islands of Morotai (*Mõr*) and *Chiaoa*, Tolo, Banggai (*Bemgaya*), and Sulu (*Çolor*) to the west of *Celebe*,[8] and they produce many foodstuffs. They come and trade in the Moluccas; they bring gold. Some of these islands also have people who are nearly white; but since it is not our intention to write about these islands, because it would mean writing about another hundred thousand, I make neither particular nor general mention of them here, except that they say that in the island of Papua, which is about eighty leagues from Banda, there are men with big ears who cover themselves with them. I never saw anyone who saw anyone else who had seen them. This story should be given no more importance than it deserves.

Having recapitulated the things about the Moluccas in accordance with what is said about them, I will not venture farther; it was only my intention to come as far as here. Whoever is able to write of the great number and infinity of islands there are from the straits of Kampar to Banda and from the straights of Singapore to the islands of Japan (*Jampom*), which are beyond China—and between this island and Banda there must be an area of more than two or three thousand leagues round—whoever is able let him speak of it. And it is certain that many of [the islands] are worth speaking about, because many have gold, but it would be never ending and tedious. I will only speak of the few in this great abundance with which Malacca is in communication now, or was in the past, and I will touch on others in general terms, so that my project may be completed, and if my project does not carry sufficient weight, may I be forgiven.

[8] This is the first recorded European mention of Celebes. Its first cartographical appearance was in Reinel's map of 1524.

These are the islands with which Malacca trades, and which trade with Malacca: *Tanjompura*,[9] the island of *Laue, Quedondoam, Samper,* Billiton (*Bilitam*), *Cate, Pamucã, Macaçar, Vdama,* Madura, in addition to those I have mentioned, as can be seen in detail earlier in this work. I will not speak of *Burney* and the Luzon (*Luções*), because I have already spoken of them in the description of China.

$$\diamond\diamond\diamond\diamond\diamond\diamond\diamond\diamond\diamond\diamond\diamond\diamond$$

11. The first Portuguese embassy to China

In the second decade of the sixteenth century, Portuguese traders in the East discovered that Europe was not the only market for Indonesian luxury products. An equally avid, and probably richer, market for spices, and for sandalwood and other aromatic woods, was mainland China. In the South China ports visiting traders could obtain return cargoes of silk and of porcelain, then exceedingly rare in Europe and expensive even in the bazaars of India. In the early fifteenth century the merchants of these southern ports had themselves carried on a flourishing foreign trade as far west as Malabar; but from the 1430's the imperial government, in the interests of security, enforced more and more strictly the rules of the Ming Code forbidding Chinese subjects to travel outside China. Foreign trade in Chinese shipping—though it could not be entirely prevented—was much diminished; visits of foreign merchants to Chinese ports, therefore, though regarded with suspicion in official circles, were welcomed by the local mercantile community, who depended on foreign trade for much of their livelihood. At the same time, the resurgence of Mongol aggressiveness and the concentration of Chinese military strength on the northern frontiers led to the neglect and decay of the southern navy and coastal defenses, so that the authorities could neither control the movement of foreign ships

---

[9] Pires' "Island" of *Tamjompura* corresponds to Tanjong Puting, on the south coast of Borneo. When Pires wrote his *Suma*, the Portuguese had not yet visited Borneo and Celebes. He was ill-informed, or mistook the information given to him, about these places he mentions as "Islands"; actually most of them were simple ports of Borneo or Celebes.

along the coast nor defend the smaller harbors against the depredations of Japanese, and later Portuguese, pirates.

The first Portuguese traders to China traveled in local junks. The first recorded visit was that of Jorge Alvárez (who later made trading voyages to Japan) in 1514. In the next few years a number of Portuguese traders, some arriving in their own ships, did business with Chinese merchants who came out, somewhat furtively, to meet them at various islands in Lintin Bay, downriver from Canton. Their reports were encouraging; and in 1517 an official Portuguese embassy was despatched from Malacca to Canton. The chief of the mission was Tomé Pires, the author of the *Suma Oriental*. He bore letters from the King of Portugal to the emperor, proposing friendship and trade and requesting a site for a factory.

The Portuguese had already made themselves respected, or at least feared, in many places on the coasts and in the islands of southern Asia, but their negotiations had been with relatively minor rulers. They had no notion of the character of the mighty state they were now approaching. The Chinese Empire was vast in size, ancient in civilization, centralized and bureaucratically administered. It was self-sufficient and supremely confident of its own unique superiority over other human societies. To its officials, the idea of the emperor negotiating with other rulers as equals was unthinkable. Embassies were allowed to enter China only for the purposes of rendering homage and tribute and seeking protection. An embassy such as that of Pires, arriving in a formidable armed fleet, was a totally new experience. Pires was received in Canton with wary and noncommittal civility, and was kept there for three years awaiting permission to proceed to Peking. Permission was eventually granted in 1520, largely because the mission had been mistakenly described by the official interpreters as a tribute-bearing embassy of the usual kind. There was even a possibility that the Chêng-tê Emperor—curious about the Portuguese and magnanimously tolerant of their uncouth ignorance—might receive the ambassador. The emperor, however, was absent on a tour when Pires arrived in Peking, and a further seven-months' wait ensued. During this time, the mistranslation of the King of Portugal's letters was discovered; complaints were received of various piracies and violations of Chinese territory committed by Portuguese ships along the coast; and the exiled Sultan of Malacca (who had for years past acknowledged a loose vassalage to the emperor) sent an embassy to report the seizure of his capital by the Portuguese and to beg for help. In 1521 the Chêng-tê Emperor died without having received Pires, a decree was issued prohibiting all trade with Europeans, and the embassy was bundled unceremoniously back to Canton. There, after a further period of indecision and delay Pires and his staff were arrested, and Pires was ordered to write to the King of Portugal instructing him in the emperor's name to restore Malacca to the sultan. On his refusal, his presents for the emperor—already rejected—were confiscated. He and his companions were manacled and placed in prison; where, one by one, they died. The date and the manner of their deaths is uncertain; but two at least were still alive in 1524, and managed in that year to smuggle out letters, which three years later reached Portugal, describing their fate and urging the king to undertake a military expedition against China. These letters are the first detailed eye-witness accounts of life in China to reach Europe since the early fourteenth century. Cristavão Vieira, in particular, was the first European since the discovery of the Cape route to visit Peking and write home describing his experience.

The extract which follows is from "Letters from Portuguese Captives in Canton," translated and edited by D. Ferguson, *The Indian Antiquary*, XXXI (January 1902), 10–30: letter of Cristavão Vieira.

WHEN *Fernão Perez* arrived at the port of China, he ordered the interpreters to write letters to the effect that there had come a captain-major and had brought an ambassador to the king of China. The interpreters wrote these according to the custom of the country, thus: "A captain-major and an ambassador have come to the land of China by command of the king of the *Firingis*[1] with tribute. They have come to beg, according to custom, for a seal[2] from the lord of the world, the son of God, in order to yield obedience to him." According to custom, for this letter we were received on land. This is the substance of the letter that they wrote, without giving an explanation of it to Fernão Perez, nor his being at any time aware of it: only the interpreters said that the letter had been well done according to custom and as they had comprehended the substance of it.

In the city of *Pinquim* [sic] within the palace of the king the letter of our lord the king was opened, and there was found

[1] Franks. Fernão Perez was the captain-major of the fleet.
[2] Barros says (Dec. III., VI. i.):—"This seal, which that emperor gives to all the kings and princes that make themselves his vassals, is of his device, and with it they sign themselves in all letters and writings, in demonstration of their being his subjects."

therein the reverse of what the interpreters had written. It therefore appeared to them all that we had entered the country of
China deceitfully, in order to spy out the land, and that it was
a piece of deception that the letter to the king was written differently from the other letters. The king thereupon commanded
that we should come no more to his palace to do reverence, and
soldiers and a guard were placed over us. The custom with ambassadors in Piquim is to place them in certain houses with large
enclosures, and there they are shut in on the first day of the
moon; and on the fifteenth day of the moon they go to the king's
palace, some on foot, and some on jades with halters of straw;
and proceed to measure their length five times before a wall of
the king's palace all in order with both knees on the ground
and head and face flat on the earth. Thus they remain until they
are commanded to rise. Five times do they do this at this wall.
Thence they return and re-enter the locked enclosures. It was
to this reverence that they commanded that we should come no
more.

The interpreters were asked why they had written a false letter and one not conformable to that of our lord the king. They
said, that they had written it according to the custom of China;
that the letter of our lord the king came closed and sealed, so
that it could not be read nor opened; that it had to be given
into the king's hands; that we were from a far country, and did
not know the custom of China, which was great; that in future
we should know it; that they were not to blame, as they had
written the letter according to custom. The mandarins were not
satisfied with the reply. They were asked each one whence they
came, and as soon as the king died they were imprisoned and
the young men their servants.

The king arrived at a town that is two leagues from the
city of *Pim* [*sic*] in January of the year 1521. He remained to
pass judgment on a relative of his who had risen against him;
and commanded him to be burnt after being hanged. There he
took up the business of our answer; because there had been
brought to him three letters against the Portuguese,—one from
two manarins in Piquim, another from the mandarins of Cantão,
and another from the Malays, the substances of which were as
follows, viz.:—

"The mandarins who went to the *Island of Trade* to receive the customs dues by order of the mandarins of Cantão beg to inform the king, that, when they had gone in such a year and day to collect the customs dues, there came *Firingi folk* with many arms and bombards, powerful people, and did not pay the dues according to custom; and they are constructing fortresses; and they have also heard say that these people had taken Malaca and plundered it and killed many people. That the king ought not to receive their present; and if he wished to receive them that they should say upon what kingdoms the kingdom of the Firingis bordered; and that he would command them that he was not willing to receive them."

The letter of the mandarins of Cantão said, that the Firingis would not pay the dues, and they took dues from the Siamese and seized them and boarded their junks and placed guards in them, and would not allow them to carry on trade or to pay dues, and had a fortress made of stone covered with tiles and surrounded with artillery, and inside many arms; and that they had come to Cantão by force, and that they carried bombards in quantities, reconnoitring the rivers; that they fired off bombards in front of the city and in other prohibited places.[3]

The Malays said, that the ambassador of the king of Portugal who was in the country of China had not come in truth, that he had come falsely to the land of China in order to deceive, and that we went to spy out the lands, and that soon we should come upon them; and that as we had set up a stone on the land and had a house we should soon have the country for our own; that thus we had done in Malaca and in other parts; that we were robbers.

A chief mandarin said, that we had asked him by letter for a residence or houses in Cantão; that, as we were Firingis, it seemed to him very bad, that in place of obedience we asked him for a residence in the country. Another mandarin said, that in the year 1520 in the Island of Trade the Firingis knocked off his cap and gave him blows and seized him when he was going to collect the customs dues by order of the mandarins of Cantão.

To these things the king replied, that "these people do not

[3] The European habit of firing blank charges from guns in celebration or salute was often misunderstood and usually disliked by eastern people.

know our customs; gradually they will get to know them." He said that he would give the answer in the city of Pequim. (He soon entered it, and the same day fell ill. Three months later he died without having given any answer.) With this reply that the king gave the grandees were not much pleased; and the king soon sent word to Cantão, that the fortress that the Portuguese had made should be demolished, and likewise the whole town; that he desired no trade with any nation; that if anyone came he was to be ordered to return. And immediately they set out on the road to Cantão that they might inquire into what had been told them, if it were true or not. The mandarins of Cantão did this only in order to plunder; they prepared armed fleets, and by deceiving them they captured by force those who came and plundered them.

As soon as we arrived at Cantão they brought us before the *pochacy*, and he ordered us to be taken to certain jail-houses that are in the store-houses of food-stuffs, and *Thome Pirez* did not wish to enter them, and the jailers put us into certain houses in which we were thirty and three days, and thence they took Thome Pirez with six persons to the prison of the *pochacy* which they call *libanco*, and me with four persons to the prison of the *tomeçi* where we were imprisoned ten months. All the goods remained in the power of Thome Pirez. They treated us like free people; we were closely watched in places separate from the prisoners. During this time the *amelçaçe* who was then there ordered Thome Pirez and all the company to be called. In like manner they summoned the Malays. He said that the king ordered that our lord the king should deliver up to the Malays the country of Malaca which he had taken from them. Thome Pirez replied that he had not come for that purpose, nor was it meet for him to discuss such a question; that it would be evident from the letter that he had brought that he knew nothing of anything else. He asked what force there was in Malaca; that he knew that there were three hundred Portuguese men there, and in *Couchim* a few more. He replied that Malaca had four thousand men of arms on sea and on land, who were now combined and then scattered; and that in *Ceilão*[4] there was a varying

---

[4] Apparently an error for Cochin.

number. With these questions he kept us on our knees for four hours; and when he had tired himself out he sent each one back to the prison in which he was kept.

The people that remained in the company of Tome Pirez were: —Duarte Fernandez a servant of Dom Felipe, Francisco de Budoya a servant of the lady commander, and Christovão d'Almeida a servant of Christovão de Tavora, Pedro de Freitas and Jorge Alvarez, I *Christovão Viera* and twelve servant lads, with five *juribassos*.[5] Of all this company there are left only I Christovão, a Persian from Ormuz, and a lad of mine from Goa. Those of us who remain alive at present are:—*Vasco Calvo*, a lad of his whom they call Gonçalo, and, as I have said, we three who are left of the company of Thome Pirez. These by saying that they belonged to the embassy escaped, and they put them with us here in this prison. We came in thirteen persons; and, as I have said, there have died Duarte Fernandez (when we went to Pequim he died in the hills, being already sick), Francisco de Bedois (when we came from Pequim he died on the road), also three or four lads in this prison by reason of the heavy fetters as I have said above, Christovão d'Almeida, also Jorge Alvarez, both Portuguese (the scrivener of the prison being fuddled with wine killed him with lashes, and he died in six days). The interpreters in Pequim were taken prisoners and killed, and their servants given as slaves to the mandarins for belonging to traitors. The head *juribasso* died of sickness, the other four were beheaded in Pequim for having gone out of the country and brought Portuguese to China. Pero de Freitas in this prison and Tome Pirez died here of sickness in the year 1524 in May. So that of all this company at present there are only two here, as I have said above.

·   ·   ·

The country of China is divided into fifteen provinces. Those that adjoin the sea are *Quantão, Foquiem, Chequeam, Namquy, Xantão,* and *Pequy*: these, although they border on the sea, also extend inland all round. *Quancy, Honão, Cuycheu, Hecheue, Cheamcy,* and *Sancy* confine, with *Pequim*, upon these provinces

[5] Interpreters.

that are in the midst:—*Queancy, Vinão, Honão*.[6] Of these fifteen
Nãoquim and *Pequim* are the chief of the whole country. Over
all Pequim is the capital where the king by law resides. *Nanquim*
lies in 28 or 29 degrees, Pequim in 28 to 39. From Cantão to
Foquē the coast runs along north-east and south-west a little
more or less. From *Foquem* to Piquim the coast runs straight
north and south. The coast winds about, which they say is a
very safe one, and having many cities and towns near the sea
on rivers. All these fifteen provinces are under one king. The
advantage of this country lies in its rivers all of which descend
to the sea. No one sails the sea from north to south; it is prohibited by the king, in order that the country may not become
known. Where we went was all rivers. They have boats and
ships broad below without number, there are so many. I am
certain that I must have seen thirty thousand including great and
small. They require little water. Certainly there are rivers for
galleys suitable for every kind of rowing foist for war. Close
to the sea the country has no wood, nor at thirty leagues from
the sea: I mean that on the coast from north to south the land
is all low, all provisions are carried, and on the rivers the wood
comes down in rafts from inland, and it is towed from more
than one hundred leagues round *Pequym* because the province
in which the king resides has no wood nor stone nor bricks:[7]
all is carried from Nanquim in large boats. If Nãoquim did not
supply it with its provisions, or other provinces, Pequym would
not be able to sustain itself, because there are people without
number and the land does not produce rice, because it is cold
and has few food-products. The king resides in this province,
which is situated at the extremity of his country, because he
is at war with some peoples called *Tazas*;[8] and if the king did
not remain there they would invade the country, because this
same Pequim belonged to these Tazas, with other provinces.

.   .   .

This province of *Cantão* is one of the best in China, from which

[6] The fifteen provinces enumerated are the following:—Kwangtung,
Fûkien, Chehkiang, Nanking, Shantung, Peking, Kwanghsî, Yünnan, Kwei-
chau, Szechwan, Shenhsî, Shanhsî, Kianghsî, Hûnan, and Honan.
[7] This was quite untrue.
[8] Tartars.

the king receives much revenue, because there are rice and food-stuffs incalculable, and all the wares of the whole country come to be shipped here by reason of the sea-port and of the articles of merchandise that come from other kingdoms to Cantão; and all passes into the interior of the country of China, from which the king receives many dues and the mandarins large bribes. The merchants live more honestly than in the other provinces which have no trade. No province in China has trade with strangers except this of Cantão: that which others may have on the borders is a small affair, because foreign folk do not enter the country of China, nor do any go out of China. This sea trade has made this province of great importance, and without trade it would remain dependent on the agriculturists like the others. However the port of the whole of the country of China is Cantão; Foquem[9] has but little trade, and strangers do not go there. Trade cannot be carried on in any other province except in Cantão, because it is thereby more suited than others for trade with strangers.

This province has thirteen cities and seven *chenos*, which are large cities that do not bear the name of cities; it has one hundred walled towns besides other walled places. All the best lies along the sea as far as Aynão on rivers which may be entered by vessels that are rowed; and those that are distant from the sea lie between rivers into which also all kinds of row-boats can go. Of the cities and towns that lie on rivers which cannot be navigated except by towing no account need by taken at the first; because when the greater obeys the lesser does not rebel. As I have said, there is under the sun nothing so prepared as this, and with people without number, and thickly populated on those borders where there are rivers (and where there are none it is not so populous, not by a fifth), of every sort of craftsman of every mechanical office, I mean carpenters, caulkers, smiths, stone-masons, tilers, sawyers, carvers: in fine that there is a super-abundance of the things that are necessary for the service of the king and of his fortresses, and from hence may be taken every year four or five thousand men without causing any lack in the country.

[9] Fukien.

The custom of this country of China is, that every man who administers justice cannot belong to that province; for instance, a person of Cantão cannot hold an office of justice in Cantão; and they are interchanged, so that those of one province govern another: he cannot be a judge where he is a native. This is vested in the literates; and every literate when he obtains a degree begins in petty posts, and thence goes on rising to higher ones, without their knowing when they are to be moved; and here they are quietly settled, when a letter comes and without his knowledge he is moved from here three hundred leagues. These changes are made in Pequim: this takes place throughout the whole country, and each one goes on being promoted. Hence it comes that no judge in China does equity, because he does not think of the good of the district, but only of stealing, because he is not a native of it, and does not know when he may be transferred to another province. Hence it comes that they form no alliances and are of no service where they govern nor have any love for the people; they do nothing but rob, kill, whip and put to torture the people. The people are worse treated by these mandarins than is the devil in hell: hence it comes that the people have no love for the king and for the mandarins, and every day they go on rising and becoming robbers. Because the people who are robbed have no vineyards nor any source of food it is necessary that they become robbers. Of these risings there are a thousand. In places where there are no rivers many people rise; those that are between rivers where they can be caught remain quiet; but all are desirous of every change, because they are placed in the lowest depth of subjection. It is much greater than I have said.

The mandarin nobles although they are mandarins hold no post of justice. Of these there are many; they are mandarins of their own residences, and have a salary from the king; while they hold office they go to fight wherever they are sent. These for any fault whatsoever are straightaway beaten and tortured like any other person of the common people. However they go on advancing in names, and according to the name so is the maintenance. These do not go out of the district of their birth, because they do not administer justice. Sometimes they have charge of

places of men of arms; however, wherever they are, they understand very little of justice, except in places with populations of
people of their own control.

The arms of the country of China are short swords of iron
with a handle of wood, and a bandoleer of *esparto* cord. This
is for the men of arms; the mandarins have of the same fashion
but finer according as they have authority. Their spears are canes,
the iron heads being spikes and hooks; pieces of wood, headpieces or helmets of tin of Flanders foil for the sake of the heat.
Before the Portuguese came they had no bombards, only some
made after the manner of the pots of Monte Mór, a vain affair.
None of the people may carry arms except they do it under
pain of death. The men of arms may not carry them at home
when they have done their duty, the mandarins give them to
them so long as they serve under them: when this is finished
they are collected at the house of the mandarin. They have wooden
cross-bows.

   .   .   .

Every person that has lands.—The whole country of China is
divided up into lots; they call each lot *quintei*: it will be sowing
land of four *alqueires*[10] of rice. Every husbandman is obliged to
pay from this land of his a certain quantity of rice. Now they
sow, then they do not; now today they have good seasons, then
bad ones. When the seasons are not favourable they become poor,
and sell their children in order to pay: if this is not sufficient,
they sell the properties themselves. They are obliged, every person that has this acreage of land, to give certain persons for
the service of the mandarins, or for each person twenty *cruzados*.
They are obliged to supply all furniture of coloured tables, chairs,
beds, ewers and other trifles for the houses of the mandarins.
Those who have not lands are obliged each one to give certain
persons; and, if he have no person, money; and, if he have no
person or money, he in person has to serve and eat at his own
cost and fee the person he serves. Besides these duties they are
liable for the following.

Throughout the whole country of China there are now rivers,
now dry land. On the high roads from stage to stage there are

[10] alqueire = 13 litres.

houses ready, with each one its mandarin clerk, where they have rice, meat, fish, fowls and every other sort of food and preparation of the kitchen; and boats with kitchens, tables, chairs and beds. They have also beasts ready, rowers for the service of the mandarins and every other person who travels by the rivers, that is, every mandarin or other person whom the king sends or the mandarins who in connection with their government carry letters; for which purpose they give them much,—if they go by land, horses; if by sea, boats, beds, and every necessary. Indeed the persons are already furnished for these houses. The persons of the districts are obliged to give this for a certain time, now some, now others: for this reason, they have nothing left that they do not spend; and if anyone refuses he is immediately imprisoned and everything is sold, and he dies in prison. No one refuses what the mandarin demands, but with head to the ground and face on the earth listens to and regards the mandarin like another lightning-flash. Hence it is that the people come to be poor; moreover for any cause whatever they are at once beaten and put in prison, and the least penalty is seven *quintals* of rice and two or three *maces* (?) of silver to them, and of these they pay five hundred and a thousand taels, whence I verily believe that the fines that are exacted for the king from the persons that are imprisoned is a very large sum of silver, and I am certain that in the prisons of Cantão there are constantly as many as four thousand men imprisoned and many women. And every day they imprison many and release fewer; and they die in the prisons of hunger like vermin. Hence the people come to have a hatred of the mandarins, and desire changes in order to obtain liberty.

The cities, towns and walled villages of the country of Chin.—All the walls are broad built on the surface of the ground: the walls have no foundations; they stand on the earth. The face of the outer part is of stone from the ground to half-way up the wall; the rest of brick. Some are all of stone. I mean the outer face; inside they are of mud. At the gateways they make great arches and great gates, and above the gates sentry-boxes of wood. From these mud-walls they remove the earth for the mud-walls. The villages and walls lie within walls and ditches. Those that I saw were all on the surface of the ground: they

have no other fortresses. The cities, towns and villages that have
walls open their gates at sunrise and shut them at sunset. They
intrust the keys to the mandarin who has charge of them: at
night he receives them, and in the morning every gate has a
person who guards it with ten or twelve persons; at night all
watch vigilantly, as they are afraid of the natives. All the houses
are protected by timber on wooden props; the walls of a few
are of mats, but in most cases of canes and mud with clay with
a facing of lime, and generally floored with small planks. Thus
they are all a very flimsy affair; and for the most part the whole
family lives within one door, and all have one surname. Each
family has a family name by which they are known: in addition
to this they have their names, Mirandas or any other cognomen.
Besides this patronymic (?) they have their own names. The oldest
person of this family has the names, in order to give an account
of how many there are; and no person can go twenty miles out
of the village where he dwells without a letter from the mandarins: if he is found without he is imprisoned as a robber; because all the roads are full of spies. For this letter they give
something: the letter declares what person he is and his age and
all for which he is given leave.

With respect to the courts of justice that there are in this city
of Cantão, the first is the *Cancheufu*, which is the court of the
city. This has twelve or thirteen mandarins and one hundred
clerks: every mandarin lives in the court where he is a mandarin.
The court of the *pochançi* has some twenty mandarins petty and
great, clerks, *chimchaes*, messengers, and other persons, with
clerks: in all there are more than two hundred. The court of
the *anchaçy* has as many other great and petty mandarins, clerks,
and other persons. The court of the *toçi* has six or seven mandarins and many clerks. The *cehi* is one who has charge of the
men of arms and of the salt: he has many clerks; and the *cuchi*
who has charge of all the affairs of justice is one who has many
clerks. The court of the *tutão* and the *choypi* and the great and
lesser *congom* and of the *tiqos*. Besides these there are some
fifteen or twenty whom I do not name. There is no doubt that
all the mandarins of this city of Cantão must have over seven or
eight thousand servants all employed at the expense of the people.
I do not speak of other great courts of the mandarins who keep

sheep, who have no charges, so that they may be reckoned as houses of men of the people. Take note that every house of those of the mandarins has terraces and freestone for the purpose of being able in each one to erect a tower, and here there is cut stone in blocks enough to build anew a Babylon. I pass over their houses of prayer and the streets which are so much carved as to defy description. Then as regards wood, one of these houses has enough to timber a fortress with ten towers. These houses have *teições* of strong gates within, all with houses and stables. Each of these houses covers enough ground to form a handsome town. The house of the *aytao* also is very large, and has great, strong, beautiful gates, and the wall at the hinges stands on the surface. Of all those of Cantão this is the abundance of the mandarins; and every day some go and others come, so that in every three years and more all have gone and others come. Since I have been in this city many crews have been changed.

As I have said of the much stone, so also of the much craft, that there is in this province of Cantão,—not one of war, all of peace,—of such a number of royal galleys and foists and brigantines, all with gunwales and beaks and masted in the manner of galleys. If into each one be put a deck and its knees they become galleys and foists and brigantines; and at first they would do instead of those of Cochi. There are also oars and rowers without number. Of these boats the best and newest should be taken, and all the rest burned. At leisure royal galleys can be built, and all the other rowing craft. These draw less water than ours, and can thus serve as well as ours in these rivers. For the sea I do not know how safe they would be; so that it would be needful to make a beginning with these, because they are very necessary, until others were made, for, if the affair proceeds as projected, there can be made here in a month ten or twelve rowing boats, because workmen and wood are in plenty, and especially when they see good payment. These boats are of much importance, because all the strength is in the rivers.

This country of China is great, and its commerce is between certain provinces of it and others. Cantão has iron, which there is not in the whole of the rest of the country of China, according to what I am informed.[11] From here it goes inland to the other

---

[11] The writer was misinformed.

side of the mountain range; and the rest lies in the vicinity of this
city of Cantão. From this they manufacture pots, nails, Chinese
trade of goods from the provinces to Cantão and from Cantão
arms and everything else of iron. They have also cordage, thread
and silk, and cotton cloths. By reason of trade all goods come
here, because this is the port whither foreigners come for this
trade of goods from the provinces to Cantão and from Cantão
to the interior, and the people are more numerous than in the
other provinces. All the goods that were coming to Cantão before
this war broke out should be kept until it is seen how things
turn out. The country inland has many, without a possibility of
their being wasted, because they would manufacture them according to the wishes of the Portuguese: I mean silks and porce-
lains.

This country cannot be sustained without trade. Goods do not
come here now, nor are there here goods and traders as were
wont, nor the fifth part, because all were destroyed on account
of the Portuguese. This city, because of foreigners' not coming
and because goods do not come from the other provinces, is at
present poor. A good trade cannot be done until those from
above come here when they learn that foreigners have arrived,
and trade has once more to be negotiated. Every day I think
that the province of Cantão is going to revolt; and the whole
country inland is bound to do likewise, because the whole is fus-
tigated after one manner. When things have been settled in one
way or another the country will carry on trade, whilst the land
will not yield such large revenues, which is a thing not to be
desired. The whole country is cultivated; and the goods that the
foreigners bring are very necessary in the country, especially in
order to effect a sale of the local ones. The country inland has
many and good articles of merchandise, many kinds of silks that
have not yet come to Cantão, because they are anxious that they
should not be rivalled, and because of its being forbidden by the
king that good wares and those of value should be sold to foreigners, only things of barter; there is also much rhubarb. I now
leave this subject and turn to that which is of more importance.

In Cantão they have not been forming fleets as they used to
do formerly. It must now be sixteen years since certain Chinese
rose in junks and turned robbers, and Cantão armed against them.

Those of Cantão were defeated; and the mandarins of Cantão made an agreement with them that they would pardon them and that they would give them land where they might live, with the condition that when other robbers should appear on the sea they should go and fight with them, and whatever they got in plunder should be theirs, excepting the women and things for the king. They gave a settlement to these robbers, some of them in Nanto, some of them in Foym, some of them in Aynameha and in other villages that lie between Nanto and Cantão: these all had junks. All the junks of Cantão were of these robbers of whom I have spoken. By the capture in the year 1521 of the junks that remained at the island[12] they became rich, and by the booty of *Syão* and Patane; and through the conquest of the two ships in the year 1522 they became so arrogant that it seemed to them that now no one could come whom they could not defeat. Wherefore in the year 1523 they prepared a fleet of one hundred junks watching for Portuguese: half of them lay in front of Nanto, and the other half at sea among the islands watching.

.   .   .

In this fleet that the Chinese prepared to watch for ours there was not one man of arms of the soldiers of China: all were people from those villages and junks taken by force and weak and low people and the majority children. Nevertheless every one of them is better than four men of arms: it is a mere mockery to talk of men of arms of this country of China. In this fleet that they sent to Nanto are some captains, it appearing to them that they could capture Portuguese as in the year 1522. If this gentry had a taste of the Portuguese sword they would soon fraternize with the Portuguese, because the most are people of floating possessions, and with little or no root in the soil. This people of Cantão is very weak in comparison with the people of the interior, who are strong. In this Cantão,—I mean in the district of Cantão and throughout the province,—because it is a region distant from the rivers, they quickly rise. They attack

[12] The Island of Trade; one of the islands in Lintin Bay—it is not clear which one—at which the Portuguese had been carrying on a regular, though illicit, trade.

villages, and kill much people: this happens every day in many
places, and they cannot do them any harm, and they send for
men to the province of Cancy which lies to the west of Cantão.
They call these *Langãs* or *Langueãs*: these are of a somewhat
better bearing; nevertheless the whole is a trumpery affair. The
Chinese say that if the Portuguese should land they would summon many of these men; and they cannot come except by river,
so that if a hundred came it would profit nothing, because when
the river was freed from their craft and our vessels were clear
and began to proceed under bombards there is nothing that would
appear within ten leagues. These Chinese of Cantão when they go
to fight with people who have risen never kill like robbers. They
surprise these abodes of robbers and kill an immense number
therein, and bring their heads and many others as prisoners: they
say that they are robbers, and there is no more need of proof.
They kill them all in a cruel manner. This they do every day.
The people is so docile and fearful that they dare not speak. It
is like this throughout the whole country of China, and it is
much worse than I have said; wherefore all the people long for
a revolt and for the coming of the Portuguese.

Going from Nanto to Cantão there lies in the middle of the
river almost adjoining the bar of Tãcoã[13] a large town also on an
island that is called *Aynãcha*. It has cut stone in the houses,
streets and churches, and in the jetty, of which could be made
a fortress like that of Goa. It has a port safe from all the winds,
all the bottom of mud, a very safe port; the main force of the
junks was here. This fortress lies above Cantão. Nanto dominates
this town of which I speak and another that is called *Xuntaeim*.
From here one could stop provisions and place Cantão in extremity, and it would capitulate in any way that the captain
pleased. I repeat, that to capture Cantão *en bloc* with a force of
two or three thousand men is better: I say two or three thousand,
not because with less the object would not be attained, only
that it is a big affair, and there are the charges of places, for
which Portuguese are needful. Six thousand would not suffice to
conquer with less than I have said and attain the end; because
the Chinese would at once rise against the city with the help of
the Portuguese.

[13] Tungkwan.

Moreover with the craft that the Portuguese bring and those that shall be made here out of their *paraos* in our fashion there will be enough to clear all the rivers. The rivers cleared, the mandarins will have to surrender perforce, or will have to flee and leave the city; then Cantão and its environs will at once be in our hands. This can be done by captains who shall bring a force of seven hundred to a thousand men; and there must remain with him the craft and large rowing boats and all the Portuguese people and Malabars; and if he find any ships he shall send them to Couchim divested of the Chinese officers that he shall find in them, because ten million will come. And if the governor will put matters in train for next year Cantão will soon be in his hands with the whole province; and he can leave therein a fortress, and in suitable places leave Portuguese people and Malabars, and can return with all his fleet laden with Chinese,—carpenters, masons, smiths, tilers, sawyers, and of every other trade, with their wives, to be left at those fortresses; for he can carry away in his fleet in junks from the country ten thousand men without causing a scarcity, and every year four thousand could leave without making a difference. This is the marvellous reason why for each Portuguese a hundred Chinese can be taken for the fortresses.

Cantão has within it a flat mount close to the wall on the north side on which stands a house that has five stories. Within the slopes of this mount are six or seven churches which have enough cut stone to build in ten days a town with walls and houses; and the churches are without number; stays, beams, doors. From here one could dominate the city. Another might be built on the edge of the water in the middle of the town where the mandarins disembark, which could be erected in five days, because there is cut stone in the streets and courts of justice sufficient to build a large walled city with towers. Another in the church that stands on the river. Just as there are stone and timber and lime in abundance, so there are workmen for this and servants. Nowhere in the whole world are there so many, and they are good servants: for a small wage for food a hundred thousand will come. And out of their *paraos* can be made galleys, foists, brigantines; of some can be made galliasses with few ribs, because the rivers do not require the strength that the sea does.

So that all these things require more time; and if written orders should be sent to engage in the work the country is prepared for everything. God grant that these Chinese may be fools enough to lose the country; because up to the present they have had no dominion, but little by little they have gone on taking the land from their neighbours; and for this reason the kingdom is great, because the Chinese are full of much cowardice, and hence they come to be presumptuous, arrogant, cruel; and because up to the present, being a cowardly people, they have managed without arms and without any practice of war, and have always gone on getting the land from their neighbors, and not by force but by stratagems and deceptions; and they imagine that no one can do them harm. They call every foreigner a savage; and their country they call the kingdom of God. Whoever shall come now, let it be a captain with a fleet of ten or fifteen sail. The first thing will be to destroy the fleet if they should have one, which I believe they have not; let it be by fire and blood and cruel fear for this day, without sparing the life of a single person, every junk being burnt, and no one being taken prisoner, in order not to waste the provisions, because at all times a hundred Chinese will be found for one Portuguese. And this done, Nanto must be cleared, and at once they will have a fortress and provisions if they wish, because it will at once be in their power; and then with the whole fleet attack Aynãcha, which lies at the bar of Tãcoam, as I have already said above having a good port. Here the ships, which cannot enter the river, will be anchored, and whatever craft they may have will be burnt; and after it has been taken if it seem good the town can be burnt, in order to terrify the Chinese. Before this has been done let a letter be sent by a Caffre black boy; and let it be sent in this manner:—

"I (then the title of the person who shall come) beg to inform the *cuhi* and the *çãci* of Cantão that so many years ago our lord the king sent a letter to the king of China and a present by Tome Pirez, who was received by the grandees and others who bear office. He was given a house in Cantão; and from there was summoned by the king of China. He went, and he saw him in *Nãquy*. Thence he ordered him to Pequim in order there to give him dispatch, saying that there was the place for giving dispatches. We have heard nothing more of him. In the year so-and-so there came a ship in search of him; it paid its dues and payments, but they armed against it to capture it. And in the year so-and-so there came in search of him five junks laden with goods; and the mandarins armed against them in order to plunder them. Doing no evil on land or giving any offence, because the junks came separately from the sea, they retired to other ships, and left the junks in port laden with many goods, quite full, without taking anything out of them. And in the year so-and-so there came five ships with an ambassador to the king of China; and the mandarins of Nãto prepared one hundred junks of robbers to entrap two of the ships by means of false messages of peace. They captured the two ships; and the three that remained did not know how that the ambassador of our lord the king had been put in chains, and his company, and all their property and clothes taken, and without food in the prisons, like the property of robbers; the embassy having been thus received by the grandees, and the present that came for the king kept, without wishing to send away the ambassador. This is not justice, but it is the justice of three thievish mandarins, namely, the *ambochim*, the *anhançi* and the *lentocim*, and the *pio* of Nanto, who for the robberies they have committed deserve all to die. Because the king of China may not know of it, this has been brought to my notice; and I have come here, and very early tomorrow I shall be in Cantão to see the city where such justice is done. Let the ambassador be sent to me before I arrive in Cantão. When he shall have been delivered over to me then we shall speak of what is to be overlooked and what are to be the consequences of that which has passed. And if you do not desire this let the blame rest with you who receive ambassadors and presents, and in order to plunder them put them in prison. This is written on such a day of the moon."

When the letter has been written and sent to ask for liberty on land for all, then enter the river with all the rowing boats; and if the answer is delayed, if it seem good, let fire be put to the town, and burn all the craft that will be of no use for service of war, and all the people that do not obey the ban shall be killed. If they are deprived of provisions for three days they will

all die of hunger. The city has a large provision house very close
to the gate on the west side within the walls; but for dividing
among the people it is nothing, because the people are without
number and each day buy what they have to eat. So that all must
die of hunger and are bound to rise against the mandarins; and
if the people rise at once the city will be in revolt. It will be
necessary to be very careful not to receive reports of delays if
many *paraos* with provisions do not arrive at the city. In Cantão
there will be idle reports, which are so many, and the population
so large, that it cannot be realised. Above all, when the craft
has been destroyed in the river, there will not appear a single
Chinese affair that has not been burnt. With this and a like slaughter
fear will arise regarding the worth of the mandarins, and they
are sure to come to blows with them. And this will have to
be done, and will take less time than I have said; because all the
people are waiting for the Portuguese. In the city provisions
cannot reach them by land, as the roads are often in rebellion;
if they do this before the arrival of the Portuguese, how much
more after it. All the rice has to come by river; and it will be
necessary to keep watch in the strait that is in the river up above
to the north a matter of half a league, by which provisions and
help may reach them. Boats can be placed there; so that, the
strait being held, so that nothing can come, all is in your power.
If the mandarins should think of fleeing, it would be to this creek:
here is their salvation. In this creek galleys could lie, and one
can come from this creek to the city by land, as it is near. There
every mandarin arrives, and thence his arrival is made known;
and then he enters, and horsemen come by land to inform the
mandarins of the city what mandarin has entered.

---

12. St. Francis Xavier's first impressions of Japan

Japan was the last major country of the East to be "discovered"—that
is to say, visited—by Europeans; though under the name "Cipangu"
the island kingdom had been known to Europeans by repute, as a syn-

onym for exotic wealth, since Marco Polo's time. Portuguese seamen, in the course of smuggling and minor depredations off the China coast, probably made contacts with Japanese *Wako* pirates in the 1530's; but the first certainly recorded European visit was by a boatload of Portuguese sailors, driven by stress of weather, in 1543. Other travelers and traders followed in the next few years, including Fernão Mendes ("Mendax") Pinto, who made several visits, though nothing which he said could be accepted without corroboration. The first clear eyewitness description was written at Malacca in 1547 by the trader Jorge Alvárez, at the request of St. Francis Xavier. Alvárez had just returned from Japan, having spent some time at the port of Yamagawa in southern Kyushu. He was accompanied by a Japanese named Yajiro, a fugitive from justice who became a Christian convert. Alvárez was a good observer and a man of some education. Besides topographical, economic, and social comment, he remarked in his report on the courtesy of the Japanese, their interest in strangers, and their willingness to listen to argument; characteristics which contrasted sharply with the indifference or contempt commonly displayed by the Chinese. These were the characteristics which above all attracted the attention of St. Francis and aroused his hopes of a fruitful Christian mission.

In 1549 Xavier himself went to Japan, with money and supplies lavishly provided by the Portuguese captain of Malacca. His party, which included Yajiro, left Malacca in May 1549 and landed at Kagoshima in August, a quick passage. He was kindly and courteously received by the *daimyo* of the province, and by other *daimyo* subsequently; probably these semi-independent feudatories hoped that the missionaries would be followed by more Portuguese traders from whom they could purchase firearms. Whatever the motive, all the Japanese with whom Xavier came in contact—even Buddhist monks—seemed pleased to see him and interested in what he had to say. The letter quoted here describes his enthusiastic response to this agreeable reception. Its description of Japanese society is in some respects superficial, as it was bound to be after a residence of only a few weeks, especially since conversations had to be interpreted by Yajiro; but it is the letter of a sympathetic, observant, educated man.

Xavier spent two years in Japan, during which time his initial enthusiasm became tempered by appreciation of the obstacles in the way of his mission. The deep hold of Buddhism he rightly considered the most formidable of these obstacles, despite the friendliness of individual Buddhist monks. In 1551 he visited Kyoto, the imperial capital, and discovered another obstacle in the prevailing anarchy and lawlessness. The *daimyo* were the real local rulers; the emperor was powerless to control his subjects, and the project of a systematic programme of conversion from the Court downwards was clearly hopeless. By 1551 Xavier became convinced that China, not Japan, was the key to the Christianizing of the East. He was to spend the last years of his life in fruitless attempts to secure admission to China. Nevertheless, as a mission his visit to Japan was a notable success. He left behind him a promising Christian community of a thousand souls; and he never lost his initial liking for the Japanese.

The extract which follows is from C. R. Boxer: *The Christian Century in Japan, 1549–1650* (Berkeley, University of California Press, 1951), pp. 401–5: Appendix I, Extracts from a letter written by Francis Xavier, S.J., to the Jesuits at Goa, dated Kagoshima, November 5, 1549.

B Y the experience which we have of this land of Japan, I can inform you thereof as follows. Firstly, the people whom we have met so far, are the best who have yet been discovered, and it seems to me that we shall never find among heathens another race to equal the Japanese. It is a people of very good manners, good in general, and not malicious; they are men of honor to a marvel, and prize honor above all else in the world. They are a poor people in general; but their poverty, whether among the gentry or those who are not so, is not considered as a shame. They have one quality which I cannot recall in any people of Christendom; this is that their gentry howsoever poor they may be, and the commoners howsoever rich they may be, render as much honor to a poor gentleman as if he were passing rich. On no account would a poverty-stricken gentleman marry with someone outside the gentry, even if he were given great sums to do so; and this they do because they consider that they would lose their honor by marrying into a lower class. Whence it can clearly be seen that they esteem honor more than riches. They are very courteous in their dealings with another; they highly regard arms and trust much in them; always carrying sword and dagger, both high and low alike, from the age of fourteen onwards. They are a people who will not submit to any insults or contemptuous words. Those who are not of gentle birth give much honor to the gentry, who in their turn pride themselves on faithfully serving their feudal lord, to whom they are very obedient. It seems to me that they act thus rather because they think that they would lose their honor if they acted contrarily, than for fear of the punishment they would receive if disobedient. They are small eaters albeit somewhat heavy drinkers, and they drink rice wine since there are no ordinary wines in these parts. They are men who never gamble, because they consider it a great dishonor, since those who gamble desire what is not theirs and hence tend to become thieves. They swear but little, and when they do it is by the Sun. There are many persons who can read and write, which is a great help to their learning quickly prayers and religious matters. It is a land where there are but few thieves in some kingdoms, and this by the strict justice which is executed against those that are, for their lives are never spared. They abhor beyond measure this vice of theft. They are a people of very good will, very sociable and very desirous of knowledge; they are very fond of hearing about things of God, chiefly when they understand them. Of all the lands which I have seen in my life, whether those of Christians or of heathens, never yet did I see a people so honest in not thieving. Most of them believe in the men of old, who were (so far as I understand) persons who lived like philosophers; many of them adore the Sun and others the Moon. They like to hear things propounded according to reason; and granted that there are sins and vices among them, when one reasons with them pointing out that what they do is evil, they are convinced by this reasoning. I discerned fewer sins in the laity and found them more obedient to reason, than those whom they regard as fathers and priests, whom they call Bonzes.

Two things have astonished me greatly about this country. The first, to see how lightly they regard great sins; and the reason is because their forebears were accustomed to live in them, from whom those of the present generation take their example; see how continuation in vices which are against nature corrupts the people, in the same manner as continual disregard of imperfections undermines and destroys perfection. The second point is to see that the laity live better in their state than the Bonzes in theirs; and withal this is so manifest, it is astonishing in what esteem the former hold the latter. There are many other errors and evils among these Bonzes, and the more learned are the worst sinners. I spoke many times with some of the wiser, chiefly with one who is highly regarded by all in these parts, both for his letters, life, and dignity, as for his great age, he being eighty years old, and called Ningit [Ninjitsu], which is to say in Japanese "truthful heart"; he is as a bishop amongst them, and if the term could be applied to him, might well be called "blessed." In many talks which I had with him, I found him doubtful, and unable to decide whether our soul is immortal, or whether it dies with the body; sometimes he told me yes, at others no, and I fear that the other learned are alike. This Ningit is so great a friend of mine, that it is a marvel to see. All, both laity and Bonzes like us very much, and are greatly astonished to see how we have come from such distant lands as from Portugal to Japan, which is more than six thousand leagues, only to speak of the things of God, and how people can save their souls by belief in Jesus Christ; saying that our coming to these lands is the work of God. One thing I tell you, for which you may give many thanks to God Our Lord, that this land of Japan is very fit for our holy faith greatly to increase therein; and if we knew how to speak the language, I have no doubt whatsoever that we would make many Christians. May it please Our Lord that we may learn it soon, for already we begin to appreciate it, and we learned to repeat the ten commandments in the space of forty days which we applied ourselves thereto.

In the place of Paulo de Santa Fé,[1] our good and true friend, we were received by the local Captain and by the Alcayde, with much benignity and love, and likewise by all the people; everyone marveling to see Fathers from the land of the Portuguese. They were not in the least surprised at Paul having become a Christian, but rather are pleased and delighted thereat, both his relatives as those who are not so, since he has been in India and seen things which they here have never seen. And the Duke [Daimyo] of this land is well affected to him, and renders him much honor, and asked many questions concerning the customs, worth, and authority of the Portuguese and of their Empire in India; and Paulo gave him a very full account of everything, whereat the Duke was greatly contented.

Here they are not now surprised at people becoming Christians,

---

[1] Yajiro.

and as a great part of them can read and write, they very soon learn the prayers; may it please God to give us tongue whereby we can speak to them of the things of God, for then we would reap much more fruit with His aid, grace, and favor. Now we are like so many statues among them, for they speak and talk to us about many things, whilst we, not understanding the language, hold our peace. And now we have to be like little children learning the language; God grant that we may likewise imitate them in true simplicity and purity of soul, striving by all means to become like them, both as regards learning the language as in showing the simplicity of children devoid of malice. And in this did God grant us great and notable favors in bringing us to these infidel lands, so that we should not neglect ourselves, since this land is wholly of idolators and enemies of Christ, and we have none in whom we can confide or trust, save only in God, for here we have neither relatives nor friends nor acquaintances, nor even some Christian piety, but only foes of Him who made the heaven and earth; and for this cause are we forced to place all our faith, hope, and trust in Christ Our Lord, and not in any living creature, since, through unbelief, all are enemies of God.

Likewise it is necessary that we should give you an account of other favors which God hath granted us, teaching us through His mercy, so that you may help us in rendering thanks to God always for them. This is, that elsewhere the abundance of bodily provisions is often the reason whereby disordered appetites are given free rein, frequently despising the virtue of abstinence, which leads to the no little detriment of men's souls and bodies. This is the origin of the majority of corporal ills, and even spiritual, and men have much difficulty in finding a means of relief, and many find that the days of their life are shortened before obtaining it, suffering all kinds of bodily pains and torments, taking physic to cure themselves which gives them more distaste to swallow than enjoyment they received from the dainties which they ate and drank. God granted us a signal favor in bringing us to these lands which lack such abundancies, so that even if we wished to minister to our bodies with these superfluities, the country does not allow of it. They neither kill nor eat anything which they rear. Sometimes they eat fish; there is rice and corn, albeit little;

there are numerous herbs, on which they live, and some fruit
but not much. This people live wonderfully healthy lives and
there are many aged. The Japanese are a convincing proof of
how our nature can subsist on little, even if it is not a pleasing
sustenance. We live in this land very healthy in body, God grant
that we may be likewise in our souls. A great part of the Japanese are Bonzes, and these are strictly obeyed in the places
where they are, even if their sins are manifest to all; and it seems
to me that the reason why they are held in such esteem is because
of their rigorous abstinence, for they never eat meat, nor fish, but
only herbs, fruit, and rice, and this once a day and very strictly,
and they are never given wine. There are many Bonzes and their
temples are of but little revenue. By reason of their continual
abstinence and because they have no intercourse with women
(especially those who go dressed in black like clergy) on pain of
death, and because they know how to relate some histories or
rather fables of the things in which they believe, it seems to me
they are held in great veneration. And it may well happen that
since they and we feel so differently about God and the method
of salvation, that we may be persecuted by them with something
stronger than words. What we in these parts endeavor to do, is
to bring people to the knowledge of their Creator and Saviour,
Jesus Christ Our Lord. We live with great hope and trust in
Him to give us strength, grace, help, and favor to prosecute this
work. It does not seem to me that the laity will oppose or per-
secute us of their own volition, but only if they ere importuned
by the Bonzes. We do not seek to quarrel with them, neither for
fear of them will we cease to speak of the glory of God, and
of the salvation of souls. They cannot do us more harm than
God permits, and what harm comes to us through them is a
mercy of God; if through them for His love, service, and zeal
for souls, He sees good to shorten the days of our life, in order
to end this continual death in which we live, our desires will be
speedily fulfilled and we will go to reign forever with Christ.
Our intentions are to proclaim and maintain the truth, however
much they may contradict us, since God compels us to seek
rather the salvation of our future than the safety of our present
lives; we endeavoring with the grace and favor of Our Lord to
fulfil this precept, He giving us internal strength to manifest the

same before the innumerable idolatries which there are in Japan.

It is well that we should give you an account of our stay in Cangoxima [Kagoshima]. We arrived here at a season when the winds were contrary for going to Miaco, [Kyoto] which is the chief city of Japan, where the King and the greatest lords of the Kingdom reside. And there is no wind that will serve us to go thither, save only five months from now, and then we will go with the help of Our Lord. It is three hundred leagues from here to Miaco, according to what they tell us, and we are like-wise told great things of that city, which is said to contain more than ninety thousand houses; there is also a great university fre-quented by students therein, which has six principal colleges and more than two hundred houses of Bonzes, and of others like friars who are called Ieguixu [Zen-shu], and of nuns who are called Hamacata [Amakata]. Besides this university of Miaco, there are five other chief universities whose names are these, Coya [Koya], Nenguru [Negoro], Feizan [Hieizen], Taninomine [Tamu no mine]. These are in the neighborhood of Miaco, and it is said that there are more than 3,500 students in each one of them. There is another university, a great way off, which is called Bandou [Bando, the Ashikaga Gakko] which is the best and biggest in Japan, and more frequented by students than any other. Bandou is a great lordship where there are six dukes, and a chief one among them, whom the others obey. This chief owes allegiance to the King of Japan who is the great King of Miaco. They tell us such things of the greatness of these lands and universities, that we would prefer to see them before affirming and writing them; and if things be as they tell us, then we will write of our experiences in detail. In addition to these principal universities, they say that there are many other smaller ones throughout the kingdom. During the year 1551, we hope to write you at length concerning the disposition that there is in Miaco and its univer-sities for the knowledge of Jesus Christ Our Lord to be spread therein. This year two Bonzes are going to India who have studied in the universities of Bandou and Miaco, and with them many other Japanese to learn the things of our law.

On St. Michael's day we spoke with the duke of this land, who gave us great honor, saying that we should keep well the books in which was written the law of the Christians, and that if it was the true and good law of Jesus Christ, it would be troublesome to the Devil. A few days afterwards he gave leave to all his vassals that those who might wish to become Christians could do so. This good news I write at the end of the letter for your consolation, and that you may give thanks unto God our Lord. It seems to me that this winter we must occupy ourselves in making a declaration concerning the Articles of Faith in Japanese, somewhat copiously, for it to be printed (because all the principal persons here know how to read and write) so that our holy faith may be understood and spread throughout many parts, since we cannot go to all. Our dearest brother Paulo will translate faithfully into his own tongue everything which is necessary for the salvation of souls.

From Cangoxima, fifth of November of the year 1549.

Your most loving brother wholly in Christ,

FRANCISCO

VI. *The Americas*

13. Columbus' landfall

Columbus was not the first European seagoing commander to land in the Americas. The Icelanders and Greenlanders preceded him by nearly five hundred years; and it is possible that in his own time fishermen from English west-country ports were fishing off Newfoundland, and may have sighted land before 1492.[1] Nevertheless, the significance of historical events must be measured by their consequences. Columbus' expedition of 1492 was the first trans-Atlantic voyage to have immediate, significant, and permanent results. Columbus, not Leif the Lucky or a nameless fisherman from Bristol, made the landfall which brought the Americas firmly within the range of European action.

The precise objects of Columbus' first voyage have been much discussed, and mystery still surrounds them. By the agreement under which he sailed, he was to "discover and acquire islands and mainland in the Ocean Sea." This standard formula doubtless included Antilla or Atlantis, if such a place existed; but almost certainly the phrase "islands and mainland" was also understood to mean Cipangu and Cathay. There was nothing fantastic, at least in theory, about a proposal to reach eastern Asia by sailing west. The earth was round; no-one suspected an intervening continent; it was a matter of winds, of currents, above all of distance. Could a ship, the stores she could carry, and the men in her, endure so far? Columbus apparently thought they could. What he proposed to do, if he actually reached "Cathay," he never explained. His ships carried no trade goods, no presents for princes, and were unarmed. He bore a letter for the "Great Khan"; but once he had arrived (as he thought) in the general neighborhood of "Cathay" he made no serious attempt to find and enter its harbors.

[1] D. B. Quinn: "The Argument for the English Discovery of America between 1480 and 1494," *Geographical Journal*, CCXVII (1961), 277–85.

Instead, he made excuses, wandered among the islands searching for gold, and eventually, having lost his flagship, set sail for home.

Columbus returned to Spain in 1493 convinced that he had found outlying islands in the archipelago of which Japan was supposed to form a part; such an archipelago as is marked, for example, on Martin Behaim's 1492 globe. He supported his conclusions by combining Marco Polo's estimate of the east-west extent of Asia, which was an overestimate; the same traveler's report of the distance of Japan from the Asian mainland—1,500 miles, a gross overestimate; and Ptolemy's estimate of the circumference of the earth, which was an under-estimate. He assumed the length of an equatorial degree of longitude to be 10 per cent shorter than Ptolemy had taught and 25 per cent shorter than the true figure. This calculation would make the westward distance from Europe to Japan less than 3,000 nautical miles. The actual great circle distance is 10,000 nautical miles; but according to Columbus' reasoning, Hispaniola and Cuba were near to where Japan ought to be. The east coast of the mainland of Cathay might well be, as Columbus stated, distant only ten days' sailing. As time went on, as more and more doubts were cast on his reliability, Columbus thought of more and more ingenious or fantastic arguments to support his main contention; to the contention itself, he clung with passionate insistence to the end of his life.

Columbus was a self-taught and extremely persuasive geographical theorist, a capable sea commander, and a careful, though not very up-to-date navigator. He never took solar observations, as far as we know, and may not have understood them. His Polaris observations were sometimes unreliable. On the other hand, his dead reckoning had an uncanny accuracy. He carried a compass rose in his head. Once he had been to a place, he could always find it again. In matters pertaining to navigation, also, he was uncommonly observant. He not only discovered the West Indies; he discovered the best way to get there, in the zone of the northeast trade winds, and the best way to return, before the westerlies of middle latitudes in the North Atlantic.

On his return to Spain, Columbus sent to Ferdinand and Isabella a letter summarizing the log or journal of his voyage, which he had kept from day to day. Subsequently, on his reception at Court, he presented the journal itself. The letter received wide and immediate publicity, but the journal was kept secret; the original of it has disappeared, and so has a copy which the Columbus family was allowed to retain. An abstract of one copy, however, was made by the Dominican missionary and historian Bartolomé de las Casas, who was a friend of the family. Las Casas quoted some parts of the journal verbatim; summarized other parts in the third person; and here and there interpolated comments of his own, as from his knowledge of the West Indies, he was well qualified to do. The Las Casas abstract was discovered in 1791 in the library of the Duque del Infantado by Martín Fernández de Navarrete, who published it in the first volume of his *Colección de Viajes* in 1825.

A better edition appeared in the *Raccolta Colombiana* in 1892. Since then there have been several other Spanish editions, and traslations have been made, some from the Navarrete version, some from the *Raccolta*, into other major European languages.

The portion of the journal quoted here describes the first West Indian landfall and the explorations immediately following. It illustrates well some of the admiral's principal characteristics: his unbreakable resolution; his persuasiveness, which included a capacity for self-deception; his inability to retreat from a predetermined conclusion. He had set out to find Asia; therefore the West Indies must somehow be fitted into Asia, however much their superficial appearance might suggest otherwise. The extract is from *The Journal of Christopher Columbus*, translated by Cecil Jane, revised and annotated by L. A. Vigneras (London, Hakluyt Society, 1960), pp. 19–41.

SATURDAY, OCTOBER 6th / He kept on his course westwards; they went forty leagues in the day and night; he reckoned thirty-three to his men. On this night Martin Alonso said that it would be well to steer south-west by west, and the admiral thought that Martin Alonso did not say this on account of the island of Cipangu;[1] and the admiral saw that, if they missed it, they would not be able to reach land so soon, and that it was better to go at once to the mainland and afterwards to the islands.

SUNDAY, OCTOBER 7th / He kept on his course to the west; they made twelve miles an hour for two hours, and afterwards eight miles an hour; and up to an hour after sunrise he went twenty-three leagues. He reckoned eighteen to his men. On this day, at sunrise, the caravel *Niña*, which went ahead as she was a fast sailer, and they all went as quickly as they could in order to be the first to sight land and secure the reward which the Sovereigns had promised to whomsoever should first sight it, hoisted a standard at the mast-head and fired a lombard, as a

[1] Marco Polo's name for Japan.

sign that they saw land; for so the admiral had ordered. He had also ordered that, at sunrise and at sunset, all the ships should join him, since these are the two periods when it is most possible to see for a distance, the mists clearing. In the evening the land, which those in the *Niña* thought they had seen, was not sighted, and a great flock of birds passed from the direction of the north to the south-west, which led him to believe that they were going to sleep on land or were, perhaps, flying from the winter which was about to come to the lands whence they came. As the admiral knew that most of the islands which the Portuguese held had been discovered through birds, on this account the admiral decided to abandon the westward course and to steer west-south-west, with the resolve to proceed in that direction for two days. He began to do so one hour before sunset. They made in the whole night a matter of five leagues, and twenty-three in the day; in the night and day together, they went in all twenty-eight leagues.

MONDAY, OCTOBER 8th / He navigated west-south-west, and day and night together they went about eleven and a half or twelve leagues, and it seems that at times in the night they made fifteen miles an hour, if the text be not corrupt. They had a sea like the river of Seville. "Thanks be to God," says the admiral, "the breeezs were softer than in April at Seville, so that it is a pleasure to be in them: they are so laden with scent." The vegetation seemed to be very fresh; there were many land birds, and they took one, and they were flying to the south-west, terns and ducks and a booby.

TUESDAY, OCTOBER 9th / He sailed south-westward; he made five leagues. The wind changed and he ran to the west by north, and went four leagues. Afterwards, in all, he made eleven leagues in the day and in the night twenty and a half leagues; he reckoned seventeen leagues to the men. All night they heard birds passing.

WEDNESDAY, OCTOBER 10th / He navigated west-south-west; they made ten miles an hour and at times twelve and sometimes seven, and in the day and night together they went fifty-nine leagues; he reckoned to the men fourty-four leagues, no more.

Here the men could now bear no more; they complained of the long voyage. But the admiral heartened them as best he could, holding out to them bright hopes of the gains which they could make, and he added that it was vain for them to complain, since he was going to the Indies and must pursue his course until, with the help of Our Lord, he found them.

THURSDAY, OCTOBER 11th / He navigated to the west-south-west; they had a rougher sea than they had experienced during the whole voyage. They saw petrels and a green reed near the ship. Those in the caravel *Pinta* saw a cane and a stick, and they secured another small stick, carved, as it appeared, with iron, and a piece of cane, and other vegetation which grows on land, and a small board. Those in the caravel *Niña* also saw other indications of land and a stick loaded with barnacles. At these signs, all breathed again and rejoiced. On this day, to sunset, they went twenty-seven leagues. After sunset, he steered his former course to the west; they made twelve miles an hour, and up to two hours before midnight they had made ninety miles, which are twenty-two leagues and a half. And since the caravel *Pinta* was swifter and went ahead of the admiral, she found land and made the signals which the admiral had commanded. This land was first sighted by a sailor called Rodrigo de Triana, although the admiral, at ten o'clock in the night, being on the sterncastle, saw a light. It was, however, so obscured that he would not affirm that it was land, but called Perro Gutierrez, butler of the King's dais, and told him that there seemed to be a light, and that he should watch for it. He did so, and saw it. He said the same also to Rodrigo Sanchez de Segovia, whom the King and Queen had sent in the fleet as *veedor*,[2] and he saw nothing since he was not in a position from which it could be seen. After the admiral had so spoken, it was seen once or twice, and it was like a small wax candle, which was raised and lowered. Few thought that this was an indication of land, but the admiral was certain that they were near land. Accordingly, when they had said the *Salve*, which all sailors are accustomed to say and chant in their manner, and when they had all been gathered together, the admiral asked and urged them to keep a good look out from

---

[2] Comptroller. His business was to keep account, on behalf of the Crown, of all valuable products acquired by the fleet.

the forecastle and to watch carefully for land, and to him who should say first that he saw land, he would give at once a silk doublet apart from the other rewards which the Sovereigns had promised, which were ten thousand maravedis annually to him who first sighted it. Two hours after midnight land appeared, at a distance of about two leagues from them. They took in all sail, remaining with the mainsail, which is the great sail without bonnets, and kept jogging, waiting for day, a Friday, on which they reached a small island of the Lucayos, which is called in the language of the Indians "Guanahaní."[3] Immediately they saw naked people, and the admiral went ashore in the armed boat, and Martin Alonso Pinzón and Vicente Yañez, his brother, who was captain of the *Niña*. The admiral brought out the royal standard, and the captains went with two banners of the Green Cross, which the admiral flew on all the ships as a flag, with an F and a Y, and over each letter their crown, one being on one side of the ✚ and the other on the other. When they had landed, they saw very green trees and much water and fruit of various kinds. The admiral called the two captains and the others who had landed, and Rodrigo de Escobedo, secretary of the whole fleet, and Rodrigo Sanchez de Segovia, and said that they should bear witness and testimony how he, before them all, took possession of the island, as in fact he did, for the King and Queen, his Sovereigns, making the declarations which are required, as is contained more at length in the testimonies which were there made in writing. Soon many people of the island gathered there. What follows are the actual words of the admiral, in his book of his first voyage and discovery of these Indies.

"I," he says, "in order that they might feel great amity towards us, because I knew that they were a people to be delivered and converted to our holy faith rather by love than by force, gave to some among them some red caps and some glass beads, which they hung round their necks, and many other things of little value. At this they were greatly pleased and became so entirely our friends that it was a wonder to see. Afterwards they came swimming to the ships' boats, where we were, and brought us parrots and cotton thread in balls, and spears and many other

[3] Probably, but not certainly, Watling's Island in the Bahamas.

things, and we exchanged for them other things, such as small glass beads and hawks' bells, which we gave to them. In fact, they took all and gave all, such as they had, with good will, but it seemed to me that they were a people very deficient in everything. They all go naked as their mothers bore them, and the women also, although I saw only one very young girl. And all those whom I did see were youths, so that I did not see one who was over thirty years of age; they were very well built, with very handsome bodies and very good faces. Their hair is coarse almost like the hairs of a horse's tail and short; they wear their hair down over their eyebrows, except for a few strands behind, which they wear long and never cut. Some of them are painted black, and they are the colour of the people of the Canaries, neither black nor white, and some of them are painted white and some red and some in any colour that they find. Some of them paint their faces, some their whole bodies, some only the eyes, and some only the nose. They do not bear arms or know them, for I showed to them swords and they took them by the blade and cut themselves through ignorance. They have no iron. Their spears are certain reeds, without iron, and some of these have a fish tooth at the end, while others are pointed in various ways. They are all generally fairly tall, good looking and well proportioned. I saw some who bore marks of wounds on their bodies, and I made signs to them to ask how this came about, and they indicated to me that people came from other islands, which are near, and wished to capture them, and they defended themselves. And I believed and still believe that they come here from the mainland to take them for slaves. They should be good servants and of quick intelligence, since I see that they very soon say all that is said to them, and I believe that they would easily be made Christians, for it appeared to me that they had no creed. Our Lord willing, at the time of my departure I will bring back six of them to Your Highnesses, that they may learn to talk. I saw no beast of any kind in this island, except parrots." All these are the words of the admiral.

"SATURDAY, OCTOBER 13th / As soon as day broke, there came to the shore many of these men, all youths, as I have said, and all of a good height, very handsome people. Their hair is not curly, but loose and coarse as the hair of a horse; all have very broad foreheads and heads, more so than has any people that I have seen up to now. Their eyes are very lovely and not small. They are not at all black, but the colour of Canaries, and nothing else could be expected, since this is in one line from east to west with the island of Hierro in the Canaries. Their legs are very straight, all alike; they have no bellies but very good figures. They came to the ship in boats, which are made of a tree-trunk like a long boat and all of one piece. They are very wonderfully carved, considering the country, and large, so that in some forty or forty-five men came. Others are smaller, so that in some only a solitary man came. They row them with a paddle, like a baker's peel, and they travel wonderfully fast. If one capsizes, all at once begin to swim and right it, baling it out with gourds which they carry with them. They brought balls of spun cotton and parrots and spears and other trifles, which it would be tedious to write down, and they gave all for anything that was given to them. And I was attentive and laboured to know if they had gold, and I saw that some of them wore a small piece hanging from a hole which they have in the nose, and from signs I was able to understand that, going to the south or going round the island to the south, there was a king who had large vessels of it and possessed much gold. I endeavoured to make them go there, and afterwards saw that they were not inclined for the journey. I resolved to wait until the afternoon of the following day, and after that to leave for the south-west, for, as many of them indicated to me, they said that there was land to the south and to the south-west and to the north-west, and that those of the north-west often came to attack them. So I resolved to go to the south-west, to seek the gold and precious stones. This island is fairly large and very flat; the trees are very green and there is much water. In the centre of it, there is a very large lake; there is no mountain, and all is so green that it is a pleasure to gaze upon it. The people also are very gentle and, since they long to possess something of ours and fear that nothing will be given to them unless they give something, when they have nothing, they take what they can and immediately throw themselves into the water and swim. But all that they do possess, they give for anything which is given to them, so that they exchange things even for pieces of broken dishes and bits of broken glass cups. I even saw one give sixteen balls of cotton for three *ceotis* of Portugal, which are a Castilian *blanca*, and in these balls there was more than an *arroba* of spun cotton.[4] I should forbid this and should not allow anything to be taken, unless it be that I command all, if there be a quantity, to be taken for Your Highnesses. It grows here in this island, but owing to lack of time, I can give no definite account; and here is also produced that gold which they wear hanging from the nose. But, in order not to lose time, I wish to go and see if I can make the island of Cipangu. Now, as it was night, they all went to land in their boats."

"SUNDAY, OCTOBER 14th / At dawn, I ordered the ship's boat and the boats of the caravels to be made ready, and I went along the island in a north-north-easterly direction, to see the other part, which lay to the east, and its character, and also to see the villages. And I soon saw two or three, and the people all came to shore, calling us and giving thanks to God. Some brought us water, others various eatables: others, when they saw that I was not inclined to land, threw themselves into the sea and came, swimming, and we understood that they asked us if we had come from heaven. One old man got into the boat, and all the rest, men and women, cried in loud voices: 'Come and see the men who have come from heaven; bring them food and drink.' Many came and many women, each with something, giving thanks to God, throwing themselves on the ground and raising their hands to the sky, and then shouting to us that we should land. But I feared to do so, seeing a great reef of rocks which encircled the whole of that island, while within there is deep water and a harbour large enough for all the ships of Christendom, the entrance to which is very narrow. It is true that inside the reef there are some shoals, but the sea is no more disturbed than the water in a well. And in order to see all this, I went this morning, that I might be able to give an account of all to Your Highnesses and also say where a fort could be built. I saw a piece of land, which is formed like an island although it is not one, on which there were six houses; it could be converted into an island in two

[4] *Blanca*, a copper coin worth half a *maravedi*. There were 750 *blancas* to a gold ducat. *Arroba* = 25 pounds weight.

days, although I do not see that it is necessary to do so, for these people are very unskilled in arms, as Your Highnesses will see from the seven whom I caused to be taken in order to carry them off that they may learn our language and return. However, when Your Highnesses so command, they can all be carried off to Castile or held captive in the island itself, since with fifty men they would be all kept in subjection and forced to do whatever may be wished. Near the said islet, moreover, there are the loveliest groups of trees that I have ever seen, all green and with leaves like those of Castile in the month of April and May, and much water. I examined the whole of that harbour, and afterwards returned to the ship and set sail. I saw so many islands that I could not decide to which I would go first. Those men, whom I had taken, made signs to me that there were very many, so many that they could not be counted, and they mentioned by name more than a hundred. Finally I sought for the largest and resolved to steer for it, which I am doing. It is five leagues away from this island of San Salvador, and of the others, some are more and some less distant. All are very flat, without mountains, and very fertile; all are inhabited and they make war upon one another, although these people are very simple and very well formed men."

"MONDAY, OCTOBER 15th / I stood off that night, fearing to come to anchor before daylight, as I did not know whether the coast was free from shoals. At daybreak, I hoisted sail. And as the island was more than five leagues distant, being rather about seven, and the tide was against me, it was about midday when I arrived at the island. I found that the side which lies towards the island of San Salvador runs north and south for a distance of five leagues, and that the other side, which I followed, runs east and west for more than ten leagues. And as from this island I saw another and larger to the west, I set sail to go all that day until night, since otherwise I should not have been able to have reached the westerly point. To this island I gave the name *Santa Maria de la Concepción*,[5] and about sunset, I anchored off the said point to learn if there were gold there, because those

[5] Now Rum Cay.

whom I had caused to be taken in the island of San Salvador told me that there they wore very large golden bracelets on the legs and arms. I can well believe that all that they said was a ruse in order to get away. It was nevertheless my wish not to pass any island without taking possession of it, although when one had been annexed, all might be said to have been. And I anchored and was there until to-day, Tuesday, when at dawn I went ashore in the armed boats and landed. The people, who were many, were naked and of the same type as those of the other island of San Salvador; they allowed us to go through the island and gave us what we asked of them. And as the wind blew more strongly across from the south-east, I was unwilling to wait and went back to the ship. A large canoe was alongside the caravel *Niña*, and one of the men of the island of San Salvador, who was in her, threw himself into the sea and went off in it, and during the evening before midnight the other threw himself overboard . . . , and went after the canoe, which fled so that there was not a boat that could have overtaken it, since we were a long way behind it. In the end it reached land and they left the canoe, and some of my company went ashore after them, and they all ran off like chickens. The boat which they had abandoned we brought on board the caravel *Niña*. To her, there now came from another direction another small canoe with a man who wished to barter a ball of cotton, and some sailors jumped into the sea and took him, because he would not come on board the caravel. I was on the poop of the ship and saw everything, and I sent for him and gave him a red cap and some small beads of green glass, which I put on his arm, and two hawks' bells, which I put in his ears, and ordered his canoe, which was also in the ship's boat, to be given back to him and sent him ashore. After that I set sail to go to the other large island which I saw to the west. I commanded that the other canoe, which the *Niña* was towing astern, should be set adrift also. Afterwards, on land, when the other, to whom I had given the things mentioned and from whom I had refused to take the ball of cotton, although he wished to give it to me, reached it, I saw that all the rest clustered round him and that he was dazzled and quite sure that we were good people and that the one who had run away had somehow wronged us and that accordingly we had carried him off. It was to create this impression that I had so acted with him, ordering him to be set free and giving him the presents, in order that we may be held in his esteem so that when Your Highnesses again send here, they may not be unfriendly. All that I gave to him was not worth four maravedis. So I departed at about ten o'clock, with a south-east wind that veered southerly, in order to pass over to the other island. It is very large and there all these men, whom I carry with me from the island of San Salvador, make signs that there is much gold and that they wear it as bracelets on their arms and on their legs, and in their ears and noses and around their necks. From this island of Santa Maria to the other was some nine leagues, from east to west, and all this side of the island runs from north-west to south-east. It seems that on this side the coast may extend for some twenty-eight leagues or more; the island is very flat, without any mountains, as are San Salvador and Santa Maria, and all the coasts are free from rocks, except that they all have some reefs near the land under water, on which account it is necessary to keep a sharp look out when it is proposed to anchor, and not to anchor very near the shore, although the waters are always very clear and the depth can be seen. At a distance of two lombard shots from land, the water off all these islands is so deep that it cannot be sounded. These islands are very green and fertile and the breezes are very soft, and it is possible that there are in them many things, of which I do not know, because I did not wish to delay in finding gold, by discovering and going about many islands. And since these men give these signs that they wear it on their arm and legs, and it is gold because I showed them some pieces of gold which I have, I cannot fail, with the aid of Our Lord, to find the place whence it comes. Being in the middle of the channel between these two islands, that of Santa Maria and this large island, to which I gave the name *Fernandina*,[6] I found a man alone in a canoe on his way from the island of Santa Maria to that of Fernandina. He was carrying with him a piece of their bread, about as large as the fist, and a gourd of water and a piece of brown earth, powdered and then kneaded, and some dried leaves, which must be a thing highly prized among them,

---

[6] Long Island.

since already at San Salvador they presented me with some of them. He also carried with him a basket of their make, in which he had a string of glass beads and two blancas, through which I knew that he came from the island of San Salvador and had crossed to that of Santa Maria and was on his way to Fernandina. He came alongside the ship. I made him come on board, as he asked to do so, and caused him to bring his canoe on board also and all that he had with him to be kept safe. I commanded that bread and honey should be given to him to eat, and something to drink, and thus I will carry him to Fernandina and will give him back all his belongings, in order to give him a good opinion of us, so that when, please God, Your Highnesses send here, those who come may receive honour and the Indians will give to us of all that they have."

"TUESDAY AND WEDNESDAY, OCTOBER 16th / I departed from the islands[7] of Santa Maria de Concepción when it was already about midday for that of Fernandina, which loomed very large to the westward, and I navigated all that day in a calm. I could not arrive in time to be able to see the bottom in order to anchor in a clear place, for it is necessary to exercise great care in this matter so as not to lose the anchors, and accordingly I stood off and on all that night until day when I came to a village, where I anchored and from which had come the man whom I had found the day before in that canoe in the middle of the channel. He had given so good a report of us that all that night there was no lack of canoes alongside the ship; they brought us water and what they had. I ordered something to be given to each of them, that is to say, some small beads, ten or a dozen of glass on a string, and some brass timbrels, of the kind which are worth a maravedi each in Castile, and some leather thongs; all these things they regarded as most excellent. When they came on board the ship, I also commanded molasses to be given to them to eat. And afterwards, at the hour of terce,[8] I sent the ship's boat ashore for water, and they with good will showed my people where the water was and themselves carried the full casks to the boat, and they were delighted to give us pleasure. This island is very

[7] I.e. modern Conception Island and Rum Cay.
[8] Nine o'clock in the morning.

large, and I am resolved to round it, because, as far as I can understand, there is in it or near it a gold mine. This island is distant from that of Santa Maria about eight leagues, almost from east to west, and this point, where I came, and all this coast runs north-north-west and south-south-east; I saw quite twenty leagues of it, but it did not end there. Now, as this is being written, I have set sail with a south wind in order to try to round the whole island and go on until I find Samoet, which is the island or city where there is gold, for so say all those who came on board the ship here, and so those from the island of San Salvador and from that of Santa Maria have told us. These people are like those of the said islands and have the same speech and manners, except that these here seem to me to be somewhat more domesticated and tractable, and more intelligent, because I see that they have brought here cotton to the ship and other trifles for which they know better how to bargain than the others did. And in this land also I saw cotton cloths made like mantillas, and the people are better disposed and the women wear in front of their bodies a small piece of cotton, which scarcely hides their secret parts. This island is very green and flat and very fertile, and I have no doubt that all the year they sow and reap Indian corn, and equally other things. I saw many trees very unlike ours, and many of them had many branches of different kinds, and all coming from one root; one branch is of one kind and one of another, and they are so unlike each other that it is the greatest wonder in the world. How great is the difference between one and another! For example: one branch has leaves like those of a cane and another leaves like those of a mastic tree, and thus, on a single tree, there are five or six different kinds all so diverse from each other. They are not grafted, for it might be said that it is the result of grafting; on the contrary, they are wild and these people do not cultivate them. No creed is known to them and I believe that they would be speedily converted to Christianity, for they have a very good understanding. There are here fish, so unlike ours that it is a marvel; there are some shaped like dories, of the finest colours in the world, blue, yellow, red and of all colours, and others painted in a thousand ways, and the colours are so fine that no man would not wonder at them or be anything but delighted to see them. There are also whales.

I saw no land animals of any kind, except parrots and lizards. A boy told me that he saw a large snake. I did not see any sheep or goats or other animals, but I have been here a very short while, as it is now midday. None the less, if there had been any I could not have failed to see one. I will describe the circuit of this island when I have rounded it."

"WEDNESDAY, OCTOBER 17th / I set out from the village at midday from my anchorage and from where I had taken water in order to round this island of Fernandina, and the wind was south-west and south. It was my wish to follow the coast of this island, from where I was to the south-east, because it all trended north-north-west and south-south-east, and I desired to take the route to the south-south-east, because in that direction, as all the Indians whom I have with me say and as another indicated, towards the south, lies the island which they call Samoet, where there is gold. And Martin Alonso Pinzón, captain of the caravel *Pinta*, in which I sent three of these Indians, came to me and told me that one of them had very definitely given him to understand that the island could be rounded more quickly in a north-north-westerly direction. I saw that the wind would not help me for the course which I wished to steer and that it was favourable for the other course, and I sailed north-north-west. And when I was about two leagues from the head of the island, I found a very wonderful harbour with a mouth, or rather it may be said with two mouths, since there is an islet in the middle, and both mouths are very narrow, and within it is more than wide enough for a hundred ships, if it be deep and clear and there be depth at the entrance. I thought it well to examine it closely and to take soundings, and so I anchored outside it, and went into it with all the ships' boats, and we saw that it was shallow. And as I thought, when I saw it, that it was the mouth of a river, I had ordered casks to be brought to take water, and on land I found some eight or ten men, who immediately came to us and showed us a village near there, where I sent the people for water, some of them with arms and some with casks, and so they took it. And as it was some distance away, I was kept there for the space of two hours. During this time I walked among the trees, and they were the loveliest sight that

I have yet seen; they seemed to be as green as those of Andalusia in the month of May, and all the trees are as different from ours as day is from night, and so is the fruit and the grasses and the stones and everything else. It is true that some trees were of the kind that are found in Castile, but yet there is a great difference, and there are many other kinds of trees which no one could say are like or can be compared with those of Castile. All these people are like those already mentioned. They are of the same type and as naked and of the same height, and they give what they have for whatever is given to them. And here I saw that some boys from the ships exchanged some little pieces of broken dishes and glass for their spears. The others, who went for the water, told me how they had been in their houses and that inside they were thoroughly swept and clean, and that their beds and coverings are like nets of cotton. They, that is the houses, are all like tents and very high and with good chimneys, but among the many villages which I have seen, I have not seen one of more than from twelve to fifteen houses. Here they found that married women wore cotton drawers, but girls did not, except some who were already eighteen years old. There are here mastiffs and small dogs, and here they found a man who had in his nose a piece of gold, which might have been half the size of a castellano,[9] on which they saw letters. I was angry with them because they had not bargained for it and given whatever might be asked, in order that it might be examined and seen what money it was, and they replied to me that they had not dared to bargain for it. After the water had been taken, I returned to the ship and set sail, navigating so far to the north-west that I discovered all that part of the island until the coast runs east and west. And afterwards all these Indians repeated that this island was smaller than the island of Samoet and that it would be well to turn back in order to arrive at it sooner. There the wind presently fell and then began to blow from the west-north-west, which was contrary for the course which we had been following. I therefore turned back and navigated all that night in an east-south-easterly direction, sometimes due east and sometimes southeast; this was done in order to keep clear from the land, because

[9] A gold coin worth 480 *maravedis.*

there were very thick clouds and the weather was very heavy. There was little wind and this prevented me from coming to land to anchor. Then this night it rained very heavily from after midnight until near daybreak, and it is still cloudy with a threat of rain. We are at the end of the island to the south-east, where I hope to anchor until the weather clears, so that I can see the other islands to which I propose to go. So it has rained, more or less, every day since I have been in these Indies. Your Highnesses may believe that this is the best and most fertile and temperate and level and good land that there is in the world."

"THURSDAY, OCTOBER 18th / When the weather had cleared, I sailed before the wind and continued the circuit of the island when I could do so, and anchored when it was not well to navigate. But I did not land, and at dawn I set sail."

"FRIDAY, OCTOBER 19th / At dawn I weighed anchor and sent the caravel *Pinta* to the east-south-east and the caravel *Niña* to the south-south-east, while I in the ship went to the south-east. I gave orders that they should follow these courses until midday, and that both should then change their course and rejoin me. And presently, before we had sailed for three hours, we saw an island to the east, towards which we steered, and all the three vessels reached it before midday, at its northern point, where there is an islet and a reef of rocks on its seaward side to the north and another between it and the main island. These men from San Salvador, whom I have with me, called this island 'Samoet,' and I named it *Isabella*.[10] There was a north wind, and the said islet lay on the course from the island of Fernandina, from which I had navigated from east to west. Afterwards the coast ran from that islet to the west and extends for twelve leagues to a cape, which I named *Cape Hermoso*.[11] It is on the west coast and it is indeed lovely, round and in deep water, with no shoals off it. At first the shore is stony and low, and further on there is a sandy beach which is characteristic of most of that coast, and there I anchored this night, Friday, until morning. All this coast, and the part of the island which I saw, is mainly

[10] Crooked Island.
[11] The southern tip of Fortune Island.

a beach; the island is the loveliest thing that I have seen, for, if the others are very lovely, this is more so. It has many trees, very green and tall, and this land is higher than the other islands which have been discovered. There is in it one elevation, which cannot be called a mountain, but which serves to beautify the rest of the island, and it seems that there is much water there in the centre of the island. On this north-eastern side, the coast curves sharply, and is very thickly wooded with very large trees. I wished to go to anchor there, in order to land and to see such beauty, but the water was of little depth and I could only anchor at a distance from the shore, and the wind was very favorable for reaching this point where I am now lying at anchor, and which I have named Cape Hermoso, because such it is. So I did not anchor within that curve and also because I saw this cape, so green and lovely, at a distance. All the other things and lands of these islands are so lovely that I do not know where to go first, and my eyes never weary of looking at such lovely verdure so different from that of our own land. I believe, moreover, that here there are many herbs and many trees which will be of great value in Spain for dyes and as medicinal spices, but I do not recognise them and this causes me much sorrow. When I arrived here at this cape, there came from the land the scent of flowers or trees, so delicious and sweet, that it was the most delightful thing in the world. In the morning, before I go from here, I will land to see what there is here at this point. There is no village, except further inland, where these men, whom I have with me, say that there is a king and that he wears much gold. Tomorrow I wish to go so far inland to find the village and to see or have speech with this king, who, according to the signs which these men make, rules all these neighbouring islands and is clothed and wears on his person much gold, although I do not put much trust in what they say, both because I do not understand them well and because they are so poor in gold that any small amount which this king may wear would seem to be much to them. This point here I call Cape Hermoso. I believe that it is an island separated from that of Samoet, and even that there is another small island between them. I make no attempt to examine so much in detail, since I could not do that in fifty years, because I wish to see and discover as much as I can, in order to return to Your Highnesses in April, if it please Our Lord. It is true that, if I arrive anywhere where there is gold or spices in quantity, I shall wait until I have collected as much as I am able. Accordingly I do nothing but go forward in the hope of finding these."

"SATURDAY, OCTOBER 20th / Today, at sunrise, I weighed anchor from the place where I was with the ship, anchored off the south-west point of this island of Samoet, to which point I gave the name *Cape de la Laguna*[12] and to the island that of Isabella, in order to steer to the north-east and east from the south-east and south. For there, as I understood from these men whom I have with me, was the village and its king. I found the water everywhere so shallow that I could not enter or navigate to that point, and I saw that, following the route to the south-west, it would be a very great detour. Therefore I determined to return by the way which I had come, to the north-north-east from the west, and to round this island in that direction, and the wind was so light that I was unable ever to proceed along the coast except in the night, and as it is dangerous to anchor off these islands except in daytime, when it is possible to see with the eye where to let go the anchor, since the bottom varies everywhere, some part being clean and some not, I proceeded to stand off under sail all this Sunday night. The caravels anchored, because they found themselves near land earlier, and they thought that from the signals which they were in the habit of making, I should come to anchor, but I did not wish to do so."

"SUNDAY, OCTOBER 21st / At ten o'clock I arrived here at this *Cape del Isleo*[13] and anchored, as did the caravels. After having eaten, I went ashore, and there was there no village but only a single house, in which I found no one, so that I believe that they had fled in terror, because in the house were all their household goods. I allowed nothing to be touched, but only went with these captains and people to examine the island. If the others, which have been already seen, are very lovely and green and fertile, this is much more so, and has large and very green trees.

[12] The southwest point of Crooked Island.
[13] The northwest point of Crooked Island.

There are here very extensive lagoons, and by them and around them there are wonderful woods, and here and in the whole island all is as green and the vegetation is as that of Andalusia in April. The singing of little birds is such that it seems that a man could never wish to leave this place; the flocks of parrots darken the sun, and there are large and small birds of so many different kinds and so unlike ours, that it is a marvel. There are, moreover, trees of a thousand types, all with their various fruits and all scented, so that it is a wonder. I am the saddest man in the world because I do not recognise them, for I am very sure that all are of some value, and I am bringing specimens of them and also of the herbs. As I was thus going round one of these lagoons, I saw a snake, which we killed, and I am bringing its skin to Your Highnesses. When it saw us, it threw itself into the lagoon and we went in after it, for the water was not very deep, until we killed it with our spears. It is seven palms in length;[14] I believe that there are many similar snakes here in these lagoons. Here I recognised the aloe, and tomorrow I am resolved to have ten quintals brought to the ship, since they tell me that it is very valuable. Further, going in search of very good water, we arrived at a village near here, half a league from where I am anchored. The inhabitants, when they saw us, all fled and left their houses and hid their clothing and whatever they had in the undergrowth. I did not allow anything to be taken, even the value of a pin. Afterwards, some of the men among them came towards us and one came quite close. I gave him some hawks' bells and some little glass beads, and he was well content and very joyful. And that this friendly feeling might grow stronger and to make some request of them, I asked him for water; and, after I had returned to the ship, they came presently to the beach with their gourds full, and were delighted to give it to us, and I commanded that another string of small glass beads should be given to them, and they said that they would come here tomorrow. I was anxious to fill all the ships' casks with water here; accordingly, if the weather permit, I shall presently set out to go round the island, until I have had speech with this king and have seen whether I can obtain from him the gold which I hear that

---

[14] *Palmo*, a span, about eight inches.

he wears. After that I wish to leave for another very large island, which I believe must be Cipangu, according to the signs which these Indians whom I have with me make; they call it 'Colba.' They say that there are ships and many very good sailors there. Beyond this island, there is another which they call "Bofio,' which they say is also very large.[15] The others, which lie between them, we shall see in passing, and according to whether I shall find a quantity of gold or spices, I shall decide what is to be done. But I am still determined to proceed to the mainland and to the city of Quisay[16] and to give the letters of Your Highnesses to the Grand Khan, and to request a reply and return with it." . . .

14. A new world

European reactions to Columbus' discoveries, and to the interpretation which he put upon them, ranged from excited optimism through skeptical questioning to flat disbelief. The discoverer's Procrustean handling of Ptolemy naturally aroused the suspicions of the learned; and except for a few gold trinkets, no evidence of Oriental wealth had been produced. Apart from gold, the commonest criterion for assessing the cultural standing of strange peoples was clothing. Civilized people wore woven fabrics, preferably silk; savages went about in skins or plaited grass or bunches of leaves. By this test, the Arawaks made an indifferent showing; they knew how to spin cotton and in some islands had some knowledge of weaving, which they employed in making hammocks; but for the most part they wore no clothes. Clearly they must be a primitive people; but did this necessarily prove Columbus wrong? Nicolò de' Conti had reported primitive peoples in some of the Asian islands. If the Caribs ate their neighbors, so—according to Conti—did the Bataks of Sumatra. Ptolemy, also, was not infallible; he had never been in Asia; wise and well-informed as he was, he too might be mistaken. What were officials, investors, and stay-at-home experts to believe? Peter Martyr, the shrewd contemporary chronicler of discovery,

[15] *Colba* is Cuba, *Bofío* Hispaniola.
[16] Quinsay, Marco Polo's name for the Great Khan's capital.

though he kept an open mind for some years, inclined to skepticism. He wrote in 1493 that Columbus had found islands and "indications of a hitherto unknown continent." The identification with Asia seemed to him "contradictory to the theories of the Ancients concerning the size of the globe." He found some support for Columbus, however, in Aristotle and Seneca, and admitted that the parrots which the expedition brought back recalled Pliny's descriptions of Indian birds.[1] Reports of the second voyage made him more skeptical: "When treating of this country one must speak of a new world, so distant is it and so devoid of civilization and religion."[2] Peter Martyr's skepticism, however, was not widely shared, in the early years, in Spain, where the general mood was one of confident hope. The Portuguese, as usual, kept their considered opinions to themselves. Publicly they seemed unmoved by Columbus' claim to have reached Asia; but they objected strongly to Spanish exploration in the tropical Atlantic, uncomfortably close to their Guinea preserve and athwart their own prospective route to India. As for Ferdinand and Isabella, they seem initially to have accepted Columbus' interpretation. In any event, reports of gold, pearls, and docile natives led them to seek papal approval of their activities, to negotiate with the Portuguese a demarcation of areas of Atlantic exploration, and to authorize further expeditions to explore and settle the West Indian Islands.

Columbus himself made three more voyages. In 1498 he sighted the northern coast of South America and discovered the mouths of the Orinoco, clearly a continental river. Two years later, the second Portuguese India fleet, commanded by Pedro Alvares Cabral, sighted the east coast of what is now Brazil, south of Cape São Roque. These and other reports revealed the presence of a landmass, possibly more than one landmass, of formidable size, lying partly within the area allocated to the Portuguese by the Treaty of Tordesillas. The nature of these lands, their relation to one another and to Asia, had still to be explained.

Amerigo Vespucci, who began the process of explanation, was a better educated person than most of the professional explorers. He was a businessman, a man of substance and indeed of some eminence in his native Florence. He first went to Spain in 1492 as a representative of the Medici, to supervise a number of marine supply contracts. His study of geography and navigation was a pastime, though one which, to judge from his letters, he pursued systematically and seriously. His residence in Seville gave him the opportunity to apply his theoretical

[1] *De orbe novo*, I, i.
[2] *Ibid.*, I, ii.

knowledge to practical ends, and in early middle age he left his business concerns to became an explorer.

Vespucci's voyages received a great deal of publicity in his own time and have been the subject of much controversy since.[3] The earliest printed accounts of them appeared in 1504, in the form of pamphlets purporting to be letters written by Vespucci. One, in Latin and addressed to Lorenzo di Pier Francesco de' Medici, under the title *Mundus Novus*, described a voyage along the west coast of the South Atlantic. Another, in a somewhat crude Italian and addressed to the Gonfaloniere Piero Soderini, described four voyages in the western regions. The pamphlets were an immediate success and went through many editions. The celebrated collection of voyages entitled *Paesi novamente retrovati*, published by Fracanzano da Montalboddo in 1507, included the *Mundus Novus*, and further attributed to Vespucci a spurious voyage to Calicut. In the same year, 1507, Martin Waldseemüller included a Latin version of the Soderini letter, under the title *Quattuor navigationes*, in his *Cosmographiae introductio*, published at St. Dié. In the introduction to this work, Waldseemüller suggested that Vespucci's name should be given to the continent whose coast he had explored. The suggestion caught the popular fancy, and the name America quickly became attached to the southern continent. Later in the century, largely through Mercator's use of it, it came to be extended to North America as well.

Mundus Novus and the *Four Voyages* are now generally, though not universally, considered by scholars to be forgeries, in the sense that they were not written by Vespucci. They were pirated accounts, partly based on genuine letters by Vespucci, partly invented. Manuscript letters more convincingly attributed to Vespucci (two of which are quoted here) were discovered in the Riccardiana in Florence in the eighteenth century. These letters, all of which are addressed to Vespucci's patron Lorenzo di Pier Francesco de' Medici, contradict the printed tracts in important particulars, and record only two voyages: the only two now generally accepted as authentic. The first was made in 1499 by Spanish ships, and at least part of the way in company with Alonso de Ojeda. It covered the coast from a point west of Cape São Roque, northwest and west to the Maracaibo Lagoon. On this voyage Vespucci made original and significant trials of a method of calculating longitude from the times of the conjunction of planets with the moon; a method too

---

[3] See G. Caraci: "Questioni e polemiche Vespucciane," *Memorie Geografiche*, vol. II (1955) and vol. III (1956).
———: "The Vespucian Problems—What Point Have They Reached?," *Imago Mundi*, XVIII (1964), 12–23.

cumbersome to be of much practical use, though it persisted in manuals of navigational theory until the late eighteenth century. In 1501 Vespucci embarked on a second voyage, under Portuguese auspices and with knowledge of Cabral's sighting of the coast of Brazil. Vespucci sailed from Lisbon to the Cape Verde Islands and thence across the Atlantic. He reached Cabral's coast in about 5°S., and followed it in a southwesterly direction for more than two thousand miles, beyond the Río de la Plata, to a point—perhaps San Julián—on the coast of Patagonia; which coast he rightly reckoned to be on the Spanish side of the Tordesillas demarcation line. Vespucci's two voyages, therefore, between them covered the greater part of the Atlantic coast of South America, revealed the continuity and immense size of that continent, and pointed the way which Solís and Magellan were later to take in seeking a western passage round it.

In the first of the two letters quoted—the letter from Seville in 1500—Vespucci apparently still accepted Columbus' theory that the coast he had explored was a remote and primitive part of Asia. He wrote in Ptolemaic terms of his hopes of rounding the "Cape of Catigara" and entering the "Great Gulf" which separated Cathay from the Golden Chersonese, Taprobana, and India *intra Gangem*. In the letter from Lisbon in 1502, describing his southern voyage, he made no mention of Ptolemy. At some time between the two dates he had reached his momentous conclusion: that the coast he was exploring belonged to a continent unconnected with Asia, unknown to the Ancients, and to Europeans wholly new.

The extracts which follow are from *Amerigo Vespucci, Pilot Major*, by Frederick J. Pohl (New York, Columbia University Press, 1944), pp. 76–89, Vespucci's letter from Seville, 1500; pp. 130–36, Vespucci's letter from Lisbon, 1502.

Vespucci's Letter from Seville, 1500

[To Lorenzo di Pier Francesco de' Medici]
Most Excellent and Dear Lord:

It is a long time since I wrote to your Excellency, solely for the reason that nothing had occurred worth remembering. My present writing will give you the news of my return from the Indies[1] a month ago by way of the ocean. By the grace of God I was brought safely to this city of Seville. I believe your Ex-

---

[1] In Vespucci's time the terms India, Indies, were used loosely to mean anywhere in or near Asia.

cellency will be pleased to hear of the success of the voyage and
of the most wonderful things which it was my lot to observe.
If I am somewhat long-winded, let my letter take the place of
fruit as a last course at table when you are in a mood for belching.

Your Excellency will please to note how with the permission of
his Highness the King of Spain, I set out with two caravels, on the
eighteenth of May, 1499, on a voyage of discovery across the
western ocean, and followed down the coast of Africa until I
reached the Fortunate Isles, which are now called the Canaries.
After I had laid in all necessary provisions, having made our
orisons and supplications, we raised sail at an island called Go-
mera, and pointed our prows to the southwest and sailed twenty-
four days with a stout breeze, without sighting land. At the end
of twenty-four days we raised land[2] and found that we had sailed
for about thirteen hundred leagues[3] to that land from the city of
Cadiz, by means of a southwest wind. Seeing the land, we gave
thanks to God, and put out our boats with about six men each,
and pulled toward the shore. We found the land heavily covered
with trees which were most amazing not only in height but in
their greenness, since they are never denuded of all their leaves.
They had a fragrant smell, being all aromatic, and gave forth
such tonic odors that we were greatly invigorated.

We followed the edge of the land in the small boats to see
whether we could discover a place to jump ashore. What a world
of shallows it was! We rowed hard all day until nightfall, but
were prevented from penetrating inland not only by the shallow-
ness but by the density of the forest through which we could
never find so much as a chimney opening. We decided, therefore,
to return to the ships, and attempt a landing in some other region.
We observed one remarkable fact in this part of the ocean. Always
when we approached within twenty-five leagues of the coast,[4]
we found the water fresh like that of a river and drank of it
and filled all our empty casks. Having rejoined the ships, we
raised anchor and set sail. We pointed our prows southward,
since it was my intention to see whether I could turn a headland
that Ptolemy calls the Cape of Catigara, which connects with

[2] The north coast of Brazil in about 4°N.
[3] If this means total distance sailed, via the Canaries, it is roughly correct.
[4] Perhaps a copyist's error for 15.

the Sinus Magnus. In my opinion we were not a great distance from it, according to computed longitude and latitude, as here-inafter stated.[5]

Sailing southward, we saw two most tremendous rivers issuing from the land, one coming from the west and flowing to the east, and having a width of four leagues, which is sixteen miles. The other flowed from south to north, and was three leagues, or twelve miles, wide.[6]

I believe these two rivers, by reason of their enormous size, create the fresh-water area in the ocean. Having observed shallows all the way down the coast, we decided to enter one of these rivers with the boats and to work along close to the bank to find either a place to jump ashore or an inhabited region. We put the boats into commission, and placed in them provisions for four days, and with twenty men well armed started upstream, and with two days of rowing worked in eighteen leagues. We attempted landing in many places, but found a thick swamp everywhere and the branches of the trees so thickly interlaced that a bird could scarcely fly through them. Thus following up the river, we saw positive signs that the hinterland was inhabited, but since the ships were in a dangerous position in case a storm had sprung up, we decided at the end of two days to return to the ships and take the will for the deed.

What we saw that was indeed a sight was an endless number of birds of ungainly shapes.[7] Some were a brilliant scarlet; others green spotted with lemon; others all green; still others black and flesh-colored. And the singing of other birds lodged among the trees was so soft and melodious that we often paused, wonder-struck at its sweetness. The trees were so beautiful and so fragrant that we thought we were in a terrestrial paradise. Not one of those trees or its fruit was like those in our part of the globe. In the river we saw a great profusion of fish of many species.

[5] Ptolemy placed "Catigara" in the extreme southeast of Asia, jutting into the Indian Ocean, and regarded it as part of a continuous continental land encircling that ocean; but Ptolemy had been proved mistaken about the Cape of Good Hope, and might similarly be mistaken about "Catigara."

[6] The Amazon and the Pará. The Amazon estuary is 150 miles wide at its mouth.

[7] Presumably toucans.

When we had regained the ships, we weighed anchor and set sail and continued to sail southward. In following this course, we stood out to sea on a leg of forty leagues. We encountered an ocean current which ran from southeast to northwest, and was so great and ran so furiously that we were terribly frightened and hastened away out of this great danger. The current was such that the waters of the Strait of Gibraltar and around the lighthouse of Messina were those of a pool by comparison. It was such that when it struck our bows we could not make any headway, even though we had a brisk fair wind. Perceiving the hazards in this floundering around, we decided to point our prows to the northwest and sail to northern parts.

As I know, if I remember correctly, that your Excellency understands something of cosmography, I have in mind to note how much we had to learn in order to navigate by means of longitude and latitude.

I certify that we sailed so far south that we entered the Torrid Zone and passed the Tropic of Cancer. You may have it as a positive fact that for several days while sailing in the Torrid Zone we saw four shadows of the sun, as the sun stood at zenith at midday. I explain it that the sun, being in our meridian, did not have any shadow, all of which I had occasion many times to demonstrate to the rest of the company, and I took as witness each one of the burly boys who do not know how the solar sphere moves through the circle of the zodiac. One time I saw the shadow to the south; at another time to the north; at another to the west; and at another to the east; and sometimes for one or two hours of the day we had no shadow at all. We sailed so far south in the Torrid Zone that we found ourselves standing under the equinoctial line and had both poles at the edge of our horizon. Having gone six degrees beyond the equator, we lost the north star altogether. The stars of Ursa Minor, or better to say, the Guards, which revolve about the pole were scarcely visible.[8]

Very desirous of being the author who should identify the

---

[8] In 1499 Polaris was about 3½ degrees from the true pole. At Vespucci's furthest south on this voyage, in late July, it would be invisible; Kochab, the brighter of the Guards, would be 10 degrees above the horizon at 7:00 p.m. and would have set before midnight.

polar star of the other hemisphere, I lost many a night's sleep in contemplation of the motion of the stars around the South Pole, in order to record which of them had the least motion and which was nearest to the pole. I was unable to succeed because of the many bad nights I had and with such instruments as I used, namely, the quadrant and the astrolabe, and other means of measuring the swing of the stars. I did not observe any star which had less than ten degrees of motion around the pole. While I was at this work, I recalled a passage of the poet Dante which occurs in the first chapter of the "Purgatorio," in which he invents a fiction of a flight into the heavens in our celestial hemisphere and his finding himself in the other hemisphere. Endeavoring to describe the Antarctic Pole, he says:

> I turned to the right hand, and gave heed
> To the other pole, and saw four stars
> Never seen save by our first parents.
> The heavens appeared to rejoice in their rays.
> O widowed northern region,
> Since thou art deprived of beholding these!

It seems to me that the poet in these verses wishes to describe by the "four stars" the pole of the other firmament, and I have no reason to doubt that what he says may be true; because I observed four stars in the figure of a cithern, which had little motion. If God grants me life and health, I hope to return at once to that hemisphere and not come back without identifying the pole. In conclusion I state that our voyage extended so far south that our distance in latitude from the city of Cadiz was sixty and one-half degrees,[9] because at the city of Cadiz the pole is elevated thirty-five and one-half degrees, and we found ourselves six degrees beyond the equator.[10]

This will suffice as to latitude. You will observe that this navigation was during the months of July and August and September, when the sun is more continuously above the horizon in our hemisphere, and describes the greater arc by day and the

[9] Obviously a copyist's error.

[10] In fact less than 3°S. Refraction, and inability to determine the true South Pole, could easily cause this error.

lesser by night. While we were at the equator or within four or six degrees of it, in July and August, the difference in length between day and night was not perceptible. Day and night were about equal, or differed very slightly, if at all.

As to longitude, I declare that I found so much difficulty in determining it that I was put to great pains to ascertain the east-west distance I had covered. The final result of my labors was that I found nothing better to do than to watch for and take observations at night of the conjunction of one planet with another, and especially of the conjunction of the moon with the other planets, because the moon is swifter in her course than any other planet. I compared my observations with the almanac of Giovanni da Montereggio, which was composed for the meridian of the city of Ferrara, correcting with calculations from the tables of King Alfonso.[11]

After I had made experiments many nights, one night, the twenty-third of August, 1499, there was a conjunction of the moon with Mars, which according to the almanac was to occur at midnight or a half hour before. I found that when the moon rose an hour and a half after sunset, the planet had passed that position in the east. That is to say that the moon was about one degree and some minutes farther east than Mars, and at midnight her position was five and a half degrees to the east, a little more or less.

By such means was made the proportion: if twenty-four hours equal three hundred and sixty degrees, what do five and a half hours equal? I found that I had come eighty-two and a half degrees. So much I computed to be the longitude from the meridian of the city of Cadiz. Giving to each degree sixteen and two-thirds leagues, I found my longitudinal distance from the city of Cadiz to be thirteen hundred and sixty-six and two-thirds leagues, which are fifty-four hundred and sixty-six and two-thirds miles. The reason why I give sixteen and two-thirds leagues to each degree is that according to Ptolemy and Alfragano the circum-

---

[11] The *Ephemerides* of Regiomontanus was first published in 1474, at Nürnberg, and was several times reprinted in the fifteenth century. It covered the years 1475–1506. The *Alfonsine Tables* were much older; they had been prepared in the thirteenth century, though they were not printed until 1483. For longitudes in western Europe the differences are slight.

ference of the earth is twenty-four thousand miles, or six thousand leagues, which being divided by three hundred and sixty comes to sixteen and two-thirds leagues for each degree. This reasoning I confirmed many times by checking with pilots their locations on charts, and I found it true and valid.[12]

It appears to me, most excellent Lorenzo, that by this voyage of mine the opinion of the majority of the philosophers is confuted, who assert that no one can live in the Torrid Zone because of the great heat, for in this voyage I found it to be the contrary.[13] The air is fresher and more temperate in this region, and so many people are living in it that their numbers are greater than those who live outside of it. Rationally, let it be said in a whisper, experience is certainly worth more than theory.

Up to this point I have told how far I sailed toward the south and toward the west. Now it remains for me to inform you of the character of the land and the nature of the inhabitants, of their customs, of the animals we saw, and of many other things most worthy of remembrance which fell under my observation. Let me say that after we turned our course toward the north, the first land that we found to be inhabited was an island[14] ten degrees from the equator. When we came up with it we saw a great multitude along the shore who stood staring at the wonderful sight. We rode at anchor about a mile from the land and manned the boats and went ashore with twenty-two men well armed. When the people saw us leaping ashore and discerned that we were of a different nature—because they have no beard or clothing, the men, like the women, appearing just as they issued from the wombs of their mothers, without covering any shame, and because of the difference of color, they being grayish and brownish yellow and we white—they had fear of us and betook themselves to the woods. With great difficulty, by means

---

[12] A confused calculation. Ptolemy estimated the circumference of the earth to be 22,500 Roman miles. The Roman mile was about 1,620 English yards, or 0.92 of an English mile. The common sea league was 3.84 Roman miles. Vespucci confused Alfragano with Albufeda; it was Albufeda who gave 66⅔ Roman miles to a degree.

[13] The opinion to which Vespucci refers persisted widely, despite the discoveries of the Portuguese; indeed, Portuguese mortality in Lower Guinea might have been held to confirm it.

[14] Trinidad.

of signs, we reassured them and negotiated with them. We discovered that they were of the breed called cannibals and that the majority of them lived on human flesh. Your Excellency may hold this for certain, that they do not eat one another among themselves, but they sail in certain vessels which they call "canoes," and with these canoes they drag their prey from the islands or mainland, from tribes which are their enemies or are not allied with them. They do not eat any women, except those they possess as slaves. And these things we verified in many places where we found such people, because we often saw the bones and skulls of some that they had devoured, and they did not deny it; the more they boasted of it, the more their enemies stood in fear of them. They are people of affable comprehension and of beautiful physique. They go entirely naked. The weapons they carry are bows and arrows and small shields. They are religious people of great courage, and very excellent bowmen. In conclusion, we had dealings with them, and they conducted us to one of their villages that lay two leagues inland. They gave us breakfast and everything we asked of them, but they gave more through fear than affection. And after we had stopped with them all one day, we returned to the ships, remaining friendly with them.

We sailed along the coast of this island and saw the inhabitants of other large villages along the seashore. We landed in a skiff and found them waiting for us, all loaded with provisions, and they gave us the wherewithal for a very good breakfast of their native dishes. Seeing they were such kind people, who treated us so well, we did not resort to seizure of anything of theirs.

We made sail and put into a gulf which is called the Gulf of Parias.[15] We rode at anchor at the mouth of a very large river, which causes the water of this gulf to be fresh. We saw a large village close to the sea, where there were so many people that we were astonished. All were unarmed. In token of peace, we went ashore in the boats, and they received us with great display of affection. They conducted us to their houses, where they had very good preparations for a collation. There they gave us three rations of wine to drink, made not of grapes but of fruit, like oldfashioned beer, and it was extremely good. There we ate

[15] The Gulf of Paria had been entered and named by Columbus in 1498.

many fresh prunelike fruits, a very peculiar sort of fruit. They gave us many other fruits all different from ours and very good to taste, and all having aromatic flavor and odor. They gave us some small pearls and eleven large ones, and they told us by signs that if we would wait several days they would go fishing and bring us many of them. Not caring to delay, we departed with many parrots of various colors and with good friendly feeling. From these people we understood that those of the island above-mentioned were cannibals and ate human flesh.

We emerged from this gulf and followed along the coast. We saw continually great numbers of people, and when they were so inclined we bargained with them, and they gave us what they had and everything we demanded of them. They all go naked as they were born, without having any shame. If all were to be related of how little modesty they have, it would be entering upon obscenity. It is better to keep silence.

After we had sailed about four hundred leagues continually along one coast, we concluded that this was mainland; that the said mainland is at the extreme limits of Asia to the eastward and at its beginning to the westward. For it often happened that we saw various animals, such as lions, red deer, wild boars, rabbits, and other land animals which are not found in islands, but only on the mainland. Going inland one day with twenty men, we saw a serpent [an anaconda]. In truth, that serpent's length was eight extended arm lengths, and its thickness as large as I am in the waist. We were very much frightened by it, and the sight of it caused us to return to the sea. Many times we happened to see most ferocious animals and huge serpents. Sailing along the coast, we discovered each day an endless number of people with various languages.

When we had sailed four hundred leagues along the coast, we commenced to find people who did not desire our friendship,[16] but stood waiting for us with their weapons, which they held in readiness, and when we approached the shore in the boats, they resisted our landing, so that we were forced to combat with them. At the end of the fight they broke from us with loss. Since they were naked, we made a great slaughter of them. It

---

[16] They had passed from an Arawak area into one inhabited by more independent and warlike Caribs.

often happened that sixteen of us fought with two thousand of them, and at the end we routed them and massacred many of them, and pillaged their houses.

Thereafter we resumed our navigation. . . . [On an island[17] off the coast] we discovered a very large population, who dwelt in houses having foundations that had been built in the water, like Venice, with much ingenuity. Marveling at them, we approved of the idea of going and looking into them. Since the inhabitants were in their houses and determined to prevent our entering any of them, they were given proof that the sword cuts; they then found it advantageous to let us in. We discovered that they kept their houses full of the finest cotton, and all the beams of their habitations were of dyewood. We took away a great deal of cotton and dyewood and returned to the ships. You must know that wherever we landed we found much cotton, and the plains were filled with cotton trees, so that all the ships throughout the world could be loaded in those regions with cotton and dyewood.

Finally we sailed another three hundred leagues along the coast, continuously finding valiant people and very often battling with them. We seized twenty of them, who were using among them seven languages, not one of which was understood by those who used the others. It is said that in the whole world there are not more than seventy-seven languages, but I declare that there are more than a thousand. I alone have heard more than forty.

After having sailed along this coast seven hundred leagues or more, without counting the great number of islands we had explored, we judged the ships to be unseaworthy, because they leaked endlessly and we could hardly reduce the water with two pumps going constantly. The men were worn down with fatigue and hardship, and the provisions were growing short. Since we found ourselves, according to the reckoning of the pilots, opposite and within one hundred and twenty leagues of an island which they call Española, discovered by the Admiral Columbus six years before, we determined to proceed to it; and, since it is inhabited by Christians, to repair our ships there and to rest the men and refit the stays; because from this island to Castile are thirteen

[17] Aruba.

hundred leagues of open water without any land. In seven days we reached this island.

We remained there about two months. We trained the ships and procured provisions. We agreed together to go in a northern direction, where we discovered more than a thousand islands[18] and found many naked inhabitants. They were all timid people of small intellect; we did what we liked with them. This last region that we discovered was very perilous to our navigation because of the reefs and shoals which we found in it. We often ran the risk of being lost. We sailed in this sea for two hundred leagues towards the northward.

Since the men were worn out from having been nearly a year at sea and were rationed down to six ounces of bread a day to eat and three small measures of water to drink, and the ships were becoming dangerously unseaworthy, the crew cried out that they wished to return to Castile to their homes and that they no longer desired to tempt fortune. Therefore we agreed to seize shiploads of the inhabitants as slaves and to load the ships with them and turn toward Spain. We went to certain islands and took by force two hundred and thirty-two persons, and then set our course for Castile.

In sixty-seven days we crossed the ocean and arrived at the islands of the Azores, which belong to the king of Portugal and are three hundred leagues from Cadiz. Here, having provided ourselves with refreshments for the passage to Castile, we encountered contrary winds and were compelled to go to the Canary Islands, and from the Canaries to the island of Madeira, and from Madeira to Cadiz.

We had been thirteen months on this voyage, having run into most awful dangers and discovered a very large country of Asia, and of islands a great plenty and for the most part inhabited. I have many times made calculations with the compass, which show that we sailed about five thousand leagues; that is, twenty thousand miles. In conclusion, we crossed the equator and went six and a half degrees to the south of it, and later returned by way of the north, going so far that the north star was at an elevation of thirty-five and a half degrees above our horizon; we sailed

18 The Bahamas.

eighty-four degrees in meridian distance from the city and harbor of Cadiz. We discovered a vast country and beheld an immense number of people, all naked and speaking various languages. Inland we saw many wild animals and various species of birds and an unlimited wealth of trees, all aromatic. We brought away pearls and virgin gold; we brought two stones—one the color of emerald, the other of amethyst, very hard, half a span in length, and three fingers thick. Their Majesties esteem them highly; the sovereigns have set them among their jewels. We brought a large piece of crystal which some jewelers say is beryl, and according to what the Indians told us they had a great abundance of it. We brought fourteen flesh-colored pearls that greatly pleased the queen; and for ourselves many other stones that seemed beautiful to us. We did not bring all these things in quantity, because we did not stay long in any one place, but were sailing continuously. When we arrived at Cadiz, we shared our slaves. We found that we had two hundred of them alive, the others that made up the total of two hundred and thirty-two having died at sea. Having sold them all, the profit that we had above the cost of the ships was five hundred ducats, which had to be divided into fifty-five shares, so that each of us received little. However, we contented ourselves with having arrived in safety with our lives, and we rendered thanks to God that on the whole voyage, of the fifty-seven Christian men whom we had, none died save two, whom the Indians killed. . . .

Vespucci's Letter from Lisbon, 1502

[To Lorenzo di Pier Francesco de' Medici]
Your Excellency, My Patron Lorenzo,

after due salutations, etc.

The last letter written to Your Excellency was from the coast of Guinea from a place which is called Cape Verde. In it you learned of the beginning of my voyage. By this present letter you will be informed in brief of the middle and end of my voyage and of what has happened up to now.

We departed from the above-mentioned Cape Verde very easily, having taken in everything necessary, such as water and wood and other requirements essential for putting to sea across the ocean wastes in search of new land. We sailed on the wind within half a point of southwest, so that in sixty-four days we arrived at a new land[19] which, for many reasons that are enumerated in what follows, we observed to be a continent. We ran the course of that land for about eight hundred leagues, always in the direction of southwest one-quarter west.

We found the land thickly inhabited. I noted there the wonders of God and of nature, of which I determined to inform Your Excellency, as I have done of my other voyages.

We coursed so far in those seas that we entered the Torrid Zone and passed south of the equinoctial line and the Tropic of Capricorn, until the South Pole stood above my horizon at fifty degrees, which was my latitude from the equator. We navigated in the Southern Hemisphere for nine months and twenty-seven days, never seeing the Arctic Pole or even Ursa Major and Minor; but opposite them many very bright and beautiful constellations were disclosed to me which always remain invisible in this Northern Hemisphere. There I noted the wonderful order of their motions and their magnitudes, measuring the diameters of their circuits and mapping out their relative positions with geometrical figures. I noted other great motions of the heavens, which would be a tedious matter to write about.

But the most notable of all the things which occurred to me in this voyage I collocated in a small work, to the end that when I reside at leisure I may apply myself to it, to win renown after my death. I was intending to send you an epitome, but His Serene Highness retains my work. When he returns it to me I will send a summary.[20]

To conclude, I was on the side of the antipodes; my navigation extended through one-quarter of the world; my zenith direction there made a right angle, at the center of the earth, with the zenith direction of the inhabitants of this Northern Hemisphere in the latitude of forty degrees. This must suffice.

Let us describe the country and the inhabitants and the animals and the plants and the other things I found in their habitations which are of general usefulness to human living.

This land is very pleasing, full of an infinite number of very tall trees which never lose their leaves and throughout the year

[19] The coast of Brazil at Cape São Roque, in 5° 26′ S.
[20] Neither work nor summary has survived.

are fragrant with the sweetest aromas and yield an endless supply of fruits, many of which are good to taste and conducive to bodily health. The fields produce many herbs and flowers and most delicious and wholesome roots. Sometimes I was so wonder-struck by the fragrant smells of the herbs and flowers and the savor of the fruits and the roots that I fancied myself near the Terrestrial Paradise. What shall we say of the multitude of birds and their plumes and colors and singing and their numbers and their beauty? I am unwilling to enlarge upon this description, because I doubt if I would be believed.

What should I tell of the multitude of wild animals, the abundance of pumas, of panthers, of wild cats, not like those of Spain, but of the antipodes; of so many wolves, red deer, monkeys, and felines, marmosets of many kinds, and many large snakes? We saw so many other animals that I believe so many species could not have entered Noah's ark. We saw many wild hogs, wild goats, stags and does, hares, and rabbits, but of domestic animals, not one.

Let us come to rational animals. We found the whole land inhabited by people entirely naked, the men like the women without any covering of their shame. Their bodies are very agile and well proportioned, of light color, with long hair, and little or no beard. I strove a great deal to understand their conduct and customs. For twenty-seven days I ate and slept among them, and what I learned about them is as follows.

Having no laws and no religious faith, they live according to nature. They understand nothing of the immortality of the soul. There is no possession of private property among them, for everything is in common. They have no boundaries of kingdom or province. They have no king, nor do they obey anyone. Each one is his own master. There is no administration of justice, which is unnecessary to them, because in their code no one rules. They live in communal dwellings, built in the fashion of very large cabins. For people who have no iron or indeed any metal, one can call their cabins truly miraculous houses. For I have seen habitations which are two hundred and twenty paces long and thirty wide, ingeniously fabricated; and in one of these houses dwelt five or six hundred persons. They sleep in nets woven out of cotton, going to bed in mid-air with no other coverture.

They eat squatting upon the ground. Their food is very good: an endless quantity of fish; a great abundance of sour cherries, shrimps, oysters, lobsters, crabs, and many other products of the sea. The meat which they eat most usually is what one may call human flesh a la mode. When they can get it, they eat other meat, of animals or birds, but they do not lay hold of many, for they have no dogs, and the country is a very thick jungle full of ferocious wild beasts. For this reason they are not wont to penetrate the jungle except in large parties.

The men have a custom of piercing their lips and cheeks and setting in their perforations ornaments of bone or stone; and do not suppose them small ones. Most of them have at least three holes, and some seven, and some nine, in which they set ornaments of green and white alabaster, half a palm in length and as thick as a Catalonian plum. This pagan custom is beyond description. They say they do this to make themselves look more fierce. In short, it is a brutal business.

Their marriages are not with one woman only, but they mate with whom they desire and without much ceremony. I know a man who had ten women. He was jealous of them, and if it happened that one of them was guilty, he punished her and sent her away. They are a very procreative people. They do not have heirs, because they do not have private property. When their children, that is, the females, are of age to procreate, the first who seduces one has to act as her father in place of the nearest relative. After they are thus violated, they marry.

Their women do not make any ceremony over childbirth, as do ours, but they eat all kinds of food, and wash themselves up to the very time of delivery, and scarcely feel any pain in parturition.

They are a people of great longevity, for according to their way of attributing issue, they had known many men who had four generations of descendants. They do not know how to compute time in days, months, and years, but reckon time by lunar months. When they wished to demonstrate something involving time, they did it by placing pebbles, one for each lunar month. I found a man of advanced age who indicated to me with pebbles that he had seen seventeen hundred lunar months, which I judged to be a hundred and thirty-two years, counting thirteen moons to the year.

They are also a warlike people and very cruel to their own kind. All their weapons and the blows they strike are, as Petrarch says, "committed to the wind," for they use bows and arrows, darts, and stones. They use no shields for the body, but go into battle naked. They have no discipline in the conduct of their wars, except that they do what their old men advise. When they fight, they slaughter mercilessly. Those who remain on the field bury all the dead of their own side, but cut up and eat the bodies of their enemies. Those whom they seize as prisoners, they take for slaves to their habitations. If women sleep with a male prisoner and he is virile, they marry him with their daughters. At certain times, when a diabolical frenzy comes over them, they invite their kindred and the whole tribe, and they set before them a mother with all the children she has, and with certain ceremonies they kill them with arrow shots and eat them. They do the same thing to the above-mentioned slaves and to the children born of them. This is assuredly so, for we found in their houses human flesh hung up to smoke, and much of it. We purchased from them ten creatures, male as well as female, which they were deliberating upon for the sacrifice, or better to say, the crime. Much as we reproved them, I do not know that they amended themselves. That which made me the more astonished at their wars and cruelty was that I could not understand from them why they made war upon each other, considering that they held no private property or sovereignty of empire and kingdoms and did not know any such thing as lust for possession, that is, pillaging or a desire to rule, which appear to me to be the causes of war and of every disorderly act. When we requested them to state the cause, they did not know how to give any other cause than that this curse upon them began in ancient times and they sought to avenge the deaths of their forefathers. In short, it is a brutal business. Indeed, one man among them confessed to me that he had shared in the eating of the flesh of more than two hundred corpses, and this I assuredly believe. It was enough for me!

As to the nature of the land, I declare it to be the most agreeable, temperate, and healthful, for in all the time that we were in it, which was ten months, none of us died and only a few fell ill. As I have already said, the inhabitants live a long time and do not suffer from infirmity or pestilence or from any unhealthy atmosphere. Death is from natural causes or from the hand of man. In conclusion, physicians would have a wretched standing in such a place.

Because we went solely to make discoveries, and departed from Lisbon with a commission to that effect, and not to seek for any profit, we did not trouble ourselves to search the land or look for any gain. Thus we did not perceive in it anything that would be profitable to anyone; not because I do not believe that the land might not produce every kind of wealth, from its wonderful nature and from the climate of the region in which it is situated. It is not surprising that we did not at once become sensible of everything there that might make for profit, since the inhabitants value neither gold nor silver nor precious stones—nothing but feathers and the previously mentioned ornaments made of bone. I hope that this Serene King will send an expedition now to inspect it and that before many years pass it will bring to this kingdom of Portugal a handsome profit and a yearly income.

We found an endless growth of very good dyewood, enough to load all the ships that nowadays sail the seas, and free from cost. The same is true of the cassia fistula.

We saw crystals and a great variety of savory and fragrant spices and drugs, but their properties are not known. The natives told us of gold and other metals and many miracle-working drugs, but I am one of those followers of Saint Thomas, who are slow to believe. Time will reveal everything.

The sky was clear there most of the time, and aglow with many bright stars, and I made notes on all of these, with their circuits. This is only a brief outline and a mere list of the things I saw in that country. Many things have been omitted, in order not to be wearisome and because you will find them in complete detail in my account of the voyage.

As yet I am remaining here at Lisbon awaiting that which the king may determine for me. Please God that what follows hereafter for me may be to promote His holy service and the salvation of my soul!

15. The first sight of Mexico

Once the continental character of "America"—that is, of South America —had been accepted, the westward search for the "Spicery" became a problem not of threading between the islands of an archipelago, but of finding a seaway round or through a landmass of unknown dimensions. The most obvious direction for the search was that of Vespucci's 1499 voyage, along the north coast. Columbus himself believed, from observation of ocean currents, that a passage of open water would be found in the western Caribbean. The Spicery, however, was not the only object of discovery. About the turn of the century a series of voyages to the Caribbean, mostly commanded by old companions of Columbus—Alonso de Ojeda, Peralonso Niño, Vicente Yáñez Pinzón— revealed that America itself had rewards to offer; modest fortunes could be made without a hazardous passage through a problematical strait.

In the first fifteen years of the sixteenth century the greater Antillean islands were settled by Spaniards, and the mainland coasts of the southern and western Caribbean were explored and also, in places, settled. No strait was found, nor any sign of the proximity of Asia. The coast trended north; promising openings—the Gulf of Urabá, the Gulf of Honduras—proved to be dead ends. Those who found them were not discouraged; they were interested less in discovery than in slaving, pearling, and gold prospecting. Even Juan de la Cosa, the eminent navigator and former companion of Columbus, turned his attention from cartography to slaving, and died in 1509 by a poisoned arrow, in a raid on the coast of what is now Colombia. The whole story was one of raiding and random prospecting rather than of systematic exploration. The Spanish colonies established in this period were undisciplined, feckless, and destructive. They caused a rapid and careless depletion of natural resources, appalling human suffering, the progressive destruction of primitive peoples, the extinction of an entire way of life. Depopulation in the islands, and consequent shortage of labor, were prominent among the factors which drove settlers on to conquest and settlement on the Central American mainland.

The first important Spanish settlement on the mainland was in Darien, an area which yielded enough gold to earn the name Castilla del Oro. Of the leaders of the enterprise, Vasco Núñez de Balboa was the ablest—indeed the only one who looked beyond immediate plunder, who showed any serious interest either in wider discovery or in planned permanent settlement. Balboa is chiefly remembered for his sighting of the Pacific in 1513; but he was also the first of the great *conquistadores* of the American mainland. His report of the South Sea created a fresh wave of speculation about the sea route to the Spicery, in discovery-minded circles in Europe; his achievements as an organizer of settlement stimulated, among adventurers in the West Indies, the search for conquest, trade, and tribute.

In 1517 and 1518 small Spanish expeditions from Cuba explored the north and west coasts of Yucatán. If they hoped to reach Balboa's South Sea, it does not appear in the records; they were looking chiefly for another, and richer, Golden Castile. Slaving, trading, and prospecting parties in the Gulf of Honduras had already heard reports from inland of a city-building people, the Maya, far richer, more skilful, and better organized than any hitherto encountered. The Yucatán Channel led the explorers into the Gulf of Mexico, where they found still more compelling evidence. It appeared that some of the settled people on the southern coast were outlying tributaries of a powerful and extensive native empire, governed from a great city lying beyond the coastal mountains, far inland. In 1519 a third and larger force from Cuba, commanded by Hernán Cortés, established itself on the coast near what is now Vera Cruz, and after some months of inquiry and reconnaissance, marched inland to find the capital city of Tenochtitlán-Mexico and to make contact with Montezuma, its reported king.

The story of Caribbean discovery is poorly reported, in the sense that few eyewitness narratives survive. Our knowledge of it is derived chiefly from the *Decades* of Peter Martyr (who never went to America) and from the *Histories* of Las Casas and Oviedo. Both Oviedo and Las Casas knew the West Indies well and described them accurately, but they were not discoverers. They arrived, one as an official, the other as a settler, in places already known and in process of settlement. The conquest of Mexico, by contrast, is very well recorded. Cortés wrote long and detailed despatches to the emperor. After his retirement in Spain, his secretary, Francisco López de Gómara, wrote a *History* based on information derived from Cortés. This excellent, though admittedly second hand narrative, provoked a counterblast, the *True History* of Bernal Díaz del Castillo. Díaz had sailed with Grijalva in 1518, had served as a foot-soldier with Cortés, and had settled in America. He wrote in old age, long after the event, but with a freshness of recollection apparently undimmed by time. The famous passage quoted here describes his first impressions of Tenochtitlán and its satellite lakeside cities, and of the first encounter with Montezuma.

The manuscript of the *True History* is preserved in Guatemala City. It has been published many times, in Spanish and in translation into other European languages. The extract which follows is from *The True History of the Conquest of New Spain*, by Bernal Díaz del Castillo, translated and edited by Alfred Percival Maudslay, (5 vols., London, Hakluyt Society, 1890) Cap. LXXXVIII (vol. II, 37–41).

THE next day, in the morning, we arrived at a broad causeway, and continued our march towards Iztapalapa, and when we saw so many cities and villages built in the water and other great towns on dry land and that straight and level causeway going towards Mexico, we were amazed and said that it was like the enchantments they tell of in the legend of Amadis, on account of the great towers and cues and buildings rising from the water, and all built of masonry. And some of our soldiers even asked whether the things that we saw were not a dream? It is not to be wondered at that I here write it down in this manner, for there is so much to think over that I do not know how to describe it, seeing things as we did that had never been heard of or seen before, not even dreamed about.

Thus, we arrived near Iztapalapa, to behold the splendour of the other caciques who came out to meet us, who were the Lord of the town named Cuitlahuac, and the Lord of Culuacan, both of them near relations of Montezuma. And then when we entered that city of Iztapalapa, the appearance of the palaces in which they lodged us! How spacious and well built they were, of beautiful stone work and cedar wood, and the wood of other sweet scented trees, with great rooms and courts, wonderful to behold, covered with awnings of cotton cloth.

When we had looked well at all of this, we went to the orchard and garden, which was such a wonderful thing to see and walk in, that I was never tired of looking at the diversity of the trees, and noting the scent which each one had, and the paths full of roses and flowers, and the many fruit trees and native roses, and the pond of fresh water. There was another thing to observe, that great canoes were able to pass into the garden from the lake through an opening that had been made so that there was no need for their occupants to land. And all was cemented and very splendid with many kinds of stone [monuments] with pictures on them, which gave much to think about. Then the birds of many kinds and breeds which came into the pond. I say again that I stood looking at it and thought that never in the world would there be discovered other lands such as these, for at that time there was no Peru, nor any thought of it. [Of all these wonders that I then beheld] today all is overthrown and lost, nothing left standing.

Let us go on, and I will relate that the caciques of that town and of Coyoacan brought us a present of gold, worth more than two thousand dollars, and Cortés gave them hearty thanks for it, and showed them much affection, and he told them through our interpreters things concerning our holy faith, and explained to them the great power of our Lord, the Emperor, and as there was much other conversation. I will not repeat it.

I must state that at that time this was a very large town, half of the houses being on land and the other half in the water, and now at this time it is all dry land and they plant corn where it was formerly lake, and it is so changed in other ways that if one had not then seen it, one would say that it is impossible that what are now fields planted with maize, could at one time have been covered with water.

.   .   .

Early next day we left Iztapalapa with a large escort of those great caciques whom I have already mentioned. We proceeded along the causeway which is here eight paces in width and runs so straight to the City of Mexico that it does not seem to me to turn either much or little, but, broad as it is, it was so crowded with people that there was hardly room for them all, some of them going to and others returning from Mexico, besides those who had come out to see us, so that we were hardly able to pass by the crowds of them that came; and the towers and cues[1] were full of people as well as the canoes from all parts of the

_____

[1] Temple-pyramids.

lake. It was not to be wondered at, for they had never before seen horses or men such as we are.

Gazing on such wonderful sights, we did not know what to say, or whether what appeared before us was real, for on one side, on the land, there were great cities, and in the lake ever so many more, and the lake itself was crowded with canoes, and in the causeway were many bridges at intervals, and in front of us stood the great City of Mexico, and we,—we did not even number four hundred soldiers! and we well remembered the words and warnings given us by the people of Huexotzingo and Tlaxcala and Tlamanalco, and the many other warnings that had been given that we should beware of entering Mexico, where they would kill us, as soon as they had us inside.

Let the curious readers consider whether there is not much to ponder in this that I am writing. What men have there been in the world who have shown such daring? But let us get on, and march along the causeway. When we arrived where another small causeway branches off (leading to Coyoacan, which is another city) where there were some buildings, like towers, which are their oratories, many more chieftains and caciques approached clad in very rich mantles, the brilliant liveries of one chieftain differing from those of another, and the causeways were crowded with them. The Great Montezuma had sent these great caciques in advance to receive us, and when they came before Cortés they bade us welcome in their language, and as a sign of peace, they touched their hands against the ground, and kissed the ground with the hand.

There we halted for a good while, and Cacamatzin, the Lord of Texcoco, and the Lord of Iztapalapa and the Lord of Tacuba and the Lord of Coyoacan went on in advance to meet the Great Montezuma, who was approaching in a rich litter accompanied by other great lords and caciques, who owned vassals. When we arrived near to Mexico, where there were some other small towers, the Great Montezuma got down from his litter, and those great caciques supported him with their arms beneath a marvellously rich canopy of green coloured feathers with much gold and silver embroidery and with pearls and chalchihuites suspended from a sort of bordering, which was wonderful to look at. The Great Montezuma was richly attired according to his usage, and he was shod with sandals [*cotoras*], for so they call what they wear on their feet, the soles were of gold and the upper part adorned with precious stones. The four chieftains who supported his arms were also richly clothed according to their usage, in garments which were apparently held ready for them on the road to enable them to accompany their prince, for they did not appear in such attire when they came to receive us. Besides these four chieftains, there were four other great caciques, who supported the canopy over their heads, and many other lords who walked before the Great Montezuma, sweeping the ground where he would tread and spreading cloths on it, so that he should not tread on the earth.

16. Cortés' description of the city of Mexico

Cortés' expedition into the Gulf of Mexico had been planned and in part financed by Diego Velázquez, conqueror and governor of Cuba. Velázquez probably contemplated a trading and slaving reconnaissance; the idea of an independent campaign of conquest was Cortés' own. It involved, of necessity, repudiating the authority of Velázquez and reporting the outcome of the campaign directly to the Crown, in the hope that success would be rewarded with confirmation and support. This was the purpose of the five *cartas-relaciones* which Cortés sent to the Emperor from New Spain between 1519 and 1526. The first of the five, indeed, is largely an *ex parte* account of Cortés' differences with Velázquez, and an ingenious—not to say unscrupulous—attempt to justify Cortés' mutinous behaviour. The other four describe Mexico and narrate the course of the conquest. They are not literary masterpieces. They have the limited vocabulary and involved construction of semi-official documents. They lack the detailed and evocative intimacy of Bernal Díaz' *True History*. They include some special pleading, some imaginative embroidery; but these features are subtle and unobtrusive, and form a relatively small part of the story. On the whole, the letters give the impression of sober and accurate records, written by a very able, intelligent and observant field commander.

The second letter is perhaps the most interesting of the five. It was written at Segura de la Frontera (Tepeaca) and relates the precautionary beaching at Vera Cruz of the ships which had brought the army from Cuba; the advance inland; the campaign against Tlaxcala which ended in a military alliance; the entry into Tenochtitlán; the kidnapping of Montezuma and his employment by the Spaniards as a puppet ruler; the intervention of Narváez, sent from Cuba with an army to bring Cortés to heel; the rising of the city population against the Spaniards; the disastrous evacuation of the *noche triste;* the retreat to Tlaxcala; and the beginnings of preparation for the final siege of Tenochtitlán. It contains a detailed description of the capital city, which is quoted here.

Tenochtitlán was something entirely new in Spanish experience. It was a big city by Spanish standards of the time, at least as big as Seville, bigger by far than Burgos or Toledo; yet it was built and inhabited by people who lacked many of the technical devices familiar to Europeans —wheeled vehicles, beasts of burden, tools of hard metal. It was efficiently governed, orderly, impressive in architecture and layout. It was also a dangerous place to occupy; built on an island, with easily invested causeways, it could—and did—become a trap for the invader; and its temple-pyramids were all potential fortresses. It is clear from all the accounts that the Spaniards were not only impressed by the place; they were also—understandably—frightened by it, and this helps to explain the atrocities which Cortés, normally a humane commander by the standards of his time, permitted and occasionally ordered. All the more remarkable that Cortés, having systematically destroyed the city in his final siege, should at once set about rebuilding it, to preserve its "renown and importance" and to make it the capital city of the kingdom of New Spain.

The second letter was first printed in Seville in 1522. It has been through many subsequent editions. The extract which follows is from Hernando Cortés: *Five Letters 1519–1526,* translated and edited by J. Bayard Morris (London, Routledge and Kegan Paul, 1928): extract from the second letter, pp. 85–98.

B UT before beginning to relate the wonders of this city and people, their rights and government, I should perhaps for a better understanding say something of the state of Mexico itself which contains this city and the others of which I have spoken, and is the principal seat of Mutezcuma. The province is roughly circular in shape and entirely surrounded by very lofty and rocky

mountains, the level part in the middle being some seventy leagues
in circumference and containing two lakes which occupy it almost
entirely, for canoes travel over fifty leagues in making a circuit
of them. One of the lakes is of fresh water, the other and larger
one of salt. A narrow but very lofty range of mountains cuts
across the valley and divides the lakes almost completely save
for the western end where they are joined by a narrow strait
no wider than a sling's throw which runs between the mountains.
Commerce is carried on between the two lakes and the cities on
their banks by means of canoes, so that land traffic is avoided.
Moreover, since the salt lake rises and falls with the tide sea
water pours from it at high tide into the fresh water lake with
the rapidity of a mountain torrent, and likewise at low tide flows
back from the fresh to the salt.

The great city of Tenochtitlan is built in the midst of this salt
lake, and it is two leagues from the heart of the city to any
point on the mainland. Four causeways lead to it, all made by
hand and some twelve feet wide. The city itself is as large as
Seville or Córdova. The principal streets are very broad and
straight, the majority of them being of beaten earth, but a few
and at least half the smaller thoroughfares are waterways along
which they pass in their canoes. Moreover, even the principal
streets have openings at regular distances so that the water can
freely pass from one to another, and these openings which are
very broad are spanned by great bridges of huge beams, very
stoutly put together, so firm indeed that over many of them ten
horsemen can ride at once. Seeing that if the natives intended
any treachery against us they would have every opportunity from
the way in which the city is built, for by removing the bridges
from the entrances and exits they could leave us to die of hunger
with no possibility of getting to the mainland, I immediately set
to work as soon as we entered the city on the building of four
brigs, and in a short space of time had them finished, so that we
could ship three hundred men and the horses to the mainland
whenever we so desired.

The city has many open squares in which markets are continuously held and the general business of buying and selling proceeds. One square in particular is twice as big as that of Salamanca and completely surrounded by arcades where there are

daily more than sixty thousand folk buying and selling. Every kind of merchandise such as may be met with in every land is for sale there, whether of food and victuals, or ornaments of gold and silver, or lead, brass, copper, tin, precious stones, bones, shells, snails and feathers; limestone for building is likewise sold there, stone both rough and polished, bricks burnt and unburnt, wood of all kinds and in all stages of preparation. There is a street of game where they sell all manner of birds that are to be found in their country, including hens, partridges, quails, wild duck, fly-catchers, widgeon, turtle doves, pigeons, little birds in round nests made of grass, parrots, owls, eagles, vulcans, sparrow-hawks and kestrels; and of some of these birds of prey they sell the skins complete with feathers, head, bill and claws. They also sell rabbits, hares, deer and small dogs which they breed especially for eating. There is a street of herb-sellers where there are all manner of roots and medicinal plants that are found in the land. There are houses as it were of apothecaries where they sell medicines made from these herbs, both for drinking and for use as ointments and salves. There are barbers' shops where you may have your hair washed and cut. There are other shops where you may obtain food and drink. There are street porters such as we have in Spain to carry packages. There is a great quantity of wood, charcoal, braziers made of clay and mats of all sorts, some for beds and others more finely woven for seats, still others for furnishing halls and private apartments. All kinds of vegetables may be found there, in particular onions, leeks, garlic, cresses, watercress, borage, sorrel, artichokes, and golden thistles. There are many different sorts of fruits including cherries and plums very similar to those found in Spain. They sell honey obtained from bees, as also the honeycomb and that obtained from maize plants which are as sweet as sugar canes; they also obtain honey from plants which are known both here and in other parts as *maguey*, which is preferable to grape juice; from *maguey* in addition they make both sugar and a kind of wine, which are sold in their markets. All kinds of cotton thread in various colours may be bought in skeins, very much in the same way as in the great silk exchange of Granada, except that the quantities are far less. They have colours for painting of as good quality as any in Spain, and of as pure shades as may be found anywhere. There are leathers of deer both skinned and in their natural state, and either bleached or dyed in various colours. A great deal of chinaware is sold of very good quality and including earthen jars of all sizes for holding liquids, pitchers, pots, tiles and an infinite variety of earthenware all made of very special clay and almost all decorated and painted in some way. Maize is sold both as grain and in the form of bread and is vastly superior both in the size of the ear and in taste to that of all the other islands or the mainland. Pasties made from game and fish pies may be seen on sale, and there are large quantities of fresh and salt water fish both in their natural state and cooked ready for eating. Eggs from fowls, geese and all the other birds I have described may be had, and likewise omelettes ready made. There is nothing to be found in all the land which is not sold in these markets, for over and above what I have mentioned there are so many and such various other things that on account of their very number and the fact that I do not know their names, I cannot now detail them. Each kind of merchandise is sold in its own particular street and no other kind may be sold there: this rule is very well enforced. All is sold by number and measure, but up till now no weighing by balance has been observed. A very fine building in the great square serves as a kind of audience chamber where ten or a dozen persons are always seated, as judges, who deliberate on all cases arising in the market and pass sentence on evildoers. In the square itself there are officials who continually walk amongst the people inspecting goods exposed for sale and the measures by which they are sold, and on certain occasions I have seen them destroy measures which were false.

There are a very large number of mosques or dwelling places for their idols throughout the various districts of this great city, all fine buildings, in the chief of which their priests live continuously, so that in addition to the actual temples containing idols there are sumptuous lodgings. These pagan priests are all dressed in black and go habitually with their hair uncut; they do not even comb it from the day they enter the order to that on which they leave. Chief men's sons, both nobles and distinguished citizens, enter these orders at the age of six or seven and only leave when they are of an age to marry, and this occurs more frequently to the first-born who will inherit their father's estates than to others. They are denied all access to women, and no woman is ever allowed to enter one of the religious houses. Certain foods they abstain from and more so at certain periods of the year than at others. Among these temples there is one chief one in particular whose size and magnificence no human tongue could describe. For it is so big that within the lofty wall which entirely circles it one could set a town of fifteen thousand inhabitants.

Immediately inside this wall and throughout its entire length are some admirable buildings containing large halls and corridors where the priests who live in this temple are housed. There are forty towers at the least, all of stout construction and very lofty, the largest of which has fifty steps leading up to its base: this chief one is indeed higher than the great church of Seville. The workmanship both in wood and stone could not be bettered anywhere, for all the stonework within the actual temples where they keep their idols is cut into ornamental borders of flowers, birds, fishes and the like, or trellis-work, and the woodwork is likewise all in relief highly decorated with monsters of very various device. The towers all serve as burying places for their nobles, and the little temples which they contain are all dedicated to a different idol to whom they pay their devotions.

There are three large halls in the great mosque where the principal idols are to be found, all of immense size and height and richly decorated with sculptured figures both in wood and stone, and within these halls are other smaller temples branching off from them and entered by doors so small that no daylight ever reaches them. Certain of the priests but not all are permitted to enter, and within are the great heads and figures of idols, although as I have said there are also many outside. The greatest of these idols and those in which they placed most faith and trust I ordered to be dragged from their places and flung down the stairs, which done I had the temples which they occupy cleansed for they were full of the blood of human victims who had been sacrificed, and placed in them the image of Our Lady and other saints, all of which made no small impression upon Muteczuma and the inhabitants. They are first remonstrated with me, for should it be known, they said, by the people of the country they would rise against me, believing as they did that to these idols were due all temporal goods, and that should they allow them to be ill used they would be wroth against them and would give them nothing, denying them the fruits of the earth, and thus the people would die of starvation. I instructed them by my interpreters how mistaken they were in putting their trust in idols made by their own hands from unclean things, and that they must know that there was but one God, Lord of all, Who created the sky, the earth and all things, Who made both them and ourselves, Who was without beginning and immortal, Whom alone they had to adore and to believe in, and not in any created thing whatsoever: I told them moreover all things else that I knew of touching this matter in order to lead them from their idolatry and bring them to the knowledge of Our Lord: and all, especially Muteczuma, replied that they had already told me that they were not natives of this land but had come to it long time since, and that therefore they were well prepared to believe that they had erred somewhat from the true faith during the long time since they had left their native land, and I as more lately come would know more surely the things that it was right for them to hold and believe than they themselves: and that hence if I would instruct them they would do whatever I declared to be best. Upon this Muteczuma and many of the chief men of the city went with me to remove the idols, cleanse the chapels, and place images of the saints therein, and all with cheerful faces. I forbade them moreover to make human sacrifice to the idols as was their wont, because besides being an abomination in the sight of God it is prohibited by your Majesty's laws which declare that he who kills shall be killed. From this time henceforth they departed from it, and during the whole time that I was in the city not a single living soul was known to be killed and sacrificed.

The images of the idols in which these people believed are many times greater than the body of a large man. They are made from pulp of all the cereals and greenstuffs which they eat, mixed and pounded together. This mass they moisten with blood from the hearts of human beings which they tear from their breasts while still alive, and thus make sufficient quantity of the pulp to mould into their huge statues: and after the idols have been set up still they offer them more living hearts which they sacrifice in like manner and anoint their faces with the blood. Each department of human affairs has its particular idol after the manner of the ancients who thus honoured their gods: so that there is one idol from whom they beg success in war, another for crops, and so on for all their needs.

The city contains many large and fine houses, and for this reason. All the nobles of the land owing allegiance to Muteczuma have their houses in the city and reside there for a certain portion of the year; and in addition there are a large number of rich citizens who likewise have very fine houses. All possess in addition to large and elegant apartments very delightful flower gardens of every kind, both on the ground level as on the upper storeys.

Along one of the causeways connecting this great city with the mainland two pipes are constructed of masonry, each two paces broad and about as high as a man, one of which conveys a stream of water very clear and fresh and about the thickness of a man's body right to the centre of the city, which all can use for drinking and other purposes. The other pipe which is empty is used when it is desired to clean the former. Moreover, on coming to the breaks in the causeway spanned by bridges under which the salt water flows through, the fresh water flows into a kind of trough as thick as an ox which occupies the whole width of the bridge, and thus the whole city is served. The water is sold from canoes in all the streets, the manner of their taking it from the pipes being in this wise: the canoes place themselves under the bridges where the troughs are to be found, and from above the canoes are filled by men who are especially paid for this work.

At all the entrances to the city and at those parts where canoes are unloaded, which is where the greatest amount of provisions enters the city, certain huts have been built, where there are official guards to exact so much on everything that enters. I know not whether this goes to the lord or to the city itself, and have not yet been able to ascertain, but I think that it is to the ruler, since in the markets of several other towns we have seen such a tax exacted on behalf of the ruler. Every day in all the markets and public places of the city there are a number of workmen and masters of all manner of crafts waiting to be hired by the day. The people of this city are nicer in their dress and manners than those of any other city or province, for since Muteczuma always holds his residence here and his vassals visit the city for lengthy periods, greater culture and politeness of manners in all things has been encouraged.

Finally, to avoid prolixity in telling all the wonders of this city, I will simply say that the manner of living among the people is very similar to that in Spain, and considering that this is a barbarous nation shut off from a knowledge of the true God or communication with enlightened nations, one may well marvel at the orderliness and good government which is everywhere maintained.

The actual service of Muteczuma and those things which call for admiration by their greatness and state would take so long to describe that I assure your Majesty I do not know where to begin with any hope of ending. For as I have already said, what could there be more astonishing than that a barbarous monarch such as he should have reproductions made in gold, silver, precious stones, and feathers of all things to be found in his land, and so perfectly reproduced that there is no goldsmith or silversmith in the world who could better them, nor can one understand what instrument could have been used for fashioning the jewels; as for the featherwork its like is not to be seen in either wax or embroidery, it is so marvellously delicate.

I was unable to find out exactly the extent of Muteczuma's kingdom, for in no part where he sent his messengers (even as much as two hundred leagues in either direction from this city) were his orders disobeyed; although it is true there were certain provinces in the middle of this region with whom he was at war. But so far as I could understand his kingdom was almost as large as Spain. Most of the lords of these various provinces resided, as I have said, for the greater part of the year in the capital, and the majority of them had their eldest sons in Muteczuma's service. The king had fortresses in all these provinces armed with his own men, and also overseers and tax-collectors to see to the services and rent which each province owed him, and which was inscribed in written characters and pictures on a kind of paper they have, by which they can make themselves understood. The manner of service rendered differed for each province according to the quality of its land, in such manner that every kind of produce that grew in the various parts of the country came to the royal hand. He was feared by all both present and distant more than was any other monarch in the world. He possessed many houses of recreation both within and without the city, each with its own special pastime, built in the most ingenious manner as was fitting for such a mighty prince: of which I will say no more than that there is not their like in all Spain. Another palace of his (not quite so fine as the one we were lodged in) had a magnificent garden with balconies overhanging it, the pillars and flagstones of which were all jasper beautifully worked. In this palace there was room to lodge two powerful princes with all their retinue. There were also ten pools of water in which were kept every kind of waterfowl known in these parts, fresh water being provided for the river birds, salt for those of the sea, and the water itself being frequently changed to keep it pure: every species of bird, moreover, was provided with its own natural food, whether fish, worms, maize or the smaller cereals. And I can vouch for it to your Majesty that those birds who ate fish alone and nothing else received some two hundred and fifty pounds of it every day, which was caught in the salt lake. It was the whole task of three hundred men to look after these birds. Others likewise were employed in ministering to those who were ill. Each pool was overhung by balconies cunningly arranged, from which Muteczuma would delight to watch the birds. In one room of this palace he kept men, women and children, who had been white since their birth, face, body, hair, eyebrows and eyelashes. He had also another very beautiful house in which there was a large courtyard, paved very prettily with flagstones in the manner of a chessboard. In this palace there were cages some nine feet high and six yards round: each of these was half covered with tiles and the other half by a wooden trellis skilfully made. They contained birds of prey, and there was an example of every one that is known in Spain, from kestrel to eagle, and many others which were new to us. Of each species there were many examples. In the covered part of every cage there was a stake on which the bird could perch and another under the wooden grating, so that the birds could go inside at nighttime and when it was raining and in the daytime come out into the sun and air. They were fed daily on chickens as their sole fare. Other large rooms on the ground floor were full of cages made of stout wood very firmly put together and containing large numbers of lions, tigers, wolves, foxes and wild cats of various kinds; these also were given as many chickens as they wanted. There were likewise another three hundred men to look after these animals and birds. In another palace he had men and women monsters, among them dwarfs, hunchbacks and others deformed in various ways, each manner of monster being kept in a separate apartment, and likewise with guards charged with looking after them.

His personal service was equally magnificent. Every morning at dawn there were over six hundred nobles and chief men present in his palace, some of whom were seated, others walking about the rooms and corridors, others amusing themselves in talk and other diversions, but none entering the actual apartment where he lay. The servants of these nobles filled two or three large courtyards and overflowed into the street, which was very large. They remained there all day, not quitting the palace until nightfall: at the time when the king took his meals food was served to them with equal profusion and rations were likewise dispensed to their servants and followers. His larders and wine cellars were open daily to all who wished to eat and drink. The meal was served by some three or four hundred youths. The dishes were innumerable since on every occasion that the king ate or drank every manner of dish was served to him, whether it were meat, fish, fruit, or herbs of whatever kind was found in the land. Since the climate is cold every plate and dish had under it a little brazier filled with lighted coals that it might not get cold. All the dishes were placed in a large hall in which he took his meals. It was almost entirely filled but kept ever fresh and clean, the King himself being seated on a small delicately fashioned leather cushion. While he ate some five or six ancient nobles stood a little way off to whom he gave morsels from his own dish. One of the youthful servitors remained on foot to place the dishes before him and remove them, and he requested from others who were further off anything which was lacking. Both at the beginning and end of the meal he was always given water with which to wash his hands, and the towel on which he dried his hands was never used again, nor likewise were the plates and dishes on which the food was brought ever used twice and the same with the little braziers which were also new for every meal. Every day he changed his garments four times, always putting on new clothes which were never worn more than once. The nobles always entered his palace barefoot, and those who were bidden to present themselves before him did so with bowed head and eyes fixed on the ground, their whole bearing expressing reverence; nor would they when speaking to him lift their eyes to his face, all of which was done to show their profound humiliation and respect. That such was the motive I am certain because certain of the nobles rebuked the Spanish soldiers for speaking to me without due shame in that they looked me full in the face, which seemed to them the height of disrespect. When Muteczuma went abroad, which was seldom, all who were with him or whom he met in the street turned away their faces and avoided looking at him, some of them prostrating themselves on the ground until he had passed. One of the nobles always preceded him bearing three long thin rods, for the purpose, as I think, of intimating the royal presence. For on his descending from the litter he bore one in his hand and carried it with him wherever he went. In short the various ceremonies which this ruler observed were so many and curious that there is not space here to recount them, and I think that not even the sultans themselves or other eastern potentates were surrounded by such pomp and display.

In this great city I was now busied in providing such things as seemed profitable to your Majesty's service, pacifying and subduing many provinces containing great numbers of large cities, towns and fortresses, discovering mines, and finding out and enquiring many secrets of these lands under the rule of Muteczuma, as also of others bordering on them of which he knew, which are so extensive and marvelous that their existence is almost incredible: all this with the goodwill and pleasure of Muteczuma and all the natives of these lands as if they had recognized from the beginning your Majesty as their natural lord and governor, and now did with no less goodwill all these things which they were bidden in your Majesty's royal name.

17. Hernando Pizarro's journey in search of gold

Shortly after the occupation of Darien rumors became current among Spaniards there of civilized and prosperous kingdoms to the south; but because of the barriers of sea, desert, and mountains, the reality—the Inca Empire governed from its remote highland capital at Cuzco—long eluded discovery. Serious exploration from Darien was first organized by a syndicate comprising two obscure soldiers of fortune from Extremadura, Francisco Pizarro and Diego de Almagro, and a priest named Luque, who apparently provided the initial capital. Pizarro and Almagro spent four years in voyages of coastal exploration, in which they collected enough evidence to encourage them to approach the emperor for a formal capitulation. Pizarro's journey to Spain coincided with the first triumphal appearance of Cortés at the Court, and his subsequent conduct of affairs was strongly influenced by Cortés' example.

Armed with a royal appointment as governor of the kingdom which he undertook to find and conquer, Pizarro sailed from Panama in 1530 with 180 men and twenty-seven horses for the conquest of Peru. His arrival at Túmbez coincided with the final stage of a succession war in which the reigning Inca, Huáscar, was defeated and dethroned by his usurping half-brother Atahuallpa. Atahuallpa, when the Spaniards landed, had not yet entered high Cuzco, but was encamped with his army near the more accessible city of Cajamarca in northern Peru. Reports of the conflict encouraged Pizarro, after establishing a base near Túmbez, to march inland in 1532 to Cajamarca. Here, by means of a surprise attack under cover of a formal conference, the Spaniards succeeded in killing most of Atahuallpa's immediate retinue and capturing the ruler himself. Almagro arrived shortly afterwards with reinforcements from Panama. The Inca forces, deprived of the authority of their ruler, were unable effectively to resist the conquerors' march on Cuzco, which was taken and sacked in November 1533. The gold and silver taken in the sack, together with the treasure of Atahuallpa's ransom, was melted down, the royal fifth subtracted, and the rest distributed; enough to make every man in the army rich for life, though few lived long to enjoy it.

After his capture at Cajamarca, but before the march on Cuzco, Atahuallpa had offered, in a vain attempt to buy his freedom, a ransom of a roomful of gold vessels and ornaments. He told Francisco Pizarro that the treasure could be collected in two months. This was over-optimistic; deliveries lagged, and Hernando Pizarro—the only one of the five Pizarro brothers who was both literate and legitimate—was sent out from Cajamarca with an escort of twenty-five men, to hurry them. Hernando had two main tasks. The first was to collect the accumulated treasure of the temple-shrine of Pachacamac. The ruins of Pachacamac remain today as one of the principal archaeological sites of coastal Peru. They housed a famous oracle, widely revered and consulted in pre-Inca times, whose prestige and wealth had grown greatly as a result of the Inca conquest of the coast. The second task was to make contact with the Inca general Chalcuchima or Chilicuchima, who was supposed to be bringing down an instalment of the ransom gold from Cuzco by way of the mountain city of Jauja. Hernando seems to have been out-witted by the priests of the Pachacamac oracle, and the loot from the shrine was disappointing; but he met Chalcuchima on the road, and that part of the ransom was duly delivered.

An account of Hernando's expedition was written by one of the officers of his escort, Miguel de Astete. Astete had been one of Ata-huallpa's captors, and was also one of those who, a little later, protested against the judicial murder of the Inca. He eventually became a prom-inent *encomendero* in the Cuzco area. Besides the present report, he wrote a short account of the conquest of Peru, which was published in 1918. He was a good observer, and his report provides the best surviv-ing description of central Peru, in the uneasy months following the capture of Atahuallpa, when the Inca system of local administration had not yet been destroyed by the invading Spaniards.

Francisco Pizarro left no record of his exploits. The first eyewitness account was written, under his instructions, by his secretary Francisco de Jérez. Jérez had sailed from Spain with Pizarro at the beginning of 1530. He accompanied the conqueror in his voyage and on his march along the Peruvian coast and across the Andes. He was an eyewitness of the events at Cajamarca and of the subsequent murder of Atahuallpa. He returned to Spain in 1534, taking the first instalments of gold and the manuscript of his narrative, *A true account of the province of Cuzco*. Into this narrative he incorporated Astete's report, which prob-ably owes its survival to this circumstance.

Jérez' *True Account* was first published at Seville in 1534 and again
at Salamanca in 1547. Both these editions are now extremely rare. It
was translated into Italian in 1535, and included in the third volume of
Ramusio's collection in 1556. The first scholarly Spanish edition appeared in 1749. It has been much quoted by later historians, notably by
Prescott. The extract which follows is from *Reports on the Discovery
of Peru*, translated and edited by Clements R. Markham (London, Hakluyt Society, 1872), pp. 74–94: the narrative of the journey made·by
the Señor Captain Hernando Pizarro, by order of the governor, his
brother, from the city of Cajamarca to Pachacamac and thence to
Jauja.

O~N~ Wednesday, the day of the Epiphany (which is vulgarly
called the Festival of the three Kings), on the 5th of January,
1533, the Captain Fernando Pizarro set out from the town of
Caxamalca with twenty horse and a few arquebusiers. On that
night he rested at some huts which were five leagues from the
town. Next day he dined at another town called Ychoca, where
he was well received. They gave him what he required for himself
and his people. On the same day he came to pass the night at
another small village called Huancasanga, subject to the town of
Guamachuco. Next morning he reached the town of Guamachuco, which is large, and is situated in a valley surrounded by
mountains. It has a beautiful view and good lodgings. The lord
of the place is called Guamanchoro, by whom the Captain and
his companions were well received. Here arrived a brother of Atabaliba, who was hurrying the gold up from Cuzco, and the Captain learnt from him that the Captain Chilicuchima was twenty
days' journey off, and that he was bringing the treasure that
Atabaliba had sent for. When he found that the treasure was so
far off, the Captain sent a messenger to the Governor, to ask
him what should be done, adding that he would not advance
until he received further orders. In this town some Indians reported that Chilicuchima was far off; and some principal men,
having been bribed, stated that Chilicuchima was only seven
leagues distant, in the town of Andamarca, with 20,000 men of
war, and that they were coming to kill the Christians and to
liberate their Lord. The chief who said this confessed that he
had dined with him on the previous day. A companion of this

chief, who was taken aside, made the same statement. The Captain, therefore, resolved to go in search of Chilicuchima, and, having mustered his men, he commenced the march. He passed that night at a small village, subject to Guamachuco, called Tambo; and there he received the same information as had been given him before. In this village he had a good watch kept all night, and next morning he continued his journey with much circumspection. Before noon he reached the town of Andamarca, but he did not find the Captain, nor any news of him, beyond what had first been stated by the brother of Atabaliba, that he was in a town called Xauxa, with much gold, and that he was on his way. In this town of Andamarca he received the reply of the Governor, which was that Chilicuchima and the gold were far off, that he had the bishop of the mosque of Pachacama in his power, and that, as to the great wealth of gold in the mosque, the Captain should make inquiries respecting the road, and if it seemed good to him to go there, he might go; as those who had gone to Cuzco would return in the meanwhile. The Captain ascertained the distance and the nature of the road to the mosque; and, although his companions were badly shod,[1] and otherwise indifferently furnished for so long a march; he considered that he would be doing good service in going to collect that gold, which the Indians would not be able to bring away; and that it was desirable to examine that land, and to ascertain whether it was suitable for Christian settlements. Although he had information that there were many rivers, and bridges of network, and long marches, and difficult passes, he yet resolved to go, and he took with him certain chiefs who knew the country.

He commenced his journey on the 14th of January, and on the same day he crossed some difficult passes, and two rivers, passing the night at a village called Totopamba, which is on a steep declivity.[2] The Indians received him well and gave him good food, and all he required for the night, and men to carry his baggage. Next day he left this village, and reached another called Corongo, where he passed the night. Half way there was a great pass of snow, and all the way there were many flocks with their

---

[1] It is not clear whether Astete means the men or the horses, or both. The Spanish word is *herrage*.

[2] On this day the party crossed from the Marañon to the coast watershed.

shepherds, who have their houses in the mountains, as in Spain. In this village they were given food, and all they required, and Indians to carry the loads. This village is subject to Guamachuco. Next day they started and came to another small village called Piga, where they passed the night. They found no inhabitants, as they had run away from fear. This was a very severe march, for they had to descend a flight of steps cut out of the stone, which was very dangerous for the horses. Next day, at dinner time, they reach a large village in a valley, and a very rapid river flowed across the road. It was spanned by two bridges close together, made of network in the following manner. They build a foundation near the water, and raise it to a great height; and from one side of the river to the other there are cables made of reeds like osiers, but as thick as a man's thigh, and they are fastened to great stones. From one cable to the other is the width of a cart. Smaller cords are interwoven between the cables, and great stones are fastened beneath, to steady them. By one of these bridges the common people cross over, and a porter is stationed there to receive transit dues; while the lords and captains use the other, which is always closed, but they opened it for the Captain and his followers, and the horses crossed over very well.

The Captain rested in this village for two days, because both men and horses were fatigued by the bad road. The Christians were very well received, and were supplied with food and all that they required. The lord of this village was called Puma-paccha. They departed from it and came to a small village, where they were given all they wanted, and near it they crossed another bridge of network, like the former one. They passed the night two leagues further on, at another village, where the people came out to receive them as friends and gave food to the Christians, and Indians to carry their loads. This day's march was through a valley covered with maize, with villages on either side of the road. The next day was Sunday. They started in the morning, and came to a village where the Captain and his companions were well received. At night they reached another village, where the people offered sheep[3] and chicha and all other necessaries. All this land has abundant supplies of maize and many

---

[3] Llamas.

flocks; and, as the Christians marched along the road, they saw the sheep crossing it. Next day, at dinner time, the Captain reached a great town called Huaras,[4] the lord of which was called Pumacapllai. He and his people supplied the Christians with provisions, and with Indians to carry the loads. This town is in a plain, and a river flows near it. Other villages were in sight, with flocks and maize fields. They had two hundred head of sheep in a yard, merely to supply the wants of the Captain and his men. The Captain departed in the afternoon, and stopped for the night at another village called Sucaracoai, where he was well received. The Lord of this village was named Marcocana. Here the Captain rested for one day, because both men and horses were tired. A strict watch was kept because the village was large, and Chilicuchima was near with 55,000 men. Next day they departed from this village, and, after marching through a valley, where there was much tilled land and many flocks, stopped for the night at a distance of two leagues, in a small village called Pachicoto. Here the Captain left the royal road which leads to Cuzco, and took that of the coast valley. Next day he stopped for the night at a place called Marcara, the chief of which was named Corcara. Here there are pastures, and at a certain time of the year they bring the flocks to browse, as they do in Castile and Estremadura. From this village the rivers flow to the sea, which makes the road very difficult, for all the country inland is very cold, and with much water and snow. The coast is very hot, and there is very little rain. The rain is not sufficient for the crops, but the waters that flow from the mountains irrigate the land, which yields abundant supplies of provisions and fruits.

Next day they departed from this village, and marching along the banks of a river, following its downward course through fields and fruit gardens, they stopped for the night at a village called Guaracanga. Next day they stopped at a large place near the sea called Parpunga. It has a strong house with seven encircling walls painted in many devices both inside and outside, with portals well built like those of Spain, and two tigers at the principal doorway. The inhabitants were filled with fear at the sight of a people never before seen, and of the horses, which astonished them still

[4] Capital of the modern Department of Ancachs, in the valley of the Santa.

more. The Captain spoke to them through the interpreter who accompanied him, to reassure them, and they then did good service.

In this village they came upon another broader road, made by the people of the coast, and bounded by walls on either side. The Captain rested for two days in this town of Parpunga to refresh his people and get them reshod. On starting again, they crossed a river in balsas, the horses swimming. He passed the night at a village called Guamamayo, which is in a ravine near the sea. Near it they had to cross another river[5] with great difficulty by swimming, for it was much swollen, and flowing rapidly. They have no bridges across these coast rivers, because they become very wide when they are swollen. The lord of this village and his people did good service in assisting to carry the baggage across, and they gave very good food to the Christians, and men to carry their loads. The Captain and his followers set out from this village on the 9th day of January, and passed the night in another village subject to Guamamayo, and three leagues from it by the road. The greater part was inhabited, and there were tilled fields, trees, fruit gardens, and a clean walled road. Next day the Captain stopped at a very large village near the sea, called Huara.[6] This town is well situated, and contains large edifices for lodging. The Christians were well served by the chiefs and the Indians, who supplied them with what they required for the day. On the following day the Captain stopped at a village called Llachu, to which he gave the name of "the town of the partridges," because there were many partridges kept in cages in all the houses. The Indians of this village were friendly and did good service. The chief of this village did not make his appearance. The Captain started rather early next morning, because he was informed that the march would be long, and he reached a large village called Suculacumbi at dinner time, a distance of five leagues. The lord of the village and his Indians were friendly, and supplied all the food that was necessary for that day. At the hour of vespers they set out from this village, in order to reach the town where the mosque is on the next day. They crossed a great river by a ford,[7] and marched along a road with a wall on

[5] The Huaman-mayu, now called La Barranca.
[6] The modern town and river of Huara and the port of Huacho.
[7] The Rimac, near the site of the future city of Lima.

each side, passing the night at a place belonging to the town, and at a distance of a league and a half from it.

The next day was Sunday, the 30th of January. The Captain departed from this village, and, without leaving groves and villages, he reached Pachacama,[8] which is the town where the mosque stands. Halfway there is another village, where the Captain dined. The lord of Pachacama and the principal men came out to receive the Captain and the Christians, and showed a desire to be friends with the Spaniards. The Captain went to lodge, with his followers, in some large chambers in one part of the town. He said that he had come, by order of the Governor, for the gold of that mosque, and that they were to collect it and deliver it up, or to convey it to where the Governor then was. All the principal men of the town and the attendants of the Idol assembled and replied that they would give it, but they continued to dissimulate and make excuses. At last they brought a very little, and said that they had no more. The Captain dissimulated also, and said that he wished to go and see the Idol they had, and he went. It was in a good house, well painted, in a very dark chamber with a close fetid smell. Here there was a very dirty Idol made of wood, and they say that this is their God who created them and sustains them, and gives them their food. At the foot of the Idol there were some offerings of gold, and it was held in such veneration that only the attendants and servants, who, as they say, were appointed by it, were allowed to officiate before it. No other person might enter, nor is any other considered worthy even to touch the walls of the house. The Captain ascertained that the Devil frequented this Idol, and spoke with his servants, saying diabolical things, which were spread over all the land. They look upon him as God, and offer many sacrifices to him. They come to this Devil, from distances of three hundred leagues, with gold and silver and cloth. Those that arrive go to the porter and beg that their gift may be accepted. He enters and speaks with the Idol, who says that he consents. Before any of his ministers may enter to minister to him, they say that they must fast for many days and refrain from women. In all the streets of this town, and at its principal gates, and

[8] The temple-city of Pachacamac.

round this house, there are many wooden Idols, which they worship as imitations of their Devil. It was ascertained from many
lords of this land that, from the town of Catamez,[9] which is at
the commencement of this government, all the people of this
coast serve this mosque with gold and silver, and offer a certain
tribute every year. There were houses and superintendents to
receive the tribute, where they found some gold, and there were
signs that much more had been taken away. Many Indians de-
posed that the gold was removed by order of the Devil. I omit
many things that might be said touching the worship of this Idol,
to avoid prolixity. But it is believed among the Indians that this
Idol is their God, that he can destroy them if they offend him
and do not serve him well, and that all the things in the world
are in his hands. The people were so shocked and terrified at
the Captain having merely gone in to see it, that they thought
the Idol would destroy all the Christians. But the Spaniards gave
the Indians to understand that they were in a great error, and
that he who spoke from the inside of the Idol was the Devil,
who deceived them. They were told that from henceforth they
must not believe him, nor do what he advised them; and were
taught other things touching their idolatries.

The Captain ordered the vault, in which the Idol was, to be
pulled down, and the Idol to be broken before all the people.
He then told them many things touching our Holy Catholic Faith,
and he taught them the sign of the cross ✤, that they might be
able to defend themselves against the Devil. This town of Pachacama is very large. Adjoining the mosque there is a house
of the Sun, well built, and situated on a hill, with five surrounding
walls. There are houses with terrace roofs as in Spain. The town
appears to be old, judging from the ruined houses it contains;
and the greater part of the outer wall has fallen. The name of
the principal lord is Taurichumbi. The neighbouring lords come
to the town to see the Captain, with presents of the products of
their land, and with gold and silver. They wondered greatly that
the Captain should have dared to enter where the Idol was, and
to see it broken.

[9] Atacames, on the coast of Ecuador.

The Lord of Malaque,[10] named Lincoto, came to offer obedience to his Majesty, and brought a present of gold and silver. The Lord of Poax, named Alincai, did the same. The Lord of Gualco,[11] named Guarilli, also brought gold and silver. The Lord of Chincha,[12] with ten of his chief men, came with a present of gold and silver. This lord said that his name was Tamviambea. The Lord of Guaxchapaicho, and the Lord of Colixa named Aci, the Lord of Sallicaimarca named Yspilo, and other principal lords of the surrounding country, brought in presents of gold and silver, which, joined to that taken out of the mosque, made ninety thousand *pesos*.[13] The Captain talked very kindly to all these chiefs, rejoicing at their coming. He commanded them, in the name of his Majesty, always to behave in the same way, and dismissed them, well satisfied.

In this town of Pachacama, the Captain Hernando Pizarro received news that Chilicuchima,[14] a Captain of Atabaliba, was at a distance of four days' journey with a large force, and with the gold; and that he would not march onwards, but declared that he was ready to fight the Christians. The Captain sent a messenger to him, urging him to continue his march with the gold, as his master was in prison; telling him that he was long behind his time, and that the Governor was angry at his delay, as he had been expected for many days. He sent many other messages, urging him to come, as he was unable to go and meet him where he then was, because the road was bad for the horses; and arranging that the one who reached a certain village on the road first should wait there for the other. Chilicuchima sent a message in reply, saying that he would do what the Captain desired, and that he had no other intention.

The Captain then set out from the town of Pachacama, to form a junction with Chilicuchima. He marched by the same

[10] Mala, a coast valley to the south of Pachacamac.
[11] Huarcu. The modern name of this rich valley is Cañete. It contains several flourishing sugar estates.
[12] The next valley, south of Cañete.
[13] It was said, according to Herrera, that the Priests concealed four hundred loads of gold and silver, and that Hernando Pizarro only collected nine hundred *castellanos*. Dec. v, lib. ii, cap. 3, p. 54.
[14] Chalcuchima.

road as he had come, until he reached Huara, which is on the coast near the sea. Then he left the coast and marched into the interior. The Captain Hernando Pizarro left the town of Huara on the 3rd of March, and advanced along a road on the bank of a river during the whole day, where there were many groves of trees. He passed the night at a village on the banks of the river. The village where the Captain slept belongs to the town of Huara, and is called Guaranga. Next day the Captain left this village, and reached another called Aillon, near the mountains. It is subject to a larger place called Aratambo, which is rich in flocks and maize crops.

On the 5th of March he passed the night at a village belonging to Caxatambo, called Chincha. On the road they had to cross a pass where the snow was very deep, reaching to the girths of the horses. This village has large flocks. The Captain remained there for two days. On Saturday, the 7th of March, he set out, and passed the night at Caxatambo. This is a large town, situated in a deep valley, where there are many flocks, and all along the road there were sheepfolds. The chief of this village is called Sachao, and he did good service to the Spaniards. At this town the Captain changed his route, in order to take the broad road by which Chilicuchima would come, which entailed a flank march of three days. Here the Captain made inquiries whether Chilicuchima had passed, in order to form a junction. All the Indians said that he had passed with the gold; but it afterwards appeared that they had been told to say this, that the Captain might be induced to march onwards; while he remained in Xauxa, with no intention of moving. The Captain, however, considered that these Indians seldom spoke the truth; so he determined, although it entailed great trouble and danger, to march to the royal road by which Chilicuchima must go, in order to ascertain whether he had already passed. If he had not gone on, the Captain resolved to seek him out, wherever he might be, as well to secure the gold as to disperse his army.

The Captain, with his followers, took the way leading to a large village called Pombo, which is on the royal road. On Monday, the 9th of March, they slept at a village, situated amongst mountains, called Diu. The chief of this village was friendly, and gave the Christians all they required for the night. The Governor started early next morning, and passed the following night in a small village of shepherds, near a lake of sweet water, about three leagues in circuit;[15] on a plain where there were large flocks of sheep with very fine wool. Next day, which was Wednesday, in the morning, the Captain and his companions reached the village of Pombo,[16] and the lords of Pombo came out to meet him, with some Captains of Atabaliba who were there with troops. Here the Captain found one hundred and fifty *arrobas* of gold, which Chilicuchima had sent, while he himself remained with his forces in Xauxa. When the Captain had taken up his quarters, he asked the Captains how it was that Chilicuchima had sent that gold, and had not come himself according to orders. They answered that it was because he was in great fear of the Christians, and also because he was waiting for more gold that was coming from Cuzco, as he did not like to come himself with so little.

The Captain Hernando Pizarro sent a messenger from this village to Chilicuchima, to let him know that as he had not come, he would go to him, and that he need have no fear. The Captain rested for one day in that village to refresh the horses, in case it should be necessary to fight. On Friday, the 14th of March, the Captain set out from the village of Pombo, with his horse and foot, to go to Xauxa. That night was passed in a village called Xacamalca, six leagues from Pombo, over level ground. On this plain there is a lake of sweet water which commences near this village, and has a circuit of eight or ten leagues.[17] The lake has villages all round its shores, and large flocks, while in its waters are birds and small fish. The father of Atabaliba had many *balsas* in this lake, which were brought from Tumbez for his amusement. A river flows out of the lake to the village of Pombo, and a branch of it is very deep and rapid. They can float by it to a bridge near the village; and those who pass pay dues as in Spain. All along the banks of this river there are large flocks,

[15] This seems to have been the lake of Lauricocha, the source of the Marañon.

[16] Pumpu of Garcilasso de la Vega, the modern Bombon.

[17] The lake of Bombon or Chinchay-cocha. It is thirty-six miles long, by six broad, and 12,940 feet above the sea. The plain or basin in which it lies is forty-five miles long. The river of Xauxa flows out of the lake.

and the name of Guadiana was given to it, because of the re-
semblance to that river in Spain.

On Saturday, the 15th of the month, the Captain left the village of Xacamalca, and after marching three leagues he came to
a house, where he and his men were well supplied with food.
He passed that night three leagues further on, at a town called
Tarma, which is on the slope of a mountain. Here he was lodged
in a painted house, which contained good rooms. The chief of
this place behaved well, both in supplying food and men to carry
loads. On Sunday morning the Captain set out rather early from
this village, having a long march before him. He caused his men
to advance in order of battle, because he suspected some treachery,
not having received any answer from Chilicuchima. At the hour
of vespers he reached a village called Yanaimalca, where the people came out to him. Here he received news that Chilicuchima
was not in Xauxa, which increased his suspicions. The Captain
was now only a league from Xauxa, so after dinner he again
marched onwards, and, having come in sight of the town, he saw
many bodies of men from a hill; but he could not make out
whether they were soldiers or townspeople who had assembled
for some festival.

As soon as the Captain arrived, and before he dismounted, he
asked for Chilicuchima, and the people answered that he was at
some other village, and that he would return next day. He had
absented himself on pretense of business until he might learn
from the Indians who came with the Captain the intentions of the
Spaniards; for he saw that he had committed a fault in not having
kept his promise, and that the Captain had come eighty leagues
in pursuit of him. These considerations made him think that the
Spaniards came to seize or kill him, and he had absented himself
from fear of them, especially of those who were on horseback.
The Captain had with him a son of the old Cuzco[18] who, when
he heard of the absence of Chilicuchima, said that he wished to
go where he was, and set out in a litter. All that night the
horses were saddled and bridled, and the lords of the town were
told that no Indian was to appear in the square, because the
horses were angry and would kill them. Next day that son of

[18] "Old Cuzco" was Huaina Cápac, the father of Huáscar and Atahuallpa.

the Cuzco returned with Chilicuchima, both in litters, and numer-
ously attended. On entering the square they alighted, and, leaving
all their servants, they went on foot, with a few attendants, to
the house occupied by the Captain Hernando Pizarro, for Chilicuchima to see him and offer his excuses for not having fulfilled
his promise, or come out to receive him. He said his business
had prevented him from doing more. The Captain asked why
he had not come to meet him, as he had promised. Chilicuchima
answered that his master Atabaliba had sent orders to him to remain where he was. The Captain then said that he felt no anger
against him, but that he must accompany him back to the Governor, who had his master Atabaliba a prisoner, and who would
keep him until he had given up the gold that had been demanded.
The Captain added that he knew how much gold there was, and
that it must be delivered up, but he assured Chilicuchima that,
although he must accompany him back, he would be well treated.
Chilicuchima replied that his Lord had sent to order him to do
otherwise, and not to go, because that country was lately conquered, and might again rebel if he left it. Hernando Pizarro
conversed with him for some time, and finally it was arranged
that they should pass the night there, and again discuss the matter
in the morning. The Captain desired to carry his point by fair
means, because he was anxious to avoid disturbances, lest it should
compromise the safety of three Spaniards who had gone to the
city of Cuzco. Next morning Chilicuchima came to the Captain's
lodging and said that, as he desired him to accompany the Spaniards, he could not refuse to obey, and that he was ready to go,
leaving another captain with the troops at Xauxa. On that day
he got together about thirty loads of gold; and after marching
for two days they met thirty or forty loads. During these days
the Spaniards kept a good look out, the horses being kept saddled
night and day; for this captain of Atabaliba had so large a force
that if he had made a night attack on the Spaniards he would
have done much mischief.

The town of Xauxa is very large. It is situated in a beautiful
valley, and enjoys a temperate climate. A very large river flows
near the town. The land is fertile. The town is built like those of
Spain, with regular streets, and many subject villages are in sight.
The town and district are very populous, and the Spaniards saw

one hundred thousand people assemble every day in the principal square. The market places and streets were also crowded. There were men whose duty it was to count all these people, and to know who came in for the service of the troops; and other men had to watch and take note of all who entered the town. Chilicuchima had stewards whose duty it was to supply provisions, and many carpenters who worked in wood, and many other men to attend upon his wants and wait on his person. There were three or four porters in his house, and both in his household service, and in everything else he imitated his Lord. He was feared throughout this land, for he was a brave warrior, and, under orders from his Lord, he had conquered more than two hundred leagues of country, and had had many encounters both in the plains and in the passes, in all of which he had been victorious, and in none had he been vanquished throughout all that land.

On Friday, the 20th of March, the Captain Hernando Pizarro departed from that city of Xauxa to return to Caxamalca, accompanied by Chilicuchima. He marched by the same road to the village of Pompo, where he stayed for the day he arrived, and one more. On Wednesday he set out from this village of Pompo, and marching over plains covered with flocks, he passed the night at some large buildings. On that day it snowed heavily. Next day he came to a village amongst the mountains called Tambo, which is near a large and deep river, where there is a bridge. There is a flight of stone steps to descend to the river, and if the position was defended, much mischief might be done. The Captain received good service from the lord of this village, and was supplied with all that he and his party required. They made a great festival out of respect for the Captain Hernando Pizarro, and because Chilicuchima accompanied him. Next day they came to a village called Tomsucancha, the lord of which, named Tillima, received them well. There were plenty of Indians fit for service; for, though the village was small, many had assembled from the surrounding country to see the Spaniards. In this village there are small sheep with very fine wool, like those of Spain. Next day they reached a village called Guaneso,[19] a march of five

[19] Huanuco.

leagues, the greater part over a paved road, with channels of water by the side. They say that the road was paved on account of the snow, which, at a certain season of the year, falls over that land. This town of Guaneso is large. It is situated in a valley, surrounded by steep mountains, the valley being three leagues in circuit. On the side leading to Caxamalca there is a long and very steep ascent. The Captain and his followers were very well received, and during the two days that they remained, the inhabitants celebrated several feasts. This town has other surrounding villages under its jurisdiction. It is a land of many flocks.

On the last day of March the Captain departed from this town, and reached a bridge over a large river, built of very stout timber. There were guards stationed there to receive transit dues, as is their custom. They passed the night at a distance of four leagues from the town, where Chilicuchima had caused all necessary preparations to be made. Next day, being the 1st of April, they reached a village called Piscomarca. It is on the slope of a very steep mountain. Its chief is named Parpay. Next day the Captain departed from this village, and, after a march of three leagues, arrived at a good village called Huari,[20] where there is a large and deep river, over which there is another bridge. This position is very strong, there being deep ravines on either flank. Chilicuchima said that here he had fought a battle with the troops of the Cuzco, who guarded the pass, defending it for two or three days. When those of Cuzco were defeated, and some of their enemies had crossed the river, they destroyed the bridge, so that Chilicuchima and his troops swam across, and killed many of the men of Cuzco.

Next day the Captain set out, and, after a march of five leagues, he passed the night at a village called Guacango. Next day he reached the large town of Piscobamba, which is on the side of a mountain. The chief is called Tauquame; and he and his people received the Captain well, and did good service to his followers. Halfway to this town, at Huacacamba, there is another deep river with two bridges of network close together, resting on a foundation of stone rising from the water; like those I have mentioned before. From one side to the other there are cables

[20] In the valley of the Marañon.

of reed, the size of a man's thigh, and between are woven many stout cords; to which large stones are fastened, for the purpose of steadying the bridge. The horses crossed this bridge without trouble; but it is a nervous thing to pass over it for the first time, though there is no danger, as it is very strong. There are guards at all these bridges, as in Spain. Next day the Captain departed from Piscobamba, and reached some buildings, after a march of five leagues. Next day he came to a village called Agoa, which is subject to Piscobamba. It is a good village among the mountains, and is surrounded by fields of maize. The chief and his people supplied what was required for the night, and next morning provided porters for the baggage. Next day the Captain marched for four leagues over a very rugged road, and passed the night at Conchuco. This village is in a hollow. Half a league before reaching it, there is a wide road cut in steps in the rock, and there are many difficult passes, and places which might easily be defended. Next day they set out, and reached a place called Andamarca, which is the point where they had diverged to go to Pachacama. At this town the two royal roads to Cuzco unite.[21] From Andamarca to Pombo[22] there are three leagues over a very rugged road; and stone steps are cut for the ascents and descents; while on the outer side there is a stone wall, to protect the traveller from the danger of slipping. If any man fell, he would be dashed to pieces; and it is an excellent thing for the horses, as they would fall if there was no flanking wall. In the middle of the road there is a bridge of stone and wood, very well built, between two masses of rock. At one end of the bridge there are well-built lodgings and a paved court, where, according to the Indians, the lords of the land had banquets and feasts when they travelled by that road.

From this place the Captain Hernando Pizarro went by the same stages as he came, until he reached the city of Caxamalca, which he entered, with Chilicuchima, on the 25th of May,[23] 1533. Here a thing was seen that had never been witnessed before since the Indies were discovered. When Chilicuchima passed through

---

[21] One leading, by Huaras, to the coast road at Parmunca; the other being the *sierra* road to Cuzco, by Xauxa.

[22] The modern Pomabamba.

[23] This should be April.

the gates of the place where his master was imprisoned, he took a light load from one of the Indian porters and put it on his back, an example which was followed by many chiefs who accompanied him. Thus laden, he and the others entered where their Lord was; and when Chilicuchima saw him, he raised his hands to the Sun, and gave thanks that he had been permitted to enjoy the sight. Then, with much reverence, and weeping, he approached his Lord, and kissed his face, hands, and feet. The other chiefs, his companions, did the same. Atabaliba maintained a mien so majestic that, though there was not a man in the kingdom that he loved more than Chilicuchima, he did not look in his face or take more notice of him than of the vilest Indians that came into his presence. This taking up of a load to enter the presence of Atabaliba is a ceremony which was performed for all the Lords who have reigned in that land. I, Miguel de Estete, the overseer, who went on the journey that the Captain Hernando Pizarro undertook, now give this account of all that happened.

MIGUEL ESTETE

18. An unsuccessful conquistador

The exploits of Cortés, Pizarro, and their like attracted the attention both of their contemporaries and of historians because of their dramatic and breathtaking success. These leaders conquered populous provinces, established cities, found productive silver mines—Potosí was discovered in 1545, Zacatecas in 1548. It should be remembered, however, that by far the greatest part of the Americas at that time was neither populous nor productive. Immense areas were traversed by Spanish explorers who, as *conquistadores*, were failures, in that they found nothing which they considered to be of value. Most sixteenth-century knowledge of what is now the southern United States, for example, was derived from two expeditions, that of Hernando de Soto, who in 1539 explored from Tampa Bay in Florida north to the Appalachians and west to the Mississippi; and that of Francisco Vázquez de Coronado. Coronado, while governor of New Galicia, the western provinces of New Spain,

was commissioned by the viceroy Antonio de Mendoza to investigate
persistent rumors of the "cities of Cíbola"; rumors originating in exaggerated reports by Fray Marcos de Niza and others of the *pueblos* of
northern New Mexico. Coronado set out from Compostela in 1540 with
a considerable armed force, and marched by way of Sonora into New
Mexico. He investigated some of the northern *pueblos* in a cursory disappointed manner, and then, lured on by Indian "guides" who clearly
had no other object than to be rid of unwelcome guests, crossed the
Río Grande and the Pecos and struck out into the prairie country,
probably as far as central Kansas. Everywhere in the plains the soldiers
found great herds of "cattle" and primitive people, "living like Arabs,"
parasitic upon the herds. Denied the opportunities of a *conquistador*,
Coronado showed little interest in those of an explorer. His reports lack
descriptive detail, as he himself apparently lacked curiosity concerning
anything except gold. There is a plaintiveness about his accounts of the
perfidy of his guides and the hardships of living on buffalo meat.

The exploits of Coronado and de Soto added much to geographical
knowledge, but they had no immediate results and added nothing to
the wealth or reputation of those who took part in them. The same is
true of the men who first explored California, or ascended the rivers of
Guiana in search of El Dorado, or discovered the route, later much
used by smugglers, up the Río de la Plata and the Paraguay River into
Upper Peru. Wounds, sickness, disappointment, and early death were
the lot of most of these eternal optimists.

The extract which follows is from *Narratives of the Coronado Expedition, 1540–1542*, edited by George P. Hammond and Agapito Rey,
(Albuquerque, University of New Mexico Press, 1940), pp. 184–90:
Letter of Francisco Vázquez de Coronado to His Majesty, giving an
account of the discovery of the province of Tiguex, October 20, 1541.

Sacred Imperial Catholic Majesty:

On April 20 of the present year I wrote to your Majesty
from this province of Tiguex,[1] in reply to your letter of last year
written at Madrid on June 11. I gave you a detailed report and
account of this expedition, which the viceroy of New Spain
ordered me to make, in the name of your Majesty, to this land
that had been discovered by Fray Marcos de Niza, provincial of

[1] Part of the Pueblo area of New Mexico, north and south of modern
Albuquerque.

the order of Saint Francis. I reported on the entire country, on the type of people, as you must have noted by my letters

While I was engaged in the conquest and pacification of the natives of this province, some Indians, natives of other provinces beyond these, told me that in their lands there were much larger pueblos and better houses than those in this land, that they had lords who governed them, and that they used gold vessels, together with other magnificent things. As I wrote to your Majesty, however, since these accounts were given by Indians and, furthermore, had been obtained by signs, I did not give them credence until I could verify them with my own eyes. Since the information seemed valuable to me, and it was befitting the service of your Majesty that it should be investigated, I decided to go with the men I have here and to see it for myself.

I set out from this province[2] on the 23rd of last April, going the way the Indians guided me. After traveling nine days I came to some plains, so vast that in my travels I did not reach their end, although I marched over them for more than three hundred leagues. On them I found so many cattle, about which I wrote to your Majesty, that it would be impossible to estimate their number. For in traveling over the plains, there was not a single day, until my return, that I lost sight of them.

After seventeen days of travel, I came upon a ranchería of the Indians who follow these cattle. These natives are called Querechos. They do not cultivate the land, but eat raw meat and drink the blood of the cattle they kill. They dress in the skins of the cattle, with which all the people in this land clothe themselves, and they have very well-constructed tents, made with tanned and greased cowhides, in which they live and which they take along as they follow the cattle. They have dogs which they load to carry their tents, poles, and belongings. These people have the best physique of any I have seen in the Indies. They could not tell me anything about the land to which the guides were taking me.

For five days I went wherever they led me, until we reached some plains as bare of landmarks as if we were surrounded by the sea. Here the guides lost their bearings because there is no-

[2] Of Tiguex.

where a stone, hill, tree, bush, or anything of the sort. There are many excellent pastures with fine grass. While we wandered aimlessly over these plains, some mounted men who went out hunting the cattle, met some Indians who were also out hunting and who are enemies of those I met at the previous ranchería. They belong to another nation of people called the Teyas. They paint their bodies and faces and are large people of very fine appearance. They, too, eat raw meat like the Querechos. They live like them and follow the cattle. From them I obtained information concerning the land where the guides were leading me, but their reports did not agree with those I had been given, for these Indians described the houses there as being of straw and hides and not of stone and several stories high, as painted by my guides. Furthermore, the land was poor in maize.

This information caused me considerable worry, and I also suffered greatly from lack of water on finding myself in those endless plains. Many times I drank some which was so bad that it tasted more like slime than water. There the guides confessed that they had not told me the truth regarding the grandeur of the houses, for they were only of straw, but that what they said concerning the large number of people and other things relating to their government was true. The Teyas contradicted this.

In view of this division of opinion among the Indians, and also because many of the people who accompanied me had not eaten anything except meat for several days, for the maize we had taken with us from this province had been exhausted, I decided to go ahead with only thirty horsemen and reach the land, see it, and give a reliable report to you of what was found there. And though it was more than forty days' travel from the place where I met these Teyas to the land where the guides were leading me, and though I realized the hardships and danger I would meet on the journey due to lack of water and maize, I thought it best to go in order to serve your Majesty. I sent the rest of the people I had with me back to this province,[3] under the leadership of Don Tristán de Arellano. For if they had all gone ahead the death of many men could not have been avoided,

[3] Tiguex.

as water was scarce and there were no other provisions except the food that they got by hunting the cattle.

With only thirty horsemen that I took with me as escort, I traveled forty-two days after leaving the army. During all this time we lived on only the meat of the bulls and cows we killed, at the cost of some horses killed by the cattle, for, as I told your Majesty, the animals are very wild and fierce. We went without water for many days and had to cook our food on cow dung, because there is no other fuel in all these plains, except along the arroyos and rivers, of which there are very few.

After traveling seventy-seven days over these barren lands, our Lord willed that I should arrive in the province called Quivira,[4] to which the guides were taking me. They had pictured it as having stone houses many stories high; not only are there none of stone, but, on the contrary, they are of straw, and the people are savage like all I have seen and passed up to this place. They have no blankets, nor cotton with which to make them. All they have is the tanned skins of the cattle they kill, for the herds are near where they live, at quite a large river. They eat the meat raw like the Querechos and the Teyas. They are enemies of one another, but they are all people of the same type. These people of Quivira have the advantage over the others in their houses and in the growing of maize. In this province, of which my guides are natives, I was received peacefully.

Although when I set out for the province I was told that I could not see it all in two months, there are not more than twenty-five towns, with straw houses, in it, nor any more in all the rest of the country that I have seen and learned about. They gave allegiance to your Majesty and placed themselves under your royal authority. The people are large. I had some Indians measured and found that they were ten spans tall. The women are comely, with faces more like Moorish than Indian women. The natives there gave me a piece of copper that an Indian chief wore suspended from his neck. I am sending it to the viceroy of New Spain, for I have not seen any other metal in this region except this and some copper jingle bells which I am

[4] Kansas.

forwarding to him. I am also sending a small amount of metal which resembles gold, but I could not find out where it was obtained, although I believe the Indians who gave it to me got it from the servants that accompanied me. I can not account for its presence or its origin otherwise.

As I have been obliged to send captains and soldiers to many places in this country to find out whether there was anything by which your Majesty could be served, the diversity of languages spoken in this land and the lack of people who understand them has been a great handicap to me, since the people in each town speak their own. And although we have searched with all diligence we have not found or heard of any towns, except those in these provinces, which do not amount to very much.

The province of Quivira is 950 leagues from Mexico by the way I came. It is at a latitude of forty degrees. The soil itself is the most suitable that has been found for growing all the products of Spain, for, besides being rich and black, it is well watered by arroyos, springs, and rivers. I found plums like those of Spain, nuts, fine sweet grapes, and mulberries.

As your Majesty has ordered, I have given the best treatment possible to the natives of this province and to others I met on my trip. They have not been injured by me in any way or by those who came with me.

I spent twenty-five days in this province of Quivira both to see and examine the land and also to find out whether there was anything farther on by which your Majesty might be served, because my guides had told me of other provinces beyond this one. The information I gathered was that there was no gold or other metal in all that country. The other provinces of which they told me are nothing more than small pueblos. In many of them they do not farm, neither do they have houses, except some built of skins and reeds. They move about following the cattle.

So the account they gave me was false—given to induce me to go there with all the army, believing that, as the route was so barren and uninhabited and lacking in water, they would take us to a place where we and our horses would starve to death. The guides admitted this much, saying that they had done it on the advice of the natives of these provinces.

Withal, after visiting the land of Quivira and obtaining the information of the region farther on, mentioned above, I returned to this province to look after the force that I had sent there and to send your Majesty a report of the nature of the land, as I had written you that I would do as soon as I had seen it. I have done everything within my power to serve you, as your faithful servant and vassal, and to discover a country where God, our Lord, might be served by extending your royal patrimony. From the moment I arrived in the province of Cíbola, where the viceroy of New Spain had sent me in the name of your Majesty, I began to explore this land for two hundred leagues and more around and beyond Cíbola, in view of the fact that nothing was found there of what Fray Marcos had said. The best I have found is this Tiguex river, where I am camping, and the settlements here. They are not suitable for settling, because, besides being four hundred leagues from the North sea, and more than two hundred from the South sea, thus prohibiting all intercourse, the land is so cold, as I have related to your Majesty, that it seems impossible for one to be able to spend the winter here, since there is no firewood or clothing with which the men may keep themselves warm, except the skins that the natives wear, and some cotton blankets, few in number.

I am sending the viceroy of New Spain a report of everything I have seen in the lands that I have traversed. And, since Don García López de Cárdenas, after working diligently and serving your Majesty well in this expedition, is leaving to kiss your hands, he will inform you of everything here as a man who has seen it, and I leave the matter in his hands.

May our Lord protect the sacred Cæsarean Catholic person of your Majesty, increasing your kingdoms and dominions, as we, your faithful servants and vassals, desire. From this province of Tiguex, October 20, 1541.

Your Majesty's humble servant and vassal, who kisses your royal feet and hands,

FRANCISCO VAZQUEZ DE CORONADO

VII. *The Pacific*

19. The first sight of the South Sea

In 1513 Vasca Núñez de Balboa, following an Indian report, marched with a small force across the Isthmus of Panama and reached the shore of the Pacific. He was not the first European to sight that ocean; Antonio de Abreu had sailed round the Pacific extremity of the Sunda Islands in the previous year. Abreu's report was kept secret, however, while Balboa's discovery received wide and early publicity. In July 1515, only nine months after the event, Peter Martyr informed the Pope that Balboa had "scaled the mountains and saluted the ocean."[1] The new discovery, moreover, disposed in the clearest and most dramatic way of the notion of a single encircling Ocean Sea. It demonstrated that there were two Ocean Seas, separated by a continental landmass which, though narrow at the point where Balboa crossed it, was known to extend in a general north-south direction for thousands of miles. The Panama coast runs east and west, so Balboa called the other ocean the South Sea, a name which it long retained in Spanish use. Its salinity proved it to be a sea. The rise and fall of its tides—eighteen feet in the Gulf of San Miguel—showed it to be an ocean of considerable extent.

Balboa's own words and actions, and the solemnity with which he "took possession," show that he was aware of the importance of the discovery. Unfortunately no eyewitness record survives. The brief passage quoted here is taken from Oviedo's *History*. Oviedo himself reached Darien in the following year. He knew Balboa personally, and after Balboa's death took charge of his papers. He knew all the participants in the exploit; and was sufficiently impressed by the importance of their achievement to record the list of their names. The third name

[1] *Opus epistolarum,* no. 537.

in the list is that of Francisco Pizarro, who later was to arrest Balboa, at the command of the governor Pedrarias Dávila, his judicial murderer; and who later still was to conquer Peru.

The extract which follows is from Gonzalo Fernández de Oviedo: *Historia general y natural de las Indias*, Part II, Book ix, cap. 3 [Editor's translation].

ON Tuesday the twenty-fifth of September[1] of the year 1513, at ten o'clock in the morning, Captain Vasco Núñez, having gone ahead of his company, climbed a hill with a bare summit, and from the top of this hill saw the South Sea. Of all the Christians in his company, he was the first to see it. He turned back toward his people, full of joy, lifting his hands and his eyes to Heaven, praising Jesus Christ and his glorious Mother the Virgin, Our Lady. Then he fell upon his knees on the ground and gave great thanks to God for the mercy He had shown him, in allowing him to discover that sea, and thereby to render so great a service to God and to the most serene Catholic Kings of Castile, our sovereigns . . .

And he told all the people with him to kneel also, to give the same thanks to God, and to beg Him fervently to allow them to see and discover the secrets and great riches of that sea and coast, for the greater glory and increase of the Christian faith, for the conversion of the Indians, natives of those southern regions, and for the fame and prosperity of the royal throne of Castile and of its sovereigns present and to come. All the people cheerfully and willingly did as they were bidden; and the Captain made them fell a big tree and make from it a tall cross, which they erected in that same place, at the top of the hill from which the South Sea had first been seen. And because the part of the coast which they first discovered was a gulf or inlet, Vasco Núñez gave it the name Gulf of Saint Michael; for the feast of the Archangel fell four days later. And he ordered that the names of all the men who were with him should be written down, so that a record should be kept of him and of them, being the first

[1] The date is probably a mistake, and should read September 27. September 25, 1513, was a Sunday.

Christians who ever saw that sea. And they all sang together the
hymn of the glorious holy fathers of the Church, Ambrose and
Augustine, led by a devout priest Andrés de Vera, who was with
them, saying with tears of joyful devotion *Te Deum laudamus,
Te Dominum confitemur.*

.   .   .

And on the twenty-ninth of the month, St. Michael's Day,
Vasco Núñez named twenty-six men, those who seemed to him
best fitted, to accompany him with their arms, and left the rest
of his force encamped at the village of Chape. He marched with
this party down to the shore of the South Sea, to the bay which
they had named Saint Michael, which was about half a league
from their camp. They found a large inlet, lined with forest,
and emerged on to the beach about the hour of vespers. The
water was low, and great areas of mud exposed; so they sat by
the shore waiting for the tide to rise, which presently it did,
rushing into the bay with great speed and force. Then Captain
Vasco Núñez held up a banner with a picture of the Blessed
Virgin, Our Lady, with her precious Son Our Lord Jesus Christ
in her arms, and below, the royal arms of Castile and León; and
with his drawn sword in his hand and his shield on his arm, he
waded into the salt sea up to his knees, and paced back and
forth, reciting "Long live the most high and most mighty mon-
archs, Don Fernando and Doña Juana, sovereigns of Castile and
Aragon and Navarre, etc., in whose names, and for the royal
crown of Castile, I now take possession, in fact and in law, of
these southern seas, lands, coasts, harbors and islands, with all
territories, kingdoms and provinces which belong to them or
may be acquired, in whatever manner, for whatever reason, by
whatever title, ancient or modern, past, present or future, without let or hindrance. And if any other prince, Christian or infidel, of whatever allegiance, standing or belief, should claim any
right to these lands or seas, I am ready and armed to defy him
and defend them in the name of the Kings of Castile, present
and future, who hold authority and dominion over these Indies,
both islands and mainland, from Arctic to Antarctic, on both
sides of the Equinoctial Line, within and without the Tropics of

Cancer and of Capricorn, as most fully, completely and lawfully belongs to Their Majesties, their heirs and successors for ever, as I declare more at length by writ setting forth their title to this their royal patrimony, now and for all time, so long as the world shall endure, until the last day of judgement." And so he performed the ceremony of taking possession, without let or hindrance, in due form of law. . . . And having done these acts and made these proclamations, binding himself to defend the royal title with sword in hand, by land and by sea against all comers, he called for witnesses. And all who were with him replied to the Captain Vasco Núñez de Balboa that they also were servants and natural vassals of the Kings of Castile and León, and were ready and armed to defend the royal territory, and to die in its defense if need be, against all the kings, princes and peoples of the world; and they recorded their testimony. And those who were present were the following:

> The Captain Vasco Núñez de Balboa,
> Andrés de Vera, Priest,
> Francisco Pizarro
> etc.

These twenty-six, and the notary Andrés de Valderrábano, were the first Christians to tread the shore of the South Sea; and they scooped up the water in their hands and tasted it, to see whether it was salt like the water of the North Sea; and finding that it was salt, and remembering where they were, they all gave thanks to God.

20. From Patagonia to the Philippines

Balboa's discovery posed questions to the academic geographers of his day analogous to those raised some years earlier by Vespucci. How were Vespucci's land and Balboa's sea to be fitted into the orthodox Ptolemaic picture of the world? Vespucci had called America a new country, and had shown it to be a continental landmass; but it might still prove to be an immense southerly peninsula of Asia. Balboa called his ocean the South Sea and did not, apparently, connect it with any sea hitherto known or suspected; but might it not, nevertheless, turn out to be identical with Ptolemy's Great Gulf? It was obvious that those who hoped to reach the "Spicery" by sailing west must cross Balboa's South Sea, and must reach that sea by surmounting or circumventing America. Surmounting America meant building ships on the west coast. Balboa tried this; so, under pressure from the Spanish Crown, did some later *conquistadores,* including Cortés. In 1519 the Crown itself dispatched Gil González Dávila and Andrés Niño from Spain, with orders to take over Balboa's ships, or build new ones, and explore the coast of the South Sea for a thousand leagues, in the hope of finding the Spice Islands. They did not get very far. Some years were to elapse before the little bush harbors of the Pacific could build ships reliable enough for long ocean passages.

Circumventing America meant finding a sea passage, a "strait," through or round it. If—as it began to appear—the Caribbean was landlocked on the west; and if—as many believed—America was joined, somewhere in the northern hemisphere, to Asia; then the strait—if it existed—could only be found by sailing south-about, by passing between America and Ptolemy's *Terra Australis*—if *that* existed—into the Great Gulf. The Plata estuary, which lay roughly on the Tordesillas boundary line, offered a possible opening. It was investigated in 1514 on behalf of Cristóbal de Haro, the international financier; and by a Spanish royal expedition commanded by Juan Díaz de Solís in 1515–16. Solís died there, killed by Indians, and the estuary was known for many years thereafter as the Río de Solís. Further south, the Patagonian coast —it was correctly believed—lay entirely on the Spanish side of the line. The discovery of a strait in that region would be extremely unwelcome to the Portuguese, who were in any event heavily committed to the Cape route to the East; but it would be much in the interest of Spain.

The appearance in Spain in 1517 of an experienced Portuguese explorer, dissatisfied with his Portuguese employment, offered a tempting opportunity. Magellan—Fernão Magalhães—had served some years in the East and had been at the taking of Malacca. He knew—though the Spanish government probably did not—that the Portuguese were already trading in the Moluccas. It is not certain whether he had himself visited those islands, but he knew their approximate position and was in correspondence with Francisco Serrão,[1] an old friend, who was actually living in Ternate. Magellan offered to discover rich islands in the East, within the Spanish demarcation and reached by an all-Spanish route. He was given command of an expedition of five ships, financed in part by the Crown and in part by private investors, notably Cristóbal de Haro. Despite Portuguese diplomatic protests and attempts at sabotage, he sailed from San Lúcar in September 1519. The fleet followed roughly the track of Vespucci's southern voyage, to the bleak bay of San Julián in Patagonia, where mutiny broke out among the Spanish officers, and was suppressed with prompt severity. Further south, in the mouth of the Strait which bears his name, Magellan lost two ships, one by wreck and one by desertion. Magellan's Strait is a most dangerous place for sailing ships, but Magellan was relatively fortunate in his weather and made a relatively prosperous passage of the Strait in thirty-eight days. Once in the Pacific, he was obliged to steer north to find a favorable wind, and his eventual ocean crossing was in a latitude well to the north of the Equator and of the Moluccas. Probably, with his weakened fleet, he hoped to find other similar islands, or perhaps part of the Asian mainland, out of reach of the Portuguese. He may even have known of the existence of the Philippines. For many weeks, however, the explorers sighted no land, save two uninhabited islands, which today cannot be certainly identified. It became clear that they were crossing no mere gulf, but a great ocean; fortunately at the time pacific. Pigafetta's cryptic reference to Catigara suggests a drastic revision of geographical ideas in the course of the voyage. A brief stay at the Thieves' Islands—the Marianas—gave them poor and grudging refreshments. Finally they made landfall at Samar in the Philippines. Here Magellan—like Columbus, a better seaman than diplomat—became involved in a local war, and he and forty of his people were killed. The fleet, now only two ships, sailed on south from the Philippines, skirted the north and east coasts of Borneo, and in November 1520 reached Tidore in the Moluccas, where it was well received by the Sultan and the local traders. One ship, the *Trinidad*, was captured by the Portuguese. The other, the *Victoria*, eluded capture, made its way out through the Banda Sea, crossed the Indian Ocean, rounded the Cape of Good Hope, and staggered back to Spain with a cargo of cloves and eighteen enfeebled survivors. Sebastian del Cano, upon whom the command had devolved, was the first captain to sail round the world.

Magellan's voyage proved that all known oceans were connected, and added one to their number. It demonstrated the separate existence

[1] See p. 109.

and the vast size of the Pacific, and showed that the world was far bigger than Ptolemy believed. It disposed finally of Ptolemy's picture of an Indian Ocean landlocked on the east. At the same time—since no one knew that Tierra del Fuego was an island—it gave *Terra Australis* a new lease of cartographical life. The revision of geographical ideas resulting from the voyage can best be seen in the famous map of Diogo Ribeiro, drawn in Spain in 1529.

Three eyewitness accounts of the voyage survive. One, the log of Francisco Albo, pilot in the *Victoria*, is little more than a list of courses and estimated positions. The second, the log of an unnamed Genoese pilot in the *Trinidad*, relates in humdrum fashion the voyage from Spain as far as the Moluccas, where author and manuscript fell into the hands of the Portuguese. The third is the narrative of Antonio Pigafetta, a Lombard who sailed with Magellan as a gentleman volunteer, returned to Spain with del Cano, and lived to tell the tale. Pigafetta clearly admired Magellan, and skips lightly over episodes such as the San Julián mutiny, which might discredit the captain-general's memory. He neither admired nor liked del Cano, and does less than justice to the prodigious feat of seamanship required to bring the *Victoria* home. Otherwise, the narrative is lively, informative, at times moving, and usually—so far as can be judged—reliable. It is one of the best of all the eyewitness accounts of the Reconnaissance. Pigafetta himself sought permission to publish it but apparently never did so. Condensed versions appeared in the course of the sixteenth century in French, Italian, and English. Ramusio included, in the first volume of the *Navigationi*, a summary, which was Englished by Richard Eden in his *Decades*. The full text of the oldest surviving manuscript, in the Biblioteca Ambrosiana in Milan, was published in Italy in 1800 and again in 1894. The standard modern text, in Italian and English, is that of Robertson, 1906. The extract which follows here begins with the departure from San Julián, after the mutiny, and ends with Magellan's arrival in the Philippines; it is taken from *Magellan's Voyage Around the World* by Antonio Pigafetta, edited and translated by James Alexander Robertson (3 vols., Cleveland, Ohio, Arthur H. Clark Co., 1906), I, 65–73, 83–117, 127–35.

LEAVING that place, we found, in 51 degrees less one-third degree, toward the Antarctic Pole, a river of fresh water. There the ships almost perished because of the furious winds; but God and the holy bodies aided them. We stayed about two months in that river in order to supply the ships with water, wood, and fish, [the latter being] one braccio in length and more, and covered with scales. They were very good although small. Before leaving that river, the captain-general and all of us confessed and received communion as true Christians.

Then going to fifty-two degrees toward the same pole, we found a strait on the day of the [feast of the] eleven thousand virgins [i.e., October 21], whose head is called Capo de le Undici Millia Vergine [i.e., cape of the Eleven Thousand Virgins] because of that very great miracle. That strait is one hundred and ten leguas or 440 millas long, and it is one-half legua broad, more or less. It leads to another sea called the Pacific Sea, and is surrounded by very lofty mountains laden with snow. There it was impossible to find bottom [for anchoring], but [it was necessary to fasten] the moorings on land 25 or 30 brazas away. Had it not been for the captain-general, we would not have found that strait, for we all thought and said that it was closed on all sides. But the captain-general who knew where to sail to find a well-hidden strait, which he saw depicted on a map in the treasury of the king of Portugal, which was made by that excellent man, Martin de Boemia,[1] sent two ships, the "Santo Anthonio" and the "Conceptione" (for thus they were called), to discover what was inside the cape de la Baia [i.e., of the Bay]. We, with the other two ships, [namely], the flagship, called "Trinitade," and the other the "Victoria," stayed inside the bay to await them. A great storm struck us that night, which lasted until the middle of next day, which necessitated our lifting anchor, and letting ourselves drift hither and thither about the bay. The other two ships suffered a headwind and could not double a cape[2] formed by the bay almost at its end, as they were trying to return to join us; so that they thought that they would have to run aground. But on approaching the end of the bay, and thinking that they were lost, they saw a small opening which did not [exceed: *crossed out in original MS*] appear to be an opening, but a sharp turn [can-

[1] Martin Behaim, the maker of the celebrated Nürnberg globe of 1493, died in Lisbon in 1506. He had been associated with Portuguese exploration, on and off, since 1480. Magellan may have known him.

[2] Probably Anegada Point.

tone].[3] Like desperate men they hauled into it, and thus they
discovered the strait by chance. Seeing that it was not a sharp
turn, but a strait with land, they proceeded farther, and found a
bay.[4] And then farther on they found another strait and another
bay larger than the first two.[5] Very joyful they immediately
turned back to inform the captain-general. We thought that they
had been wrecked, first, by reason of the violent storm, and second, because two days had passed and they had not appeared, and
also because of certain [signals with] smoke made by two of
their men who had been sent ashore to advise us. And so, while
in suspense, we saw the two ships with sails full and banners
flying to the wind, coming toward us. When they neared us in
this manner, they suddenly discharged a number of mortars, and
burst into cheers. Then all together thanking God and the Virgin Mary, we went to seek [the strait] farther on.

After entering that strait, we found two openings, one to the
southeast, and the other to the southwest.[6] The captain-general
sent the ship "Sancto Anthonio" together with the "Concitione"
to ascertain whether that opening which was toward the southeast had an exit into the Pacific Sea. The ship "Sancto Anthonio"
would not await the "Conceptione," because it intended to flee
and return to Spagnia—which it did. The pilot of that ship was
one Stefan Gomes, and he hated the captain-general exceedingly,
because before that fleet was fitted out, the emperor had ordered
that he be given some caravels with which to discover lands, but
his Majesty did not give them to him because of the coming of
the captain-general, On that account he conspired with certain
Spaniards, and next night they captured the captain of their ship,
a cousin of the captain-general, one Alvaro de Meschita, whom
they wounded and put in irons, and in this condition took to
Spagnia. The other giant whom we had captured was in that
ship, but he died when the heat came on. The "Conceptione," as
it could not follow that ship, waited for it, sailing about hither
and thither. The "Sancto Anthonio" turned back at night and
fled along the same [port: crossed out in original MS] strait. We

[3] The "First Narrows."
[4] St. Philip's Bay.
[5] The "Second Narrows" and Broad Reach.
[6] Either side of Dawson Island.

had gone to explore the other opening toward the southwest. Finding, however, the same [port: crossed out in original MS] strait continuously, we came upon a river which we called the river of Sardine [ie., Sardines], because there were many sardines near it. So we stayed there for four days in order to await the two ships. During that period we sent a well-equipped boat to explore the cape of the other sea. The men returned within three days, and reported that they had seen the cape and the open sea. The captain-general wept for joy, and called that cape, Cape Dezeado [i.e., Desire], for we had been desiring it for a long time. We turned back to look for the two ships, but we found only the "Conceptione." Upon asking them where the other one was, Johan Seranno,[7] who was captain and pilot of the former ship (and also of that ship that had been wrecked) replied that he did not know, and that he had never seen it after it had entered the opening. We sought it in all parts of the strait, as far as that opening whence it had fled, and the captain-general sent the ship "Victoria" back to the entrance of the strait to ascertain whether the ship was there. Orders were given them, if they did not find it, to plant a banner on the summit of some small hill with a letter in an earthen pot buried in the earth near the banner, so that if the banner were seen the letter might be found, and the ship might learn the course that we were sailing. For this was the arrangement made between us in case that we went astray one from the other. Two banners were planted with their letters—one on a little eminence in the first bay, and the other in an islet in the third bay where there were many sea-wolves and large birds. The captain-general waited for the ship with his other ship near the river of Isleo, and he had a cross set up in an islet near that river, which flowed between high mountains covered with snow and emptied into the sea near the river of Sardine. Had we not discovered that strait, the captain-general had determined to go as far as seventy-five degrees toward the Antarctic Pole. There in that latitude, during the summer season,

[7] The similarity of the names has led some scholars to think that this Serrano or Serrão was a Portuguese, perhaps the brother of the Francisco Serrão who had settled in Ternate (see p. 109) and who supplied Magellan with information about the Moluccas. Pigafetta says Serrano was a Spaniard. The matter has never been completely resolved.

there is no night, or if there is any night it is but short, and so in the winter with the day. In order that your most illustrious Lordship may believe it, when we were in that strait, the nights were only three hours long, and it was then the month of October. The land on the left-hand side of that strait turned toward the southeast and was low. We called that strait the strait of Patagonia. One finds the safest of ports every half legua in it, water, the finest of wood (but not of cedar), fish, sardines, and missiglioni, while smallage,[8] a sweet herb (although there is also some that is bitter) grows around the springs. We ate of it for many days as we had nothing else. I believe that there is not a more beautiful or better strait in the world than that one.

.   .   .

Wednesday, November 28, 1520, we debouched from that strait, engulfing ourselves in the Pacific Sea. We were three months and twenty days without getting any kind of fresh food. We ate biscuit, which was no longer biscuit, but powder of biscuits swarming with worms, for they had eaten the good. It stank strongly of the urine of rats. We drank yellow water that had been putrid for many days. We also ate some ox hides that covered the top of the mainyard to prevent the yard from chafing the shrouds, and which had become exceedingly hard because of the sun, rain, and wind. We left them in the sea for four or five days, and then placed them for a few moments on top of the embers, and so ate them; and often we ate sawdust from boards. Rats were sold for one-half ducado apiece, and even then we could not get them. But above all the other misfortunes the following was the worst. The gums of both the lower and upper teeth of some of our men swelled, so that they could not eat under any circumstances and therefore died.[9] Nineteen men died from that sickness, and the giant together with an Indian from the country of Verzin. Twenty-five or thirty men fell sick [during that time], in the arms, legs, or in another place, so that but few remained well. However, I, by the grace of God, suffered no sickness. We sailed about four thousand leguas during those three months and twenty days through an open stretch in that Pacific Sea. In truth it is

[8] A herb resembling parsley, still common and widely eaten in Patagonia.
[9] Scurvy; a constant refrain in the long voyages of discovery.

very pacific, for during that time we did not suffer any storm. We saw no land except two desert islets, where we found nothing but birds and trees, for which we called them the Ysolle Infortunate [i.e., the Unfortunate Isles]. They are two hundred leguas apart. We found no anchorage, [but] near them saw many sharks. The first islet lies in fifteen degrees of south latitude, and the other in nine. Daily we made runs of fifty, sixty, or seventy leguas at the catena or at the stern.[10] Had not God and His blessed mother given us so good weather we would all have died of hunger in that exceeding vast sea. Of a verity I believe no such voyage will ever be made [again].

When we left that strait, if we had sailed continuously westward we would have circumnavigated the world without finding other land than the cape of the eleven thousand Virgins.[11] The latter is a cape of that strait at the Ocean Sea, straight east and west with Cape Deseado of the Pacific Sea. Both of those capes lie in a latitude of exactly fifty-two degrees toward the Antarctic Pole.

The Antarctic Pole is not so starry as the Arctic. Many small stars clustered together are seen, which have the appearance of two clouds of mist.[12] There is but little distance between them, and they are somewhat dim. In the midst of them are two large and not very luminous stars, which move only slightly. Those two stars are the Antarctic Pole. Our loadstone, although it moved hither and thither, always pointed toward its own Arctic Pole, although it did not have so much strength as on its own side. And on that account when we were in that open expanse, the captain-general, asking all the pilots whether they were always sailing forward in the course which we had laid down on the maps, all replied: "By your course exactly as laid down." He answered them that they were pointing wrongly—which was a fact—and that it would be fitting to adjust the needle of navigation, for it was not receiving so much force from its side. When we were in

[10] An obscure sentence. The *catena* was a crossbeam in the forepart of the ship, to which cables were bitted. The "chip" log, streamed over the stern, was not in use in Magellan's day, as far as is known. Possibly they measured their speed by the time taken for bits of flotsam to float by from *catena* to stern.

[11] I.e. the easternmost cape of the Strait.

[12] The Magallanic clouds, *nubecula major* and *nubecula minor*.

the midst of that open expanse, we saw a cross with five extremely bright stars straight toward the west, those stars being exactly placed with regard to one another.[13]

During those days we sailed west northwest, northwest by west, and northwest, until we reached the equinoctial line at the distance of one hundred and twenty-two degrees from the line of demarcation. The line of demarcation is thirty degrees from the meridian, and the meridian is three degrees eastward from Capo Verde. We passed while on that course, a short distance from two exceedingly rich islands, one in twenty degrees of the latitude of the Antarctic Pole, by name Cipangu, and the other in fifteen degrees, by name Sumbdit Pradit.[14] After we had passed the equinoctial line we sailed west northwest, and west by north, and then for two hundred leguas toward the west, changing our course to west by south until we reached thirteen degrees toward the Arctic Pole in order that we might approach nearer to the land of cape Gaticara. That cape (with the pardon of cosmographers, for they have not seen it), is not found where it is imagined to be, but to the north in twelve degrees or thereabouts.[15]

About seventy leguas on the above course, and lying in twelve degrees of latitude and 146 in longitude, we discovered on Wednesday, March 6, a small island to the northwest, and two others toward the southwest, one of which was higher and larger than the other two. The captain-general wished to stop at the large island and get some fresh food, but he was unable to do so because the inhabitants of that island entered the ships and stole whatever they could lay their hands on, so that we could not protect ourselves. The men were about to strike the sails so that we could go ashore, but the natives very deftly stole from us the small boat that was fastened to the poop of the flagship. Thereupon, the captain-general in wrath went ashore with forty armed men, who burned some forty or fifty houses together with many boats, and killed seven men. He recovered the small boat, and we

[13] The Southern Cross.

[14] Cipangu is Japan; Sumbdit Pradit may be Antilla, marked "Septé Cidade" on the Behaim globe.

[15] Cape Catigara, supposed to lie at the southeastern extremity of Ptolemy's Great Gulf.

departed immediately pursuing the same course. Before we landed, some of our sick men begged us if we should kill any man or woman to bring the entrails to them, as they would recover immediately.

When we wounded any of those people with our crossbow-shafts, which passed completely through their loins from one side to the other, they, looking at it, pulled on the shaft now on this and now on that side, and then drew it out, with great astonishment, and so died. Others who were wounded in the breast did the same, which moved us to great compassion. Those people seeing us departing followed us with more than one hundred boats for more than one legua. They approached the ships showing us fish, feigning that they would give them to us; but then threw stones at us and fled. And although the ships were under full sail, they passed between them and the small boats [fastened astern], very adroitly in those small boats of theirs. We saw some women in their boats who were crying out and tearing their hair, for love, I believe, of those whom we had killed.

Each one of those people lives according to his own will, for they have no seignior. They go naked, and some are bearded and have black hair that reaches to the waist. They wear small palm-leaf hats, as do the Albanians. They are as tall as we, and well built. They have no worship. They are tawny, but are born white. Their teeth are red and black, for they think that is most beautiful. The women go naked except that they wear a narrow strip of bark as thin as paper, which grows between the tree and the bark of the palm, before their privies. They are goodlooking and delicately formed, and lighter complexioned than the men; and wear their hair which is exceedingly black, loose and hanging quite down to the ground. The women do not work in the fields but stay in the house, weaving mats, baskets [casse: literally boxes], and other things needed in their houses, from palm leaves. They eat cocoanuts, camotes [batate], birds, figs one palmo in length [i.e., bananas], sugarcane, and flying fish, besides other things. They anoint the body and the hair with cocoanut and beneseed oil. Their houses are all built of wood covered with planks and thatched with leaves of the fig-tree [i.e., banana-tree] two brazas long; and they have floors and windows. The rooms and the beds are all furnished with the most beautiful palmleaf mats. They sleep on palm straw which is very soft and fine. They use no weapons, except a kind of a spear pointed with a fishbone at the end. Those people are poor, but ingenious and very thievish, on account of which we called those three islands the islands of Ladroni [i.e., of thieves].[16] Their amusement, men and women, is to plough the seas with those small boats of theirs. Those boats resemble *fucelere*, but are narrower, and some are black, [some] white, and others red. At the side opposite the sail, they have a large piece of wood pointed at the top, with poles laid across it and resting on the water, in order that the boats may sail more safely. The sail is made from palmleaves sewn together and is shaped like a lateen sail. For rudders they use a certain blade resembling a hearth shovel which have a piece of wood at the end. They can change stern and bow at will [literally: they make the stern, bow, and the bow, stern], and those boats resemble the dolphins which leap in the water from wave to wave. Those Ladroni [i.e., robbers] thought, according to the signs which they made, that there were no other people in the world but themselves.

At dawn on Saturday, March sixteen, 1521, we came upon a high land at a distance of three hundred leguas from the islands of Latroni—an island named Zamal [i.e., Samar]. The following day, the captain-general desired to land on another island which was uninhabited and lay to the right of the above mentioned island, in order to be more secure, and to get water and have some rest. He had two tents set up on the shore for the sick and had a sow killed for them. On Monday afternoon, March 18, we saw a boat coming toward us with nine men in it. Therefore, the captain-general ordered that no one should move or say a word without his permission. When those men reached the shore, their chief went immediately to the captain-general, giving signs of joy because of our arrival. Five of the most ornately adorned of them remained with us, while the rest went to get some others who were fishing, and so they all came. The captain-general seeing that they were reasonable men, ordered food to be set before them, and gave them red caps, mirrors, combs, bells, ivory,

[16] Now the Marianas.

bocasine, and other things. When they saw the captain's courtesy, they presented fish, a jar of palm wine, which they call *uraca* [i.e., arrack], figs more than one palmo long [i.e., bananas], and others which were smaller and more delicate, and two cocoanuts. They had nothing else then, but made us signs with their hands that they would bring *umay* or rice, and cocoanuts and many other articles of food within four days.

Cocoanuts are the fruit of the palmtree. Just as we have bread, wine, oil, and milk, so those people get everything from the tree. They get wine in the following manner. They bore a hole into the heart of the said palm at the top called palmito [i.e., stalk], from which distils a liquor which resembles white must. That liquor is sweet but somewhat tart, and [is gathered] in canes [of bamboo] as thick as the leg and thicker. They fasten the bamboo to the tree at evening for the morning and in the morning for the evening. That palm bears a fruit, namely, the cocoanut, which is as large as the head or thereabouts. Its outside husk is green and thicker than two fingers. Certain filaments are found in that husk, whence is made cord for binding together their boats. Under that husk there is a hard shell, much thicker than the shell of the walnut, which they burn and make therefrom a powder that is useful to them. Under that shell there is a white marrowy substance one finger in thickness, which they eat fresh with meat and fish as we do bread; and it has a taste resembling the almond. It could be dried and made into bread. There is a clear, sweet water in the middle of that marrowy substance which is very refreshing. When that water stands for a while after having been collected, it congeals and becomes like an apple. When the natives wish to make oil, they take that cocoanut, and allow the marrowy substance and the water to putrefy. Then they boil it and it becomes oil like butter. When they wish to make vinegar, they allow only the water to putrefy, and then place it in the sun, and a vinegar results like [that made from] white wine. Milk can also be made from it for we made some. We scraped that marrowy substance and then mixed the scrapings with its own water which we strained through a cloth, and so obtained milk like goat's milk. Those palms resemble date-palms, but although not smooth they are less knotty than the latter. A family of ten persons can be supported on two trees, by utilizing them week about for the wine; for if they did otherwise, the trees would dry up. They last a century.

Those people became very familiar with us. They told us many things, their names and those of some of the islands that could be seen from that place. Their own island was called Zuluan and it is not very large. We took great pleasure with them, for they were very pleasant and conversable. In order to show them greater honor, the captain-general took them to his ship and showed them all his merchandise—cloves, cinnamon, pepper, ginger, nutmeg, mace, gold, and all the things in the ship. He had some mortars fired for them, whereat they exhibited great fear, and tried to jump out of the ship. They made signs to us that the abovesaid articles grew in that place where we were going. When they were about to retire they took their leave very gracefully and neatly, saying that they would return according to their promise. The island where we were is called Humunu; but inasmuch as we found two springs there of the clearest water, we called it Acquada da li buoni Segnialli [i.e., "the Watering-place of good Signs"], for there were the first signs of gold which we found in those districts.

We found a great quantity of white coral there, and large trees with fruit a trifle smaller than the almond and resembling pine seeds. There are also many palms, some of them good and others bad. There are many islands in that district, and therefore we called them the archipelago of San Lazaro, as they were discovered on the Sabbath of St. Lazarus. They lie in ten degrees of latitude toward the Arctic Pole, and in a longitude of one hundred and sixty-one degrees from the line of demarcation.

At noon on Friday, March 22, those men came as they had promised us in two boats with cocoanuts, sweet oranges, a jar of palm-wine, and a cock, in order to show us that there were fowls in that district. They exhibited great signs of pleasure at seeing us. We purchased all those articles from them. Their seignior was an old man who was painted [i.e., tattooed]. He wore two gold earrings [*schione*] in his ears, and the others many gold armlets on their arms and kerchiefs about their heads. We stayed there one week, and during that time our captain went ashore daily to visit the sick, and every morning gave them cocoanut water from his own hand, which comforted them greatly. There are people living near that island who have holes in their ears so large that they can pass their arms through them. Those people are caphri, that is to say, heathen. They go naked, with a cloth woven from the bark of a tree about their privies, except some of the chiefs who wear cotton cloth embroidered with silk at the ends by means of a needle. They are dark, fat, and painted. They anoint themselves with cocoanut and with beneseed oil, as a protection against sun and wind. They have very black hair that falls to the waist, and use daggers, knives, and spears ornamented with gold, large shields, fascines, javelins, and fishing nets that resemble rizali; and their boats are like ours.

On the afternoon of holy Monday, the day of our Lady, March twenty-five, while we were on the point of weighing anchor, I went to the side of the ship to fish, and putting my feet upon a yard leading down into the storeroom, they slipped, for it was rainy, and consequently I fell into the sea, so that no one saw me. When I was all but under, my left hand happened to catch hold of the clew-garnet of the mainsail,[17] which was dangling [*ascosa*] in the water. I held on tightly, and began to cry out so lustily that I was rescued by the small boat. I was aided, not, I believe, indeed, through my merits, but through the mercy of that font of charity [i.e., of the Virgin]. That same day we shaped our course toward the west southwest between four small islands, namely, Cenalo, Hiunanghan, Ibusson, and Abarien.

On Thursday morning, March twenty-eight, as we had seen a fire on an island the night before, we anchored near it. We saw a small boat which the natives call *boloto* with eight men in it, approaching the flagship, A slave belonging to the captain-general, who was a native of Zamatra [i.e., Sumatra], which was formerly called Taprobana, spoke to them. They immediately understood him, came alongside the ship, unwilling to enter but taking a position at some little distance. The captain seeing that they would not trust us, threw them out a red cap and other things tied to a bit of wood. They received them very gladly, and went away quickly to advise their king. About two hours later we saw

[17] *Sic* in Robertson's translation; but "mainsheet" seems a more likely rendering. [Ed.]

two balanghai coming. They are large boats and are so called [by those people]. They were full of men, and their king was in the larger of them, being seated under an awning of mats. When the king came near the flagship, the slave spoke to him. The king understood him, for in those districts the kings know more languages than the other people. He ordered some of his men to enter the ships, but he always remained in his balanghai, at some little distance from the ship until his own men returned; and as soon as they returned he departed. The captain-general showed great honor to the men who entered the ship, and gave them some presents, for which the king wished before his departure to give the captain a large bar of gold and a basketful of ginger. The latter, however, thanked the king heartily but would not accept it. In the afternoon we went in the ships [and anchored] near the dwellings of the king.

Next day, holy Friday, the captain-general sent his slave, who acted as our interpreter, ashore in a small boat to ask the king if he had any food to have it carried to the ships; and to say that they would be well satisfied with us, for he [and his men] had come to the island as friends and not as enemies. The king came with six or eight men in the same boat and entered the ship. He embraced the captain-general to whom he gave three porcelain jars covered with leaves and full of raw rice, two very large orade,[18] and other things. The captain-general gave the king a garment of red and yellow cloth made in the Turkish fashion, and a fine red cap; and to the others (the king's men), to some knives and to others mirrors. Then the captain-general had a collation spread for them, and had the king told through the slave that he desired to be casi casi with him, that is to say, brother. The king replied that he also wished to enter the same relations with the captain-general. Then the captain showed him cloth of various colors, linen, coral [ornaments], and many other articles of merchandise, and all the artillery, some of which he had discharged for him, whereat the natives were greatly frightened. Then the captain-general had a man armed as a soldier, and placed him in the midst of three men armed with swords and daggers, who struck him on all parts of the body. Thereby was the king rendered al-

18 Perhaps *dorados*, the fish.

most speechless. The captain-general told him through the slave that one of those armed men was worth one hundred of his own men. The king answered that that was a fact. The captain-general said that he had two hundred men in each ship who were armed in that manner. He showed the king cuirasses, swords, and bucklers, and had a review made for him. Then he led the king to the deck of the ship, that is located above at the stern; and had his sea-chart and compass brought. He told the king through the interpreter how he had found the strait in order to voyage thither, and how many moons he had been without seeing land, whereat the king was astonished. Lastly, he told the king that he would like, if it were pleasing to him, to send two of his men with him so that he might show them some of his things. The king replied that he was agreeable, and I went in company with one of the other men.

When I reached shore, the king raised his hands toward the sky and then turned toward us two. We did the same toward him as did all the others. The king took me by the hand; one of his chiefs took my companion: and thus they led us under a bamboo covering, where there was a balanghai, as long as eighty of my palm lengths, and resembling a fusta. We sat down upon the stern of that balanghai, constantly conversing with signs. The king's men stood about us in a circle with swords, daggers, spears, and bucklers. The king had a plate of pork brought in and a large jar filled with wine. At every mouthful, we drank a cup of wine. The wine that was left [in the cup] at any time, although that happened but rarely, was put into a jar by itself. The king's cup was always kept covered and no one else drank from it but he and I. Before the king took the cup to drink, he raised his clasped hands toward the sky, and then toward me; and when he was about to drink, he extended the fist of his left hand toward me (at first I thought that he was about to strike me) and then drank. I did the same toward the king. They all make those signs one toward another when they drink. We ate with such ceremonies and with other signs of friendship. I ate meat on holy Friday, for I could not help myself. Before the supper hour I gave the king many things which I had brought. I wrote down the names of many things in their language. When the king and the others saw me writing, and when I told them their words, they

were all astonished. While engaged in that the supper hour
was announced. Two large porcelain dishes were brought in,
one full of rice and the other of pork with its gravy. We ate
with the same signs and ceremonies, after which we went to
the palace of the king which was built like a hayloft and was
thatched with fig [i.e., banana] and palm leaves. It was built up
high from the ground on huge posts of wood and it was necessary to ascend to it by means of ladders.[19] The king made us sit
down there on a bamboo mat with our feet drawn up like
tailors. After a half-hour a platter of roast fish cut in pieces was
brought in, and ginger freshly gathered, and wine. The king's
eldest son, who was the prince, came over to us, whereupon the
king told him to sit down near us, and he accordingly did so.
Then two platters were brought in (one with fish and its sauce,
and the other with rice), so that we might eat with the prince.
My companion became intoxicated as a consequence of so much
drinking and eating. They used the gum of a tree called *anime*
wrapped in palm or fig [i.e., banana] leaves for lights. The king
made us a sign that he was going to go to sleep. He left the prince
with us, and we slept with the latter on a bamboo mat with pil-
lows made of leaves. When day dawned the king came and took
me by the hand, and in that manner we went to where we had
had supper, in order to partake of refreshments, but the boat
came to get us. Before we left, the king kissed our hands with
great joy, and we his. One of his brothers, the king of another
island, and three men came with us. The captain-general kept him
to dine with us, and gave him many things.

.   .   .

Those people are heathens, and go naked and painted. They wear
a piece of cloth woven from a tree about their privies. They are
very heavy drinkers. Their women are clad in tree cloth from
their waist down, and their hair is black and reaches to the
ground. They have holes pierced in their ears which are filled
with gold. Those people are constantly chewing a fruit which
they call *areca*, and which resembles a pear. They cut that fruit
into four parts, and then wrap it in the leaves of their tree which

[19] A type of construction still common in the Philippines.

they call *betre* [i.e., betel]. Those leaves resemble the leaves of the mulberry. They mix it with a little lime, and when they have chewed it thoroughly, they spit it out. It makes the mouth exceedingly red. All the people in those parts of the world use it, for it is very cooling to the heart, and if they ceased to use it they would die. There are dogs, cats, swine, fowls, goats, rice, ginger, cocoanuts, figs [i.e., bananas], oranges, lemons, millet, panicum, sorgo, wax, and a quantity of gold in that island. It lies in a latitude of nine and two-thirds degrees toward the Arctic Pole, and in a longitude of one hundred and sixty-two degrees from the line of demarcation. It is twenty-five from the Acquada, and is called Mazaua.[20]

We remained there seven days, after which we laid our course toward the northwest, passing among five islands, namely, Ceylon, Bohol, Canighan, Baybai, and Gatighan.[21] In the last-named island of Gatighan, there are bats as large as eagles. As it was late we killed one of them,[22] which resembled chicken in taste. There are doves, turtle-doves, parrots, and certain black birds as large as domestic chickens, which have a long tail.[23] The last mentioned birds lay eggs as large as the goose, and bury them under the sand, through the great heat of which they hatch out. When the chicks are born, they push up the sand, and come out. Those eggs are good to eat. There is a distance of twenty leguas from Mazaua to Gatighan. We set out westward from Gatighan, but the king of Mazaua could not follow us [closely], and consequently, we awaited him near three islands, namely, Polo, Ticobon, and Pozon.[24] When he caught up with us he was greatly astonished at the rapidity with which we sailed. The captain-general had him come into his ship with several of his chiefs at which they were pleased. Thus did we go to Zubu from Gatighan, the distance to Zubu being fifteen leguas.

At noon on Sunday, April seven, we entered the port of Zubu, passing by many villages, where we saw many houses

[20] Now Limasaua.

[21] Leyte, Bohol, Canigao, the northern part of Leyte, and Possibly Apit, on the west coast of Leyte.

[22] Fruit bats, "flying foxes." They are certainly as large as crows. The skins are used as fur in some parts of the Philippines.

[23] The mound-building *megapodes*.

[24] The Camotes: Poro, Pasijan, and Pansón.

built upon logs. On approaching the city, the captain-general ordered the ships to fling their banners. The sails were lowered and arranged as if for battle, and all the artillery was fired, an action which caused great fear to those people. The captain sent a foster-son of his as ambassador to the king of Zubo with the interpreter. When they reached the city, they found a vast crowd of people together with the king, all of whom had been frightened by the mortars. The interpreter told them that that was our custom when entering into such places, as a sign of peace and friendship, and that we had discharged all our mortars to honor the king of the village. The king and all of his men were reassured, and the king had us asked by his governor what we wanted. The interpreter replied that his master was a captain of the greatest king and prince in the world, and that he was going to discover Malucho; but that he had come solely to visit the king because of the good report which he had heard of him from the king of Mazaua, and to buy food with his merchandise. The king told him that he was welcome [literally: he had come at a good time], but that it was their custom for all ships that entered their ports to pay tribute, and that it was but four days since a junk from Ciama [i.e., Siam] laden with gold and slaves had paid him tribute. As proof of his statement the king pointed out to the interpreter a merchant from Ciama, who had remained to trade the gold and slaves. The interpreter told the king that, since his master was the captain of so great a king, he did not pay tribute to any seignior in the world, and that if the king wished peace he would have peace, but if war instead, war. Thereupon, the Moro merchant said to the king *Cata raia chita* that is to say, "Look well, sire." "These men are the same who have conquered Calicut, Malaca, and all India Magiore [i.e., India Major]. If they are treated well, they will give good treatment, but if they are treated evil, evil and worse treatment, as they have done to Calicut and Malaca." The interpreter understood it all and told the king that his master's king was more powerful in men and ships than the king of Portogalo, that he was the king of Spagnia and emperor of all the Christians, and that if the king did not care to be his friend he would next time send so many men that they would destroy him.

21. From the Philippines to Fukien: the first Spanish embassy to China

Magellan's expedition, and especially del Cano's visit to the Moluccas, was a direct challenge to Portugal. It produced a long series of outwardly civil negotiations in Europe, about the position of the islands in relation to an eastern extension of the Tordesillas line of demarcation. In the islands it produced a state of open war, in which the Spaniards had the worst of it. They could not, either by sending ships through Magellan's Strait, or by building them on the Pacific coast of New Spain, provide adequate support for an establishment at Tidore. In 1527 Charles V conceived the idea of transferring to Portugal, for a cash payment, his depreciating claim; and this transaction was formally incorporated in the Treaty of Zaragoza in 1529. Nothing was said about the Philippines—which produced no spices—and for more than thirty years nothing much was done, though Portuguese traders sometimes visited the islands, and the Spanish ships of the Villalobos expedition in 1542 spent some months at Mindanao on their way to the Moluccas. The information brought back by survivors of that disastrous venture was used by Ramusio. In 1565 an expedition from New Spain, commanded by Miguel López de Legazpi, established the first Spanish settlement in Sebu. Manila, on the island of Luzon, was occupied in 1571. It quickly became an important commercial *entrepôt*, where Spanish merchants used Mexican silver to buy silk, porcelain, and other Chinese products from Chinese merchants who frequented the port.

In 1575 the Spaniards in Manila engaged and defeated a Chinese pirate fleet which had caused much damage on the coast of Fukien and which was being pursued by the naval forces of that province. Naval cooperation was probably the only acceptable gift which Europeans at that time could offer to Chinese high officials. In recognition of this service the Chinese naval commander offered to conduct emissaries from the governor of the Philippines to the viceroy of Fukien; an opportunity such as the Portuguese had long coveted and never obtained. An embassy consisting of two soldiers and two religious accordingly visited Fukien, and was courteously received. Nothing came of it; the naval alliance was short-lived, and it was not until after the turn of the century that Ricci and his fellow Jesuits received permission to reside in Peking. Nevertheless, the embassy was important as the first meeting on equal terms between educated Europeans and high officials of the Ming Empire. Two of the envoys at least wrote reports which have survived, but only one has been published, that of Martín de Rada, the distinguished Augustinian scholar and missionary. Rada was both perceptive and diligent. His report contains a most interesting and valuable account of Ming China in its period of rigid isolation, when it was almost unknown to Europeans. Though Rada found his Chinese hosts trying at times, he acquired a healthy respect not only for their civilized ways but also for their numbers, their strength, and their powers of organization. His respect was shared by Philip II, who wisely and realistically refused to have anything to do with plans for aggression against China.

The extract which follows is from *South China in the Sixteenth Century*, edited by C. R. Boxer (London, Hakluyt Society, 1953): "Relation of the things of China which is properly called Taybin," by Fr. Martín de Rada, O.E.S.A., pp. 260–5, 271–8, 282–97.

[*Introduction*]

T HE country which we commonly call China was called by Marco Polo the Venetian the kingdom of Cathay, perhaps because it was then so called; for when he came there, which was about the year 1312, it was ruled by the Tartars.[1] The natives of these islands call China "Sangley," and the Chinese merchants themselves call it Tunsua; however its proper name nowadays is Taybin,[2] which name was given it by the King, Hombu,[3] who drove the Tartars out of China; just as formerly at different times it had other names such as Hanton, Tungzonguam, Tong Gu, Cantay.[4]

The things which we will treat herein concerning this kingdom

---

[1] Marco Polo was in China 1275–1292. Fray Martín de Rada was the first modern European to identify China, correctly and convincingly, with Marco Polo's Cathay.

[2] Ta Ming, or Great Ming Dynasty, which ruled China from 1368 to 1644.

[3] Hung-Wu, reign-title of the first Ming emperor, T'ai-tsu.

[4] These are corrupted renderings of the Amoy vernacular versions of earlier Chinese dynasties, Han, T'ang, Sung, etc.

will be part of them seen with our own eyes, part taken from their own printed books and descriptions of their country, because they take an interest in themselves; for not only do they have general and particular descriptions of their country, but printed books thereof, wherein are described in detail all the provinces, cities, towns, and frontier posts and garrisons, and all the particularities thereof, and the families and tributaries and tributes, and the gains which the King derives from each one of them.[5] Seven of these books came into my hands, different editions by different authors and of different dates, so that by comparing them with each other the truth could be thus better known. Withal as they are a people who know very little geography, geometry, or even arithmetic, they draw their illustrations very crudely, and even their distances and circuits very falsely, so that it is impossible to reconcile them in many places; however, I followed that which seemed to me most truthful, comparing it all with some of their rutters which came to my hands. As regards the distances, I greatly reduced them in some places from those stated in their books, because, even taking the distances separately and afterwards adding them together, they are very wrongly added in the books. Thus as regards the size of the country and the distances, what is stated hereafter will be much less than what is found in their books, but I feel it will be more exact, and I leave the truth to subsequent experience when all the country will have been travelled. But in everything else I will follow what is written in their books, and we will call the country Taybin, because that is its proper name.

As for the name of China or Sina, I do not know where the Portuguese could have got it from;[6] unless it be from some village or point of that name which they found in those parts, and which name they gave to the whole country. . . .

However, there is no point in arguing about names, for the first discoverer calls the land by the name which he wishes, and it is left with it for ever.

[5] Rada is probably referring to provincial and regional histories and topographies, generally described by modern writers as "gazetteers."

[6] The generally accepted derivation is from the Ch'in or Ts'in dynasty of 221–207 B.C.

1. *Of the size of the kingdom of Taybin and its situation*

The kingdom of Taybin must be almost a thousand leagues long and four hundred broad, with a circuit of nearly two thousand and five hundred leagues. It is bounded on the east and on the south side by the Eastern Indian Sea of Further India, which the ancients called Serica. It is bounded on the other and western side by a very large river which rises in some lakes about fifty leagues from the sea, and running many leagues towards the north, finally passes by the end of the wall which divides China from Tartary; and running for almost a hundred leagues outside the wall, it bends towards the east and enters China, almost dividing it in the middle, and finally flows into the sea in the province of Nanquim [Nanking or Kiangnan], after having run winding in and out for more than a thousand leagues of land.[7]

On the north side [of China] is a magnificent boundary-wall of squared stone which is one of the most notable works which have been made in the world; for it must be about six hundred leagues long, and seven fathoms high, and six fathoms broad at the bottom and three at the top, and according to what they say it is all faced with tiles. This boundary-wall was built by the King Cincio nearly eighteen hundred years ago according to their histories.[8] And although beyond the said wall there are many cities and towns as frontier garrisons against the Tartars, in which the king of China appoints two viceroys and three captain-generals, yet because this is something acquired and added since the expulsion of the Tartars, they are not counted in the kingdom of Taybin, even though they are subject thereto.

The sea-coast of this kingdom is almost eight hundred leagues in extent. Beginning in 20° latitude, it runs in a nearly east-northeasterly direction as far as 25°, where lies the city of Hoc-

[7] There may be confusion here between the Huangho or Yellow River, and the Yangtse, though both rivers at that period had their respective outlets to the sea in the province of Nanking. The reference to the Great Wall indicates, however, that it was mainly the Yellow River which Rada had in mind.

[8] The original wall as built by Shih Huang-ti of the Ch'in dynasty (221–210 B.C.) extended from the present province of Kansu to Liaotung. It was considerably repaired and improved in the Ming Dynasty, particularly during the reign of Ch'êng-hua (1464–1487).

chiu,[9] and thence north-east to latitude 29°; and thence the coast bends northwards, and sometimes north-north-east, as far as about latitude 45°, whence the coast bends again to the east, forming a sea like the Adriatic or Gulf of Venice, beginning at the province of Santoan [Shantung] and running for a hundred leagues towards the north-west.[10] From the end of this gulf as far as the capital or principal city of the kingdom of Taybin where the King resides and which is called Suntien,[11] it is not more than three days journey by a river upstream, but this river cannot be navigated by large ships. In my opinion, Suntien will be in about 50° latitude.

All this coast from latitude 29° where lies the city of Nin[g]po —or Liampo as they call it in the maps—is clean and has very good ports, according to what they say. At any rate from what we could see of the coast of Hocquien,[12] it afforded great store of good harbours and deep and clean anchorages. For all along the coast are innumerable islands which all belong to the country of Taybin. Many of them are inhabited and many others are uninhabited, and thus the sea between them seems like rivers. However, from Ningpo upwards until after passing all the province of Nanquim, there are many sandbanks. And from there onwards they say that the coast is clean, although the entrance of that gulf which I said begins at the province of Santon [Shantung], is said to be a very wild and dangerous sea; in such sort that they do not dare to cross it from point to point, but only by coasting it.

Besides these islands which lie near to the coast, there are a very large number of [other] great and populous islands; these I will describe as they are depicted in their draughts. Beginning at the extremity of the province of Canton, which we said lies in latitude 20°, from thence nearly forty leagues to seaward, they say lies the great and populous island of Cauchi[13] which is tributary

[9] Foochow; from the Amoy vernacular form Hok-chiu.
[10] The gulf of Pei-Chihli or Liaotung. Some of these latitudes are wrong.
[11] Shun-t'ien-fu, the official name for the city and prefecture of Peking.
[12] Fukien.
[13] Hainan Island is here confused with Annam under the Chinese name of Chiao-chih.

to China. Over against the province of Hocquien [Fukien] . . . lies towards the northeast of it the island of Zuansin, and from thence towards the northeast, Lusin. To the east of this lies Siaugy, and from here towards the north-west lies the Lesser Leuquiu, the which lies to the east of Hocchiu [Foochow]. Then towards the north, lies the Greater Leuquiu. These islands are called Los Lequios in our maps.[14] More towards the north is Humal, over against Chetcan.[15] From thence to the northwards lies Gitpon,[16] which we call the Japones, and further north than the Japones lies Tauçian.[17] And near the strait at the entrance of the gulf of Santon [Shantung] is Tanhay and at the furthest extremity of Taybin is Halecan.[18]

We had neither time nor opportunity to enable us to learn the names of the peoples and nations which border on the land of Taybin, and therefore we here make mention only of those whom we call Tartars and whom they call Tacsuy. These are they with whom they have had more wars and disputes than with any other nation soever, and who have given them most cause for concern.

$\cdot$ $\cdot$ $\cdot$

4. Of the fighting-men, garrisons and weapons

In all the provinces of Taybin, there is a very great number of fighting-men, some of whom are natives of the provinces wherein they serve, and who are called *Cun,* and who form the largest part. These men do not wear arms, nor do they use them, nor (I believe) do they even keep them in their houses; for although we entered into many houses, we did not see weapons in any of them. They are merely men who are appointed to man the city walls for defence when necessity arises, and each one has his allotted place to which he has to repair. Where we saw this most

[14] The Lesser Liu-chiu are here identified with Western Formosa, the Greater with the islands now known as the Ryukyu.
[15] Chekiang.
[16] Japan.
[17] Chao-hsien, Chosen, or Korea.
[18] Possibly a reference to the Yalu River, which formed the boundary between China and Korea.

clearly was in Hocchiu, where, as the wall is faced with bricks, it has many casemates, and in each of them is inscribed the name of the squadron which has to repair thither, and each squadron consists of about ten men. These same men are responsible for rebuilding their section of the wall if the top or some other part of it falls down. At regular intervals along the wall there was a house with a garret above it; these are used as sentinels' posts or guardrooms during the time of siege; and in each one of these is inscribed the name of the captain (whom they style Cey or Çon), who has to repair thither with his men. There was a distance of about one hundred ordinary paces on the wall of Hocchiu between one guardroom and another, and some seventeen, twenty, or twenty-two casemates, and similarly in the other cities and towns. Even where the wall is not faced with brick, it has its openings in the battlements, inscribed with the names of those who have to man the walls and who are called Cun.[19] This post and duty is hereditary from father to son, and being styled soldiers they do not pay tribute.

The other sort of soldiers are strangers from other provinces who serve for wages, and among these must be counted the guards of the viceroys, governors, captains and justices, and all the men who serve these and the ministers of justice, sheriffs, constables and executioners, and likewise all the sailors who man the royal fleets and ships. As all these are reckoned among the number of fighting-men and garrisons, their number reaches an incredible total, amounting to 4,178,500 foot and 780,000 horse, distributed in the manner following,—

Province	Foot	Horse
Paquiaa (Peking)	1,141,100	229,000
Canton (Shantung)	223,800	99,000
Sansi (Shansi)	152,600	32,900
Holam (Honan)	140,000	15,900
Siamcay (Shensi)	130,000	61,000
Susuan (Ssŭch'üan)	120,000	10,000
Oucun (Hukuang)	310,000	72,600

[19] Hereditary militia.

Province	Foot	Horse
Lanquiaa (Nanking)	840,000	70,000
Chitcan (Chekiang)	160,000	40,000
Cansay (Kiangsi)	110,000	30,000
Hocquien (Fukien)	200,000	—
Cuanton (Kuangtung)	157,000	—
Holan (Yünnan)	170,000	80,000
Cunsay (Kuangsi)	100,000	12,000
Cuichiu (Kueichou)	160,000	37,400

Of these strangers, the bodyguards of the captains and governors and the guards of the city gates are continuously under arms. Their weapons are arquebusses, pikes and halberds, and other kinds of hafted weapons, some with scimitars and others made like sickles to cut the legs, and others with three prongs, as likewise scimitars and shields. They also use bows and arrows in war, both ahorse and on foot; and these archers hold a monthly review and are very skilful with their weapons. We saw one in Hocchiu under two captains, each having about six hundred men, and it was admirable to see how speedy and skilful they were in what they had to do, even though their manœuvres were not done in ordered array as we are wont to do, but in crowds and all huddled very close together.

Their artillery (at least that which we saw, and although we entered an armoury in Hocchiu) is most inferior, for it consists only of small iron guns.[20] On their walls they have neither bastions nor cavaliers[21] from which to play their artillery, but all their strength is concentrated on their gates. They make great use of incendiary bombs of gunpowder, particularly on board ship, and they put inside them many iron crowsfeet, in sort that nobody can walk thereon. They also use fire-arrows wherewith to burn the ship's timbers; also large numbers of great javelins with iron barbs on long shafts, as also broad-swords of half a fathom for boarding.

[20] The Chinese had employed artillery since the beginning of the twelfth century, but Ming writers admitted that Chinese guns were inferior to those of the "Franks" or *Fo-lang-chi*.

[21] Turrets.

5. Of the population of the kingdom of Taybin and tributers and tributes[22]

Although it is not possible to state exactly the number of people that there are in such great and populous kingdoms, nor is it to be found in any of their books, yet some idea can be gained of the infinite number of people from the register of the tributers and other things which are recorded. And moreover some indication of their multitude is given by the fact that the fighting-men alone number nearly five millions. However, as regards taxes in general, it should be noted that in the provinces of Taybin the people are divided into households, some of which are gentry and the others tributers.

The gentry are known by the square bonnets which they wear, something like a clergyman's biretta, whereas the tributers have a round one. The gentry are nearly as numerous as the tributers, as we saw in all the places through which we passed.[23] Some of the tax-paying households pay at the rate for six or eight or less tributers, although their households are much more numerous, as many of them told us, among whom was one called Jacsiu, who told us that there were seventy men in his household, and that he did not pay more taxes than for seven. Another told us that there were about sixty men in his, and that he only paid taxes for four. In sort that the register of the tributers is much less [than it ought to be]; although the number of tributers is thus recorded in the register of the families and tributers of each province which is reproduced herewith:

Province	Households	Tributers
Paquiaa (Peking)	418,789	3,413,254
Santon (Shantung)	770,555	6,759,675
Sansi (Shansi)	589,959	5,084,015
Holam (Honan)	589,296	5,106,107
Siamsay (Shensi)	363,207	3,934,176
Susuan (Ssŭch'üan)	164,119	2,104,270

[22] Tax-payers and taxes.

[23] Rada was mistaken in suggesting that the scholar-gentry (whom he calls *hidalgos*) as a class were exempt from taxation. Officials and certain other groups were exempt from poll tax.

Province	Households	Tributers
Oucun (Hukuang)	531,686	4,325,590
Lamaquiaa (Nanking)	1,962,818	9,967,439
Chetcan (Chekiang)	1,242,135	4,515,471
Cansay (Kiangsi)	1,583,097	7,925,185
Hocquien(Fukien)	509,200	2,082,677
Cuanton (Kuangtung)	483,380	1,978,022
Cuynsay (Kuangsi)	186,090	1,054,767
Onilam (Yünnan)	132,958	1,433,110
Cuyiuchiu (Kueichou)	148,957	5,132,891

Thus the total of the households which there are in all the fifteen provinces is 9,676,246, and the tributers are 60,187,047. And in this accompt, the cities of the salt-makers are not included, nor the others which we said were outside the jurisdiction and register of the fifteen provinces, because they and their subjects are not included in this register. Neither are many others, because they bring no profit to the king beyond sustaining the frontier garrisons of the western marches, and therefore no accompt is made of them in the books, save only their names are listed. But these contain not a few people, for in the seven cities of the salt-makers alone, an incredible number of villages are registered in the books as pertaining to them, —they say that there are 1,177,525 villages, which, even if they do not average more than thirty householders apiece, would amount to more than 35,000,000 people. From this it will be seen what an infinite number of people there are in this kingdom; and in truth all the country through which we travelled was an ant-hill of people, and I do not believe that there is as populous a country in the world. The taxes which are levied each year by the king, when reduced to our weights and measures are as follows.

Silver	2,863,211 ducats
hulled rice	60,171,832 *fanegas*
barley	29,391,982 *fanegas*
another kind of grain [*sic*][24]	139,535 *quintals*

[24] Possibly maize, then of relatively recent introduction from the New World. A *fanega* was approximately a bushel; *quintal* a hundredweight; *arroba* about 25 pounds.

salt	5,990,262 *fanegas*
silken pieces of 14 varas	205,598
cotton cloth	130,870
raw silk	47,676 pounds
clean cotton ('algodon limpio')	12,856 *arrobas*
pieces of linen	3,077
petates	2,590

All this is what they say belongs to the king, and is exclusive of all that is given to the judges, viceroys, governors, justices, captains and soldiers, for that is not included in this register. Only, we have included in the amount of rice, eight million fanegas, which is what is given for the rations of the king's bodyguard and for the city of Peking.

.   .   .

7. *Of the manner of the people and of their customs and clothes.* The people of Taybin are all, on the one hand, white and well-built, and when they are small children they are very fair, but when they grow up they become ugly. They have scant beards and small eyes. They are proud to have a great head of hair. They let it grow long and coil it up in a knot on the crown of the head. They then put on it a hair-net, parted in the centre, to hold and fix the hair in position, wearing on top of it a bonnet made of horse-hair. This is their ordinary headgear, although their captains' bonnets are of another kind, made of finest thread, and underneath a hair-net of gold thread. They take a good time each morning in combing and dressing their hair. The women do not make use of any hair-ornaments save only some garland, or jewelry of silver or gold, which they fix on the coils of their hair.

The women are very secluded and virtuous, and it was a very rare thing for us to see a woman in the cities and large towns, unless it was an old crone. Only in the villages, where it seemed that there was more simplicity, the women were more often to be seen, and even working the fields. They are accustomed since babyhood to bind and cramp the feet in such a way that they deform them, leaving all the toes below the great toe twisted underneath.

The men often let the fingernails of one of their hands grow very long, and are very proud thereof, as we saw by many of them whose fingernails were as long as their fingers. Their ordinary dress is of cotton-linen, dyed either blue or black, except when they wear mourning. Their dress is then made of another kind of coarse linen, and the nearer their kinship to the deceased, the coarser is the linen of their dress. Their ordinary dress is a long loose upper-coat reaching down to the stockings, and a pair of long narrow drawers, and shoes made of straw. Some of them put underneath the coat, instead of a shirt, a silken net-work vest and a very wide mesh through which you can put your finger; and the captains who accompanied us, when indoors, took off their coats because of the heat, and went about in this net-work vest and their drawers. The pages of the captains ordinarily go with their hair coiled up on top and secured with a thread and bodkin thrust through. They wear stockings and straw shoes, likewise woven, but which look like nothing so much as silk mesh.

The important people, and captains and governors, wear long silken gowns, usually of damask, reaching down to the ground, with large and wide sleeves, and wide and large boots of dark colour, with the point of the toe turned up. To put them on, they first tie a large linen fillet round their feet and legs. The boots and bonnets which differ serve to distinguish those who are officers of justice, or captains, and so forth. As a rule they have a great lion[25] embroidered on the breast and back of these silk gowns. The bonnets of the common people are round, and those of the gentry square like clergymen's birettas, and all these are of horsehair, save when they wear mourning as we have said above. The viceroys, governors, captains, and ministers of justice when at home wear a bonnet like a bishop's small mitre with golden welts and embroidery. But when they go out in the streets or sit upon their thrones, they wear a kind of bonnet, the back half of which stands up nearly six inches and which moreover has, as it were, two wings or large ears sticking straight

[25] I.e. dragon.

out at the sides. These bonnets are worn by all the ministers of justice, and captains and viceroys. However, if any one of these captains or justices goes to interview one of his superiors, then he does not wear such a bonnet, but takes along a state-umbrella.

The King's bonnet, as I have seen it depicted in many places, is of the same shape as that of the justices, save that it is square, and the two wings which we described are not so large, nor placed at the two sides, but are high on the back part, sticking up like horns. The bonnet of the secretaries or scriveners likewise has its ears, but they are made very differently from the others. The bonnets of the judges and the councillors of the king also differ from the others in the placing and shape of the ears. The bonnets of the students are shaped like letter-carriers or caskets, highly gilded and polished. Those of their friars are shaped like mitres, but differently from the captains' described above; and they fashion something like rosettes out of the folds of the front part of these bonnets, so that by the form of the bonnet you can know who a person is and what office he has.

They are a plain, humble and obliging people, save only the mandarins who set themselves up as gods. They are great workers and very active in their trades, so that it is astounding to see how diligently they furnish their works, and in this they are most ingenious. There are to be found entire streets for each trade.

With the exception of the mandarins and soldiers in garrisons, everyone has his own proper employment. Although they have little sumpter-mules and little asses and pack-horses, they also employ men to carry burdens, like the natives of New Spain. But one Chino will carry as much as three Indians of New Spain, and thus laden they will go almost as well as a horse. It is easier to find men for carrying burdens than it is animals; nay, many times they dispute with and strike each other over who will carry the burden. Thus when we approached a place whence we were to begin the next day's journey, no sooner were we descried from the village or the ploughed fields, than many people ran out to meet us, vying with each other as to who should take some of the burdens; and many times they took them over from those who were carrying them as much as half a league before the village, in order to stake their claim to carry it on the next day, solely for the gain and pay thereof; and at times they came to fisticuffs as to who should carry it. Their manner of carrying the burden is in two bundles or hampers slung at either end of a pole carried over their shoulder. If it is a very heavy burden or chest, they carry it slung from a pole between two of them. They usually travel six or seven leagues a day, and when they put down their burden they return to their own village,—I suppose that they return there to sleep.

When their principal men go out, even if it is only to visit a friend in the city, they go in large canopied chairs, carried like biers on men's shoulders. The other people go either ahorse or afoot. When the sun is fiercest everyone carries his own sunshade and a fly-whisk, however poor or lowly he may be. If any common man, through illness or exhaustion, wishes to go in a chair, he has to go in a lowly little chair of cane, forasmuch as only the captains and justices can go in the large and covered ones. The higher their dignity, the richer their chair. The principal persons have their chairs all decorated with broad and well-wrought bands of ivory on gilded planks which are very fine and well worth seeing. There is in each community-house a great quantity of chairs of different kinds, for the visitors who come there to make use of, according to their quality.

They are a people who use many compliments and civilities. They do not doff their bonnet or hat to anybody, but when they meet each other, instead of doffing their bonnet, they put their hands in their sleeves, and clasping them together they lift them up as high as their breast. And when they wish to be more courteous, instead of making reverence as we do, they make a deep bow, with their hands in their sleeves as described above, their hands reaching nearly to the ground, and their head lower than their knees; and then straightening up, they bring their hands close to their breast. And they are not satisfied with one of these bows, but make three or four, or more. If four or five of them meet together, each one makes his bows. Even when they are discussing business, from time to time they put their hands in their sleeves and raise them to their breast.

They have scores of other kinds of ceremonies. Both in dealing with as in receiving or in going out to accompany any superior, they kneel down on both knees, and putting their hands in their sleeves and up to their breast, they bend their head down until their forehead touches ground, and this they do three times or more. While they are speaking, they never get up, but listen and answer on their knees to what is said to them. Even to us, the common people sometimes spoke on their knees, and bowed their heads to the ground. And some of those who had been in Manila laughed at the Spaniards who did not bend more than one knee in church, saying that if anyone had bowed in that way on only one knee to a mandarin, he would have been soundly whipped. For this reason, those who have to deal very often with a mandarin are wont to carry along some knee-pads. Likewise, when one goes to visit another, he usually takes a docket stating that he has come to kiss his hand, which he gives him after having made his bows. When one comes to visit another, after having made their bows and being seated, a household servant comes with a tray of as many cups of hot water as there are persons seated. This water is boiled with certain somewhat bitter herbs, and with a little morsel of conserve in the water. They eat the morsel and sip the hot water. Although at first we did not care much for that hot boiled water, yet we soon became accustomed to it and got to like it, for this is always the first thing which is served on a visit.

8. Of their manner of eating, and of their banquets

The principal food of all Chinos is rice, for although they have wheat and sell bread kneaded therefrom, yet they do not eat it save as if it were a fruit. Their chief bread is cooked rice, and they even make a wine from it which is comparable with a reasonable grapewine and might even be mistaken for it. They eat seated at tables, but they do not use table-cloths or napkins; for they do not touch with their fingers anything that they are going to eat, but they pick up everything with two long little sticks. They are so expert in this, that they can take anything, however small, and carry it to their mouth, even if it is round, like plums and other such fruits. At the beginning of a meal they eat meat without bread, and afterwards instead of bread they eat three or four dishes of cooked rice, which they likewise eat with their chopsticks, even though somewhat hoggishly. At banquets, a table is placed for each guest, and when the banquet is a formal one, each guest gets many tables, and to explain this I would like to recount what sort of banquets they offered us, and the way in which they were served.

In a large room, at the top of the hall, they placed seven tables in a row for each one of the Religious, and along the side-walls five tables for each of the Spanish laymen who were there, and three tables for each of the Chinese captains who accompanied us. And next to the doors of the hall, opposite the Religious, sat the captains who had invited us, each one at his own table. In our room they had arranged on one side three tables bearing the covers for each one of us. All these tables were loaded as much as they could be with plates and dishes of food, save that only the principal table contained cooked meats, and all the uncooked food was on the other tables which were for grandeur and display. There were whole geese and ducks, capons and hens, gammons of bacon and other chops of pork, fresh pieces of veal and beef, many kinds of fish, a great quantity of fruits of all kinds, with elegant pitchers and bowls and other knicknacks all made of sugar, and so forth. All this which was put upon the tables, when we got up therefrom, was put into hampers and carried to our lodgings. In sort that everything which is put there for display all belongs to the guests.

Outside the door of the house where the banquet was held, was arrayed the whole bodyguard of our host, with their weapons, drums and musical instruments which they began to play when we arrived. The captains who were to be present at the banquet came out halfway into the courtyard to receive us, and without making any courtesy or bow we went together to a reception-room which was in front of the banqueting-hall, where we made our bows one by one according to their custom. With many ceremonies we seated ourselves there, each on a chair, and they forthwith brought the hot water [tea] which I have described above. When we had drunk this, we conversed for a short space, and then went to the banqueting-hall, where, after many ceremonies and courtesies which I omit to avoid tediousness, they conducted each one of us individually to the table where we were to sit. On this table the captains placed the first dish and a little cup full of wine. When everyone was seated, the music began to play, consisting of tamborets, gitterns, re-

becks, lutes with a big arch, and they played continuously for
as long as the banquet lasted.

Other persons in the middle of the hall acted a play, and what
we saw were elegant representations of old stories and wars,
whose plot was explained to us beforehand, so that although we
did not understand the words yet we well understood what was
happening. In Hocchiu [Foochow], besides the plays, there was
a tumbler who did fine tricks, both on the ground and on a
stick. Although the table be full of food, there is never any
pause in the flow of broths and dressed meats. As long as the
banquet lasts they drink healths heartily, although not with gob-
lets but, as it were, in little saucers. In drinking they are a
temperate people as far as we could see. They do not drink
wine continually but only water; and when they drink wine
they drink it very hot, and they sip it like a broth, although they
gave it us cold, as they knew that we did not drink it hot. They
think it mean of the host to rise first from the table, but on the
contrary as long as the guests are there, more and more dainties
are continually served until they wish to get up. Even after we
got up, they asked us to sit down again, begging us to wait for
another one or two dishes, and this they did two or three times.
Their manner of acting is with chanting, and they also usually
act puppet-plays which go through all their motions, and men
behind the scenes say what has to be spoken.

In their food they are not great meat-eaters, but on the contrary in our experience their principal food is fish, eggs, vegetables, broths and fruit. The things which we saw like unto our
own (apart from many other different kinds) were fish, wheat,
barley, rice, beans, millet and *borona*. There were kine and buffaloes, and they say that there are also sheep the land inward; and
we also saw pigs, goats, and hens like ours and others which
have black flesh and are more tasty,[26] and likewise capons and
godwits. We did not see any game, because in the region where
we were there was no waste-land for them, but they say there
is some the land inward. We saw birds of prey, likewise geese
and royal ducks, and great store of doves and turtle-doves. Of

[26] The black-fleshed fowl of Fukien are mentioned by Marco Polo. Their
origin has been the subject of much discussion.

fruits, there are white and black grapes in vines, although we did not see any wine made therefrom, and I do not believe they know how to make it. Also oranges and lemons of many kinds, and large citrons, pears, apples, wild pears, peaches, plums, mulberries, nuts, chestnuts, jujubes, pumpkins, cucumbers, water-melons, cabbages, coleworts, turnips, radishes, garlic, onions, and many other fruits and vegetables peculiar to the country. They have much sugar and they make many and very good conserves.[27] Even in the squares and streets they have dwarf trees in pots and tubs, and I do not know with what ingenuity they grow them that though so small they can yet bear fruit, because we saw them laden with fruit. They also have a kind of tree from the fruit of which they take something like tallow, whereof throughout the whole country they make candles to give light, and which anyone would think was animal fat.[28] They have coconut-palms in the southern provinces but not in Hocquien [Fukien] nor north thereof. They have horses although small ones, and asses, mules and donkeys. We saw good ones and droves of them.

9. *Of the buildings, husbandry, mines and other things which there are in this country*

Their manner of building is always low without any stories, although in a very few places we saw some little houses with upper stories, and over the gates of the cities they usually have some galleries and large halls. There are also some towers of idols, built square and of a good height, which have many fenestrations on all four sides, wherein they place their idols. We saw two of these in Chiunchiu,[29] and another two in Hocchiu [Foochow], and another three at the top of some hills. One of these last is at the very entrance of the haven, on a great hill which the call Gousou, which can be seen from afar off at sea and can serve as a sea-mark for the port.

The houses of the great men, even though they are not storied,

[27] Marco Polo mentions sugar production in Fukien.

[28] Vegetable tallow, obtained from the tallow-tree (*Sapium sebiferum*), which is common in all the warmer parts of China.

[29] The first mention in European literature of the famous twin pagodas of the K'ai-Yuan temple at Ch'üan-chou. They were built in the thirteenth century.

are very large and they occupy a great space, for they have courtyards and more courtyards, and great halls and many chambers and kitchen-gardens. These halls are ordinarily higher up than the ground by three or four steps of very large and beautiful flagstones. The foundations are usually of square stone, and are built on the ground of each room to the height of about a *vara*.[30] They then place thereon some pillars or posts of pinewood on bases of stone; the keystones on top are very well wrought and the ceiling covered with tiles. The floor is well paved with bricks set very close together, although without lime, and sometimes paved with flagstones. Between the pillars they have thin walls of lath and plaster over wattle frames strengthened with great bars of wood and first daubed with clay on both sides and then plastered. The walls of the courtyards and kitchen-gardens are of tamped earth plastered on the outside. We saw one house in Tangoa which was well worth seeing, with a very fine pond all paved with flagstones, and with arbours and paths above the water, and very fine tables made from single slabs of stone. Of similar form are the royal community-houses which we said above were in all the towns, some being larger and others smaller. The houses of the common people are like the little houses of the Moriscos. Each one occupies about fourteen feet of street frontage, and they usually consist of two rooms with a small courtyard in between. The room which abuts on the street is divided into two, the front part serving as a shop.

The main streets are very broad, and they all have a large number of triumphal arches, some of very well wrought stone and others of wood. For every great man prides himself on leaving as a memorial such an arch, inscribed with his name and the year it was built, and other notable things which he did. These main streets serve as market-places, and there are to be found in them every kind of meat, fish, fruits and vegetables; and stalls selling books, paper, knives, scissors, bonnets, shoes, straw sandals, etc. As these main streets are so wide, there is a good space left in the middle, with room to pass between the stalls and the houses, although the stalls stretch from one end of the street to the

[30] The Spanish *vara* was a little less than an English yard.

other. The other streets are all filthy little alleys. Their way of
building walls has been described above. They are all of square
stone, although daubed with clay without lime, and then the
joints are plastered over on the outside. Their lime is made from
oyster-shells and mussels. Their highways are paved with flagstones, and there are many well wrought bridges of stone. The
tombs of the principal people are usually outside the towns
and cities, and are built of stone. In front of the grave, facing
the road, is a very large flagstone erected on a tortoise or
some other animal, hewn from one large stone slab. On the
tombstone are inscribed the achievements of the man who is
buried there.

Most of their husbandry is by irrigation, in so far as we could
see, and greatly abounds in rivers and waters. With certain buck-
ets fixed to wooden water-wheels, they easily irrigate all their
crops, and even on top of the hills they have irrigated crops. I
think they give the land but little rest, for when we went to
Hocchiu [Foochow] we found all the land tilled in this way.
Some of the rice had not yet been transplanted, some had just
been, some was more advanced, some was fairly grown, and
some was being harvested. On our return, we saw the same kind
of activity, for another crop was already planted where the
first had been harvested, and elsewhere another was being gathered in. They till the soil with hoes and ploughs. They have mills
both to cleanse the rice from the straw as to make meal, and
they are hand-mills, although we saw a few water-mills.

There is a great abundance of silk and cotton, sugar and
musk throughout all the country, as also many drugs.[31] There are
mines of all kinds of metals, iron, steel, copper, latten[32] in great
abundance and very cheap, and also lead and tin. They say that
there are mercury mines in the province of Namquin. The mines
of gold and silver which are listed in their books are as follows.[33]

[31] I.e. spices and medicinal plants.
[32] Zinc, important as an ingredient in brass.
[33] Silver and gold mines were a natural subject of interest; but Chinese
production of precious metals did not compare with that of the New World.
China was short of silver; a fact of great economic importance to the
Spaniards at Manila.

Province	District	Mines
Paquiaa [Peking]	Poam	Silver
Santon [Shantung]	Tinchiu	Gold
Oucum [Hukuang]	River Buchian	Silver
	River Sinchiu	Gold
Namquien [Nanking]	Linquoy	Silver
Chetcan [Chekiang]	Unchiu	Gold
Hocquien [Fukien]	Hocchiu [Foochow]	Silver
	Ciuchiu [?Ch'üan-chou]	Gold and Silver
Cuinsay [?Kuangsi]	Quinoan	Silver
Quanton [Kuangtung]	Yanchiu [Lien-chou]	Pearl-fishery

Despite all this, most of the people are poor, as there are so many of them; and thus everything is very cheap, and all things are sold by weight, even birds and firewood. We did not see any kind of money save only in the district of the city of Cunchiu [Chüan-chou] and its appendages, where there was a stamped copper money with a hole bored through the middle of it. They gave us 312 and 320 of these pieces for four rials.

Everywhere else (and also there) everything is bought by weight with little bits of silver which weigh what they call a *Nio*. One of these *nio* weighs eleven rials in our money; and one *nio* equals ten *lacuns* and one *lacun* equals ten *phou* and one *phou* equals ten *dis*, in sort that they divide eleven rials of our weight into a thousand parts.

We also saw poor people who went begging through the streets, especially blind. Although they are so numerous a people they do not throw anything away. They do not waste a bone or horn, but make a thousand things thereof, as also of straw and grass, and they make use of everything in some way or other.

Their ships are somewhat slow and ill-made, although they sail very well before the wind and well enough close-hauled. They do not have sea-cards but they do have some manuscript rutters.[34] They also have a compass-needle, but not like ours, for it is only a very sensitive little tongue of steel which they touch with a loadstone. They place it in a little saucer full of sea-

---

[34] Rada was mistaken. Ming China had both charts and written sailing directions.

water and on which the winds are marked. They divide the compass into twenty-four parts, and not into thirty-two as we do.

As regards their paper, they say it is made from the inside pith of canes. It is very thin, and you cannot easily write on both sides of the paper, as the ink runs through. They sell the ink in little slabs, and write with it after moistening it in some water. For pens they use extremely fine little brushes. Their letters are the most barbarous and difficult of any which have yet been discovered, for they are characters rather than letters. They have a different character for every word or thing, in sort that even if a man knows ten thousand characters he cannot read everything. Thus he who can read the most is the wisest among them.

There came into our hands printed books of all the sciences, both astrology and astronomy, as physiognomy, chiromancy, arithmetic, and of their laws, medicine, fencing, and of every kind of their games, and of their gods. In all of these (save only in medicinal matters, wherein like herbalists they know from experience the virtues of herbs and depict them as we do in the book of Dioscorides), in everything else there is nothing to get hold of, since they have nothing more than the smell or shadow of the substance. For they do not know anything of geometry, nor do they have compass-dividers, nor can they reckon beyond simple addition, subtraction and multiplication.[35] They think that the sun and the moon are human, that the sky is flat, and that the earth is not round. It is true that, like the natives of these islands,[36] they recognize many of the stars, and by their relative positions they calculate the seasons for sowing and

[35] Rada is unfair in his cursory dismissal of Chinese mathematics and astronomy. It is true that mathematical studies were in a dormant condition at this time; but some of the older works contained material which, in some respects at least, was actually in advance of the methods that were later introduced by Ricci and the Jesuits. Geometry was altogether new to Ming China, but the ancient Chinese were acquainted with trigonometry, both plane and spherical, as well as with algebra and other branches of mathematics. A. Wylie: *Notes on Chinese Literature* (ed. Shanghai, 1922), pp. 106–119; Dyer-Ball: *Things Chinese*, p. 355.

[36] I.e. the Philippines, where Rada wrote his report after returning from Fukien.

harvesting; and they know thereby when the north-east and south-west monsoon winds begin, and when it is the season for storms or heats,—but since these Indians, although savages, know such things, it is obvious that the Chinos know them much better. I also saw sundials in the city of Hocchiu [Foochow], but they were ill-made, as if by ignorant people, and did not give the exact hour. All their divination is usually done by casting lots.

When they know that someone of good family can read really well, he is examined by one called a Ja Ju, and if he is found sufficiently able he is given what we would call a bachelor's degree. They place two silver nosegays in his ears, and he is taken on horseback in procession through the city with flags and minstrels in front. We saw one of these in Hocchiu [Foochow], and he was a noble youth. When they receive that degree they are thenceforth fitted to exercise some office of justice; for nobody who cannot read and write well (and knows the court language besides) can become a governor or his deputy.

In each province they have a different speech, although they are all rather similar—just as those of Portugal, Valencia and Castile resemble each other. The script of China has this peculiarity, that since not letters but characters are used, then the same document can be read in all the tongues of China; although I saw documents written in the court script which was different from that of Hocquien [Fukien]. However, the one style and the other can be read in both tongues.

VIII. *By the Arctic to Cathay*

§§§§§§§§§§§§§§§§§§§§§§§§§§§§§§§§§§§§§§§

22. In the wake of the Norsemen

The first European discoverers of America, so far as is known, were Norse adventurers. These wanderers from a harsh northern home—by turns farmers, traders, and pirates, endlessly daring, incurably land-hungry—were the best seamen of the Europe of their day, and possessed the best oceangoing ships. They occupied Iceland—where Irish wanderers had probably preceded them—in the ninth and tenth centuries. Latecomers to Iceland went further, and established farming communities in southwest Greenland. To the west and southwest of Greenland they found other lands: Helluland or Baffin Land, good for nothing save perhaps hunting; Markland or Labrador, where they could get timber, precious in treeless Greenland; and Vinland, which offered good pasture as well as timber and the wild grapes which (probably) gave the place its name. Attempts were made to settle in Vinland. The location of these attempted settlements has long been a subject of controversy; northern Newfoundland is the likeliest place, though voyages of reconnaissance may have gone further south, perhaps to New England or even further. Wherever Vinland was, the settlements were soon abandoned; the settlers were too few, the natives too many and too hostile. The Greenlanders, however, continued to visit Markland and Vinland, so long as they had adequate ships, and the Vinland story was recorded, with considerable wealth of detail, in Icelandic sagas.

In the later Middle Ages the Greenland settlements fell on evil days. Regular contact with Europe ceased about the middle of the fourteenth century and at some unknown later date, perhaps in the early sixteenth, the last settlement died out or was abandoned. The existence of Greenland, however, was known in Iceland, Denmark, and Norway, and even the Vinland story was probably remembered there, though doubtless in a hazy fashion. Vinland was marked on at least one fifteenth-century map. The celebrated "Vinland map," believed to have been drawn in Switzerland about 1440, and to have been based in part on Scandinavian information, shows Greenland in remarkably accurate outline, and southwest of it a large island, conventional in shape, but clearly labeled "Vinland."

It is impossible to say how much, if at all, Scandinavian traditions about Vinland the Good affected the south European seamen who were the pioneers of the European Reconnaissance. Portugal and Denmark were in fairly regular diplomatic contact in the later fifteenth century, and the Corte-Real family may have heard stories. John Cabot's expeditions sailed from Bristol, home port of traders and fishermen long familiar with Icelandic waters. It is probable that fishermen rather than explorers first reopened the northern navigation. Fishermen would be interested in the sea rather than the land, and if they found productive banks, would probably keep the information to themselves; but they may, in the course of their voyages, have sighted unfamiliar land, and the explorers may have questioned them and followed up their answers. One of the documents quoted here indicates that expeditions to the western Atlantic had been sailing regularly from Bristol since 1491. There are other indications of still earlier voyages in search of "Brasill." The pioneers of the Reconnaissance were not concerned, as the Vikings had been, to find homes for themselves and pasture for their cattle; nor were they particularly interested in fish; their business was to find sea routes to places where spices grew. The northern routes, though unattractive in themselves, offered Atlantic crossings with relatively short stretches of open ocean, and frequent favorable easterly winds, especially in the early summer. Land in the northwestern Atlantic might well prove to be part of the northeastern coast of Asia; it might prove feasible, having found this rumored land, to follow the coast southwest as far as the cities of Cathay, far to the west of Columbus' deceptive islands. Some such plan was probably in the minds of Cabot and the brothers Corte-Real. Cabot made voyages in 1497 and 1498, and possibly an earlier voyage, under license from Henry VII; the Corte-Real brothers between them made three voyages for the Portuguese Crown in 1500–1502. These voyages together revealed long stretches of coast in Greenland, Labrador, Newfoundland, Nova Scotia, perhaps (from Cabot's last voyage) New England. The results of Cabot's discoveries, with English banners attached, are shown in Juan de la Cosa's map of 1500. The explorers noted dense shoals of cod and great stands of timber suitable for ships' masts; but they found no spices. Cabot nevertheless reported that he had reached the extremities of Asia, and subsequent cartographical evidence suggests that some reputable geographers accepted this interpretation.

No eyewitness accounts of the Cabot and Corte-Real voyages have survived. The extracts which follow indicate some contemporary reactions. They are:

1. Letter from Raimondo de Raimondi de Soncino to the Duke of Milan, December 18, 1497 in *Calendar of State Papers, Milan*, vol. I, no. 552.
2. Letter from John Day (an English merchant resident in Spain) to the Lord Grand Admiral, edited and translated by L. A. Vigneras: *Canadian Historical Review*, XXXVIII (1957), 219–28.
3. Letter from Pedro de Ayala, Spanish ambassador in England, to the Spanish sovereigns, July 25, 1498, edited and translated by H. P. Biggar in *Precursors of Jacques Cartier*, (Ottawa, Government Printing Bureau, 1911), pp. 29–9.
4. Letter from Pietro Pasqualigo, Venetian ambassador in Portugal, to his brothers in Venice, October 19, 1501, from *Paesi novamente retrovati* (Vicenza, 1507), lib. VI, cap. cxxvi, edited and translated by J. A. Williamson in *The Cabot Voyages and Bristol Discovery Under Henry VII* (Cambridge, Hakluyt Society, 1962), pp. 24–6.

All four extracts are included in Williamson, *op. cit.*

Raimondo de Soncino to the Duke of Milan

[LONDON, 18 December, 1497] Perhaps amid the numerous occupations of your Excellency, it may not weary you to hear how his Majesty here has gained a part of Asia, without a stroke of the sword. There is in this Kingdom a man of the people, Messer Zoane Caboto by name, of kindly wit and a most expert mariner. Having observed that the sovereigns first of Portugal and then of Spain had occupied unknown islands, he decided to make a similar acquisition for his Majesty. After obtaining patents that the effective ownership of what he might find should be his, though reserving the rights of the Crown, he committed himself to fortune in a little ship, with eighteen persons. He started from Bristol, a port on the west of this kingdom, passed Ireland, which is still further west, and then bore towards the north, in order to sail to the east, leaving the north on his right hand after some days. After having wandered for some time he at length arrived at the mainland, where he hoisted the royal standard, and took possession for the king here; and after taking certain tokens he returned.

This Messer Zoane, as a foreigner and a poor man, would not have obtained credence, had it not been that his companions, who are practically all English and from Bristol, testified that he spoke the truth. This Messer Zoane has the description of the world in a map, and also in a solid sphere, which he has made, and shows where he has been. In going towards the east he passed far beyond the country of the Tanais. They say that the land is excellent and temperate, and they believe that Brazil wood and silk are native there. They assert that the sea there is swarming with fish, which can be taken not only with the net, but in baskets let down with a stone, so that it sinks in the water. I have heard this Messer Zoane state so much.

These same English, his companions, say that they could bring so many fish that this kingdom would have no further need of Iceland, from which place there comes a very great quantity of the fish called stockfish. But Messer Zoane has his mind set upon even greater things, because he proposes to keep along the coast from the place at which he touched, more and more towards the east, until he reaches an island which he calls Cipango, situated in the equinoctial region, where he believes that all the spices of the world have their origin, as well as the jewels. He says that on previous occasions he has been to Mecca, whither spices are borne by caravans from distant countries. When he asked those who brought them what was the place of origin of these spices, they answered that they did not know, but that other caravans came with this merchandise to their homes from distant countries, and these again said that the goods had been brought to them from other remote regions. He therefore reasons that these things come from places far away from them, and so on from one to the other, always assuming that the earth is round, it follows as a matter of course that the last of all must take them in the north towards the west.

He tells all this in such a way, and makes everything so plain, that I also feel compelled to believe him. What is much more, his Majesty, who is wise and not prodigal, also gives him some

credence, because he is giving him a fairly good provision, since
his return, so Messer Zoane himself tells me. Before very long
they say that his Majesty will equip some ships, and in addition
he will give them all the malefactors, and they will go to that
country and form a colony. By means of this they hope to make
London a more important mart for spices than Alexandria. The
leading men in this enterprise are from Bristol, and great seamen,
and now they know where to go, say that the voyage will not
take more than a fortnight, if they have good fortune after leaving Ireland.

I have also spoken with a Burgundian, one of Messer Zoane's
companions, who corroborates everything. He wants to go back,
because the Admiral, which is the name they give to Messer
Zoane, has given him an island. He has given another to his bar-
ber, a Genoese by birth, and both consider themselves counts,
while my lord the Admiral esteems himself at least a prince.

I also believe that some poor Italian friars will go on this voyage, who have the promise of bishoprics. As I have made friends
with the Admiral, I might have an archbishopric if I chose to go
there, but I have reflected that the benefices which your Excellency reserves for me are safer, and I therefor beg that possession may be given me of those which fall vacant in my absence,
and the necessary steps taken so that they may not be taken away
from me by others, who have the advantage of being on the spot.
Meanwhile I stay on in this country, eating ten or twelve courses
at each meal, and spending three hours at table twice every day,
for the love of your Excellency, to whom I humbly commend
myself.

London, the 18th of December, 1497

John Day to the Lord Grand Admiral[1]

Your Lordship's servant brought me your letter. I have seen its
contents and I would be most desirous and most happy to serve

[1] According to Dr. Vigneras, who found the document in the Simancas
archive, the personage to whom this letter was addressed may have been—as
the superscription suggests—Fadrique Enríquez, Marqués de Tarifa, Admiral
of Castile; or it may have been Christopher Columbus. Columbus was in
Spain at the time; and though not entitled to it, was sometimes addressed
in official communications as *Almirante mayor*. [Ed.]

you. I do not find the book Inventio Fortunata,[2] and I thought
that I (or he) was bringing it with my things, and I am very
sorry not to find it because I wanted very much to serve you. I am
sending the other book of Marco Polo and a copy of the land
which has been found. I do not send the map because I am not
satisfied with it, for my many occupations forced me to make it
in a hurry at the time of my departure; but from the said copy
your Lordship will learn what you wish to know, for in it are
named the capes of the mainland and the islands, and thus you will
see where land was first sighted, since most of the land was discovered after turning back. Thus your Lordship will know that
the cape nearest to Ireland is 1800 miles west of Dursey Head
which is in Ireland, and the southernmost part of the Island of the
Seven Cities is west of Bordeaux River, and your Lordship will
know that he landed at only one spot of the mainland, near the
place where land was first sighted, and they disembarked there
with a crucifix and raised banners with the arms of the Holy
Father and those of the King of England, my master; and they
found tall trees of the kind masts are made, and other fir trees,
and the country is very rich in grass. In that particular spot, as I
told your Lordship, they found a trail that went inland, they saw
a site where a fire had been made, they saw manure of animals
which they thought to be farm animals, and they saw a stick half
a yard long pierced at both ends, carved and painted with brazil,
and by such signs they believe the land to be inhabited. Since he
was with just a few people, he did not dare advance inland beyond the shooting distance of a cross-bow, and after taking in
fresh water he returned to his ship. All along the coast they found
many fish like those which in Iceland are dried in the open and
sold in England and other countries, and these fish are called in
England "stockfish"; and thus following the shore they saw two
forms running on land one after the other, but they could not
tell if they were human beings or animals; and it seemed to them
that there were fields where they thought might also be villages,

[2] *Inventio Fortunata*, a tract on the Arctic regions, written about 1360
by an English friar, probably Nicholas of Lynn, describing voyages which
he claimed to have made. The tract had considerable influence on fifteenth-
century geographical thonght. It is now lost, and known only from an
abstract made by Mercator.

and they saw a forest whose foliage looked red. They left England toward the end of May, and must have been on the way 35 days before sighting land; the wind was east-north-east and the sea calm going and coming back, except for one day when he ran into a storm two or three days before finding land; and going so far out, his compass needle failed to point north and marked two rhumbs below. They spent about one month discovering the coast and from the above mentioned cape of the mainland which is nearest to Ireland, they returned to the coast of Europe in fifteen days. They had the wind behind them, and he reached Brittany because the sailors confused him, saying that he was heading too far north. From there he came to Bristol, and he went to see the King to report to him all the above mentioned; and the King granted him an annual pension of twenty pounds sterling to sustain himself until the time comes when more will be known of this business, since with God's help it is hoped to push through plans for exploring the said land more thoroughly next year with ten or twelve vessels—because in his voyage he had only one ship of fifty "toneles" and twenty men and food for seven or eight months—and they want to carry out this new project. It is considered certain that the cape of the said land was found and discovered in the past by the men from Bristol who found "Brasil" as your Lordship well knows. It was called the Island of Brasil, and it is assumed and believed to be the mainland that the men from Bristol found.

Since your Lordship wants information relating to the first voyage, here is what happened: he went with one ship, he fell out with his crew, he was short of supplies and ran into bad weather, and he decided to turn back.

Magnificent Lord, as to other things pertaining to the case, I would like to serve your Lordship if I were not prevented in doing so by occupations of great importance relating to shipments and deeds for England which must be attended to at once and which keep me from serving you: but rest assured, Magnificent Lord, of my desire and natural intention to serve you, and when I find myself in other circumstances and more at leisure, I will take pains to do so; and when I get news from England about the matters referred to above—for I am sure that everything has to come to my knowledge—I will inform your Lordship of all that would not be prejudicial to the King my master. In payment for some services which I hope to render you, I beg your Lordship to kindly write me about such matters, because the favour you will thus do me will greatly stimulate my memory to serve you in all the things that may come to my knowledge. May God keep prospering your Lordship's magnificent state according to your merits. Whenever your Lordship should find it convenient, please remit the book or order it to be given to Master George.

I kiss your Lordship's hands,
Johan Day

Pedro de Ayala to the Spanish sovereigns

[LONDON, 25 July, 1498] . . . I think Your Highnesses have already heard how the king of England has equipped a fleet to explore certain islands or mainland which he has been assured certain persons who set out last year from Bristol in search of the same have discovered. I have seen the map made by the discoverer, who is another Genoese like Columbus, who has been in Seville and at Lisbon seeking to obtain persons to aid him in this discovery. For the last seven years the people of Bristol have equipped two, three [and] four caravels to go in search of the island of Brazil and the Seven Cities according to the fancy of this Genoese. The king made up his mind to send thither, because last year sure proof was brought him they had found land. The fleet he prepared, which consisted of five vessels, was provisioned for a year. News has come that one of these, in which sailed another Friar Buil, has made land in Ireland in a great storm with the ship badly damaged. The Genoese kept on his way. Having seen the course they are steering and the length of the voyage, I find that what they have discovered or are in search of is possessed by Your Highnesses because it is at the cape which fell to Your Highnesses by the convention with Portugal. It is hoped they will be back by September. I let [? will let] Your Highnesses know about it. The king has spoken to me several times on the subject. He hopes the affair may turn out profitable. I believe the distance is not 400 leagues. I told him that I believed the islands were those found by Your Highnesses, and although I gave him the main reason, he would not have it. Since I believe Your Highnesses will already have notice of all this and also of the chart or mappemonde which this man has made, I do not send it now, although it is here, and so far as I can see exceedingly false, in order to make believe that these are not part of the said islands. . . .

London, 25th July, 1498

Pietro Pasqualigo to his brothers in Venice

[LISBON, 19 October, 1501] On the eighth of the present month arrived here one of the two caravels which this most august monarch sent out in the year past under Captain Gaspar Corterat to discover land towards the north; and they report that they have found land two thousand miles from here, between the north and the west, which never before was known to anyone. They examined the coast of the same for perhaps six hundred to seven hundred miles and never found the end, which leads them to think it a mainland. This continues to another land which was discovered last year in the north. The caravels were not able to arrive there on account of the sea being frozen and the great quantity of snow. They are led to this same opinion from the considerable number of very large rivers which they found there, for certainly no island could ever have so many nor such large ones. They say that this country is very populous and the houses of the inhabitants of long strips of wood covered over with the skins of fish. They have brought back here seven natives, men and women and children, and in the other caravel, which is expected from hour to hour are coming fifty others. These resemble gypsies in colour, features, stature and aspect; are clothed in the skins of various animals, but chiefly of otters. In summer they turn the hair outside and in winter the opposite way. And these skins are not sewn together in any way nor tanned, but just as they are taken from the animals; they wear them over their shoulders and arms. And their privy parts are fastened with cords made of very strong sinews of fish, so that they look like wild men. They are very shy and gentle, but well formed in arms and legs and shoulders beyond description. They have their faces marked like those of the Indians, some with six, some with eight, some with less marks. They speak, but are not understood by anyone, though I believe that they have been spoken to in every possible language. In their land there is no iron, but they make knives out of stones and in like manner the points of their arrows. And yet these men have brought from there a piece of broken gilt sword, which certainly seems to have been made in Italy. One of the boys was wearing in his ears two silver rings which without doubt seem to have been made in Venice, which makes me think it to be mainland, because it is not likely that ships would have gone there without their having been heard of. They have great quantity of salmon, herring, cod and similar fish. They have also great store of wood and above all of pines for making masts and yards of ships. On this account his Majesty here intends to draw great advantage from the said land, as well by the wood for ships, of which they are in want, as by the men, who will be excellent for labour and the best slaves that have hitherto been obtained. This has seemed to me worthy to be notified to you, and if anything more is learned by the arrival of the captain's caravel, I shall likewise let you know.

23. North America a continent

The discovery of a rich fishery on the Newfoundland Banks was an event of great economic significance for sixteenth-century Europe, and fishermen from England, France, Portugal, and the Vascongado were quick to exploit it. The lands which fringed the fishery on the north and west, on the other hand, were for many years neither exploited nor systematically explored; understandably, since to governments and investors interested in the spice trade, those uncivilized, sparsely inhabited shores had little to offer. Cartographers were concerned, however, to place the new discoveries in their correct relation with the known continents, and for the purpose of finding routes to Asia this was obviously of practical importance. Greenland—often labeled Labrador—was variously shown in sixteenth-century maps as an island or as a peninsula, whether of northwestern Europe, of northeastern Asia, or of some separate polar continent. The newly discovered lands—Labrador,

Newfoundland, Nova Scotia, to give them their modern names—might be joined to Greenland; they might be a distinct insular landmass or archipelago, separated from Greenland by a stretch of sea; or they might—as in the de la Cosa map—be part of a long continental coast running continuously southwest to the region of the Spanish Antilles. Italian maps of the first quarter of the century favored an "Asian" interpretation. The Contarini-Rosselli map of 1506, the Ruysch map of 1507–8, the Vesconte Maggiolo map of 1511, all show the recently discovered coasts, roughly in the longitude of the eastern Antilles, as the Atlantic seaboard of a great promontory jutting eastward from northeast Asia, with its southern coast trending first west and then south, to the point of Mangi, in Cathay. In these maps the Spanish discoveries in the Caribbean are separated by a broad sea passage both from the English and Portugese landfalls in the northwest and from the mainland of Asia.

The first explorer to make a thorough search for this passage was the Florentine Giovanni da Verrazzano, a privateer settled at Dieppe and turned discoverer, who in 1524 commanded an expedition in the west Atlantic under license from the King of France. The expedition consisted of a single ship. It was financed by a syndicate of Italian silk-merchants in Lyons, and its object was the discovery of a sea passage to the East in temperate latitudes. Verrazzano sailed west from Madeira, reached the Carolina coast in about 34° N., and coasted north and east as far as Newfoundland. The results of his voyage appear in the Maggiolo map of 1527 and in Girolamo Verrazzano's map of 1529. These maps showed clearly that, far from a broad and easy waterway to Cathay, there existed on the western side of the north Atlantic a landmass as formidable as that which Vespucci had discovered in the south.

On his return Verrazzano wrote to Francis I a letter summarizing the experiences of the voyage. The original of this letter is lost; three later versions of it, which differ considerably one from another, exist. One is the printed version in the third volume of Ramusio's *Navigationi*, which also appears in English translation in Hakluyt's *Voyages*. The second is a late sixteenth-century manuscript copy, commonly known as the Carli letter, in the National Library of Florence; it was edited and published in 1841, and several times subsequently. The third, commonly known as the Cèllere Codex, is the most complete and convincing of the three. It was found in a private library in Rome and published, with an English translation by E. Hagaman Hall, in 1910. This translation, in a slightly revised form, was included in Phelps-Stokes' *Iconography of Manhattan Island*.

The extract which follows is abridged from I. N. Phelps-Stokes, *The*

Iconography of Manhattan Island (6 vols., New York, Robert H. Dodd, 1922), IV, 15–19.

WE started from the deserted rock near the Island of Madeira belonging to the Most Serene King of Portugal commencing 1524, with the said Dauphine, on the XVII of the month of January past, with fifty men, furnished with victuals, arms and other instruments of war and naval munitions for eight months; departing, we sailed westward with an east southeast wind blowing with sweet and gentle mildness. In XXV days we sailed eight hundred leagues. The XXIIII day of February we experienced as severe a storm as ever any man who has navigated experienced. From which, with divine aid and the goodness of the ship, enabled by its glorious name and fortunate destiny to resist the violent waves of the sea, we were saved. We pursued our navigation continuously toward the west, bearing somewhat to the north. In XXV more days we sailed more than 400 leagues, where there appeared to us a new land never before seen by anyone, ancient or modern.

At first it appeared rather low; having approached to within a quarter of a league, we perceived, by the great fires built on the shore of the sea, that it was inhabited. We saw that it extended toward the south; following it, to find some port where we could anchor with the ship and investigate its nature, in the space of fifty leagues we did not find a port or any place where it was possible to stay with the ship. And having seen that it trended continually to the south, in order not to meet with the Spaniards, we decided to coast along it again toward the north, where we found the same place that we started from. We anchored by the coast, sending the small boat to land. We saw many people, who came to the shore of the sea and seeing us approach fled, sometimes halting, turning back, looking with great admiration. Reassuring them by various signs, some of them approached, showing great delight at seeing us, marveling at our clothes, figures and whiteness, making to us various signs where we could land more conveniently with the small boat, offering us of their foods.

We were on land, and I shall tell Your Majesty briefly what we were able to learn of their life and customs:

They go altogether naked except that at the private parts they wear some skins of little animals similar to martens, a girdle of fine grass woven with various tails of other animals which hang around the body as far as the knees; the rest nude; the head likewise. Some wear certain garlands of feathers of birds. They are of black color not much unlike the Saracens; their hair is black and thick, and not very long, which they tie together back on the head in the shape of a little tail. As for the symmetry of the men, they are well proportioned, of medium stature, and rather exceed us. In the chest they are broad, their arms well built, the legs and other parts of the body well put together. There is nothing else to remark, except that they incline somewhat to broadness in the face; but not all, for in many we saw the face clear-cut. The eyes are black and large, the glance intent and quick. They are not very strong, of keen intelligence, swift and the greatest runners. From what we were able to learn by experience, they resemble in the last two respects the Orientals, and mostly those of the farthest regions of China. We were not able to learn in detail of the life and customs of these people because of the shortness of the stay we made on land, on account of there being few people and the ship anchored in the high sea.

The sea-shore is all covered with fine sand XV feet high, extending in the form of little hills about fifty paces wide. Near by appears the spacious land, so high that it exceeds the sandy shore, with many beautiful fields and plains, full of the largest forests, some thin and some dense, adorned and clothed with palms, laurels, cypresses, and other varieties of trees unknown in our Europe. We baptized this land "Forest of Laurels" and a little farther down on account of the beautiful cedars it was given the name "Field of Cedars"; which, for a long distance, exhale the sweetest odors, the property of which we were not able to learn. We think that, partaking of the Orient, on account of the surroundings, they are not without some drugs or aromatic liquor. And other riches, gold and other, to which land of such a color has every tendency. It abounds in many animals, stags, deer, hares; likewise in lakes and pools of living water, with many kinds of birds, adapted and convenient for every pleasure of the chase.

This land lies in 34 degrees like Carthage and Damascus. The

air salubrious, pure and with moderate heat and cold; in those
regions gentle winds blow, and those which prevail most continuously are west-north-west and west, in summer time, at the
beginning of which we were in those regions; the sky clear and
serene with infrequent rains, and if sometimes owing to the south
winds the air gathers in clouds or darkness in an instant, not lasting, it is dispelled, and the air again becomes pure and clear; the
sea tranquil and not boisterous, the waves of which are placid.
And although the shore always tends to lowness, and is barren of
ports, it is not troublesome to sailors, being entirely clear and
without any rocks; so deep that within only four or five paces
from land are found, regardless of flood or ebb, XX feet of water,
the depth of the sea increasing in uniform proportion; with such
good holding-ground that any ship howsoever afflicted by the
tempest can never perish in those parts unless it breaks its cable.
. . . We called it Annunciata from the day of arrival, where is
found an isthmus[1] a mile in width and about 200 long, in which
from the ship, was seen the oriental sea between the west and
north. Which is the one, without doubt, which goes about the
extremity of India, China and Cathay. We navigated along the said
isthmus with the constant hope of finding some strait or true
promontory at which the land would end toward the north in
order to be able to penetrate to those blessed shores of Cathay.
To which isthmus was given by the discoverer the name Isthmus
of Verrazanio: as all the land found was named Francesca after
our Francis.

Having departed thence, following always the shore which
turned somewhat toward the north, we came in the space of
fifty leagues to another land which appeared much more beautiful and full of the largest forests. Anchoring at which, XX men
going about two leagues inland, we found the people through
fear had fled to the woods. Searching everywhere, we met with
a very old woman and a young woman of from XVIII to XX
years of age, who through fear had hidden themselves in the grass.
The old one had two little girls whom she carried on her shoulders, and back on her neck she carried a boy, of about eight

[1] This imaginary "Isthmus of Verrazanio" is shown on the Maggiolo map
of 1527. Verrazzano's error has never been convincingly explained. It was
never seriously pursued by explorers. [Ed.]

years. Having approached towards them, they began to scream, and the old woman to make signs to us that the men had fled to the woods. We gave them to eat of our food, which the old woman accepted with great gusto; the young woman refused everything and with anger threw it to the ground. We took the boy away from the old woman to carry him to France, wishing also to take the young woman, who was of much beauty and of tall stature, it was not however possible for us to conduct her to the sea, on account of the very great cries which she uttered. And having to pass through some woods, being far from the ship, we decided to leave her, carrying only the boy.

These we found lighter colored than the previous ones, dressed in certain grasses which grow, pendant from the branches of the trees, and which they weave with various ends of wild hemp. The head bare in the same way as the others. Their food in general consists of pulse which they have in abundance, differing in color and size from ours, of excellent and delightful flavor; besides, from hunting, fishes and birds, which they take with bows and with snares. They make the bows of tough wood, and arrows of reeds, placing at the extremities bones of fishes and of other animals. The beasts in this part are much wilder than in our Europe because they are continually molested by the hunters. We saw many of their boats constructed from a single tree twenty feet long, four wide, which are not fashioned with stones, iron or other kind of metals, because in all this land, in the space of two hundred leagues which we traveled, only one stone of any kind was seen by us. They help themselves with fire, burning such part of the wood as is necessary for the hollowing of the boat, also of the stern and prow, so that, sailing, it is possible to endure the waves of the sea.

The land in situation, goodness and beauty, is like the other; the forests open, full of various kinds of trees, but not of such fragrance, on account of being farther north and colder. We saw in that land many vines growing wild, which, rising, entwine themselves around the trees, as they are accustomed to do in Lombardy; which, if they had a perfect system of culture by agriculturists, without doubt would produce excellent wines, because we found many times the dry fruit of those vines sweet and agreeable, not different from ours. They are held in esteem

by them (the inhabitants) because wherever they grow, they
lift up the surrounding bushes in order that the fruit may be able
to mature. . . .

At the end of a hundred leagues we found a very agreeable
situation located within two small prominent hills, in the midst of
which flowed to the sea a very great river[2] which was deep
within the mouth; and from the sea to the hills of that place with
the rising of the tides, which we found eight feet, any laden ship
might have passed. On account of being anchored off the coast
in good shelter, we did not wish to adventure in without knowledge of the entrance. We were with the small boat, entering the
said river to the land, which we found much populated. The
people, almost like the others, clothed with the feathers of birds
of various colors, came toward us joyfully, uttering very great
exclamations of admiration, showing us where we could land with
the boat more safely. We entered said river, within the land,
about half a league, where we saw it made a very beautiful lake
with a circuit of about three leagues; through which the Indians
went, going from one and another part with XXX of their little
boats, with innumerable people, who passed from one shore and
the other in order to see us. In an instant, as is wont to happen in
navigation, a gale of unfavorable wind blowing in from the sea,
we were forced to return to the ship, leaving the said land with
much regret because of its commodiousness and beauty, thinking
it was not without some properties of value, all of its hills showing indications of minerals. . . .

We came to another land . . . which we found as pleasing as
it is possible to express, adapted to every kind of cultivation—
grain, wine, oil. Because in that place the fields are from XXV to
XXX leagues wide, open and devoid of every impediment of
trees, of such fertility that any seed in them would produce the
best crops. Entering then into the woods, all of which are pene-
trable by an army of any size in any way whatsoever, and
whose trees, oaks, cypresses, and others, are unknown in our
Europe, we found cherries, plums and filberts, and many kinds of
fruits different from ours. Animals there are in very great number, stags, deer, lynx, and other species, which they capture in

[2] The Hudson.

the same way as the other animals with snares and bows which
are their principal arms. Whose arrows are worked with great
beauty, placing at the end, instead of iron, emery, jaspar, hard
marble, and other sharp stones, which they used instead of iron
in cutting trees, making their boats from a single trunk of a tree,
hollowed with wonderful skill, in which from fourteen to XV
men may go comfortably; the oar short, broad at the end, worked
solely with the strength of the arms at sea without any peril with
as much speed as pleases them.

We saw their habitations, circular in form, of XIIII to XV
paces compass, made from arched saplings, bent in the form of an
arbor, separated one from the other, without system of architecture, covered with mats of straw ingeniously worked which protect them from rain and wind. There is no doubt that if they
had the perfection of methods which we have, they would build
magnificent edifices, for all the maritime coast is full of blue
rocks, crystals and alabaster; and for such cause is full of ports
and shelters for ships. They transport the said houses from one
place to another according to the fertility of the site and the
season in which they live. Carrying away only the mats, immediately they have other habitations made. There live in each a
father and family to a very large number, so that in some we
saw XXV and XXXV souls. Their food is like that of the others:
of pulse (which they produce with more system of culture than
the others, observing the full moon, the rising of the Pleiades and
many customs derived from the ancients), also of the chase and
fish. . . .

The land is situated in the parallel of Rome, in forty and two-
thirds degrees, but somewhat colder on account of chance and not
on account of nature. . . . The shore of said land runs from west
to east. The mouth of the port (which on account of its beauty
we called "Refugio") looks toward the south, half a league wide,
after entering which between east and north it extends XII
leagues, where, widening itself, it makes an ample bay of about
XX leagues in circuit. In which are five little islands of much
fertility and beauty, full of high and spreading trees, among
which a fleet of any size, without fear of tempest or other impediment of fortune, could rest secure. Turning thence toward
the south to the entrance of the port, on one side and the other

are very charming hills with many brooks, which from the height, to the sea discharge clear waters. . . .

Being supplied with our every necessity, the sixth day of May we departed from said port, following the shore, never losing sight of the land. We sailed one hundred and fifty leagues, within which space we found shoals which extend from the continent into the sea fifty leagues. Upon which there was over three feet of water; on account of which great danger in navigating, we survived with difficulty and baptized it "Armellini,"[3] finding it of the same nature and somewhat higher with some mountains, with a high promontory which we named "Pallavisino" which all indicated minerals. We did not stop there because the favorableness of the weather served us in sailing along the coast. The shore ran to the east.

Within the space of fifty leagues, holding more to the north, we found a high land full of very thick forests, the trees of which were pines, cypresses and such as grow in cold regions. The people all different from the others, and as much as those passed were of kind manners, these were full of uncouthness and vices, so barbarous that we were never able, with howsoever many signs we made them, to have any intercourse with them. They dress in the skins of bear, lynxes, sea-wolves, and other animals. The food, according to that which we were able to learn through going many times to their habitations, we think is of the chase, fish and some products which belong to a species of roots which the ground yields by its own self. They do not have pulse, nor did we see any signs of cultivation, nor would the ground, on account of its sterility, be adapted to produce fruit or any grain. If, trading at any time with them, we desired their things, they came to the shore of the sea upon some rock where it was very steep, and—we remaining in the small boat—with a cord let down to us what they wished to give, continually crying on land that we should not approach, giving quickly the barter, not taking in exchange for it except knives, hooks for fishing, and sharp metal. They had no regard for courtesy, and when we had nothing more to exchange, departing, the men made at us all the signs of contempt and immodesty which any brute creature

---

[3] The shoals off Cape Cod.

could make. Contrary to their wish, XXV of us armed men were inland two and three leagues, and when we descended to the shore they shot at us with their bows, sending forth the greatest cries, then fled into the woods. We do not know any thing of any considerable value in this land except the very great forests, with some hills which possibly have some metal, because on many natives we saw "pater-nosters" of copper in the ears.

We departed, skirting the coast between east and north, which we found very beautiful, open and bare of forests, with high mountains back inland, growing smaller toward the shore of the sea. In fifty leagues we discovered XXXII islands, all near to the continent, small and of pleasing appearance, high, following the turns of the land, among which were formed most beautiful ports and channels, as are formed in the Adriatic Gulf, in the Illyrias and Dalmatia. We had no knowledge of the peoples and think they were like the others, devoid of morals and culture.

Navigating between east-south-east and north-north-east in the space of CL leagues we came near the land which the Britons found in the past, which stands in fifty degrees, and having consumed all our naval stores and victuals, having discovered six hundred leagues and more of new land, furnishing ourselves with water and wood, we decided to turn toward France. . . .

It remains for me to narrate to Your Majesty the order of said navigation as it bears on Cosmography. . . .

My intention was in this voyage to reach Cathay and the extreme east of Asia, not expecting to find such an obstacle of new land as I found; and if for some reason I expected to find it, I thought it to be not without some strait to penetrate to the Eastern Ocean. And this has been the opinion of all the ancients, believing certainly our Western Ocean to be one with the Eastern Ocean of India without interposition of land. This Aristotle affirms, arguing by many similitudes, which opinion is very contrary to the moderns and according to experience untrue. Because the land has been found by them, unknown to the ancients, to be another world with respect to the one which was known to them, it manifestly shows itself to be larger than our Europe and Africa and almost Asia, if we estimate correctly its size; as briefly I will give Your Majesty a little account of it.

Beyond the equator, distant from the meridian of the Fortunate Islands toward the west 20 degrees, the Spaniards (that is, Magellan) have navigated 54 degrees toward the south, where they have found land without end. . . .

On the other hand, we, in this voyage, made by order of Your Majesty beyond 92 degrees, etc. from said meridian toward the west to the land we first found in 34 degrees (land near Temistitan),[4] navigated 300 leagues between east and north and almost 400 leagues to the east uninterruptedly along the shore of the land, attaining to 54 degrees, leaving the land that the Lusitanians (that is, Bacalaia, so called from a fish) found a long time ago, which they followed farther north as far as the Arctic circle leaving the end unknown. Therefore the northern latitude joined with the southern, that is, 54 degrees with 66 degrees, make 120 degrees, more latitude than Africa and Europe contain, because joining the extremity of Europe, which the limits of Norway form, and which stand in 71 degrees, with the extremity of Africa, which is the Promontory of Good Hope in 35 degrees, makes only 106 degrees, and if the terrestrial area of said land corresponds in extent to the sea-shore, there is no doubt it exceeds Asia in size.

In such way we find the globe of the Earth much larger than the ancients have held and contrary to the Mathematicians who have considered that relatively to the water, the land was smaller, which we have found by experience to be the reverse.

All this land or New World which above I have described is connected together, not adjoining Asia nor Africa; it may join Europe by Norway and Russia; which would be false according to the ancients, who declare almost all the north from the promontory of the Cimbri to have been navigated to the east, going around as far as the Caspian Sea. . . .

I hope we shall have soon better assurance of this, with the aid of Your Majesty, whom God Almighty prosper in everlasting glory, that we may see the perfect end of this our cosmography, and that the sacred word of the evangelist may be accomplished: "Their sound has gone out into all the earth."

[4] I.e. Tenochtitlán—Mexico.

24. The St. Lawrence not a strait

Verrazzano's voyage narrowed considerably the areas in which a sea passage might be found between the North Atlantic and the South Sea. The Maggiolo map of 1527 still marked a *streito dubitoso* leading from the Gulf of Mexico; but exploration in that area was politically out of the question, except for Spaniards, who were already undeceived. The only remaining possibilities lay much further north. Verrazzano himself had been cautious in his guessing; but the hankering for symmetry, still characteristic of much of the geographical theory of the time, encouraged the hope that a strait might exist to the north of North America, corresponding to that which Magellan had found to the south of South America. For northern Europeans the logical next step was a more careful investigation of the Baccalaos, the codfish coasts, known only to fishermen since the time of Cabot and Corte-Real. In 1534 the French Crown despatched Jacques Cartier of St. Malo with two ships for this purpose. Cartier came of fishing stock. He was one of the ablest and most thorough, as well as one of the most intrepid of sixteenth-century explorers. In the spring of 1534 he sailed from St. Malo to Cape Bonavista and made a careful survey of the north coast of Newfoundland; sailed through the Strait of Belle Isle and, despite constant dangers from ice, examined both the Labrador and Newfoundland shores of the Strait; and explored the Gulf of St. Lawrence as far as the western shore of Anticosti Island. The following year Cartier sailed boldly up the St. Lawrence as far as ships could go, to the Lachine Rapids near where Montreal was later to be built, and diligently collected native information which showed the St. Lawrence to be a river and not a strait. He and his people wintered up the river, and suffered the inevitable hardships of cold and scurvy; though they relieved the disease to some extent by drinking an infusion of the leaves of a tree— probably hemlock—which the Indians showed them. The following spring they returned, by way of Anticosti, Cape Breton, and Cape Race, to St. Malo.

Cartier's exploration of the St. Lawrence was a notable achievement; but its positive results—French settlement and the development of the fur trade—lay far in the future. Roberval's attempt to plant a colony in 1541 failed. The kingdom of Saguenay, rich in precious metals, of which the explorers heard, or thought they heard, from Indians, proved an illusion. The immediate and important result of Cartier's exploration was negative: he found no strait. If the strait existed, it was further north. Cartier's own *Relations*, worked up, apparently, from the logs or journals kept on the voyages, record a succession of disappointments; of promising openings explored and found to be rivers, bays, or inlets. The extracts which follow are from *The Voyages of Jacques Cartier*, translated and edited by H. P. Biggar (Ottawa, Government Printing Bureau, 1924), pp. 44–57, 99–111, 168–70.

[*Part of the first voyage. The fleet was at the western mouth of Northumberland Strait, which runs between Prince Edward Island and the coast of New Brunswick, and which Cartier wrongly took for a bay*]

On the following day [Thursday], the second of July [1534], we caught sight of the coast to the north of us,[1] which joined that already explored, and we saw that this [mouth of Northumberland strait] was a bay about twenty leagues deep and as many in width. We named it St. Leonore's bay. We went in our long-boats to the cape on the north and found the water so shallow that at the distance of more than a league from shore there was a depth of only one fathom. Some seven or eight leagues to the north-east of this cape [Escuminac point], lay another cape,[2] and between the two there is a bay,[3] in the form of a triangle, which ran back a long way; and so far as we could see the longest arm stretched north-east. This [Miramichi] bay was everywhere skirted with sandbanks and the water was shallow. Ten leagues from shore the depth was twenty fathoms. From the last-mentioned cape to the said [?] point and headland the distance is fifteen leagues. And when we were opposite to this cape we had sight of more land and a cape[4] which lay to the north of us, one quarter north-east in full view. During the night [Thursday-

[1] Escuminac Point.
[2] Blackland Point.
[3] Miramichi Bay.
[4] Cap d'Espoir.

Friday, July 2-3] the weather turned bad with much wind; and
we deemed it advisable to lie to until the morning of [Friday],
the third day of July, when the wind came west; and we headed
north in order to examine this coast, which was a high land lying
to the north-north-east of us beyond the low shores.[5] Between
these low shores and the high lands was a large bay and opening,
with a depth in some places of fifty-five fathoms and a width of
about fifteen leagues.[6] On account of this depth and width and of
the alteration in the coast-line, we had hopes of discovering
here a strait like the one at the strait of Castles.[7] This [Chaleur]
bay runs east-north-east and west-south-west. The land along
the south side of it is as fine and as good land, as arable and as
full of beautiful fields and meadows, as any we have ever seen;
and it is as level as the surface of a pond. And that on the north
side is a high mountainous shore, completely covered with many
kinds of lofty trees; and among others are many cedars and spruce
trees, as excellent for making masts for ships of 300 tons and
more, as it is possible to find. On this [north] shore we did not
see a single spot clear of timber, except in two places near the
water's edge, where there were meadows and very pretty ponds.
The middle of this bay lies in latitude 47° 30′ and in longitude
73°.[8]

The cape on the south shore was named Hope cape for the
hope we had of finding here a strait.[9] And on [Saturday] the
fourth of the said month [of July], being St. Martin's day, we
coasted along the north shore [of Chaleur bay] in order to find
a harbour, and entered a small bay and cove[10] completely open to
the south, with no shelter from that wind. We named it St.
Martin's cove. We remained in this cove from [Saturday] the
fourth until [Sunday] the twelfth of July. And while there, we

[5] Miscou Island is low and sandy, so that they could see over it the high
ground on the north side of Châleur Bay.

[6] Châleur Bay.

[7] That is to say, they hoped to find here a strait similar to the Strait of
Belle Isle.

[8] The latitude of Châleur Bay is about 48°10′N. The longitude extends
from 67° to 68°45′W. of Paris. It would be less from St. Malo, and less still
from Ferro in the Canaries, from which longitude was then commonly
reckoned.

[9] North point on Miscou Island.

[10] Port Daniel.

set out on Monday the sixth [of July], after hearing mass, in one of our long-boats, to examine a cape and point of land, that lay seven or eight leagues to the west of us,[11] and to see in which direction the coast ran. And when we were half a league from this point, we caught sight of two fleets of Indian canoes that were crossing from one side [of Chaleur bay] to the other, which numbered in all some forty or fifty canoes. Upon one of the fleets reaching this point, there sprang out and landed a large number of Indians, who set up a great clamour and made frequent signs to us to come on shore, holding up to us some furs on sticks. But as we were only one boat we did not care to go, so we rowed towards the other fleet which was on the water. And they [on shore], seeing we were rowing away, made ready two of their largest canoes in order to follow us. These were joined by five more of those that were coming in from the sea, and all came after our long-boat, dancing and showing many signs of joy, and of their desire to be friends, saying to us in their language: *Napou tou daman asurtat*, and other words, we did not understand. But for the reason already stated, that we had only one of our long-boats, we did not care to trust to their signs and waved to them to go back, which they would not do but paddled so hard that they soon surrounded our long-boat with their seven canoes. And seeing that no matter how much we signed to them, they would not go back, we shot off over their heads two small cannon. On this they began to return towards the point, and set up a marvellously loud shout, after which they proceeded to come on again as before. And when they had come alongside our long-boat, we shot off two fire-lances which scattered among them and frightened them so much that they began to paddle off in very great haste, and did not follow us any more.

The next day [Tuesday, July 7] some of these Indians came in nine canoes to the point at the mouth of the cove, where we lay anchored with our ships.[12] And being informed of their arrival we went with our two long-boats to the point where they were, at the mouth of the cove. As soon as they saw us they began to run away, making signs to us that they had come to barter with us; and held up some furs of small value, with which they

[11] Paspebiac Point.
[12] West Point at the mouth of Port Daniel.

clothe themselves. We likewise made signs to them that we
wished them no harm, and sent two men on shore, to offer them
some knives and other iron goods, and a red cap to give to their
chief. Seeing this, they sent on shore part of their people with
some of their furs; and the two parties traded together. The
savages showed a marvellously great pleasure in possessing and
obtaining these iron wares and other commodities, dancing and
going through many ceremonies, and throwing salt water over
their heads with their hands. They bartered all they had to such
an extent that all went back naked without anything on them;
and they made signs to us that they would return on the morrow
with more furs.

On Thursday the eighth of the said month [of July] as the
wind was favourable for getting under way with our ships, we
fitted up our long-boats to go and explore this [Chaleur] bay;
and we ran up it that day some twenty-five leagues. The next
day [Friday, July 10], at daybreak, we had fine weather and
sailed on until about ten o'clock in the morning, at which hour
we caught sight of the head of the bay, whereat we were grieved
and displeased. At the head of this bay, beyond the low shore,
were several very high mountains. And seeing there was no
passage, we proceeded to turn back. While making our way
along the [north] shore, we caught sight of the Indians on the
side of a lagoon and low beach, who were making many fires
that smoked. We rowed over to the spot, and finding there was an
entrance from the sea into the lagoon, we placed our long-boats
on one side of the entrance. The savages came over in one of
their canoes and brought us some strips of cooked seal, which they
placed on bits of wood and then withdrew, making signs to us
that they were making us a present of them. We sent two men on
shore with hatchets, knives, beads and other wares, at which the
Indians showed great pleasure. And at once they came over in a
crowd in their canoes to the side where we were, bringing furs
and whatever else they possessed, in order to obtain some of our
wares. They numbered, both men, women and children, more
than 300 persons. Some of their women, who did not come over,
danced and sang, standing in the water up to their knees. The
other women, who had come over to the side where we were,
advanced freely towards us and rubbed our arms with their

hands. Then they joined their hands together and raised them to heaven, exhibiting many signs of joy. And so much at ease did the savages feel in our presence, that at length we bartered with them, hand to hand, for everything they possessed, so that nothing was left to them but their naked bodies; for they offered us everything they owned, which was, all told, of little value. We perceived that they are people who would be easy to convert, who go from place to place maintaining themselves and catching fish in the fishing-season for food. Their country is more temperate than Spain and the finest it is possible to see, and as level as the surface of a pond. There is not the smallest plot of ground bare of wood, and even on sandy soil, but is full of wild wheat, that has an ear like barley and the grain like oats, as well as of pease, as thick as if they had been sown and hoed; of white and red currant-bushes, of strawberries, of raspberries, of white and red roses and of other plants of a strong, pleasant odour. Likewise there are many fine meadows with useful herbs, and a pond where there are many salmon. I am more than ever of opinion that these people would be easy to convert to our holy faith. They call a hatchet in their language, *cochy*, and a knife, *bacan*. We named this bay, Chaleur bay [i.e. the bay of Heat].

.   .   .

[*Part of the second voyage. The fleet had passed through the Strait of Belle Isle and was heading west along the north shore*] On the following day [Saturday], the last day of July, we continued our way along that coast, which runs east and west, one quarter south-east, and is skirted all along with islands and shoals and is very dangerous coast. The distance from the cape at St. German's islands[13] to the point where the islands end, is about seventeen and a half leagues. And at the point where the islands end, there is a fine headland, covered with large, high trees.[14] This coast is fringed all along with sandy beaches, and with no sign of a harbour, as far as cape Thiennot,[15] where it turns north-west. This cape lies some seven leagues from the last of the islands; and we recognized it from our former voyage.

[13] Cape Whittle. The islands end at Kegashka bay, forty miles beyond.
[14] Kegashka Point.
[15] Natashkwan Point.

On this account we sailed on all night [Saturday-Sunday, July 31-August 1] to the west-north-west until daylight, when the wind came ahead, whereupon we looked out for a harbor in which to anchor. We found a nice little harbour[16] some seven and a half leagues beyond cape Thiennot, lying among four islands which stretch out into the gulf. We named it "St. Nicholas's harbour"; and on the nearest island we set up a large wooden cross for a land-mark. One must keep this cross to the north-east, then head for it and leave it to starboard. You will find a depth of six fathoms and anchorage in the harbour in four fathoms. One must beware of two shoals, one on each side, half a league out. This whole coast is very dangerous and is full of reefs. Though one would think it contained many good harbours, there are shoals and reefs everywhere. We remained in that harbour from that day [Sunday, August 1] until Sunday, August 8, when we set forth and made our way towards cape Rabast, on the coast towards the south.[17] This cape lies some twenty leagues south-west of the above [Pashashibu] harbour. On the following day we had a head wind and since we found no harbours along this south coast, we sailed north to a point some ten leagues beyond the former [Pashashibu] harbour where we discovered a very fine large bay,[18] full of islands and with good entrances and anchorage for any weather that might prevail. This bay may be known by a large island which stretches out beyond the others like a headland[19] and on the mainland, some two leagues off, stands a mountain having the form of a shock of wheat. We named this bay "St. Lawrence's bay."

On [Friday] the thirteenth of that month, we set out from St. Lawrence's bay and heading towards the west, made our way as far as a cape on the south side,[20] which lies some twenty-five leagues west, one quarter south-west of St. Lawrence's harbour. And it was told us by the two Indians whom we had captured on our first voyage, that this cape formed part of the land on the

[16] Pashashibu Bay.
[17] On Anticosti Island, and still so called.
[18] Pillage Bay.
[19] Ste. Génevieve Island.
[20] West Point on Anticosti Island.

south which was an island;[21] and that to the south of it lay the route from Honguedo,[22] where we had seized them when on our first voyage, to Canada;[23] and that two days' journey from this cape and island, began the kingdom of the Saguenay, on the north shore as one made one's way towards this Canada. Some three leagues from this cape, there is a depth of more than 100 fathoms; and none of us ever remembers having seen so many whales as we saw that day off this cape.

After passing through the strait [of St. Peter] on the previous night, the next day which was our Our Lady's day of August, [Sunday] the fifteenth of that month, we had sight of land towards the south, which turned out to be a coast with marvellously high mountains. The above-mentioned [West] cape on the island [of Anticosti], which we named "Assumption island," and a cape on this high [Gaspé] shore,[24] lie east-north-east and west-south-west; and the distance from one to the other is twenty-five leagues. The north shore, when one is some thirty leagues off, looks higher than the south shore. We coasted this south shore from that day, [Sunday], until noon on Tuesday, when the wind came out of the west. We then headed north in order to make our way towards the high coast we saw in that direction. And on reaching it, we found that the shore was low and flat at the water's edge, but that beyond this low shore there were mountains. This coast runs east and west, one quarter south-west. Our Indians told us that this was the beginning of the Saguenay and of the inhabited region; and that thence came the copper they call *caigneldazé*. The distance from the south to the north shore is about thirty leagues; and there is a depth of more than 200 fathoms. The two Indians assured us that this was the way to the mouth of the great river of Hochelaga[25] and the route towards Canada, and that the river grew narrower as one approached Canada; and also that farther up, the water became

[21] Anticosti.

[22] Gaspé.

[23] I.e. the region along the St. Lawrence from Grosse Island on the east to a point between Québec and Three Rivers on the west.

[24] Probably Fame Point, allowing for compass variation, now about 27° W. in this area.

[25] I.e. the St. Lawrence.

fresh, and that one could make one's way so far up the river that they had never heard of anyone reaching the head of it. Furthermore that one could only proceed along it in small boats. In view of these statements and of their assertion that no other passage existed, the Captain [Cartier] was unwilling to proceed further until he had explored the remainder of the north shore to see if there was a strait there; for on account of our passing over to the south shore, the coast from St. Lawrence's bay onward had not been visited.

On Wednesday, August 18, the Captain ordered the ships to head back and to steer in the opposite direction; and we coasted the north shore, which runs north-east and south-west in the form of a semi-circle. It is a high shore though less so than the south shore. And on the following day, Thursday, we came to seven very high islands, which we named the "Round islands."[26] They lie some forty leagues from the south shore, and stretch out into the gulf to a distance of three or four leagues. Opposite to them commences a low shore covered with trees, which we coasted with our long-boats on the Friday [August 20]. Some two or more leagues from shore lie several very dangerous sand-bars which become bare at low water. At the end of this low shore, which continues for some ten leagues, is a fresh-water river [Moisie], which enters the gulf with such force that at a distance of more than a league from shore, the water is as fresh as spring water. We entered this river with our long-boats and at the mouth of it found a depth of only a fathom and a half. Up this river were several fish in appearance like horses[27] which go on land at night but in the day-time remain in the water, as our two Indians informed us. We saw a great number of fish up this river.

At dawn on the following morning [Saturday], the twenty-first of the said month, we set sail and made our way along this shore until we had examined all the omitted portion, and had arrived at Assumption island which we had explored on leaving this coast. And when we had made certain that we had examined the whole coast and that no strait existed, we returned

[26] Sept-isles.
[27] Walruses.

to our ships, which were at the above-mentioned Seven islands, where there are good harbours with eighteen and twenty fathoms and sandy bottom.

[*From Sept-isles the fleet sailed upstream as far as the Indian village of Hochelaga, on the site of modern Montreal, where they were well received, and where they finally accepted the fact that the St. Lawrence was not a strait*]

On issuing forth from the village we were conducted by several of the men and women of the place up the above-mentioned mountain, lying a quarter of a league away, which was named by us "Mount Royal." On reaching the summit we had a view of the land for more than thirty leagues round about. Towards the north there is a range of mountains, running east and west,[28] and another range to the south. Between these ranges lies the finest land it is possible to see, being arable, level and flat. And in the midst of this flat region one saw the river [St. Lawrence] extending beyond the spot where we had left our long-boats. At that point there is the most violent rapid it is possible to see, which we were unable to pass.[29] And as far as the eye can reach, one sees that river, large, wide and broad, which came from the south-west and flowed near three fine conical mountains, which we estimated to be some fifteen leagues away. And it was told us and made clear by signs by our three local Indian guides, that there were three more such rapids in that river, like the one where lay our long-boats; but through lack of an interpreter we could not make out what the distance was from one to the other. They then explained to us by signs that after passing these rapids, one could navigate along that river for more than three moons.[30]

[28] The Laurentian Hills.
[29] The Lachine Rapid.
[30] The distance from Montreal to the headwaters of Lake Superior by the great lakes is 1,550 miles.

25. The northeast passage leads to Russia

To northern navigators and geographical theorists who habitually used globes, it seemed obvious that there should be a more direct route to Cathay across the Arctic than round the Cape of Good Hope. Most sixteenth-century maps show the polar area as open sea, with large but widely separated islands. In the second half of the century a considerable number of voyages were planned, most of them in England, to search for passages between these islands, either to the northeast or to the north-west. The "Company of merchant adventurers for discovery of regions, dominions, islands and places unknown" had as its first Master old Sebastian Cabot who, though born in England, had been pilot-major of Spain, and who survived as a living link between the maritime Renais-sance of the Mediterranean and the Elizabethan seamen. Cabot lived in the memory of his father's achievements. Disappointed in the north-west and in the Río de la Plata, he was determined in old age to see the northeast explored. In 1553 the company despatched a fleet of three ships under Sir Hugh Willoughby with the express intention of sailing to Cathay by way of a northeast passage. The ships were separated by a storm off the Lofoten Islands, and two of them, including Willough-by's flagship, were never heard of again. The third, the *Edward Bona-ventura*, commanded by the senior navigator, Richard Chancellor, rounded North Cape, entered the White Sea, and reached Archangel. There Chancellor—who was a competent diplomat as well as a fine sea-man—learned for the first time of the power and wealth of the Russian emperor. After long haggling with the local people, he and some of his officers set off on an astonishing journey in horse-drawn sleighs, in winter, from Archangel to Moscow.

Russia at that time was almost completely isolated from other civil-ized countries. It was hemmed in by nomad peoples to the south and east; it was allowed no intercourse with militant Catholic Poland to the west. Sparse supplies of Oriental luxury goods came up the great rivers which flow into the Black Sea and the Caspian. Equally sparse were the supplies of European commodities which came up the Baltic by a route monopolized by the German Hanse. Ivan the Terrible, therefore, welcomed the English adventurers both as merchants and as civilized strangers. The visit led to a series of diplomatic exchanges, not only on commercial matters, but extending even to tentative suggestions of alliance and royal marriage.

Chancellor's search for the northeast passage was continued later by Linschoten, Bärents, and others; but none of them got further than Novaya Zemlya. No ship—until Nordenskiöld's *Vega* in 1878, and in more modern times Russian ice-breakers—penetrated to the Pacific by that route. The principal results of their discoveries were incidental: the opening of English, and later Dutch trade with Russia, and the Arctic whale fishery, based on Spitzbergen, which began in the early seventeenth century, and ended only with killing-out of the whales.

The extract which follows is from *The Principal navigations . . . of the English nation,* by Richard Hakluyt (12 vols., Glasgow, Maclehose, 1903), II, 246–55: Clement Adams' narrative of Richard Chancellor's voyage to Russia in 1553.

T HE very same day in the afternoone, about foure of the clocke, so great a tempest suddenly arose, and the Seas were so outragious, that the ships could not keepe their intended course, but some were perforce driven one way, and some another way, to their great perill and hazard: The generall with his lowdest voyce cried out to Richard Chanceler, and earnestly requested him not to goe farre from him: but hee neither would nor could keepe companie with him, if he sailed still so fast: for the Admirall was of better saile then his shippe. But the said Admirall (I knowe not by what meanes) bearing all his sailes, was caried away with so great force and swiftnesse, that not long after hee was quite out of sight, and the third ship also with the same storme and like rage was dispersed and lost us.

The shippe boate of the Admirall (striking against the shippe,) was overwhelmed in the sight and viewe of the Mariners of the Bonadventure: and as for them that are already returned and arrived, they know nothing of the rest of the ships what was become of them.

But if it be so, that any miserable mishap have overtaken them, If the rage and furie of the Sea have devoured those good men, or if as yet they live, and wander up and downe in strange Countreys, I must needs say they were men worthy of better fortune, and if they be living, let us wish them safetie and a good returne: but if the crueltie of death hath taken holde of them, God send them a Christian grave and Sepulchre.

Nowe Richard Chancelor with his shippe and company being thus left alone, and become very pensive, heavie, and sorrowfull, by this dispersion of the Flette, hee (according to the order before taken,) shapeth his course for Wardhouse in Norway, there to expect and abide the arrivall of the rest of the shippes. And being come thither, and having stayed there for the space of 7. days, and looked in vaine for their comming, hee determined at length to proceede alone in the purposed voyage. And as hee was preparing himselfe to depart, it happened that hee fell in company and speech with certaine Scottishmen: who having understanding of his intention, and wishing well to his actions, beganne earnestly to disswade him from the further prosecution of the discoverie, by amplifying the dangers which hee was to fall into, and omitted no reason that might serve to that purpose. But hee holding nothing so ignominious and reproachfull, as inconstancie and levitie of minde, and perswading himselfe that a man of valour could not commit a more dishonourable part then for feare of danger to avoyde and shunne great attempts, was nothing at all changed or discouraged with the speeches and words of the Scots, remaining stedfast and immutable in his first resolution: determining either to bring that to passe which was intended, or els to die the death.

And as for them which were with Master Chancelor in his shippe, although they had great cause of discomfort by the losse of their companie (whom the foresaid tempest had separated from them,) and were not a little troubled with cogitations and perturbations of minde, in respect of their doubtfull course: yet notwithstanding, they were of such consent and agreement of minde with Master Chancelor, that they were resolute, and prepared under his direction and government, to make proofe and triall of all adventures, without all feare or mistrust of future dangers. Which constancie of minde in all the companie did exceedingly increase their Captaines carefulnesse: for hee being swallowed up with like good will and love towards them, feared lest through any errour of his, the safetie of the copanie should bee indangered. To conclude, when they sawe their

desire and hope of the arrivall of the rest of the shippes to be
every day more and more frustrated, they provided to sea
againe, and Master Chanceler held on his course towards that
unknowen part of the world, and sailed so farre, that hee came
at last to the place where hee found no night at all, but a continual light and brightnesse of the Sunne shining clearely upon
the huge and mightie Sea. And having the benefite of this
perpetuall light for certaine dayes, at the length it pleased God
to bring them into a certaine great Bay, which was of one hun-
dreth miles or thereabout over. Whereinto they entred, and
somewhat farre within it cast ancre, and looking every way
about them, it happened that they espied a farre off a certaine
fisher boate, which Master Chanceler, accompanied with a fewe
of his men, went towards to common with the fishermen that
were in it, and to knowe of them what Countrey it was, and
what people, and of what maner of living they were: but they
being amazed with the strange greatnesse of his shippe, (for
in those partes before that time they had never seene the like)
beganne presently to avoyde and to flee: but hee still following
them at last overtooke them, and being come to them, they
(being in great feare, as men halfe dead) prostrated themselves
before him, offering to kisse his feete: but hee (according to his
great and singular courtesie,) looked pleasantly upon them, com-
forting them by signs and gestures, refusing those dueties and
reverences of theirs, and taking them up in all loving sort from
the ground. And it is strange to consider howe much favour
afterwards in that place, this humanitie of his did purchase to
himselfe. For they being dismissed spread by and by a report
abroad of the arrivall of a strange nation, of a singular gentle-
nesse and courtesie: whereupon the common people came together offering to these newe-come ghests victuals freely, and
bound by a certaine religious use and custome, not to buy any
forreine commodities, without this knowledge and consent of
the king.

By this time our men had learned that this Countrey was
called Russia, or Moscovie, and that Ivan Vasiliwich (which was
at that time their Kings name) ruled and governed farre and
wide in those places. And the barbarous Russes asked likewise
of our men whence they were, and what they came for: where-

unto answere was made, that they were Englishmen sent into
those coastes, from the most excellent King Edward the sixt,
having from him in commandement certaine things to deliver to
their King, and seeking nothing els but his amitie and friendship,
and traffique with his people, whereby they doubted not, but
that great commoditie and profit would grow to the subjects of
both kingdomes.

The Barbarians heard these things very gladly, and promised
their aide and furtherance to acquaint their king out of hand
with so honest and a reasonable request.

In the meane time Master Chanceler intreated victuals for his
money of the governour of that place (who together with
others came aboord him) and required hostages of them likewise for the more assurance of safetie to himselfe and his
company. To whom the Governours answered, that they knewe
not in that case the will of their king, but yet were willing in
such things as they might lawfully doe, to pleasure him: which
was as then to affoord him the benefit of victuals.

Nowe while these things were a doing, they secretly sent a
messenger unto the Emperour, to certifie him of the arrivall of
a strange nation, and withall to knowe his pleasure concerning
them. Which message was very welcome unto him, insomuch
that voluntarily hee invited them to come to his Court. But if
by reason of the tediousnesse of so long a journey, they thought
it not best so to doe, then hee graunted libertie to his subjects
to bargaine, and to traffique with them: and further promised,
that if it would please them to come to him, hee himselfe
would beare the whole charges of poste horses. In the meane time
the governours of the place differed the matter from day to day,
pretending divers excuses, and saying one while that the consent
of all the governours, and another while, that the great and
waightie affaires of the kingdome compelled them to differ their
answere: and this they did of purpose, so long to protract the
time, until the messenger (sent before to the king) did returne
with relation of his will and pleasure.

But Master Chanceler, (seeing himselfe held in this suspense
with long and vaine expectation, and thinking that of intention
to delude him, they posted the matter off so often,) was very

instant with them to performe their promise: Which if they would not doe, hee tolde them that hee would depart and proceede in his voyage. So that the Moscovites (although as yet they knew not the minde of their king) yet fearing the departure in deede of our men who had such wares and commodities as they greatly desired, they at last resolved to furnish our people with all things necessarie, and to conduct them by land to the presence of their king. And so Master Chanceler beganne his journey, which was very long and most troublesome, wherein hee had the use of certaine sleds, which in that Countrey are very common, for they are caried themselves upon sleds, and all their carriages are in the same sort, the people almost not knowing any other maner of carriage, the cause whereof is the exceeding hardnesse of the ground congealed in the winter time by the force of the colde, which in those places is very extreme and horrible, whereof hereafter we will say something.

But nowe they having passed the greater part of their journey, mette at last with the Sleddeman (of whom I spake before) sent to the king secretly from the Justices or governours, who by some ill happe had lost his way, and had gone to the Sea side, which is neere to the Countrey of the Tartars, thinking there to have found our ship. But having long erred and wandered out of his way, at the last in his direct returne, hee met (as hee was comming) our Captaine on the way. To whom hee by and by delivered the Emperours letters, which were written to him with all courtesie and in the most loving maner that could be: wherein expresse commandement was given, that post horses should bee gotten for him and the rest of his company without any money. Which thing was of all the Russes in the rest of their journey so willingly done, that they began to quarrell, yea, and to fight also in striving and contending which of them should put their post horses to the sledde: so that after much adoe and great paines taken in this long and wearie journey, (for they had travailed very neere fifteene hundred miles) Master Chanceler came at last to Mosco the chiefe citie of the kingdome, and the seate of the king: of which citie, and of the Emperour himself, and of the principall cities of Moscovie, wee will speake immediately more at large in this discourse.

Of Moscove, which is also called Russia

Moscovie, which hath the name also of Russia the white, is a
very large and spacious Countrey, every way founded with
divers nations. Towards the South and the East, it is compassed
with Tartaria: the Northren side of it stretcheth to the Scytian
Ocean: upon the West part border the Lappians, a rude and
savage nation, living in woods, whose language is not knowen
to any other people: next unto these, more towards the South,
is Swecia, then Finaldia, then Livonia, and last of all Lituania.
This Countrey of Moscovie, hath also very many and great
rivers in it, and is marish ground in many places: and as for the
rivers, the greatest and most famous amongst all the rest, is that,
which the Russes in their owne tongue call Volga, but others
know it by the name of Rha. Next unto it in fame is Tanais,
which they call Don and the third Boristhenes which at this day
they call Neper. Two of these, to wit, Rha, and Boristhenes
yssuing both out of one fountaine, runne very farre through the
land: Rha receiving many other pleasant rivers into it, & running from the very head or spring of it towards the East, after
many crooked turnings and windings, dischargeth it selfe, and
all the other waters and rivers that fall into it by divers passages
into the Caspian Sea. Tanais springing from a fountaine of great
name in those partes, and growing great neere to his head,
spreds it selfe at length very largely, and makes a great lake:
and then growing narrowe againe, doth so runne for certaine
miles, untill it fall into another lake, which they call Ivan: and
there-hence fetching a very crooked course, comes very neere
to the river Volga: but disdaining as it were the company of any
other river, doth there turne it selfe againe from Volga, and
runnes toward the South, and fals at last into the Lake of Mæotis.
Boristhenes, which comes from the same head that Rha doth,
(as wee sayde before) carieth both it selfe, and other waters
that are neere unto it, towards the South, not refusing the mixture of other small rivers: and running by many great and large
Countreys fals at last into Pontus Euxinus. Besides these rivers,
are also in Moscovie certaine lakes, and pooles, the lakes breede
fish by the celestiall influence: and amongst them all, the chiefest
and most principall is called Bealozera, which is very famous by
reason of a very strong towre built in it, wherein the kings of

Moscovie reserve and repose their treasure in all time of warre and danger.

Touching the Riphean mountaines, whereupon the snow lieth continually, and where hence in times past it was thought that Tanais the river did spring, and that the rest of the wonders of nature, which the Grecians fained and invented of olde, were there to be seene: our men which lately came from thence, neither sawe them, nor yet have brought home any perfect relation of them, although they remained there for the space of three moneths, and had gotten in that time some intelligence of the language of Moscovie. The whole Countrey is plaine and champion, and few hils in it: and towards the North it hath very large & spacious woods, wherein is great store of Firre trees, a wood very necessarie, and fit for the building of houses: there are also wilde beastes bred in those woods, as Buffes, Beares, and blacke Wolves, and another kinde of beast unknowen to us, but called by them Rossomakka: and the nature of the same is very rare and wonderfull: for when it is great with yong, and ready to bring foorth, it seeketh out some narrow place betweene two stakes, and so going through them, presseth it selfe, and by that meanes is eased of her burden, which otherwise could not be done. They hunt their buffes for the most part a horsebacke, but their Beares a foot, with woodden forkes. The north parts of the Countrey are reported to be so cold, that the very ice or water which distilleth out of the moist wood which they lay upon the fire is presently congealed and frozen: the diversitie growing suddenly to be so great, that in one and the selfe same firebrand, a man shall see both fire and ice. When the winter doth once begin there it doth still more & more increase by a perpetuitie of cold: neither doth that colde slake, untill the force of the Sunne beames doth dissolve the cold, and make glad the earth, returning to it againe. Our mariners which we left in the ship in the meane time to keepe it, in their going up onely from their cabbins to the hatches, had their breath oftentimes so suddenly taken away, that they eftsoones fell downe as men very neere dead, so great is the sharpenesse of that colde climate: but as for the South parts of the Countrey, they are somewhat more temperate.

Of *Mosco the chiefe Citie of the kingdome, and of the Emperour thereof*

It remaineth that a larger discourse be made of Mosco, the principall Citie of that Countrey, and of the Prince also, as before we have promised. The Empire and government of the king is very large, and his wealth at this time exceeding great. And because the citie of Mosco is the chiefest of al the rest, it seemeth of it selfe to challenge the first place in this discourse. Our men say, that in bignesse it is as great as the Citie of London, with the suburbes thereof. There are many and great buildings in it, but for beautie and fairenesse, nothing comparable to ours. There are many Townes and Villages also, but built out of order, and with no hansomnesse: their streetes and wayes are not paved with stone as ours are: the walles of their houses are of wood: the roofes for the most part are covered with shingle boords. There is hard by the Citie a very faire Castle, strong, and furnished with artillerie, whereunto the Citie is joyned directly towards the North, with a bricke wall: the walles also of the Castle are built with bricke, and are in breadth or thickenesse eighteene foote. This Castle hath on the one side a drie ditch, on the other side the river Moscua, whereby it is made almost inexpugnable. The same Moscua trending towards the East doth admit into it the companie of the river Occa.

In the Castle aforesaide, there are in number nine Churches, or Chappels, not altogether unhansome, which are used and kept by certaine religious men, over whom there is after a sort, a Patriarke, or Governour, and with him other reverend Fathers, all which for the greater part, dwell within the Castle. As for the kings Court and Palace, it is not of the neatest, onely in forme it is foure square, and of lowe building, much surpassed and excelled by the beautie and elegancie of the houses of the kings of England. The windowes are very narrowly built, and some of them by glasse, some other by lettisses admit the light: and whereas the Palaces of our Princes are decked, and adorned with hangings of cloth of gold, there is none such there: they build and joyne to all their wals benches, and that not onely in the Court of the Emperour, but in all private mens houses.

26. The northwest passage leads nowhere

The possibility of a northwest passage to the Pacific had weightier support, both from ancient and modern geographers, than the northeast. Sir Humphrey Gilbert's persuasive *Discourse* on the subject gives an impressive list of authorities. After Cartier's failure, attention became fixed on the wide stretch of sea between Greenland and Labrador. Martin Frobisher, on his first voyage to that region in 1576, claimed to have found a strait; in fact the deep inlet known as Frobisher Bay. He also found quantities of a dense and heavy black rock which he and others believed to be gold ore. Frobisher made two more voyages in the same region, and the third, like that of Cartier, was intended to establish a colony; but the colony was not planted, the strait was not found, and the ore yielded no gold.

Frobisher's work was continued—unhampered by gold strikes or colonizing plans—by Davis, by Hudson, by a long series of explorers, mostly English, extending down to the nineteenth century. As in the northeast, so in the northwest, the seaway to the Pacific was found to be choked with ice. As in the northeast, so in the northwest, the chief results of the search were incidental: the enlargement of geographical knowledge; the discovery, in Hudson's Strait and Bay, of a backdoor to the richest fur-producing region in the world; and the development of a characteristically English school of navigators and explorers.

The extract which follows is from *The Three Voyages of Martin Frobisher*, edited by Rear-Admiral Richard Collinson (London, Hakluyt Society, 1867), pp. 72–6.

He . . . continued hys course towardes the north-weast, knowing that the sea at length must needes have an endyng, and that some lande shoulde have a beginning that way; and determined, therefore, at the least, to bryng true proofe what lande and sea the same myght bee, so farre to the northweast- wardes, beyonde anye man that hathe heeretofore discovered. And the twentieth of July hee hadde sighte of a highe lande, whyche hee called Queene Elizabeth's Forlande, after hyr Majesties name, and sayl-

ing more northerlie alongst the coast he descried another forlande
with a greate gutte, bay, or passage, deviding as it were, two
maynelands or continents asunder. There he met with store of
exceeding great ise al this coast along, and covetng still to continue his course to the northwardes, was alwayes by contrarie
winde deteyned overthwarte these straytes, and could not get
beyonde. Within few days after he perceyved the ise to be well
consumed and gone, eyther there engulfed in by some swifte cur-
rants or in draftes caried more to the southwardes of the same
straytes, or else conveyed some other way; wherefore he determined to make profe of this place to see how far that gutte had
continuance, and whether he mighte carrie himselfe through the
same into some open sea on the backe syde, whereof he conceyved
no small hope, and so entred the same the one-and-twentieth of
July, and passed above fyftie leagues therein, as hee reported, having upon eyther hande a greate mayne or continent; and that land
uppon hys right hande as he sayled westward, he judged to be the
continente of Asia, and there to bee devided from the firme of
America, whiche lyeth uppon the lefte hande over against the
same.

This place he named after his name Frobisher's Streytes, lyke as
Magellanus at the south-weast ende of the worlde having discovered the passage to the South Sea (where America is divided
from the continente of that lande whiche lyeth under the south
pole), and called the same straites Magellanes streightes. After
he hadde passed 60 leagues into this foresayde strayte hee wente
ashore, and founde signe where fire had bin made.

He saw mightie deere y^t seemed to be mankind, which ranne
at him, and hardly he escaped with his life in a narrow way,
where he was faine to use defence and policie to save his life.

In this place he saw and perceyved sundry tokens of the peoples resorting thither, and being ashore upon the toppe of a hill,
he perceived a number of small things fleeting in the sea afarre
off, whyche hee supposed to be porposes or seales, or some kinde
of strange fishe; but coming nearer, he discovered them to be
men in small boates made of leather. And before he could
descende downe from the hyll certain of those people had almost cut off his boate from him, having stollen secretly behinde

the rocks for that purpose, where he speedily hasted to his
boate and bente himselfe to his holberte, and norrowly escaped
the daunger and saved his bote. Afterwards he had sundry con-
ferences with them, and they came aboarde his ship, and brought
him salmon and raw fleshe and fishe, and greedily devoured the
same before our mens faces. And to shewe their agilitie, they
tryed many maisteries upon the ropes of the ship after our
mariners fashion, and appeared to be very strong of theyr armes
and nimble of their bodies. They exchanged coates of seale and
beares skinnes, and suche like, with oure men, and received
belles, looking-glasses, and other toyes in recompence thereof
againe. After great curtesie and many meetings, our mariners,
contrarie to theyr captaines dyrection, began more easily to
trust them, and five of oure men going ashore, were by them
intercepted with theyr boate, and were never since heard of to
this daye againe. So that the captaine being destitute of boate,
barke, and al company, had scarcely sufficient number to conduct back his bark againe. He coulde nowe neither convey himselfe ashore to rescue his men (if he had bin able), for want
of a boate; and again, the subtile traytours were so warie as
they would after that never come within our mens danger. The
captaine, notwithstanding, desirous to bring some token from
thence of his being there, was greatly discontented that he had
not before apprehended some of them. And therefore to deceive
the deceivers he wrought a prettie pollicie, for knowing well
how they greatly delighted in our toyes, and specially in belles,
he rang a pretie lowbel, making wise that he would give him
the same that would come and fetch it. And bycause they
would not come within his daunger for feare, he flung one bell
unto them, which of purpose he threw short that it might fal
into the sea and be lost. And to make the more greedie of the
matter he rang a lowder bell, so that in the ende one of them
came neare the ship side to receive the bell, which, when he
thought to take at the captaine's hand he was thereby taken
himself; for the captain being redily provided, let the bel fal
and caught the man fast, and plucked him with maine force
boate and al into his bark out of the sea. Whereupon, when he
founde himself in captivitie, for very choller and disdain, he bit

his tong in twayne within his mouth: notwithstanding, he died not thereof, but lived untill he came in England, and then he died of colde which he had taken at sea.

Nowe with this newe pray (whiche was a sufficient witnesse of the captaines farre and tedious travell towards the unknowne partes of the worlde, as did well appeare by this strange Infidel, whose like was never seen, red, nor harde of before, and whose language was neyther knowne nor understoode of anye) the saide Captain Frobisher retourned homeward, and arrived in England in August folowing, an. 1576, where he was highly commended of all men for his great and notable attempt, but specially famous for the great hope he brought of the passage to Cataya, which he doubted nothing at all to find and passe through in those parts, as he reporteth.

And it is especially to be remembered at the first arrivall in those partes, there laye so great store of ise all the coaste along so thicke togither, that hardely his boate coulde passe unto the shoare. At lengthe, after diverse attempts, he commaunded his company if by anye possible meanes they could get ashore, to bring him whatsoever thing they could first find, whether it were living or dead, stocke or stone, in token of Christian possession, which thereby he toke in behalfe of the Queenes most excellent Majestie, thinking that therby he might justify the having and enjoying of ye same things that grew in these unknowne partes.

Some of his companye broughte floures, some greene grasse, and one brought a peece of a blacke stone, much lyke to a seacole in coloure, whiche by the waight seemed to be some kinde of mettall or mynerall. This was a thing of no accompt in the judgement of the captain at the first sight. And yet for novelty it was kept, in respect of the place from whence it came.

After his arrival in London, being demanded of sundrie his friendes what thing he had brought them home of that country, he had nothing left to present them withall but a peece of this black stone. And it fortuned a gentlewoman, one of ye adventurers wives, to have a peece thereof, which by chance she threw and burned in the fire, so long, that at the length being taken forth and quenched in a little vinegre, it glistered with a bright Marquesset of golde. Whereupon the matter being called in some question, it was brought to certain goldfinders in London to make assay therof, who indeed found it to hold gold, and that very ritchly for the quantity. Afterwards, the same goldfinders promised great matters thereof if there were anye store to be found, and offred themselves to adventure for the serching of those partes from whence the same was brought. Some, that had great hope of the matter, sought secretly to have a lease at hir Majesties hands of those places, whereby to enjoy the masse of so great a publike profit unto their owne private gaines.

In conclusion, the hope of the same golde ore to be founde, kindled a greater opinion in the heartes of many to advaunce the voyage againe. Whereupon preparation was made for a newe voyage against the yeare following, and the captaine more specially directed by commission for the searching more of this golde ore than for the searching any further of the passage. And being wel accompanied with diverse resolute and forward gentlemen, hir Majestie then lying at the right honourable the Lord of Warwicks house in Essex, came to take theyr leaves, and kissing hir highnesses hands, with gracious countenance and comfortable words departed towardes their charge.

IX. *The Explorer's Trade*

27. Sailing directions

The Portuguese were pioneers not only in oceanic exploration, but
also in the tasks of organizing and systematizing the results of exploration. The explorers went out under royal auspices; their masters
expected them to record their voyages in detail, step by step, so that
others coming after could follow their routes and develop their discoveries. From the accumulated experiences of discovery and later
seaborne trade were built up the *roteiros*, books of sailing directions,
giving courses and distances from place to place, navigational hazards,
and descriptions by which navigators could recognize salient features
of a coast. The *roteiros*, later imitated by Dutch and English compilers,
were the ancestors of the pilot-books of modern times. They were
treated as secret documents by the Portuguese government—at least in
so far as they dealt with eastern seas—and probably many have perished.

Esmeraldo de situ orbis is the earliest surviving Portuguese *roteiro*
which can be dated with confidence. It was written between 1505 and
1508. Its author[1] promised in his introduction to describe Africa and
Asia, but the work as it has survived contains directions only for West
and South Africa. Possibly the Indian Ocean sections were suppressed
for reasons of security. The directions in the *Esmeraldo* are less laconic
than many of their kind; they include historical notes on discoveries
and information about local trade. The section quoted here deals with
the stretch of coast between Cape Palmas, on what is now the Ivory
Coast, and the Portuguese factory-fortress of São Jorge da Mina on
the Gold Coast, modern Ghana. The accuracy of its information can
be assessed to some extent by comparison with the modern *Africa Pilot*.

The extract which follows is from *Esmeraldo de situ orbis* by Duarte

---

[1] See p. 110.

Pacheco Pereira, translated and edited by George H. T. Kimble (London, Hakluyt Society, 1937), Book II, Chapters IV and V, pp. 114–21.

Chapter IV: Concerning the routes and landmarks from Cabo das Palmas to the Castle of S. Jorge da Mina

WE must notice the difference in the direction of the coast beyond Cabo das Palmas, for beyond this cape it runs in one direction, and on this side of the cape, along the coast of Malagueta, in another: any pilot going to these parts should observe this and the latitude of this cape, and he will then make no mistake, even if he does not know this country as we now know it after the experience of many years.

Item. Eight leagues beyond Cabo das Palmas is a river called Rio de S. Pedro;[1] they lie W.S.W. and E.N.E. This river has a small mouth, but as we are not accustomed to enter it and have no practical knowledge of it, we will therefore not write about that which is unknown to us, although the coast itself we have come to know well enough from years of experience.

Item. From Rio de S. Pedro to Rio de S. André is twenty-five leagues, and between them is a narrow cape, called Cabo da Praya,[2] which has on the W. side some fields called "the rice fields." Farther on the land forms a bay[3] having a broad headland at its entrance and a white rock like an islet standing in the sea.[4] All this coast is inhabited. A little beyond this bay along the sea are six or seven hills;[5] these are eight leagues distant from Rio de S. André. The coast lies W. by S. and E. by N. Rio de S. André[6] has a wide mouth, and when opposite it you can see above its mouth some trees in the interior which look like pine-trees; half a league up the river there is an island in mid-stream. From the ricefields to this river you will find a muddy bottom with some patches of sand if you anchor half a league from the

---

[1] Name retained to the present day.
[2] Drewin (or Moncho) Point (*vide Africa Pilot*, Part 1, p. 316).
[3] Victoria Gulf (or Bay) (*vide Africa Pilot*, Part 1, p. 316).
[4] Boulakba Rocks (*vide Africa Pilot*, Part 1, p. 316).
[5] The Drewin Highland.
[6] Sassandra (or St. Andrew) River.

shore in twenty fathoms; at a league from land the depth is fifty fathoms. But as we have not yet had any experience or traffic at this Rio de S. André we will say no more of it here, except that we have learnt that the country is densely populated and this river, like all the other rivers of Guinea, is rife with fever.

Item. Three leagues beyond the Rio de S. André you find tall red cliffs[7] along the coast, extending for four or five leagues; these lie E. and W. with respect to the river and are composed of very red clay and are the landmark for the said R. de S. André.

Item. From the red cliffs to Rio d'Alaguoa[8] is eight leagues, and the coast lies W. by S. and E. by N. The landmarks of this Rio d'Alaguoa are a wood, like a pinewood, above its mouth in the interior, and the fact that this river flows along the coast till it reaches a village[9] where in our day there are four palm-trees, each standing apart by itself; on the farther side of this village is a very large lake, which you cannot see unless you climb the ship's mast. All this coast has a good clean bottom as far as Cabo das Tres Pontas; we do not know if there is any commerce here.

Item. Seven leagues beyond Rio d'Alaguoa there are seven villages, which are very well populated, extending seven or eight leagues along the coast; the coast runs E. and W. and is composed entirely of beach of a reddish sand. The country is densely wooded and the depth near the shore is thirty or forty fathoms, but it is less than this two leagues out at sea. The negroes of this coast are great fishermen and their canoes have fo'castles. They wear hooded caps like those of shepherds; they go naked and are idolaters. We call them "Beiçudos." [10] They are evil people and there is no commerce here.

Item. From the seven villages to Rio de Mayo[11] is twelve leagues; the mouth of this river is not large and the country round it is very low, marshy and well-wooded. We know nothing of what trade there may be in this country, but only know that it is densely populated.

[7] Cf. *Africa Pilot*, Part I, p. 319.
[8] I.e. Lahu River.
[9] Grand Lahu (?) (*vide Africa Pilot*, Part I, p. 320).
[10] I.e. "the thick-lipped."
[11] I.e. Komoë River.

Item. From Rio de Mayo to Rio de Soeyro[12] is ten leagues. This Rio de Soeyro was discovered by Soeyro da Costa at the bidding of King Afonso V. Whoever sails from the shore past the seven villages to this Rio de Soeyro, must sail E. and S., close in to the shore, and by this course he will not go wrong.

Item. From Rio de Soeyro to the Serra de Santa Apolonia[13] is twelve leagues; the coast lies W. N. W. and E. S. E. Six leagues beyond these hills you will see a fortress[14] which Our Lord King Manuel ordered to be built, where yearly there is obtained in barter thirty to forty thousand doubloons of good gold. The country is called Axem and is very subject to fever. The merchandise exchanged for gold consists of brass bracelets, basins of the same metal, red and blue cloth, linen neither very coarse nor very fine, and "lanbens," that is, a kind of mantle made like the shawls of Alentejo, with stripes of red, green, blue and white, the stripes being two or three inches wide. They are made in the city of Ouram[15] and in Tenez in the kingdom of Tremecem, in Bona and Estora[16] of the kingdom of Bogia, and also in Tunez and in other parts of Berbery. This is the principal merchandise used for the barter of gold in Axem, besides other articles of less value.

To continue our description of the Serra de Santa Apolonia; it is not as high as the ignorant may imagine, but consists of eight or ten hills of reasonable height on the coast, covered with woods. However, because the rest of the country is very low these hills seem quite high. He who leaves Cabo das Palmas for the castle of S. Jorge da Mina should sail E. by N.; at 130 leagues along the route he will find the Serra de Santa Apolonia opposite him; in order not to lose his way his correct course will lie outside the bay.

Item. The Serra de Santa Apolonia and Cabo das Tres Pontas[17]

[12] I.e. Assini River: to this day the hills behind the mouth of this river are called after da Costa, who was one of the captains employed by Fernão Gomes during the period of his Guìnea trading lease.

[13] Cf. *Africa Pilot*, Part 1, p. 325.

[14] A fort—St. Anthony's—still commands the bay in which the port of Axim is situated.

[15] I.e. Oran.

[16] I.e. Stora in Argelia in the province of Constantina, to the northwest of Philippeville.

[17] I.e. Cape Three Points.

lie N.W. by W. and S.E. by E. and they occupy fifteen leagues
of the route. One may anchor opposite this Serra in twenty fathoms
on a muddy bottom a league from the shore. Twelve leagues beyond this Serra is an islet close to the mainland; it is very rugged
and white with the guano of birds. A little over half a league
from this islet is an island near to the coast; this island has a tree
in its centre and on the side on which the sea beats it is of a reddish
colour. From there to Cabo das Tres Pontas is three leagues. I do
not know why this cape was called thus, for there are six or seven
points, on all of which the sea beats; they are all of broken rock,
and he who doubles the central point doubles them all. The landmarks of this cape are that the coast there turns to the N.E. and
that its latitude is 4° 30′ N.[18] The pilot or captain who is ignorant of this country should observe the trend of the coast and he
will find that it follows two directions: from Cabo das Tres
Pontas to Serra de Santa Apolonia it lies N.W. by W. and S.E. by
E.; and from there it trends N.E., the latitude increasing.

Item. From Cabo das Tres Pontas to the islets of Anda[19] is
four leagues; the coast runs S.W. and N.E., and these islands are
very close to the shore; in the same neighbourhood there are some
red cliffs. The region of Anda extends for seven or eight leagues;
it contains a gold mine, which although not very large, yields
20,000 doubloons or more; the gold is taken to be bartered at the
Castle of S. Jorge da Mina and at the fortress of Axem of which
we have spoken above. The negroes of this country live on millet, fish and yams, together with a little meat; they are naked from
the waist up, are uncircumcised and heathen, but, God willing,
they will soon become Christians.

Item. The islet of Anda and the Rio de Sam Joham[20] lie S.W.
and N.E. and occupy eight leagues of the route. This river is very
small and narrow; there is only a fathom and a half at its mouth
at high tide, and its mouth cannot be seen until one is quite close
to it. There is here a town called Samaa[21] of some 500 inhabitants, where the first gold in this country was obtained in barter,

---

[18] Actually 4° 46′ N.
[19] Abokori Islet (?).
[20] Pra River. It enters the sea in Shama Bay.
[21] I.e. Shama which, today, has a population of about 2,400 (*vide Africa
Pilot*, Part I, p. 337).

and it was at that time called Mina. It was discovered at the bidding of King Afonso V by Joham de Santarem and Pedro d'Escobar,[22] knights of his household, in the month of January of the year of Our Lord 1471. These captains carried as pilots a certain Alvaro Estevez, an inhabitant of the town of Lagos, and a certain Martim Estevez, citizen of Lisbon, Alvaro Estevez being the man most skilled in his profession in Spain at that time. The landmark of the Rio de S. Joham and of the town of Samaa is a very large bay over two leagues in circuit and a good league across from point to point; almost in the centre of the bay is the mouth of the river. This bay is full of shallows and a ship should anchor in ten or twelve fathoms on a clean sandy bottom a league from the shore and not go farther in.

Item. From the bay of Samaa to the village of Torto is three leagues; the route lies W.S.W. and E.N.E. The lord of this village was squint-eyed, hence its name. It has a great reef of rock on which the sea breaks violently,[23] running more than half a league into the sea, so that one should keep well out. From here to the castle of S. Jorge da Mina is three leagues.

Chapter V: Concerning the Castle of S. Jorge da Mina and when it was built

In the paragraph before last we related how the excellent prince, King Afonso V ordered the discovery of Mina and what captains and pilots he sent for the purpose. We must now tell how his son the most serene prince, King John of Portugal after the death of his father ordered the foundation of the Castle of S. Jorge da Mina. At the bidding of this magnanimous prince it was built by Dieguo d'Azambuja, a knight of his household and High Commander of the Order of S. Bento. On the 1st of January in the year of Our Lord 1482 he took with him nine caravels, each with its captain, very honourable men, under his command, together with two urcas of 400 tons laden with lime and building stone and other material for this work. There was much trouble with

[22] These men, like Soero da Costa, were chosen by Fernão Gomes to forward the exploration of West Africa. Pedro d'Escobar subsequently accompanied Diogo Cão to the Congo and acted as one of Vasco da Gama's pilots on his first voyage to India.

[23] Kassi Reefs (?) (vide Africa Pilot, Part I, p. 338).

the negroes, who wished to prevent the work, but it was finally
finished, despite them, with all diligence and zeal, and it was
necessary for the refuge and defence of all of us. At a later date
the same King John, seeing that this was necessary, ordered the
work to be added to. This, as we know, was the first stone building in the region of the Ethiopias of Guinea since the creation of
the world. Through this fortress trade so greatly increased by
the favour of Our Lord that 170,000 doubloons of good fine gold,
and sometimes much more, are yearly brought thence to these
realms of Portugal; it is bartered from the negro merchants who
bring it thither from distant lands. These merchants belong to
various tribes; the Bremus,[24] Atis,[25] Hacanys,[26] Boroes,[27] Mandin-
guas,[28] Cacres, Andeses or Souzos,[29] and many others which I
omit for the sake of brevity. In exchange they take away much
merchandise, such as "lanbens," which is the principal article of
commerce (we described this in the ninth paragraph of the fourth
chapter of this second book), red and blue cloth, brass bracelets,
handkerchiefs, corals, and certain red shells which they prize as
we prize precious stones; white wine is also greatly prized, and
blue beads, which they call "coris," and many other articles of
various kinds. These people have hitherto been heathen, but some
of them have now become Christians; I speak of those who dwell
near the castle, for the merchants come from far and have not
the same intercourse with us as these neighbours and accordingly
continue in their false idolatry. The profit of this trade is five for
one, or more, but the country is much subject to fever, and white
men often die here. The latitude of this castle is 5° 30′ N. of the
Equator,[30] and on a clear night one can see the Pole Star elevated
the same number of degrees above the horizon. For a clearer understanding we have given here a painting from sight of the
castle, as it appears at the present time. Here there is an abundance of fish, upon which the negroes live, but they keep few

[24] The Ebrié tribes of the Ivory Coast (?).
[25] The Attié tribes located inland from the Ebrié tribes (?).
[26] I.e. the Akans who at the present time inhabit both Gold Coast and
Ashanti territory (see A. W. Cardinall: *The Gold Coast*, 1931, p. 9).
[27] The natives of the Bouré gold-mining region in the upper Niger (?).
[28] Mandingos.
[29] The Susu (or Soso or Soussou) peoples of the Fouta Djallon Mountains.
[30] Actually 5° 05′ N.

cattle; however, there are many wild beasts such as ounces, elephants, buffaloes, gazelles and many other kinds, and also birds of various kinds, some of them being very beautiful. The negroes in this country go about naked, save for a loin-cloth or a piece of striped cloth, which they consider a very noble garment. They live on millet and palm-wine (though they prefer our wine) with fish and a little game. Our lord the King sends out yearly twelve small vessels laden with merchandise; these bring back to this realm the gold which the factor of his Highness obtains there by barter. Besides these vessels, three or four ships go out laden with provisions, wine and other articles which are needed there. The merchants who bring the gold to this fortress bring no asses or beasts of burden to carry away the merchandise, which they buy for three times and more its value in Portugal. Our people who are sent out by the most serene King in his ships buy slaves 200 leagues beyond the castle, by rivers where there is a very large city called Beny,[31] whence they are brought thither [to Mina?]. What we have said of this is sufficient for our purpose, [which] solely concerns the commerce of our lord the King.

28. The uses of astronomy

Esmeraldo de situ orbis, as its ambitious (if cryptic) title suggests, was intended by its author to be more than a simple set of sailing directions. It was to be a description of the world. It contains a general essay on cosmography, including some eccentric speculation on the source of the Nile, and a guide to navigational practice. The cosmographical description is of no particular interest. It is based on conventional classical, scriptural, and medieval authorities, and seems to have been included in order to provide a façade of book-learning. The navigational information, on the other hand, is eminently practical and clearly the product of experience. The chapter on tides is somewhat muddled,

[31] Benin.

and the author skates lightly over the problem—in his day insoluble—
of ascertaining longitude. The use of celestial observations for determining latitude, on the other hand, is clearly and succinctly described.
In general, the book is the best available contemporary account of the
skill and knowledge of up-to-date ocean navigators in the first decade
of the sixteenth century.

The extract which follows is from *Esmeraldo de situ orbis* by Duarte Pacheco Pereira, translated and edited by George H. T. Kimble
(London, Hakluyt Society, 1937) Book I, Chapters IV–XII, pp. 21–35.

*Chapter VI: Concerning the advantage of knowing how to count
the world's degrees of longitude and latitude*

SINCE we have promised in this work of ours to deal with navigation and the things of the sea, it is reasonable that we should
fulfil our promise; and because the subject of astronomy is so well
established as to be of great advantage to the matter in hand, we
have thought it well to set down here the degrees by which some
places known to us are distant from the Equator in the direction
of the North or of the South Pole. And since it is necessary to
explain the manner of counting the globe's degrees of latitude
and longitude to the common unlettered people and especially to
the mariners who sail across the surface of the sea of the world
(they will derive great benefit if they will learn this, seeing that
they sail afar to many countries and lands), we have set here a
table of places, cities, lands and islands and their degrees of distance from the Equator towards the Poles, and later on we will
say how the longitude and latitude of the globe must be taken.

*Chapter VII: Table of the latitude of the following places
located north of the Equator*

	degrees	minutes		degrees	minutes
Iherusalem	33	00	Ancron[1]	33	00
Egipto	29	50	Fugua do Egipto[2]	29	00
Babilonia	33	30	Damiata	31	00
Meca	21	40	Anburi[3]	20	00
Damasco	33	00	Alcansatina[4]	45	00

[1] Corruption for Acre?
[2] Head of Nile Delta?
[3] Corruption for Anbur near Barcelona?
[4] Corruption?

All four names are found in
Zacuto's *Almanach perpetuum*
(1525).

	degrees	minutes		degrees	minutes
Rodes	36	00	Seguovea	40	57
Sardenha	38	00	Burguos	42	18
Cezilia[5]	37	00	Santiaguo[9]	43	07
Roma	42	00	Valença[10]	39	52
Alixandria	31	00	Albuquerque[11]	38	37
Genova	42	30	Tolosa[12]	43	00
Napoles	40	40	Viana Provincie[13]	44	00
Constantinopla	43	00	Brujas[14]	52	00
Captor[6]	31	20	Collonha Agripina[15]	51	00
Paris	48	00	Argentina[16]	47	00
Lisboa	39	00	Constancia	46	00
Santarem	40	00	Augusta Vindelicor-		
Covilhan	41	00	[um][17]	46	00
Medelim in Castile[7]	38	50	Suecia[18]	62	00
Tanger	35	15	Norvegia	54	00
Sevilha	37	15	Buda in Hungary	47	00
Salamanca	41	19	Vilhana[19]	39	16
Cordova	37	44	Mérida	39	08
Toledo	39	54	Niebla	37	44
Legion[8]	43	08	Narbona	40	43
Camora	41	43	Hyta[20]	40	49
Touro	41	44	Cadafalso[21]	40	19
Ávilla	40	44	Cáceres	39	44
Valhadolid	41	51	Trosilho[22]	39	27
Medina del Campo	41	22	Pisa	42	30
Benavente	39	11	Veneza	45	00

[5] Sicily.

[6] In southeast Spain. The portolan charts of the fourteenth and fifteenth centuries mark Captor midway between Malaga and Almeria.

[7] Near Badajoz.

[8] Leon in Old Castille. Its Roman name was Legio.

[9] I.e. Santiago de Compostela.

[10] I.e. Valencia in Cáceres.

[11] A town situated to the southeast of Valencia in the province of Badajoz.

[12] Tolosa near S. Sebastian? Toulouse?

[13] Vienne in Dauphiné?

[14] Bruges.

[15] Roman name of Cologne.

[16] Strasburg.

[17] Roman name of Augsburg.

[18] Sweden.

[19] Fillena in Valencia?

[20] Hita in Old Castille.

[21] Cadalso in the province of Cáceres.

[22] Trujillo to east of Cáceres.

	degrees	minutes		degrees	minutes
Arzila	36	00	Taragona	41	53
Perepinha[23]	42	30	Narbona	42	00
Panplona	43	30	Cartagena	36	00
Logronho	42	20	Requena[35]	40	16
Agueda[24]	41	08	Alcantara	40	30
Lorca[25]	38	11	Madrid	40	24
Murcia	38	38	Jaem	37	56
Tortosa	41	21	Guadalajara	40	45
Barcelona	42	19	Alcalá	40	30
Granada	37	39	Tordelaguna[36]	39	58
Verona	42	00	Colonia[37]	51	00
Cuencua	40	30	Buarcos in Portugal[38]	40	35
Soria	41	38	O Porto in Portugal	41	40
Almaria[26]	37	30	Caminha	42	30
Atença[27]	41	08	Ilha Terceira of the		
Vitoria	42	46	Azores	39	00
Sena[28]	42	30	Cabo de Finis terra	43	45
Feez	33	00	Sorlingua[39]	..	..
Cepta[29]	35	20	Hoexante[40]	..	..
Aljazira[30]	37	22	Ho de Sines[41]	38	00
Talaveira[31]	39	58	Ilha de São Miguel of		
Écija[32]	39	33	the Azores	38	00
Palença	42	00	Cabo de São Vincente	37	00
Valença[33]	39	36	Calez[42]	37	00
Daroca[34]	41	20	Cabo de São Vincente	37	00
Saraguoça	41	30	Ilha da Madeira	33	30

[23] Perpignan.
[24] Near Aveiro in Portugal.
[25] Near Murcia.
[26] Almeria.
[27] Atienza in New Castille.
[28] Siena in Tuscany.
[29] Ceuta.
[30] Algeciras.
[31] Talavera in New Castille.
[32] Near Cordoba.
[33] Valencia, capital of the province of that name.
[34] Near Calatayud.
[35] Near Valencia.
[36] Torre laguna in New Castille.
[37] Cologne.
[38] Near Coimbra.
[39] Scilly Isles (*vide* portolan charts, e.g. Catalan Atlas, *c.* 1375).
[40] Ushant.
[41] Cape Sines in Southern Portugal.
[42] Cadiz.

	degrees	minutes		degrees	minutes
Cabo de Cantim	33	30	Cabo da Verga	09	20
Trapana in Cezilia	36	30	Ilhas dos Idolos	09	00
Ilha de Xio[43]	38	00	Auguada da Serra		
Cabo de Santo Angelo			Lyoa	08	00
in Morea	36	00	Cabo de Santa Anna	07	20
Maguadaxo in Ethiopia	02	30	Cabo do Monte	06	40
Cochim in India	09	00	Rio dos Cestos de		
Ilha d'Anjadiva in			Costa da Malagueta	05	50
India[44]	15	00	Cabo das Palmas	04	00
Calecut in India	11	20	Castello de Sam Jorze		
Cananor in India	12	00	da Mina	05	30
Coulam in India[45]	08	00	Rio da Volta	06	30
Xaul in India[46]	22	00	Rio do Laguo	05	15
Melinde in Ethiopia	03	00	Rio Fermoso	..	..
Ilhas do Fayal e do			Rio dos Escravos	..	..
Pico	38	30	Cidade do Benin	..	..
Hazamor	33	40	Cabo Fermoso	..	..
Cabo de Guer	31	25	Ilha de Ferna do Poo	..	..
Cabo de Nam	30	20	Serra Guerreira	03	00
Ilha de Forte Ven-			Ilha de Santo Antonio,		
tura in the Canaries	28	00	also called Ilha do		
Cabo de Bojador	27	10	Principe	03	00
Angra dos Ruivos	25	00	Ilha de Sam Thomé	01	00
Angra dos Cavallos	24	00	Ilha de Cori Mori near		
Rio do Ouro	23	35	Persia[48]	21	00
Cabo das Barbas	21	30	Ilha da Boa Vista	15	50
Cabo Branco	20	20	Ilha do Sal near Ilha		
Rio de Çanaguá	15	20	da Boa Vista	16	30
Cabo Verde and Anfra			Ilhas de S. Nicolao,		
de Bezeguiche	14	20	Santa Luzia, Sam		
Cabo dos Mastos	14	20	Vincente. All these		
Ilha de Sam Thiago de			four islands close		
Cabo Verde	15	20	together, near the		
Rio de Guambea[47]	13	00	Ilha da Boa Vista	16	40
Rio Grande	11	00			

[43] Chios.
[44] Anjidiv Is., about 50 miles S.S.E. of Goa.
[45] Quilon in Travancore.
[46] Chaul, south of Bombay.
[47] Gambia River.
[48] Kuria Muria Isles off the south coast of Arabia.

These are the latitudes of the following places located south of the Equator:

	degrees	minutes		degrees	minutes
Rio do Guabam on the equator	00	00	Cabo das Agulhas	35	00
			Auguada de Sam Bras	34	30
Cabo de Lopo Gonçalvez	00	10	Rio do Infante	33	15
Rio do Padram[49]	07	00	Ilheo da Cruz	..	..
Cabo . . . y fuso[49]	10	45	Ilheos de Sam		
Angra das Aldeas	16	20	Christova	32	40
Mangua das Areas	17	00	Ponta de Santa Luzia	30	00
Cabo Negro	18	00	Ponta de Santa Martha	26	00
Angra da Balea	21	00			
Cabo do Padram	23	00	Cabo das Correntes	24	00
Angra da Comceipçam	25	30	Cabo de Sam		
Angra de Sam Thomé	27	40	Sebastiam	20	30
Angra das Voltas	29	00	Çofalla in Ethiopia	20	00
Morros da Pedra	31	00	Ilhas Primeiras	16	00
Angra de Santa Elena	32	30	Monsombique	15	00
Cabo de Boa			Cabo Delgado	10	00
Esperança	34	30	Quiloa	09	00
			Mombaça	04	30

These are the latitudes of the following places located south of the Equator in the land of Brazil:

	degrees	minutes		degrees	minutes
Angra de Sam Roque	03	30	Porto Seguro	18	00
Santa Maria d'Arabida	05	00	Rio de Santa Luzia	19	20
Cabo de Santo			Ilha de Santa Barbara	20	20
Agostinho	08	15	Rio dos Harefeẽs	24	40
Rio de Sam			Cabo Frio	25	00
Francisco	10	00	Ilha de Santa Crara	24	40
Auguada de Sam			Ilha de . . . Fernahu[50]	27	00
Miguel	10	00	Ilha de Santo Amaro	28	30
Porto Real	14	00	Ilha d'Acemsam[51]	21	00
Angra de Todolos			Angra Fermosa	15	00
Santos	15	40	Ilha de Sam Lourenco	04	00

[49] Ponta das Camboas? (*vide* book III, chap. 2). Text corrupt.
[50] Text corrupt.
[51] Ascension Isle.

Chapter VIII: Concerning the Equator and the understanding of the earth's degrees of longitude and latitude

We hold it to be a true and certain fact of astronomy that the Equator divides into two equal parts the circumference of the world, running from east to west and back to the east; being set at the center of the globe it is distant ninety degrees from the Arctic Pole, which the mariners call the North, and likewise ninety degrees from the Antarctic Pole, which they call the South. A man standing with the Equator as his zenith will see the two poles level on the horizon.[52] Since these terms "zenith" and "horizon" are only understood by the learned, we have thought it well to explain them here in order to instruct those who have no knowledge of this matter; they must know then that the zenith is nothing but an imaginary point in the sky immediately above our head, and if a thousand men are standing together, or separate, or more or less than a thousand, each will have his own zenith. The horizon is where it seems to us that the sky joins the sea or the earth and is called the "determinator"[53] of our vision since we cannot see beyond. Thus he who reaches a point where he has the Equator for zenith will see the two poles equally touching the horizon, as I have said, and if he travels until he has the Arctic or Antarctic Pole as zenith he will see the Equator as the horizon. Further, you must know that the degrees of latitude of the surface and circumference of the world are counted from

[52] Pacheco presumably had in mind the polar circles of the celestial sphere and not the terrestrial sphere. Our polar (or arctic and antarctic) circle is fixed: his varied according to the viewpoint of the observer. His was the arctic circle of the Greeks, which was drawn on the celestial sphere parallel to the equator and tangential to the observer's horizon, and it therefore separated the circumpolar stars that are always above the horizon from the stars that rise and set with respect to his (the observer's) horizon. Since the altitude of the celetial pole is always the same as the latitude of the oberver, the arctic circles would become zero for him at the Equator: and, again, he would have no arctic circles if stationed south of the Equator, nor would he have any antarctic circles if stationed north of the Equator. Conversely, if the observer were at either of the poles the circle of the Equator would become zero for him, that is, the Equator would be his horizon—as Pacheco says lower down. (*Vide* Strabo: *Geography*, Book II, Chap. 2, para. 2, note, Loeb edition.)

[53] The word used by Pacheco—*determinador*—is the etymological definition of the Greek word *horizonte*, which the Romans translated by *circulus finitor* and *circulus finiens*.

the Equator towards the poles, and the number of degrees that either pole is raised above the horizon (which is also called the circle of the hemisphere) gives the number of degrees that a place, or man standing at that place, is distant from the Equator. The degrees of longitude are counted from orient to occident,[54] which the mariners call east and west, and this is difficult to ascertain because they have no firm and fixed point [of reference] as are the poles[55] for the latitudes, and of this I will say no more.

Chapter IX: Concerning the course of the sun towards the tropics.

Twice in the year the sun crosses the Equator, giving two equinoxes, one on the eleventh of March,[56] when the sun is at the first point of Aries; the other on the fourteenth of September, when the sun is at the first point of Libra; at which times the day is equal to the night throughout the world. Moving from Aries the sun in its course gives us a high solstice, and proceeding till the twelfth day of June[58] enters the tropic and sign of Cancer, beyond which it never passes. This is called the summer solstice, and the sun's greatest declination from the Equator towards this region is 23° 33′ [north].[57] The sun then turns again and retires from Cancer and enters the sign of Libra on the fourteenth day of September[56] as I have said; proceeding, it gives us a low solstice until it reaches the tropic and sign of Capricorn

[54] As a general rule, longitude used to be reckoned from the prime meridian which Ptolemy had used, namely that of the Fortunate Isles (i.e. Canaries) which were situated in the Western Ocean at what was regarded as the westernmost limit of the habitable earth. Accordingly the longitudes of places in the Old World came to be counted from west to east. Pacheco must have known that this was the practice of his own day, and therefore we can only suppose that he is guilty of a verbal slip in writing "from orient to occident" (but cf. R. Bacon: *Opus Majus—Mathematica*, Chap. 16, p. 208, Burke's edition).

[55] Text slightly corrupt.

[56] These dates are anterior to the reform of the calendar which took place in 1582 under Pope Gregory, when 11 days (5 to 14 October inclusive) were passed over.

[57] Up to the time of Pedro Nunes (*Tratado da carta de marear*) the most commonly given value of the sun's maximum declination was 23° 33′—the figure adopted by Zarkali. The corresponding value given by Regiomontanus (*Ephemerides*) was 23° 30′. Nunes discussed the 3 minutes, and finding them unimportant dropped them. Pacheco compromised, adopting Zarkali's figure for the northern, and Regiomontanus's for the southern, declination.

on the twelfth day of December.[56] This is called the winter
solstice; its greatest declination is 23° 30′ [south] and this is its
farthest limit. Thus it goes working and illuminating with its
rays throughout the year, passing through the twelve signs of
the Zodiac, entering and dwelling in one each month and leaving it to enter another. Because the altitudes of the poles calculated by the degrees of the sun's declination are required for
fixing the latitude and distance of certain places north and south
of the Equator we will write here the manner of doing this,
since without this explanation nothing certain can be done. However he who wishes to understand this must first know how many
degrees and minutes the sun declines daily and travels from the
Equator towards either of the tropics; and when this is known
and also the time when the sun's declination must be added to
the degrees of its altitude, or when the same declination of altitude is to be taken away or when there is no declination, then
the degrees and latitude from the Equator towards either of the
tropics and poles will be known.

*Chapter X: How the degrees of the sun's altitude are to be added
to its declination or the declination to be deducted from the altitude*

The altitude of the sun should be taken exactly at noon with
the astrolabe or quadrant. He who takes it on the eleventh of
March, and on the fourteenth of September, and finds it to be
90°, which is its maximum altitude, may know for certain that
he is on the Equator and has it for his zenith; for at any other
time except these two equinoctial days of March 11th and
September 14th, the sun does not reach an altitude of 90° at the
Equator. He who takes the altitude on these two days and finds
it to be fifty or sixty or eighty degrees, or more or less, but
still under ninety, will not have the Equator for zenith; to ascertain his latitude he must deduct the number of degrees of altitude
from 90° and this will give him the number of degrees from the
Equator towards either of the tropics.

Item. He who takes the altitude of the sun of the twelfth
of June and finds it to be ninety degrees may know for certain
that he is under the tropic of Cancer and so at a latitude of
23° 33′ from the Equator. If he finds an altitude of 90° on the

twelfth of December he will be under the tropic of Capricorn. On these days one or other of the tropics will be his zenith and he will be in the aforesaid latitude, namely, 23° 33′ from the Equator.

Item. The astronomers have decided that the distance from the Equator towards each of the tropics should be called the torrid zone and the "table"[58] of the sun. The sun pursues its course in this table throughout the year; while it rises to an altitude of 90° at the Equator and the tropics, as I have said in the preceding chapter, it also ascends during the course of the twelve months in travelling between these points that number of degrees in the said torrid zone. A man may be at such a place on any of the days of the year, and when the sun rises to an altitude of 90° it will be the zenith of his table; when he finds the altitude to be 90°, let him look at the table of the sun's declinations for the declination of that day. Let him then deduct his number from the 90° and the remainder will give the degrees of latitude that he is distant from the Equator in the direction of either tropic.

Item. If a man is at a place where the sun is between him and the Equator, whether the Equator be towards the Arctic or towards the Antarctic pole, let him first find the number of degrees of the sun's declination on that day and subtract them from the degrees of the sun's altitude; if he subtracts the remainder from 90° he will have the number of degrees of latitude he is from the Equator in the direction of either tropic.

Item. If a man is situated between the sun and the Equator, towards either pole, he must first take the sun's declination for the day from the table of declinations and add its degrees to those of the sun's altitude, then subtract from 90° and the resulting number will give his distance in degrees of latitude from the Equator towards either tropic; but if the sum of the degrees of altitude and the degrees of declination exceed 90°[59],

[58] Cf. Martín Cortés: *The Art of Navigation*, Chap. 2 (translated by R. Eden).

[59] A moment's reflection will show that when the observer is between the sun and the Equator the sum of the sun's noon altitude and declination must always be more than 90°, so that Pacheco's equation for this case should read: latitude (north or south) equals declination plus altitude minus 90°.

then the 90° must be subtracted and the resulting sum will give the degrees of latitude.

Item.   If you are in a place where the Equator is between you and the sun, whether towards one pole or the other, first find in the tables of declination the degrees of the sun's declination for that day, then take the sun's altitude, adding its degrees to those of the declination and then subtract 90°. The result will give the degrees of latitude that you are distant from the Equator towards either tropic.

He who would understand this work of ours must know the months in which the sun moves from the Equator to the tropic of Cancer and similarly to the tropic of Capricorn, as I have said in chapter 9; for if he knows the time of the sun's course towards either region and its declinations and the differences of the shadows it makes according to the month in which it is this side or that side of the Equator, he will be able to understand this work.

Chapter XI: How to compute the ebb and flow of the sea in the greater part of Spain and likewise in other regions where there are tides

With very good reason we have based one part of our work on the art of navigation, as we have pointed out at the end of the Prologue to this book; and since we must make use of it in all our voyages by sea, we must briefly explain the calculation of the moon's course, by which we can know the ebb and flow of the sea; for those who know this calculation for the tides will be able easily to learn them and will know why the mariners say that in the greater part of this country of Spain they flow northeast and southwest. When these are known they will be able to judge by them if the tides elsewhere flow northeast and southwest, as in Spain, or wherein they differ. Thus we shall be able to know, wherever we are, either inland far from the sea or coming from the deep sea in search of land to enter some river, how the tide stands, judging by the phases of the moon and considering how many days have elapsed from the time of the conjunction and new moon to the day and hour for which we require to know the tide; with this knowledge our ships will be able to enter safely rivers and other places for which it is necessary[60] to know the state of the tide, without actually seeing its ebb and flow.

Item. We must first note that the astronomers have affirmed that from the time the moon is new and in conjunction with the sun, which the common people call *"antrelunho,"* to the time when the conjunction and new moon recur, there is an interval of 29 days, 12 hours and 33 minutes;[61] and in every 24 hours (which is a natural day) after the conjunction, the moon draws away from the sun four-fifths of an hour and continues in this course during 14½ natural days, 16 minutes and one second,[62] at the end of which time it is opposite the sun and full. It then begins to hide itself gradually and to conceal from our sight the light it receives from the sun, approaching the sun each natural day after the time of its opposition and full moon four-fifths of an hour again, until there is a fresh conjunction and a new moon; and this is the monthly movement of the moon as displayed before our eyes.

Item. There is a difference between the astronomers and the mariners concerning the course of the moon, for the astronomers say that during each natural day of twenty-four hours from the time of the conjunction and new moon to the time when it is full and in opposition to the sun, the moon draws away from the sun four-fifths of an hour and then similarly approaches the sun four-fifths of an hour daily until it is again in conjunction, as we have already explained in the preceding paragraph in this chapter; but the mariners affirm that the moon recedes from and approaches the sun only three-quarters of an hour in each natural day, which is equivalent to a quarter point on the compass. Accordingly there is a difference between them of a twentieth of an hour; and although the astronomers may be right in this matter and the mariners wrong, the difference of

[60] The text is corrupt at this point.

[61] M. Cortés gives 29 days 12 hours 44 minutes, which is the more usual figure, and correct to 3 seconds.

[62] It is difficult to see how Pacheco arrived at this figure, for the "opposition" was usually regarded as occurring exactly halfway through the lunar cycle. The general reckoning was 14 days 18 hours 22 minutes after conjunction.

three minutes is so slight that it makes no difference, introducing neither difficulty nor palpable error into the calculation of the tides of which we hope to treat. We will therefore follow the opinion of the mariners, since the tides are more easily calculated by the compass than in any other way, according to the ancient practice of mariners.

Chapter XII: How it is necessary, in order to learn the tide, to know how to read the compass

He who wishes to learn to calculate the tides must first know all the points of the compass with its quarter points and half points, since this is the essential foundation of this matter and without it there can be no certainty. The mariners and pilots who practised this [art] of old first learned the points of the compass, quarter points and half points, and deduced therefrom the rhythm of the ebb and flow of the sea in the province of Spain and in other regions according to the difference of the tides, beginning from the Rio de Barbate in Andaluzia to Galiza[63] and the greater part of Bizcaya, calculating six hours ebb and six hours flow as follows: northwest and southeast, low tide; north and south, half way to high tide; northeast and southwest, high tide; east and west, half way to ebb. Now it must be understood that when the moon is in the northwest and southeast the tide will be low on the coast of Spain, and when it is in the northeast and southwest the tide will be high along the whole of the coast of Spain and along the coast of Berbery from the straits of Cepta; this is always so, whether the moon be new or half or full.

Item. The mariners say, what is indeed true, that from point to point of the compass there is an interval of three hours, the eight points making in all twenty-four hours or a natural day, and that each quarter point represents three quarters of an hour and each half point one hour and a half, and thus it [the day? sun?] advances regularly through all its points, half points and quarter points. When the moon is new and in conjunction with the sun, being in the southeast, the hour will be nine o'clock

[63] I.e. the province of Galicia in northwest Spain.

and the tide will be low on the coast of Spain outside the straits; for this reason the mariners say "northwest and southeast, low tide," since when the moon is in the northwest, whether it be new or in any other phase, there will be the same low tide. On the same day when the sun passes, with the moon in conjunction, to southeast by south the tide will be one-eighth full; when it passes farther to the southsoutheast it will be a quarter full; when it reaches south by east the tide will be three-eights full. When the sun, with the moon in conjunction, is in the south it will be midday and the tide will be half full, and therefore the mariners say "north and south, half-flow," for when the moon is in the north it makes the same tide; when the sun and moon together are south by west the tide will be five-eighths full, and when they are southsouthwest the tide will be seven-eighths full, and when the sun and the moon together reach the southwest the tide will be high on the coast of Spain; it will then be three hours after noon. Therefore the mariners say "northeast and southwest, full tide," for the moon causes this same tide when it is in the northeast no matter what its phase, either in conjunction with the sun or away from it.

Item.   When the sun and moon are in conjunction on the day of the new moon, when they pass from the southwest to southwest by west the tide will have ebbed one-eighth, and when they are at westsouthwest, a quarter; and when they are west by south, three-eighths; when they both reach the west it will be half ebb (each quarter point representing one-eighth of the tide). Therefore the mariners say "eastwest, half ebb," for when the moon is in the east it causes the same tide.

Item.   When the sun and the moon in conjunction go from the west to west by north the tide will have ebbed five-eighths; when they pass to westnorthwest it will have ebbed three-quarters, at northwest by west it will have ebbed seven-eighths, and when they reach the northwest it will be low tide. Therefore the mariners say "northwest and southeast, low tide."

Item.   When the sun and moon in conjunction are at northwest by north the tide will be one-eighth full, and at northnorthwest a quarter; and at north by west three-eighths, on the coast of Spain[64] as we have already said; therefore the mariners say "northeast and southwest, full tide."

Item.   When the sun and moon, as we have mentioned above, are in northeast by east, the tide will have ebbed one-eighth, when they are in the eastnortheast, one-quarter; when in east by north, three-eighths, and when in the east, half ebb; therefore the mariners say "east and west, half ebb."

Item.   Because the moon in every twenty-four hours (or one natural day) after its conjunction recedes from the sun one quarter point of the compass it was fitting that we should explain in the first section of this twelfth chapter why we began to calculate the tides at nine o'clock in the morning when the sun and moon were in conjunction in the southeast; and now having gone through all the points of the compass and explained about the tides[65], and twenty-four hours having passed since we began this work, and the moon being three-quarters of an hour behind the sun, it no longer makes the tide as on the previous day but three-quarters of an hour later, which is one quarter point of the compass. Because of this it is well that what we have explained should be known and we will end in the southeast where we began.

Item.   When the sun and moon pass from the east to east by south the tide will have ebbed five-eighths, and when they are in the southeast seven-eighths[66]; and when the sun is southeast by south and the moon southeast it will be low tide on the coast of Spain outside the Straits. For this reason the mariners say "northwest and southeast, low tide." We have already said that twenty-four hours after the conjunction of the sun with the moon the tide is three-quarters of an hour later, and forty-eight hours after the conjunction it is an hour and a half later, each

[64] There is a lacuna in the text at this point. Judging by the context the original presumably contained the indications of the state of the tide when the sun is in north, north by east, northnorthest, northeast by north and northeast.

[65] Text corrupt.

[66] Pursuing Pacheco's reasoning, if the tide has ebbed five-eighths when the sun is east by south, it will have ebbed three-quarters when it is eastsoutheast and seven-eighths when it is southeast by east. Low tide, then, will occur when the sun is again in the southeast. But, by hypothesis, low tide should occur a quarter point later, i.e. when the sun is southeast by south.

twenty-four hours representing one quarter point of the compass; he who wishes to calculate the tide must therefore see in what point of the compass the sun is and then count the number of days which have passed since the conjunction, counting a quarter point of the compass for each twenty-four hours up to fifteen days or less, and according to the position of the moon will be the tide; that is to say, if it is in the southeast it will be low tide and if in the southeast by south the tide will be one-eighth full, and so on, as we have already explained. When this mode of calculating the tides of Spain is known it will be possible to infer whether the tides in other regions are the same or different.

29. The complete navigator

The principles of navigation changed little in the course of the sixteenth century, but increasing experience of oceanic voyages brought increasing sophistication and confidence in its practice. Navigation proper —navigation out of sight of land—became more and more clearly distinguished from pilotage, which is navigation within soundings. Similarly, manuals of navigation became more clearly distinguished from sailing directions, though the two types of information were still often bound in the same volume. Pilotage was the stock in trade of any competent master mariner; oceanic navigation was the preserve of a relatively small aristocracy of experts, who nevertheless were expected to be skilled in pilotage also.

Many manuals of navigation were compiled in the sixteenth century, in Portugal, Spain, the Netherlands, France, and England. Bourne's *Regiment for the Sea* was one of the best, and the first to be written and published in English. Bourne was a practical man and wrote with the needs of practical men in mind. The clarity and simplicity of his instructions are in welcome contrast to the longwinded complexity of some of his predecessors. His book enjoyed a considerable vogue in England and the Netherlands, and was superseded only by the excellent and highly original work of John Davis at the end of the century. In the brief section quoted here, Bourne defines the art of navigation as understood in the third quarter of the sixteenth century including pilotage, and describes the attributes of the successful navigator.

The extract which follows is from *A Regiment for the Sea* (1574), by William Bourne, edited by E. G. R. Taylor (Cambridge, Hakluyt Society, 1963), pp. 168–71.

What Nauigation is

NAUIGATION is this, how to direct his course in the Sea to any place assigned, and to consider in that direction what things may stande with him, & what things may stand against him, hauing consideration how to preserue the ship in all stormes and chaunges of weather that may happen by the way, to bring the ship safe vnto the port assigned, and in the shortest time.

The vse of Nauigation

The vse thereof is this, fyrste to knowe how that the place dothe beare from him, by what winde or poynte of the compasse, and also how farre that the place is from hym, and also to consider the streame, or tide gates, Currents, which way that they do set or driue the ship, and also to consider what daungers is by the waye, as rockes and sandes, and suche other lyke impedimentes, and also if that the wynde chaunge or shifte by the waye, to consider which way to stand, and direct his course vnto the most aduantage to attayne vnto the port in shortest time: and also if anye stormes doe happen by the way, to consider how for to preserue the shippe and the goodes, and too bring hir safe vnto the porte assigned. And also it is moste principally to be considered and foreseene, that if they haue hadde by occasion of a contrarye tempest, for too goe very muche out of the course or way, too knowe then howe that the place dothe then beare, that is to say, by what poynte of the compasse the place dothe stande from you: and also how farre it may be from you. Whyche way to bee knowne is this: firste to consider by what poynte that the shippe hath made hir way by, and how fast and swiftly that the shippe hathe gone, and to consider how often that the shippe hath altered hir course, and how muche that she hathe gone at euery tyme, and then to

consider all thys in youre platte or carde, and so you may gyue
an neere gesse, by what poynte or wynde it beareth from you,
and also howe farre it is thither. And also you may haue a
greate helpe by the Sunne or Starres, to take the heigthe of
the Pole aboue the horizon, and also in some place you may
gesse by the sounding, bothe by the depth, and also by the
grounde. And also it is very meete and necessarye to knowe
any place, when that hee dothe see it.

Of instrumentes to vse at the Sea
for to take the heigthe of the Sunne
or any Starres

All instrumentes too take the heighte of the Sunne or anye
Starre, the originall of the making thereof, it is eyther a circle or
the parte of a circle, whose division is the .360. parte of a circle
what forme soeuer that it hathe, as your crosse staffe, it is
marked according vntoo the proportion of a circle, and euery
one of the degrees, is the equall parte of a circle, the three
hundred and sixtie part. &c.

The vse of the Instruments

The vse of the Instrumentes, as Astrolobes or common Rings, or
the crosse staffe, is to take the heigth of the sune or other
stars, whose vses doe folow heere after in the boke.

What manner of persons be meetest to take
charge of Shippes in Nauigation

As touching those persons that are meete to take charge, that is
to say, to be as master of ships in Nauigation, he ought to be
sober and wise, and not to be light or rash headed, not to be to
fumish or hasty, but such a one as can wel gouern himselfe, for
else it is not possible for him to gouerne his cōpany well: he
ought not to be to simple, but he must be suche a one as must
keepe his companie in awe of him (by discretion) doing his
companie no iuiurie or wrong, but to let thē haue that which
men ought to haue, and then to see vnto them that they doe
their laboure as men ought to doe in all points. And the principall point in gouernment is, to cause himself both to be feared
& loued, & that groweth principally by this meanes, to cherishe

men in well doing, and those men that be honestly addicted, to let them haue reasonable preheminence, so that it be not hurtfull vnto the Marchaunt nor to himselfe, and to punishe those that be malefactors and disturbers of their company, and for smal faults, to giue them gentle admonition to amende them: and principally these two pointes arte to be foreseene by the maisters. (that is) to serue God himselfe, and to see that all the whole companie do so in like maner, at suche conuenient time as it is meete to be done: the second point is, that the master vse no play at the dise or cards, neither (as near as he cā) to suffer any, for yᵉ sufferance thereof may do very much hurt in diuers respects: And furthermore, the maister ought to be suche a one, as dothe knowe the Moones course, whereby he doth knowe at what time it is a full Sea, or a lowe water, knowing in what quarter or part of the skye, that the Moone doth make a full Sea at that place, and also the master ought to bee acquainted, or knowe that place well, that he doth take charge to goe vnto (except that he haue a Pilot) and also he that taketh charge vpon him, ought to be expert, how the tydegates or currentes doe set from place vnto place: and not to bee ignorant of such daungers as lyeth by the way, as rocks, sandes, or bankes, and also most principally he ought to bee such a one, as can very well directe his courses vnto any place assigned, and to haue capacitie howe for to handle or shift himselfe in foule weather or stormes. And also it behoueth him too be a good coaster. that is to say, to knowe euery place by the sight thereof. And also he that taketh charge for long voyages, ought to haue knowledge in plats or cardes, and also in such instrumentes as be meet to take the heigth of the Sunne or any Starre, and to haue capacitie to correcte those instrumentes, and also he ought to be such a one, that can calculate the Sunnes declination, or else to haue some true regiment, and also he ought to knowe howe to handle the Sunnes declination, when that he hath taken the heigth of the Sunne.

30. The minor horrors of the sea

We know relatively little about the details of life at sea in the fifteenth and sixteenth centuries. Sailors were practical men, little given to writing. Explorers kept journals, but rarely troubled to include information about a daily round which to them was familiar, and which they took for granted. The best accounts of ships' routine and conditions on board ship were written by landlubbers who, for one reason or another, made sea voyages as passengers. The letter which follows is the best of the surviving documents of this type. By 1573, when it was written, the trans-Atlantic crossing, pioneered by Columbus eighty-one years earlier, had become familiar to many sailors; not a commonplace, for it was always hazardous, but reasonably predictable and regular. Considerable numbers of Spanish ships—over a hundred in some years—crossed annually to the West Indies and the mainland coasts of America: out with the trade winds, with a stop at the Canaries; home with the westerlies, with a stop at the Azores. The average size of the ships had increased steadily since Columbus' day, charts and navigational techniques had considerably improved; but it is likely that the details of shipboard life were much the same.

Eugenio de Salazar was a judge who had a long and distinguished career in the Indies service. He served successively as governor of Tenerife in the Canaries; judge in the *audiencia* (appeal court) of Santo Domingo in the island of Hispaniola; *fiscal* in the *audiencia* of Guatemala; judge in the *audiencia* of Mexico; and councillor of the Indies. He left behind a considerable volume of allegorical poetry and a number of interesting and amusing private letters, of which this, written to a friend in Spain, is one. It describes the voyage from Tenerife to Santo Domingo, which Salazar made in order to take up his appointment there.

Most Spanish ships at that time had religious names, and *Nuestra Señora de los Remedios* was among the favorites. Four or five ships of that name were in the Indies trade in Salazar's time; but only one is recorded as plying between Tenerife and Santo Domingo, and we may with reasonable confidence identify her as Salazar's ship. She was a small ship by the standards of the Indies trade: 120 tons, with a crew of thirty, according to the Seville registers.[1] She first appears in the registers in 1552, outward bound from San Lúcar to Puerto Rico. In 1563 she came into the possession of Juan Núñez, and for eight years was based at Tenerife, making regular passages to Santo Domingo, out one year, back the next, under Baltazar Núñez (perhaps a son or brother) as master. In the early 1570's she seems to have changed hands, and for the rest of her life had a different master each trip. Her last recorded voyage was in 1577. Salazar, then, traveled in a small and aging vessel, out of a minor port, away from the formal discipline of the main annual convoys, and with a new master unfamiliar with his ship. It is not surprising that he found it uncomfortable.

The extract which follows is from *Cartas de Eugenio de Salazar* (Madrid, 1866), pp. 36–57: "Carta escrita al licenciado Miranda de Ron." [Editor's translation.]

To the Licentiate Miranda de Ron:

Qui navigant mare, enarrant pericula ejus. Those who go to sea may speak of the perils of the deep; and since I have just had to make a sea voyage, for my sins, I write to tell you about my maritime sufferings; though I must admit that they included (thank God) no pirates or shipwrecks.

I was in the island of Tenerife when my new appointment[1] came through, and I had to make my own arrangements for getting to Hispaniola. I inquired about sailings, and eventually booked passage, at great expense, in a ship called the *Nuestra Señora de los Remedios*—better by name than by nature, as it turned out. Her master assured me that she was a roomy ship, a good sailer, seaworthy, sound in frames and members, well rigged and well manned. Accordingly, on the day we were to sail and at the hour of embarkation, Doña Catalina[2] and I, with all our household, presented ourselves on the bank of the Styx. Charon, with his skiff, met us there, ferried us out to the ship, and left us on board. We were given, as a great privilege, a tiny cabin, about two feet by three by three; and packed in there, the movement of the sea upset our heads and stomachs so horribly that we all turned white as ghosts and began to bring up

---

[1] H. and P. Chaunu: *Séville et l'Atlantique* (11 vols., Paris, 1955), vols. II and III *passim*.

[1] As judge in the *audiencia*, or appeal court, of Santo Domingo.

[2] His wife.

our very souls. In plain words, we were seasick; we vomited, we gagged, we shot out of our mouths everything which had gone in during the last two days; we endured by turns cold depressing phlegm, bitter burning choler, thick and heavy melancholy. There we lay, without seeing the sun or the moon; we never opened our eyes, or changed our clothes, or moved, until the third day. Then, lying in the darkness, I was startled by a voice nearby which cried out, "Blessed be the light of day, and the Holy True Cross, and the Lord of Truth, and the Holy Trinity; blessed be the day and the Lord who makes it; blessed be the day and the Lord who sends it"; and then the voice recited the prayers, Our Father and Hail Mary; and then said, "Amen. God give us good weather and a prosperous voyage; may the ship make a good passage, Sir Captain, and master, and all our good company, amen; so let us make, let us make a good voyage; God give your worships good day, gentlemen aft and forward." I was somewhat reassured when I heard this, and said to my wife, "Madam, though I fear we may be in the Devil's house, I still hear talk of God. I will get up and go out, and see what is happening—whether we are moving, or being carried away." So I dressed as well as I could, and crawled out of the whale's belly or closet in which we lay. I discovered that we were riding on what some people call a wooden horse, or a timber nag, or a flying pig; though to me it looked more like a town, a city even. It was certainly not the city of God that the sainted Augustine talked about; I saw no churches, nor courts of justice: nobody says mass there, nor do the inhabitants live by the laws of reason. It is a long narrow city, sharp and pointed at one end, wider at the other, like the pier of a bridge; it has its streets, open spaces and dwellings; it is encircled by its walls—that is to say, its planking; at one end it has its forecastle, with more than ten thousand knights in barracks, and at the other its citadel, so strong and firmly built that a puff of wind could tear it from its foundations and tip it into the sea. It has its batteries, and a gunner to command them; it has chain-wales, foresail, fore topsail, main course, topsail and topgallant, bonnet and second bonnet. It has a capstan, the bane of the sailors because of the labor of turning it, and of the passengers because of the noise it makes; one or two fountains, called pumps, the water from which is unfit for tongue and palate to taste, or nostrils to smell, or even eyes to see, for it comes out bubbling like Hell and stinking like the Devil. The dwellings are so closed-in, dark, and evil-smelling that they seem more like burial vaults or charnelhouses. The entrances to these dwellings are openings in the deck, which they call companionways or hatches, and anyone who goes through them can say goodbye to the order, the comfort and the pleasant smells of dwellings on the earth; since, indeed, these lodgings seem to be the caves of Hell (even if they are not so in fact) it is only natural that those who enter them should do so through holes in the ground, as if they were being buried. There is such a complicated network of ropes and rigging on every side, that the men inside it are like hens or capons being carried to market in grass or netting coops.

There are trees in the city, not fragrant with gums and aromatic spices, but greased with fish-oil and stinking tallow. There are running rivers, not of sweet, clear, flowing water, but of turbid filth; full not of grains of gold like the Cibao or the Tagus, but of grains of very singular pearl—enormous lice, so big that sometimes they are seasick and vomit bits of apprentice.

The ground of this city is such, that when it rains the soil is hard, but when the sun is hot the mud becomes soft and your feet stick to the ground so that you can hardly lift them. For game in the neighborhood, there are fine flights of cockroaches —they call them *curianas* here—and very good rat-hunting, the rats so fierce that when they are cornered they turn on the hunters like wild boars. The lamp and the *aguja*[3] of the city are kept at night in the binnacle, which is a chest very like the commodes which some gentlemen keep in their bedrooms. The city is dark and gloomy, black without and pitch-black within; black ground and walls, dark inhabitants, swarthy officers. In sum, from bowspirit to bonaventure, from stem to stern, from hawse-holes to tiller-port, from the port chains to the starboard topgallant

---

[3] This seems to be a somewhat labored pun. *Aguja* means a needle. In a city, it can mean a spire or steeple. In a ship the *aguja de marear* is, of course, the compass.

yardarms, from one side to the other, there is nothing for which a good word can be said; except indeed that, like women, it is a necessary evil.

There is in the city a whole community of people, all with their duties and dignities in strict (if not angelic) hierarchy. The wind is the real owner and master; the navigator governs as his deputy. The captain is responsible for defense; and though this captain is no Roldán, the ship is full of *roldanas* and has dashing *bigotes—bigotas*, even.[4] The master has charge of the general work of the ship; the bo'su'n, of stowing and breaking out the cargo. The able seamen work the ship; the ordinary seamen help the able seamen; and the boys wait on the able seamen and the ordinary seamen, sweep and scrub, chant the prayers, and keep watch. The bo'su'n's mate[5] is no Franciscan; he has charge of the ship's boat, sees to the water supply, and looks out for ways of cheating the passengers. The steward is responsible for the food. The caulker is the engineer who fortifies the city and secures the posterns through which the enemy might enter. The city has a surgeon-barber, to scrape the sailors' heads and bleed them when they need it. In general, the citizens of this city have as much faith, charity and friendship as sharks encountering in the sea.

I watched the navigator, the wind's lieutenant, seated in all his dignity upon his wooden throne; there he sits, an imitation Neptune, claiming to rule the sea and its waves. From time to time the sea unseats him with an unexpected lurch, so that he has to hold on to the pommel of his saddle to avoid a ducking in salt water. From there he rules and governs; "since Lanzarote out of Brittany came," no knight has been more faithfully served. Certainly I have never seen a gang of rogues obey more promptly, or earn their wages better, than these sailors; for when he shouts, "up forrard there," they come tumbling aft in a moment, like conjured demons, all their eyes on him and mouths open, awaiting his command. He gives the helmsman his orders

[4] Another series of untranslatable puns. *Roldana* = the sheave of a block; *bigote* = mustache, also in nautical slang the bow-wave of a ship; *tener bigotes* = to be bold or obstinate; *bigota* or *vigota* = a deadeye.

[5] *Guardián;* which, in the Franciscan Order, is the title of the head of a province.

—"Port your helm—steady as you go—bear up, don't let her yaw—steer sou'-sou'-west—watch out for that whipstaff or you'll break the hinge—keep her full and by." In the same way he orders the other seamen, "Hoist the t'gallant—lower the fore-topsail—hoist the foresail—haul the tack aboard—harden in the spritsail a little— set the main course—bend on the bonnet—pass the points through the eyelets, quick—take in the mizen—furl it on the yard in the gaskets—man the jeers—grease the halliard block—belay the halliard round the cleat—haul in the topsail sheets—two hands out on the yard arms—check away the halliards—ease to the lifts—grease the parral-trucks and ribs—rig the parrals, pass them round the mast— cast off the gaskets—hold onto that tack—gather aft the main sheet —turn up round the bitts—haul out the tack to windward—haul taut the bowline—haul up that buntline—clew up—haul away on that brace—turn up—make fast those backstays—well the clewlines— set up the stays—slip that toggle through and free the line— man the pump—make sure the collar is secure—work the brake till she sucks—clear the well—clear out the scuppers." When the master gives his orders it is astonishing to see the diligence and speed of the sailors in carrying them out. In a moment some will be up on the main crosstrees; some running up the ratlines holding on to the shrouds; some riding on the yards; some on the lower mastheads clinging to the caps, or swarming up the topmasts and hanging from the trucks; some on deck, hauling and gathering aft the sheets; some climbing and swinging about in the rigging like monkeys in the trees, or like the souls of those who fell from Heaven and stayed suspended in the air.

And when they hoist the sails—to hear the sailors singing as they work! for they hoist to the time of the chanty, like an ox-team straining in time to the leader's bell. The leading hand begins the song—most of these leading hands are Levantines—and calls out:

> *bu iza—o dio*
> *ayuta noi—o que somo*
> *servi soy—o voleamo*
> *ben servir—o la fede*
> *mantenir—o la fede*
> *de cristiano—o malmeta*

lo pagano—sconfondí
y sarrahin—torchi y mori gran mastin
o fillioli—dabrahin
o non credono—que ben sia
o non credono—la fe santa
en la santa fe—di Roma
o di Roma—está el perdon
o San Pedro—gran varon
o San Pablo—son compañon
o que rueque—a Dio por nos
o por nosotros—navegantes
en este mundo—somos tantes
o ponente—digo levante
o Levante—se leva el sol
o ponente—resplandor
fantineta—viva lli amor
o jóvel home—gauditor

As the leader chants each couplet, all the others reply in chorus "oh—oh" and haul away at the jeers to hoist the sail.

I was fascinated to watch the city and the activities of its people, and intrigued to hear the marine (or malign) language, which I could follow no better than heathen gibberish; and I doubt whether Your Honor, for all his cleverness, has understood all the words and phrases I have written. If any have escaped you, look them up in Antonio's word-book; and if you don't find them, ask the sailors in the town of Illescas to translate, for this jargon is much used there; but don't ask me. I have only learnt the sounds of the words and cries of this complicated language, without understanding the meanings, and I chatter them like a cageful of parrots. It is enough for me to have made in forty days as much progress as the student from Lueches, who studied Latin four years at the University of Alcalá de Henares; when he presented himself to be ordained with the first tonsure, the Archbishop of Toledo asked him, "What does *Dominus vobiscum* mean?" and he in reply construed as follows: "*Do*, I give, *minus*, less, *vobiscum*, to fools." "That is my way too," said the Archbishop, "Go back to your books, and when you have learnt a little elementary grammar, we will give you the crown you ask," and he sent him away with his head still unshaven. But it is not surprising that I should know a little of this jargon; I have worked hard at it, and use it constantly in my ordinary speech. If I want something to drink I say "Let go the mainsheet"; if something to eat, "Set the spritsail."[6] If I need a napkin I say "Open up the sail locker." When I go to the galley I say "The pots are boiling nicely"; when it is time for a meal, I call out "Set the mizen"; when a sailor lifts his elbow more than usual I say "Now she sucks"; and when somebody breaks wind—as often happens—I cry "Down aft, there!" So the use of this argot has become a habit which I cannot now break.

I would pass the time listening to the master giving his orders and watching the sailors carrying them out, until the sun was high in the sky; and then I would see the ship's boys emerge from the half-deck with a bundle of what they called table cloths; but alas, not white or handsomely embroidered. They spread out these damp and dirty lengths of canvas in the waist of the ship, and on them piled little mounds of broken biscuit, as white and clean as the cloths, so that the general effect was that of a cultivated field covered with little heaps of manure. They would then place on the "table" three or four big wooden platters full of beefbones without their marrow, with bits of parboiled sinew clinging to them. They call the platters *saleres*, and so have no need of salt-cellars. When the meal is laid out, one of the boys sings out, "Table, table, Sir Captain and master and all the company, the table is set, the food is ready; the water is drawn for his honor the captain, the master and all our good company. Long live the King of Castile by land and by sea! Down with his enemies, cut off their heads! The man who won't say 'amen' shall have nothing to drink. All hands to dinner! If you don't come you won't eat." In a twinkling, out come pouring all the ship's company saying "amen," and sit on the deck round the "table," the bo'sun at the head and the gunner on his right, some crosslegged, some with legs stretched out, others squatting or reclining, or in any posture they choose; and without pausing for grace these knights of the round table

---

[6] *Cebadera*, an Andalusian nosebag, a baggy rectangle of canvas slung between the shafts of a cart; hence, from its shape and its position in the ship, the spritsail.

whip out their knives or daggers—all sorts of weapons, made
for killing pigs or skinning sheep or cutting purses—and fall
upon those poor bones, stripping off nerves and muscles as if
they had been practicing anatomy at Guadalupe or Valencia all
their lives; and before you can say a *credo*, they leave them as
clean and smooth as ivory. On Fridays and vigils they have beans
cooked in salt water, on fast days salt cod. One of the boys takes
round the mess-kettle and ladles out the drink ration—a little
wine, poor thin stuff, not improved by the baptism it receives.
And so, dining as best they can, without ceremony or order,
they get up from the table still hungry.

The captain, the master, the navigator and the ship's notary
dine at the same time, but at their own mess; and the passengers
also eat at the same time, including myself and my family, for in
this city you have to cook and eat when your neighbors do,
otherwise you find no fire in the galley, and no sympathy. I
have a squeamish stomach, and I found these arrangements very
trying; but I had no choice but to eat when the others were
hungry, or else to dine by myself on cold scraps, and sup in
darkness. The galley—"pot island" as they call it—is a great
scene of bustle and activity at meal times, and it is amazing how
many hooks and kettles are crowded on to it; there are so many
messes to be supplied, so many diners and so many different
dinners. They all talk about food. One will say, "Oh for a bunch
of Guadalajara grapes!"; another, "What would I give for a dish
of Illescas berries?"; somebody else, "I should prefer some turnips
from Somo de Sierra"; or again, "For me, a lettuce and an arti-
choke head from Medina del Campo"; and so they all belch out
their longings for things they can't get. The worst longing is for
something to drink; you are in the middle of the sea, surrounded
by water, but they dole out the water for drinking by ounces,
like apothecaries, and all the time you are dying of thirst from
eating dried beef and food pickled in brine; for My Lady Sea
won't keep or tolerate meat or fish unless they have tasted her
salt. Even so, most of what you eat is half-rotten and stinking, like
the disgusting fu-fu that the *bozal* negroes eat. Even the water,
when you can get it, is so foul that you have to close your eyes
and hold your nose before you can swallow it. So we eat and drink
in this delectable city. And if the food and drink are so exquisite,

what of the social life? It is like an ant-heap; or, perhaps, a melt-
ing-pot. Men and women, young and old, clean and dirty, are all
mixed up together, packed tight, cheek by jowl. The people
around you will belch, or vomit, or break wind, or empty their
bowels, while you are having your breakfast. You can't complain
or accuse your neighbors of bad manners, because it is all allowed
by the laws of the city. Whenever you stand on the open deck,
a sea is sure to come aboard to visit and kiss your feet; it fills your
boots with water, and when they dry they are caked with salt, so
that the leather cracks and burns in the sun. If you want to walk
the deck for exercise, you have to get two sailors to take your arms,
like a village bride; if you don't, you will end up with your
feet in the air and your head in the scuppers. If you want to
relieve yourself—leave it to Vargas![7] You have to hang out over
the sea like a cat-burglar clinging to a wall. You have to placate
the sun and its twelve signs, the moon and the other planets,
commend yourself to all of them, and take a firm grip of the
wooden horse's mane; for if you let go, he will throw you and
you will never ride him again. The perilous perch and the splash-
ing of the sea are both discouraging to your purpose, and your
only hope is to dose yourself with purgatives.

There is always music in the city: the sighing of the wind
and the roaring of the sea as the waves strike the ship.

If there are women on board (and no city is without them)
what a caterwauling they make with every lurch of the ship!
"Mother of God, put me back on shore!" but the shore is a
thousand miles away. If it rains in torrents, there are, it is true,
roofs and doorways for the people to shelter; if the sun beats
down, enough to melt the masts, there are shady places where
you can escape it, and food and drink (of sorts) to refresh you.
But if you are becalmed in the midst of the sea, the victuals
running out and no water left to drink, then indeed you have
need of comfort; the ship rolling night and day; your seasick-
ness, which you thought you had left behind, returning; your
head swimming; then there is no recourse but prayer, till the

[7] A very involved pun. Don Francisco Vargas was an *alcalde* at the Court
of Isabella the Catholic, to whom the queen often entrusted awkward
problems. The phrase *"provéalo Vargas"*—"let Vargas attend to it"—became
proverbial. *Proveerse* also is slang for "relieve oneself."

wind gets up again. When the sails are filled, and drawing well, they are a beautiful sight; but when the wind draws ahead, and the canvas slats against the masts, and the ship can make no headway, then life in her becomes a misery. If the navigator is inexperienced, and does not know when to look out for the land, or how to avoid reefs and shoals, you may seem one minute to be sailing in open water, and the next be fast aground, filling with water and about to drown. If the ship is a sluggish sailer, as ours was, she will hardly move with the wind before the beam. The other ships in company must constantly haul their luff, lie to and wait for her, or else take her in tow. But when she has a fair wind on the beam she will forge ahead, heeling well over to the wind; and we are all seasick once again.

Everything in the city is dark by day and pitch-black by night; but in the first watch of the night, after supper (which is announced in the same way as dinner), the city is reminded of God by the voice of the boy who sets the lamp in the binnacle. He cries, "Amen, and God give us good-night, Sir Captain, master and all the company." After that, two boys come on deck and say prayers, *Pater Noster*, *Ave Maria* and *Salve Regina*. Then they take their places to watch the hour-glass, and chant, "Blessed was the hour when God was born, Saint Mary who bore him and Saint John who baptized him. The watch is set, the glass is running. We shall make a good passage, if God wills." When the sand has run through the glass, the boy on watch sings out, "That which is past was good, better is that which is to come. One glass is gone, the second is running; more will run, if God wills; keep a good count, for a prosperous voyage; up forward there, attention and keep a good watch." The look-outs in the bows reply with a shout, or rather a grunt, to show that they are awake. This is done for each glass, that is, every half-hour, until morning. At midnight the boy calls the men who are to keep the middle watch. He shouts "Turn out, turn out, the watch; turn out, turn out, hurry along, the navigator's watch; time is up, show a leg, turn out, turn out." The rest of us sit up till then; but after midnight we can no longer keep our eyes open, and we all go off to the accommodation allotted to us. I creep into my little hutch with my family, and we doze fitfully, to the sound of the waves pounding the ship. All night we rock about as if we were sleeping in hammocks; for anyone who travels in a ship, even if he is a hundred years old, must go back to his cradle, and sometimes he is rocked so thoroughly that the cradle overturns and he ends up in a heap with cradles and seachests on top of him.

We sailed on alone for the first six days; for the eight other ships which left Santa Cruz harbor in Tenerife in our company all disobeyed the instructions which the judge of the *Contratación de Indias* sent us, and each went off on his own during the first night. What pleasure can a man have on board a solitary ship at sea? No land in sight, nothing but lowering sky and heaving water; he travels in a blue-green world, the ground dark and deep and far below, without seeming to move, without seeing even the wake of another ship, always surrounded by the same horizon, the same at night as in the morning, the same today as yesterday, no change, no incident. What interest can such a journey hold? How can he escape the boredom and misery of such a journey and such a lodging?

It is pleasant to travel on land, well mounted and with money in your purse. You ride for a while on the flat, then climb a hill and go down into the valley on the other side; you ford a running river and cross a pasture full of cattle; you raise your eyes and watch the birds flying above you; you meet all kinds of people by the way and ask the news of the places they have come from. You overtake two Franciscan friars, staves in their hands, skirts tucked into their girdles, riding the donkeys of the seraphic tradition, and they give you "Good-day and thanks be to God." Then, here comes a Jeronymite father on a good trotting mule, his feet in wooden stirrups, a bottle of wine and a piece of good ham in his saddle-bag. There will be a pleasant encounter with some fresh village wench going to town scented with pennyroyal and marjoram, and you call out to her, "Would you like company, my dear?" Or you may meet a traveling whore wrapped up in a cloak, her little red shoes peeping below the hem, riding a hired mule, her pimp walking beside her. A peasant will sell you a fine hare to make a fricassée; or you may buy a brace of partridge from a hunter. You see in the distance the town where you intend to sleep or stop for a meal, and already feel rested and refreshed by the sight. If today you stay in some village where the food is scanty and bad, tomorrow you may be in a hospitable and well-provided city. One day you will dine at an inn kept by some knife-scarred ruffian, brought up to banditry and become a trooper of the *Santa Hermandad;* he will sell you cat for hare, billy-goat for mutton, old horse for beef and watered vinegar for wine; yet the same day you may sup with a host who gives you bread for bread and wine for wine. If, where you lodge, tonight, your hostess is old, dirty, quarrelsome, querulous and mean, tomorrow you will do better and find a younger one, clean, cheerful, gracious, liberal, pious and attractive; and you will forget the bad lodging of the previous day. But at sea there is no hope that the road, or the host, or the lodging will improve; everything grows steadily worse; the ship labors more and more and the food gets scantier and nastier every day.

On the first Saturday out, we were still alone; and on that day, at the usual time for prayers, we held a solemn service in the city, a *Salve* and sung litany with full choir. They put up an altar with images and lighted candles. First of all the master asked, "Are we all here?" and the company responded "God be with us." Then the master: "Let us say the *Salve*, and pray for a good passage; we will say the *Salve*, and our passage will be prosperous." So we begin the *Salve;* we all sing together, we all give tongue—no fancy harmonies, but all eight keys at once. Sailors are great dividers; just as they divide each wind into its eight points, so they break the eight notes of the scale into thirty-two, diverse and perverse, resonant and dissonant. Our *Salve* was a storm, a hurricane of music. If God and his Holy Mother, and the saints to whom we prayed, attended to our singing voices and not to our hearts and spirits, it would have done us no good to beg for mercies with such raucous bawling. After the *Salve* and the litany the master, who acts as priest, continues: "Let us say together the creed in honor of the holy apostles, and ask them to intercede with Our Lord Jesus Christ, to give us a safe passage"; and all who believe the creed recite it. Then one of the boys, who acts as acolyte: "Let us say the Hail Mary for ship and company"; the other boys respond, "May our prayer be received," and we all recite the *Ave.* At the end the boys all stand and say, "Amen, God give us good-night, etc."; and so ends the celebration for the day. This takes place every Saturday.

The next day, Sunday, in the morning, we sighted our vice-commodore, and she saluted us (for we were the flagship of the convoy); and we sailed contentedly in company for the next fifteen days. Then one morning the look-out at the masthead called out "Sail ho!" This caused great excitement, for to merchantmen, sailing as we were without escorting warships, any stranger is an object of suspicion; even the smallest may turn out to be a pirate. "Two sail!" cried the look-out, and doubled our alarm; "three sail"; and by this time we were convinced that we had to deal with corsairs. You may imagine how I felt, with my wife and children all on board. The gunner began to give the orders to clear away for action; the ports were opened for the falcons and culverins; the guns were loaded and run out, and small arms were mustered. Women began to shriek, "Why did we come here, miserable wretches? Whatever possessed us, to go to sea?" Those who had money or jewels ran to hide them in the dark corners of the frames and futtock-timbers. We all stood by with our weapons at the best points of vantage we could find—for the ship had no nettings—all ready to defend ourselves; and we could see the same preparations on board the vice-commodore. The three ships drew closer, on a course to intercept. One was a very big ship, and caused much ironical speculation among the sailors. Some said she must be the Florentine galleon; "More likely the *Bucentaur*," said others; "She's the English *Minion*"—"No, she looks like the *Cacafogo* out of Portugal." Although there were three of them, they approached us at first as cautiously as we them; but when they came near enough for recognition, they saw who we were, and we recognized them as friends. They were, in fact, three of the missing ships of our own convoy; and all our fears vanished in the pleasure of reunion. Even so, the sea played us another trick. The big ship closed us to speak, and as she bore down on us her helmsman misjudged his distance, and put us all in fear of our lives. His beakhead collided with out poop and holed us on the quarter so that the water poured in. Our city might have been taken by the forces of the sea within the hour; but our people ran to work and soon repaired the damage. It was an alarming experience for Doña Catalina, whose cabin was in that part of the ship. When the volleys of abuse had died down (though not the pounding of hearts) our fears were washed away with the salt water, and we greeted one another with relief and joy. The three stragglers promised to keep in sight of the flagship in future. We hoisted our flag at the mainmast head, mounted a crossbow on the poop, and lit our stern lantern at night. The other ships, when they closed us to salute, took care to come up under our lee; and all our subsequent operations were carried out in good order. The form of greeting each morning is a call on the bosun's whistle and a shout, "Good passage to you!"—bellowed loud enough to frighten anyone out of their wits; to hear this "Good voyage" unexpectedly one day would be enough to give one a bad voyage for a year of days.

We ran with a stiff northeast wind for the next four days; and the navigator and the sailors began to sniff the land, like asses scenting fresh grass. It is like watching a play, at this time, to see the navigator taking his Pole Star sights; to see him level his cross-staff, adjust the transom, align it on the star, and produce an answer to the nearest three or four thousand leagues. He repeats the performance with the midday sun; takes his astrolabe, squints up at the sun, tries to catch the rays in the pinhole sight, and fiddles about endlessly with the instrument; looks up his almanac; and finally makes his own guess at the sun's altitude. Sometimes he overestimates by a thousand degrees or so; sometimes he puts his figure so low that it would take a thousand years to complete the voyage. They always went to great pains to prevent the passengers knowing the observed position and the distance the ship had made good. I found this secretiveness very irritating, until I discovered the reason for it; that they never really knew the answer themselves, or understood the process. They were very sensible, as I had to admit, in keeping the details of this crazy guesswork to themselves. Their readings of altitudes are rough approximations, give or take a degree or so; yet on the scale of their instruments the difference of a pin's head can produce an error of five hundred miles in the observed position. It is yet another demonstration of the inscrutable omnipotence of God, that the vital and intricate art of navigation should be left to the dull wits and ham fists of these tarpaulin louts. You hear them discussing it among themselves: "How many degrees does Your Honor make it?" and one says "Sixteen," another "Barely twenty," and yet a third, "Thirteen and a half." Then somebody will ask, "How far does Your Honor reckon we are from land?"; one answers, "I make it forty leagues," another, "A hundred and fifty," and the third says, "This morning I reckoned ninety-two." It may be three or it may be three hundred; they never agree, either with one another or with the truth.

In the middle of all these vain conflicting arguments among masters, navigators, and sailors who claimed to be graduates in the art, on the twenty-sixth day out, God be praised, we sighted land; and how much lovelier the land appears from the sea than the sea from the land! We saw Deseada—appropriately named—and Antigua, and set our course between them, leaving Deseada to the east. We ploughed on; Santa Cruz hove in sight to windward, and we passed it at a distance; we reached San Juan del Puerto Rico and coasted along the shore some way, keeping a careful watch on Cape Bermejo, which is a notorious haunt of pirates. We recognized Mona and the Monitos—easy to identify, even at a distance—looked for Santa Catalina but failed to see it; and eventually came in sight of Saona, the land of the blessed saint, and blessed sight to us. All this time we were repeatedly soaked by downpours of rain; but we made light of them, and thought ourselves lucky to have been spared hurricanes.

In the general rejoicing at the sight of our destination, the navigator—the wind's lieutenant and deputy, who held the reins of the wooden horse—grew a little careless, and allowed the ship to fall away to leeward of the harbor, so that we had to beat with short boards in order to regain lost ground; with the result that it was already dark when we arrived off the mouth of the Santo Domingo River. We had to feel our way in, sounding as we went, and find a sheltered place to anchor for the night. We should certainly have looked very foolish if we had allowed ourselves to drift into danger, and perhaps founder, so close to the shore. We let go two anchors and a good length of cable and (thanks be to God) rode safely through the night. I did not allow any of my people ashore, because the authorities had not yet been warned of my arrval. It was the most disagreeable night of the whole voyage, for the ship pitched abominably, and our stomachs rebelled as they had done on the first day out. But I will weary you no more with the perils and miseries of the sea; except to ask you to imagine, if life can be so uncomfortable with fair winds and a relatively calm sea, what it must be like to experience contrary winds, encounters with pirates, mountainous seas and howling gales. Let men stay on firm ground and leave the sea to the fishes, say I.

Next day at dawn our city came to life, with much opening of trunks and shaking out of clean shirts and fine clothes. All the people dressed in their best, especially the ladies, who came out on deck so pink and white, so neat, so crimped, curled and adorned, that they looked like the granddaughters of the women we had seen each day at sea.

The master went ashore, and I sent my servant with a message of greeting to the president of the court. Boats began to put out to the ship; and since there was a head wind and the ship had to be warped up the river, my family and I went ashore directly in a launch which they sent for us. So we reached the longed-for land, and the city of Santo Domingo. We were kindly welcomed; and after a few days' rest I took my seat on the Bench, and here I stay for as long as God wills, without any desire to cross the sea again. I hope soon to hear that you also have the appointment which you deserve. Doña Catalina and the children send their respects and best wishes.

List of Works Cited

This is a simple list of the works quoted or mentioned in the foregoing text or notes. Where a work not originally written in English has been translated, the best available English edition is the one listed; otherwise, the best available edition in the original language.

I

Francesco Balducci Pegolotti, ed. A. Evans: *La practica della mercatura*, Cambridge, Mass., 1936.

H. Yule, ed.: *Cathay and the Way Thither*, 3 vols., 2nd edn, London, 1913–16.

Marco Polo, ed. A. C. Moule and Paul Pelliot: *The Description of the World*, 2 vols., London, 1938.

Pierre d'Ailly, trans. Edwin F. Keever: *Imago Mundi*, Wilmington N.C., 1948.

Joannes de Sacro Bosco (John of Holywood), ed. Joaquin Bensaude: "Tractado da sphera do mundo," in *Regimento do astrolabio e do quadrante*, Munich, 1914. (Facsimile edition of the unique Munich copy of the earliest printed navigation manual.)

Claudius Ptolemaeus, ed. and trans. E. L. Stevenson: *The Geography of Claudius Ptolemy*, New York, 1932.

Roger Bacon, ed. and trans. Robert B. Burke: *Opus majus*, Oxford, 1928.

Ibn Battuta, ed. and trans. H. A. R. Gibb: *The Travels of Ibn Battuta*, vols. I and II, Cambridge, 1958–62.

II

Malcolm Letts, ed. and trans.: *Mandeville's Travels, Texts and Translations*, 2 vols., London, 1953.

R. H. Major, ed.: *India in the Fifteenth Century*, London, 1857: "The travels of Nicolò de' Conti . . . as related by Poggio Bracciolini, in his work entitled *Historia de varietate fortunae*, Lib IV."

III

Gomes Eannes de Azurara, ed. Charles Raymond Beazley and Edgar Prestage. *The Chronicle of the Discovery and Conquest of Guinea*, 2 vols., London, 1896.

G. R. Crone, ed.: *The Voyages of Cadamosto*, London, 1937.

Duarte Pacheco Pereira, ed. and trans. George H. T. Kimble: *Esmeraldo de situ orbis*, London, 1937.

IV

E. G. Ravenstein, ed. and trans.: *A Journal of the First Voyage of Vasco da Gama*, London, 1898.

João de Barros, ed. António Baião: *Decadas*, 4 vols., Lisbon, 1945–6.

Damião de Gois: *Crónica do Seriníssimo Senhor Rei Dom Manoel*, 4 vols., Coimbra, 1926.

G. Ferrand: *Introduction à l'astronomie nautique arabe*, Paris, 1928.

T. A. Shumovskii, trans. M. Malkiel-Jirmounsky: *Tres roteiros desconhecidos de Ahmad ibn-Madjid, o piloto árabe de Vasco da Gama*, Lisbon, 1960.

Ludovico di Varthema, trans. J. W. Jones, ed. R. C. Temple: *The Itinerary of Ludovico di Varthema of Bologna from 1502 to 1508*, London, 1928.

Duarte Barbosa, ed. and trans. Mansel Longworth Dames: *The Book of Duarte Barbosa*, 2 vols., London, 1918–21.

V

Tomé Pires, ed. and trans. Armando Cortesão: *Suma Oriental*, 2 vols., London, 1944 (includes also *The Book of Francisco Rodrigues*).

Giovanni Battista Ramusio: *Delle navigationi e viaggi*, 3 vols., Venice, 1550–59.

D. Ferguson, ed. and trans.: "Letters from Portuguese captives in Canton," *The Indian Antiquary*, XXXI, January 1902.

C. R. Boxer: *The Christian Century in Japan, 1549–1650*, Berkeley, 1951.

VI

Christopher Columbus, trans. Cecil Jane, ed. L. A. Vigneras, *The Journal of Christopher Columbus*, London, 1960.

Martín Fernández de Navarrete: *Colección de los viages y descubrimientos, que hicieron por mar los Españoles*, 5 vols., Buenos Aires, 1945–6.

Raccolta di documenti e studi pubblicati dalla R. Commissione Colombiana, per il quarto centenario della scoperta dell' America, 13 vols., Rome, 1892–6. [The standard collection of Columbus material.]

Pietro Martyr d'Anghiera, ed. and trans. F. A. McNutt: *De orbe novo*, 2 vols., New York, 1912.

G. Caraci: "Questioni e polemiche Vespucciane," *Memorie Geografiche*, vol. II (1955) and vol. III (1956).

Fracanzano de Montalboddo: *Paesi novamente retrovati, Vicenza*, 1507.

Frederick J. Pohl: *Amerigo Vespucci, Pilot Major*, New York, 1944.

Bernal Díaz del Castillo, ed. and trans. Arthur Percival Maudslay: *The True History of the Conquest of New Spain*, 5 vols., New London, 1890.

Hernando Cortés, ed. and trans. J. Bayard Morris: *Five Letters 1519–1526*, London, 1928.

Francisco López de Gómara, ed. and trans. Lesley Byrd Simpson: *Cortés, The Life of the Conqueror by His Secretary*, Berkeley, 1964.

Clements R. Markham, ed. and trans.: *Reports of the Discovery of Peru*, London, 1872.

Miguel de Estete (Astete), Carlos M. Larrea, ed.: "El descubrimiento y la conquista del Peru," *Boletín de la Sociedad Ecuatoriana de Estudios Históricos Americanos*, vol. I (1918).

George P. Hammond and Agapito Rey, ed. and trans.: *Narratives of the Coronado expedition 1540–1542*, Albuquerque, 1940.

Garcilaso de la Vega, el Inca, trans. Harold V. Livermore: *The Royal Commentaries of the Incas and the General History of Peru*, 2 vols., Austin, 1966.

Bartolemé de las Casas, ed. A. Millares Carlo, intro. L. Hanke: *Historia de las Indias*, Mexico, 1951.

Antonio de Herrera y Tordesillas, trans. John Stevens: *The General History of America*, 6 vols., London, 1725.

VII

Gonzalo Fernández de Oviedo, ed. Juan Pérez de Tudela Bueso: *Historia general y natural de las Indias*, 5 vols., Madrid, 1959.

Antonio Pigafetta, ed. and trans. James Alexander Robertson: *Magellan's Voyage Around the World*, 3 vols., Cleveland, 1906.

C. R. Boxer, ed. and trans.: *South China in the Sixteenth Century, Being the Narratives of Galeote Pereira, Fr. Gaspar da Cruz, O.P., Fr. Martín de Rada O.E.S.A.* (1550–1575), London, 1953.

VIII

J. A. Williamson, ed.: *The Cabot Voyages and Bristol Discovery under Henry VII*, Cambridge, 1962.

R. A. Skelton: Thomas E. Marston and George D. Painter: *The Vinland Map*, New Haven, 1965.

D. B. Quinn: "The Argument for the English Discovery of America between 1480 and 1494," *Geographical Journal*, CCXVII (1961), 277–285.

H. P. Biggar: *Precursors of Jacques Cartier*, Ottawa, 1911.

I. N. Phelps-Stokes: *The Iconography of Manhattan Island*, 6 vols., New York, 1915–28, vol. II, 1922.

H. P. Biggar, ed. and trans.: *The Voyages of Jacques Cartier*, Ottawa, 1924.

Sir Humphrey Gilbert: "A Discourse of a Discovery for a New Passage to Cataia," in D. B. Quinn, ed.: *The Voyages and Colonising Enterprises of Sir Humphrey Gilbert*, 2 vols., London, 1940.

Richard Hakluyt: *The Principal Navigations . . . of the English Nation*, 12 vols., Glasgow, 1903.

Richard Collinson, ed.: *The Three Voyages of Martin Frobisher*, London, 1867.

IX

Strabo: *The Geography of Strabo*, with an English translation by Horace Leonard Jones, Loeb Classical library, London, 1917.

Martín Cortés, trans. Richard Eden: *The Arte of Navigation*, London, 1561.

John Davis: *The Seamans Secrets*, London, 1955; *The Worlds Hydrographical Discription*, London, 1595, both in A. H. Markham, ed.: *John Davis, Voyages and Works*, London, 1880.

William Bourne, ed. E. G. R. Taylor: *A Regiment for the Sea*, Cambridge, 1963.

Eugenio de Salazar: *Cartas*, Madrid, 1866.

H. and P. Chaunu: *Séville et l'Atlantique*, 11 vols., Paris, 1955.

The Africa Pilot, Parts I–III, London, 1929–30.

Suggestions for General Reading

The great discoveries aroused eager public interest at the time, and books on the subject were among the "bestsellers" of the sixteenth and seventeenth centuries. Accounts of voyages—some of which have been quoted here—descriptions of newly found territories, atlases, pamphlets, and treatises urging exploration and settlement, and general annals of discovery, appeared in great numbers. The work of interpreting this great mass of evidence is still going on, and some of the questions which it raises are still matters of acute controversy. The story, moreover, is worth retelling, and is constantly retold, for its adventurous excitement as well as for its social, economic, and scientific significance. The resulting literature is enormous, and of very uneven merit. Mention is made here of a small selection of books in English of a general character which may be found suggestive or useful for reference.

A general discussion of the whole subject is J. H. Parry. *The Age of Reconnaissance* (London, 1963). J. N. L. Baker. *A History of Geographical Discovery and Exploration* (London, 1937) contains a highly condensed narrative. Interesting and important essays on the discoveries are contained in V. T. Harlow, ed.: *Voyages of the Great Pioneers* (London, 1929) and A. P. Newton, ed.: *The Great Age of Discovery* (London, 1932). B. Penrose: *Travel and Discovery in the Renaissance* (Cambridge, Mass., 1955) is a good narrative of voyages with an excellent survey of the literature. Donald Lach: *Asia in the Making of Europe*, vol. I, "The Century of Discovery," (Chicago, 1965), has an excellent chapter on the spice trade.

The best accounts of medieval geographical knowledge are C. R. Beazley: *The Dawn of Modern Geography* (3 vols.,

Oxford, 1896-1906); A. P. Newton, ed.: *Travel and Travellers of the Middle Ages* (London, 1930); and G. H. T. Kimble: *Geography in the Middles Ages* (London, 1938). On the legacy of classical geographers, the definitive work is J. O. Thomson: *History of Ancient Geography* (Cambridge, 1948). The literature on Ptolemy is very large, as might be expected. H. N. Stevens: *Ptolemy's Geography* (London, 1908) is a descriptive guide to the numerous editions of this work. E. L. Stevenson, ed.: *The Geography of Claudius Ptolemy* (New York, 1932) is the best English translation.

There is no satisfactory single account of the development of shipping in our period. Most historians of sail concentrate attention on later centuries. For our purposes the best are R. C. Anderson: *The Sailing Ship* (London, 1926), and G. S. Laird Clowes: *Sailing Ships; Their History and Development* (2 parts, London, 1931-6). There is a good chapter on shipbuilding by G. P. B. Naish in C. Singer and others, eds.: *A History of Technology* (5 vols., Oxford, 1957), vol. III. The same volume has chapters on gunnery and navigation. Among English books on navigation, with good chapters on our period, the most useful are J. B. Hewson: *A History of the Practice of Navigation* (London, 1951); E. G. R. Taylor: *The Haven-finding Art* (London, 1956); and L. C. Wroth: *The Way of a Ship: an Essay on the Literature of Navigational Science* (Portland, Maine, 1937). C. M. Cipolla: *Guns, Sails and Empires* (New York, 1956), is weak on shipping but contains interesting information on the early history of gun-founding.

On the cartography of the Reconnaissance, the literature is extensive and much of it highly technical. Two indispensable basic works are A. E. Nordenskiöld: *Facsimile-atlas to the Early History of Cartography* (Stockholm, 1889); and by the same author: *Periplus: an Essay on the Early History of Charts and Sailing Directions* (Stockholm, 1897). Two notably good brief summaries are G. R. Crone: *Maps and Their Makers* (London, 1953) and R. A. Skelton: *Explorers' Maps* (London, 1958)—the last profusely illustrated. For their beauty and technical perfection, as well as for their scholarly excellence, three collections of facsimile maps and charts should be mentioned: E. L. Stevenson: *Maps Illustrating*

Early Discovery and Exploration in America, 1502–1530 (New
Brunswick, 1906); *Mapas españoles de America, siglos XV–XVII,*
edited by a committee of the Real Academía de Historia (Madrid,
1951); and A. Cortesão and A. Teixeira de Mota, eds.: *Portugaliae
monumenta cartographica* (with English text) (5 vols., Lisbon,
1960).

A fascinating account of the African trade which helped to
stimulate early Portuguese exploration is given in E. W. Bovill:
The Golden Trade of the Moors (Oxford, 1958). The best survey
in English of the Portuguese African voyages is E. Prestage: *The
Portuguese Pioneers* (London, 1933); of the African coastal trade,
J. W. Blake: *European Beginnings in West Africa, 1454–1578* (London, 1937). The story of the discovery of the sea route to India is
well told in K. G. Jayne: *Vasco da Gama and His Successors,
1460–1580* (London, 1910), and more recently and breezily in
H. H. Hart: *Sea Road to the Indies* (New York, 1950); the effect
of the discovery upon the maritime situation in the Indian Ocean is
described in G. A. Ballard: *Rulers of the Indian Ocean* (London,
1928). R. S. Whiteway: *The Rise of Portuguese Power in India*
(London, 1899) is still valuable. On Alboquerque, E. Sanceau:
Indies Adventure (London, 1936) is vivid and reliable.

Of the enormous and often controversial literature on Columbus the best and most convincing account is S. E. Morison: *Admiral of the Ocean Sea* (2 vols. Boston, 1942). It has the special
merit of concentrating on Columbus' achievements as a seaman.
G. E. Nunn: *The Geographical Conceptions of Columbus* (New
York, 1924) is a useful though somewhat technical study. A good,
though perhaps too laudatory book on Vespucci is F. J. Pohl:
Amerigo Vespucci, Pilot Major (New York, 1944). On Magellan
and his successors the best short works in English are J. C. Beaglehole. *The Exploration of the Pacific* (London, 1934) and C. M.
Parr: *Ferdinand Magellan, Circumnavigator* (New York, 1964).

Many books have been written about the Spanish conquests in
America. Perhaps the best single-volume narrative is F. A. Kirkpatrick: *The Spanish Conquistadores* (London, 1934). C. O. Sauer:
The Early Spanish Main (Berkeley, 1965) is an admirable account by
a distinguished historical geographer of the exploration and settlement of the Caribbean area. W. H. Prescott's two great literary
classics: *The History of the Conquest of Mexico* and *The History of*

the Conquest of Peru have their place in all bibliographies; there are many editions. More modern accounts of the principal episodes of the conquest are F. A. MacNutt: *Fernando Cortés and the Conquest of Mexico* (New York, 1909) and P. A. Means: *Fall of the Inca Empire and Spanish Rule in Peru, 1530–1780* (New York, 1932).

Of early exploration of North America, the best brief general account is J. B. Brebner: *The Explorers of North America* (London, 1933). The works of H. P. Biggar on Cartier and on his precursors have already been mentioned (p. 368). Francis Parkman's *Pioneers of France in the New World* is a great literary classic, of the same vintage and the same order of distinction as Prescott's work on the Spanish conquests.

Finally, a word on the sixteenth-century collections of voyages and their editors, to whom we owe a great part of our knowledge of the whole story. The three most important collections are those of Fracanzano da Montalboddo, Ramusio, and the younger Richard Hakluyt. The first of these, *Paesi novamente retrovati*, was first published in Vicenza in 1507. It is composed largely of Americana, the accounts of Columbus, Pinzón, and Vespucci being the most important; but it also includes Cadamosto's account of his voyages to Guinea and the narrative of the voyage of da Sintra; two letters of Girolamo Sernigi, an Italian merchant in Lisbon, describing da Gama's expedition; and a full narrative of Cabral's voyage, written by a participant. The *Paesi* had six Italian editions, six French, and two German. It was the principal vehicle by which news of the discoveries was spread throughout Renaissance Europe.

Giovanni Battista Ramusio was the most celebrated figure in Italian geographical literature of the sixteenth century. He spent more than thirty years collecting narratives of voyages. The first volume of his *Delle navigationi e viaggi* was published in Venice in 1550. It includes Leo's *Africa;* the accounts of Cadamosto, da Gama, Cabral, and Vespucci, all taken from the *Paesi;* Varthema's travels; Alvares' account of Abyssinia; descriptions of India and adjacent lands by Tomé Lopes, Duarte Barbosa, and Andrea Corsale; the journeys of Conti and Santo Stefano; and Pigafetta's journal of the Magellan voyage. The second volume, which appeared posthumously in 1559, contains a composite version of several texts of Marco Polo; Hayton of Armenia; the Venetian missions to Persia; Paolo Giovio's book on the Turks; and in a second edition (1574), the journeys of William of Rubruck and Odoric of Pordenone, Heberstein's travels in Russia, and the apocryphal voyages of the Zeni to Greenland. The third volume (Venice, 1556) is devoted to America, and includes Peter Martyr's first three *Decades;* the entire 1535 edition of Oviedo; Cortés' second, third, and fourth Letters; Cabeza de Vaca's account of his wanderings; the expedition of Coronado; the voyages of Ulloa and Alarcón along the Pacific coast; Jérez' account of the conquest of Peru; Orellana's voyage down the Amazon; and accounts of the exploits of Verrazzano and Cartier. The collection as a whole is the most important single source of our knowledge of the Reconnaissance. Unfortunately there is no modern edition.

Hakluyt was a propagandist and translator as well as a collector, and was responsible for rendering into English many Italian, Portuguese, and French discovery narratives. His great work, however, was *The Principall Navigations, Voiages and Discoveries of the English nation,* the first, single-volume edition of which appeared in London in 1589. Hakluyt—a better archivist and editor than Ramusio—in general adopted Ramusio's plan of a work in three parts. The first deals with the Levant Company, early travels in the Near and Middle East, and the early voyages to West Africa; the second concerns the search for the northeast passage, the travels in Russia and Central Asia of Jenkinson and his successors; the third narrates exploits in the western hemisphere, such as the voyages of Hawkins and Frobisher, Hariot's account of the Roanoke colony, promotion literature of Gilbert and Peckham, and the voyages of Drake, Davis, and Cavendish. The second edition, which appeared in three volumes in 1598, 1599, and 1600, was greatly expanded, to more than twice the length of the first. This is Hakluyt's masterpiece, a splendid work of history and sourcebook of geography, the great prose epic of Elizabethan maritime endeavor; and unlike Ramusio, Hakluyt has (in 12 volumes, Glasgow, 1903-5) a worthy modern edition.

Chronological List

Principal events mentioned in text or notes

1404   Clavijo's embassy to Samarkand
1406   Jacobus Angelus' translation of Ptolemy's *Geography*
1410   Pierre d'Ailly's *Imago Mundi*
1415   Portuguese took Ceuta
1419   Prince Henry Governor of Algarve
       Nicolò de' Conti departed for the East
1420   (*c.*)   Beginnings of Portuguese settlement in Madeira
1432   (*c.*)   Portuguese rediscovery of the Azores
1434   Gil Eannes rounded Cape Bojador
1437   Abortive Portuguese attack on Tangier
1441   (*c.*)   First slave cargoes brought back from West Africa
1442   Nuno Tristão sighted Cape Branco
1443   Nuno Tristão landed on Arguim Island
1444   Nicoló de' Conti returned from the East
1445   Dinis Dias sighted Senegal and Cape Verde
       (*c.*)   Beginnings of Portuguese settlement in the Azores
1446   Nuno Tristão killed off the Gambia
1448   Conti's exploits recorded by Poggio Bracciolini
       Andrea Bianco's chart of West Africa
1455   Cadamosto's first voyage
       Bull *Romanus pontifex*
1456   Cadamosto's second voyage. Cape Verde Islands sighted.
       Mouth of Gambia explored
1457   "Genoese" world map
1459   Fra Mauro's map of the world

1460 Death of Prince Henry of Portugal
      (c.)   Pedro da Sintra reached Sierra Leone
1462 Pedro da Sintra passed Cape Mensurado and entered Gulf
          of Guinea
1467 Grazioso Benincasa's chart of West Africa
1469 Guinea trade leased to Fernão Gomes
1471 Gomes' captains passed Cape Three Points
1473 (c.)   Portuguese visited Benin
1474 Fernando Po Island discovered
      Lopo Gonsalves discovered southern trend of Gaboon coast
          and reached Cape St. Catherine
      Afonso V consulted Toscanelli about easiest route to the
          Indies
1475 Outbreak of Succession War between Portugal and Cas-
          tile
      Fighting in Canaries and off West Africa
      First printed edition of Ptolemy's text
1478 Rome edition of Ptolemy, with maps
1479 Treaty of Alçacovas
1480 (c.)   English voyages in search of "Brasill" probably
          began about this time
1481 Accession of João II
1482 Diogo Cão departed on his first voyage
      Castle of São Jorge da Mina founded on Gold Coast
1483 Diogo Cão explored lower reaches of Congo. Reached Cape
          Santa María
      Ulm edition of Ptolemy's Geography
      (c.)   First printed edition of Imago Mundi
      (c.)   First printed edition of Marco Polo
1484 Diogo Cão returned to Portugal. False reports of rounding
          Africa
1485 Diogo Cão departed on second voyage
1486 Diogo Cão reached Cape Cross
1487 Pedro da Covilhã sent to the East
      Bartolomeu Dias departed on Cape voyage
1488 Dias returned with news of discovery of Cape of Good
          Hope
      Pedro da Covilhã in India

1490 Pedro da Cavilhã's report (probably) sent to Lisbon
  (*c.*)   Henricus Martellus' world map
  (*c.*)   Soligo's chart of "Ginea Portugalexe"
1492 Columbus departed on first trans-Atlantic voyage; discovered Hispaniola and other islands
  Martin Behaim's globe completed
  Amerigo Vespucci arrived in Spain
1493 Columbus returned to Spain. Bulls of Demarcation issued
  Columbus departed on second trans-Atlantic voyage. Visited Cuba and Jamaica
1494 Treaty of Tordesillas
1495 Columbus returned from second voyage
1497 Vasco da Gama departed on first voyage to India
  John Cabot's first (recorded) North Atlantic voyage
1498 Vasco da Gama at Calicut
  Columbus departed on third trans-Atlantic voyage. Discovered mouths of Orinoco, Trinidad, Gulf of Paría
  John Cabot's second (recorded) North Atlantic voyage
1499 Vasco de Gama returned to Portugal
  Ojeda and Juan de la Cosa off Guina and Venezuela coasts
  Vespucci departed with Ojeda on (probably) first voyage
  Niño and Guerra discovered Margarita pearl fishery
  Vincente Yáñez Pinzón off the Amazon (or Orinoco)
1500 Pedro Alvares Cabral departed for India. Sighted east coast of Brazil
  Gaspar Corte-Real's first North Atlantic voyage
  Bastidas off Colombia coast
  Juan de la Cosa's map
1501 Vespucci departed on (probably) second voyage. Explored east coast of South America
  Gaspar Corte-Real's second North Atlantic voyage
1502 Vasco da Gama departed on second voyage to India
  Ludovico di Varthema departed for the East
  Miguel Corte-Real's North Atlantic voyage
  Columbus departed on fourth voyage
  "Cantino" world map
  (*c.*)   "Canerio" world map
  (*c.*)   "King-Hamy" world map

1503 Columbus explored coast of Honduras and Nicaragua
1504 Columbus returned to Spain for last time
1506 Death of Columbus
      Contarini-Rosselli world map
1507 First Portuguese landing in Ceylon
      Johan Ruysch's world map
      Paesi novamente retrovati published
      Waldseemüller's world map
1508 Capture of Ormuz by Alboquerque's fleet
      Ocampo explored Cuba
      Ponce de León explored Puerto Rico
1509 Portuguese defeated Egyptian and Gujerati fleet off Diu
      Expeditions of Ojeda and Nicuesa to Gulf of Urabá
      Esquivel in Jamaica
      (?) Sebastian Cabot's voyage in search of Northwest Passage
1510 Capture of Goa by Alboquerque's fleet
      Publication of Varthema's *Itinerary*
1511 Capture of Malacca by Alboquerque's fleet
      Peter Martyr's first *Decade* published, with map of Carib-
          bean
      Vesconte Maggiolo's world map
1512 Antonio d'Abreu and Francisco Serrão departed from Mal-
          acca to explore eastern archipelago. Visited parts of
          Borneo, Celebes, and Moluccas, and sighted West
          Pacific
1513 Francisco Serrão in Ternate
      Ponce de León landed in Florida
      Balboa crossed Isthmus of Panama and sighted East Pacific
      Francisco Rodrigues' MS chart of the Spice Islands
      Strasburg edition of Ptolemy's *Geography*
1514 Pedrarias Dávila in Darien
1515 Solís left Spain in search of the Strait
1516 (c.)   Beginnings of clandestine trade at Canton
      Solís in the Río de la Plata
      Waldseemüller's *Carta marina navigatoria*
1517 Thomé Pires' embassy arrived at Canton.
      Hernández de Córdoba's voyage along Yucatán coast
1518 Grijalva's voyage into Gulf of Mexico

1519   Magellan departed from Seville on voyage into Pacific
       Cortés departed from Cuba on expedition to Mexico
       Pedarias Dávila founded Panama
       Pedro Reinel's chart of Indian Ocean

1520   Magellan discovered the Strait
       Thomé Pires arrived in Peking
       Rodrigo de Lima and Francisco Alvares reached Abyssinia
       Cortés in Tenochtitlán—Mexico. Montezuma captured
       Alonso de Pineda explored North coast of Gulf of Mexico

1521   Magellan reached the Philippines. Death of Magellan
       Del Cano reached Tidore
       Thomé Pires imprisoned
       Seige and capture of Mexico
       Lucas Vázquez de Ayllón explored coast of the Carolinas

1522   Del Cano returned to Spain

1524   Verrazzano departed from Madeira to explore east coast
         of North America
       Estevão Gomes' voyage along east coast of North America

1525   Verrazzano returned to France

1526   Jorge de Meneses discovered New Guinea
       Sebastian Cabot left Spain in search of a nearer route to the
         Pacific

1527   Francisco Alvares returned to Portugal from Abyssinia
       Sebastian Cabot explored the Río de la Plata
       Spaniards began exploration of Pacific coast of Tehuántepec
       Vesconte Maggiolo's map of North America

1528   Narváez landed in Florida. Cabeza de Vaca set out to walk
         to Mexico

1529   Treaty of Zaragoza
       Cabot returned to Spain
       Diogo Ribeiro's world chart
       Girolamo da Verrazzano's chart of North America

1530   Pizarro sailed from Panama

1531   Pizarro landed in Peru

1532   Atahuallpa captured at Cajamarca

1533   Cuzco taken by Spaniards
       Belalcázar's expedition to Quito
       Heredia founded Cartagena

1534   Cartier's first voyage to the St. Lawrence
1535   Cartier's second voyage to the St. Lawrence
       Lima founded
       Almagro left Cuzco for Chile
1536   Cartier returned to France
       Quesada explored Magdalena River
1537   Almagro returned from Chile to Cuzco
       Juan de Ayolas explored Paraguay River and founded
          Ascunción
       Fernão Mendes Pinto left Portugal for the East
1538   Quesada founded Bogotá
1539   DeSoto's expedition from Florida to the Mississippi
       Gulf of California explored by Francisco de Ulloa
1540   Portuguese fleet entered the Red Sea
       Coronado departed in search of Cíbola. Expedition into
          prairie
       Gonzalo Pizarro's expedition left Quito for the Amazon
          forest
       Valdivia left Cuzco to conquer Chile
1541   Cartier's third voyage to the St. Lawrence
1542   Coronado returned to Mexico
       Orellana traveled down the Amazon
       Gonzalo Pizarro returned to Quito
1543   First Portuguese visit to Japan
       California coast explored by Juan Rodríguez Cabrillo
1549   St. Francis Xavier arrived in Japan
1550   First volume of Ramusio's *Navigationi*
1551   St. Francis left Japan
1553   Chancellor's voyage to Russia
1556   Burrough's voyage to Vaigach Island and Novaya Zemlya
       Third volume of Ramusio's *Navigationi*
1557   Fernão Mendos Pinto returned to Portugal
       Portuguese established at Macao
1559   Second volume of Ramusio's *Navigationi*
1564   López de Legazpi left Mexico to settle in Philippines
       Ortelius' world map
1565   Urdaneta returned from Philippines to Mexico
1567   Mendaña's expedition into Pacific
1568   Mendaña discovered Solomon Islands

1569   Mercator's world chart
1570   Ortelius' *Theatrum orbis terrarum*
1576   Frobisher's first voyage in search of Northwest Passage
1577   Drake left England on voyage of circumnavigation
       Frobisher's second voyage
1578   Frobisher's third voyage
1580   Voyage of Pet and Jackman in search of Northwest Passage
       Drake returned to England
1585   Davis' first voyage in search of Northwest Passage
1586   Davis' second voyage
1587   Davis' third voyage
1589   First edition of Hakluyt's *Principall Navigations*
1594   Linschoten's voyage to Kara Sea
1596   Bärent's voyage to Bear Island, Spitzbergen, and Novaya
       Zemlya
1598   Second edition of Hakluyt's *Principal Navigations*, vol. I
1599   Hakluyt, vol. II
1600   Hakluyt, vol. III